MUIRHEAD LIBRARY OF PHILOSOPHY

AN admirable statement of the aims of the Library of Philosophy was provided by the first editor, the late Professor J. H. Muirhead, in his description of the original programme printed in Erdmann's *History of Philosophy* under the date 1890. This was slightly modified in subsequent volumes to take the form of the following statement:

'The Muirhead Library of Philosophy was designed as a contribution to the History of Modern Philosophy under the heads: first of different Schools of Thought—Sensationalist, Realist, Idealist, Intuitivist; secondly of different Subjects—Psychology, Ethics, Aesthetics, Political Philosophy, Theology. While much had been done in England in tracing the course of evolution in nature, history, economics, morals and religion, little had been done in tracing the development of thought on these subjects. Yet "the evolution of opinion is part of the whole evolution".

'By the co-operation of different writers in carrying out this plan it was hoped that a thoroughness and completeness of treatment, otherwise unattainable, might be secured. It was believed also that from writers mainly British and American fuller consideration of English Philosophy than it had hitherto received might be looked for. In the earlier series of books containing, among others, Bosanquet's *History of Aesthetic*, Pfleiderer's *Rational Theology since Kant*, Albee's *History of English Utilitarianism*, Bonar's *Philosophy and Political Economy*, Brett's *History of Psychology*, Ritchie's *Natural Rights*, these objects were to a large extent effected.

'In the meantime original work of a high order was being produced both in England and America by such writers as Bradley, Stout, Bertrand Russell, Baldwin, Urban, Montague, and others, and a new interest in foreign works, German, French, and Italian, which had either become classical or were attracting public attention, had developed. The scope of the Library thus became extended into something more international, and it is entering on the fifth decade of its existence in the hope that it may contribute to that mutual understanding between countries which is so pressing a need of the present time.'

The need which Professor Muirhead stressed is no less pressing today, and few will deny that philosophy has much to do with enabling us to meet it, although no one, least of all Muirhead himself, would regard that as the sole, or even the main, object of philosophy. As Professor Muirhead continues to lend the distinction of his name to the Library of Philosophy it seemed not inappropriate to allow him to recall us to these aims in his own words. The emphasis on the history of thought also seemed to me very timely; and the number of important works promised for the Library in the near future augur well for the continued fulfilment, in this and other ways, of the expectations of the original editor.

H. D. LEWIS

MUIRHEAD LIBRARY OF PHILOSOPHY

General Editor: Professor H. D. Lewis
Professor of Philosophy, University College, Bangor

The Analysis of Mind. By BERTRAND RUSSELL. 6th impression.

Analytic Psychology. By PROFESSOR G. F. STOUT. 2 Vols. 5th Impression.

Attention. By PROFESSOR W. B. PILLSBURY. 2nd Impression.

Coleridge as Philosopher. By PROFESSOR J. H. MUIRHEAD.

Contemporary American Philosophy. Edited by PROFESSOR GEORGE P. ADAMS and PROFESSOR WM. PEPPERELL MONTAGUE. Two Vols.

Contemporary British Philosophy. Edited by PROFESSOR J. H. MUIRHEAD. Two Vols. in One. 3rd Impression.

Contemporary British Philosophy. Third Series. Edited by H. D. LEWIS.

Contemporary Indian Philosophy. Edited by RADHAKRISHNAN and PROFESSOR J. H. MUIRHEAD.

Dialogues on Metaphysics. By NICHOLAS MALEBRANCHE. Translated by Morris Ginsberg.

Elements of Constructive Philosophy. By PROFESSOR J. S. MACKENZIE. 2nd Impression.

Ethics. By NICOLAI HARTMANN. Translated by Stanton Coit. 3 Vols.

God and Personality. By PROFESSOR CLEMENT C. J. WEBB. 3rd Impression.

The Good Will: A Study in the Coherence Theory of Goodness. By PROFESSOR H. J. PATON.

The Great Problems. By BERNARDINO VARISCO. Translated by Professor R. C. Lodge.

Hegel's Science of Logic. Translated by W. H. JOHNSTON and L. G. STRUTHERS. 2 Vols. 2nd Impression.

History of Aesthetic. By DR. B. BOSANQUET. 4th Edition. 5th Impression.

History of English Utilitarianism. By PROFESSOR E. ALBEE.

History of Philosophy. By J. E. ERDMANN.
Vol. I. *Ancient and Mediæval.* 5th Impression.
Vol. II. *Modern.* 6th Impression.
Vol. III. *Since Hegel.* 7th Impression.

History of Psychology. By PROFESSOR G. S. BRETT. Edited by R. S. PETERS. Abridged one volume edition.

Human Knowledge. By BERTRAND RUSSELL.

A Hundred Years of British Philosophy. By Dr. Rudolf Metz. Translated by Professor J. W. Harvey, Professor T. E. Jessop, Henry Sturt. 2nd Impression.

Ideas: A General Introduction to Pure Phenomenology. By Edmund Husserl. Translated by W. R. Boyce Gibson.

Identity and Reality. By Emile Meyerson. Translated by Kate Loewenberg.

Indian Philosophy. By Radhakrishnan. 2 Vols. Rev. 2nd Edition.

The Intelligible World: Metaphysics and Value. By Professor W. M. Urban.

Introduction to Mathematical Philosophy. By Bertrand Russell. 2nd Edition. 8th Impression.

Kant's First Critique. By H. W. Cassirer.

Kant's Metaphysic of Experience. By Professor H. J. Paton.

Know Thyself. By Bernardino Varisco. Translated by Dr Guglielmo Salvadori.

Language and Reality. By Wilbur Marshall Urban.

Matter and Memory. By Henri Bergson. Translated by N. M. Paul and W. S. Palmer. 6th Impression.

Modern Philosophy. By Guido de Ruggiero. Translated by A. Howard Hannay and R. G. Collingwood.

Moral Sense. By James Bonar.

Natural Rights. By D. G. Ritchie. 3rd Edition.

Nature, Mind, and Modern Science. By E. Harris.

The Nature of Thought. By Brand Blanshard, B.Sc., Ph.D. 2nd Impression.

The Phenomenology of Mind. By G. W. F. Hegel. Translated by Sir James Baillie. Revised 2nd Edition. 3rd Impression.

Philosophy and Political Economy. By J. Bonar. 4th Impression.

The Platonic Tradition in Anglo-Saxon Philosophy. By Professor J. H. Muirhead.

The Principal Upanisads. By Radhakrishnan.

Some Main Problems of Philosophy. By G. E. Moore.

A Theory of Direct Realism; and The Relation of Realism To Idealism. By J. E. Turner.

The Ways of Knowing: or, The Methods of Philosophy. By Professor W. P. Montague. 4th Impression.

Time and Free Will. By Professor Henry Bergson. Translated by F. G. Pogson. 6th Impression.

The Muirhead Library of Philosophy

EDITED BY H. D. LEWIS

ON SELFHOOD AND GODHOOD

ON SELFHOOD
AND
GODHOOD

The Gifford Lectures
delivered at the University of St. Andrews
during Sessions 1953-54 and 1954-55
revised and expanded

BY

C. A. CAMPBELL

*Professor of Logic and Rhetoric
in the
University of Glasgow*

LONDON: GEORGE ALLEN & UNWIN LTD
NEW YORK: THE MACMILLAN COMPANY

FIRST PUBLISHED IN 1957

TO RUTH

PRINTED IN GREAT BRITAIN
in 11pt. *Imprint type*
AT THE UNIVERSITY PRESS
ABERDEEN

PREFACE

THIS work is a much revised, and in some parts much expanded, version of the Gifford Lectures which were delivered in the University of St. Andrews during Sessions 1953-54 and 1954-55. Departures from the oral version have been dictated in the main by three considerations:

In the first place, there are manifest limits to the closeness of texture that is reasonable in philosophic argument addressed to a lecture audience, which has to grasp what is being said at once or not at all. A lecturer shows some disrespect for his listeners if his mode of presentation takes no account of this. On the other hand, should he come to revise his lectures for publication, he would show some disrespect for his readers if he did not see fit to tighten his argument in many places well beyond what was appropriate to the spoken word.

In the second place, it has seemed to me not to make good sense that, in its printed form, my twenty lectures should continue each to consist of approximately the number of words that could be conveniently uttered in fifty-five minutes. Philosophical argument does not readily lend itself to such tidy division into uniform blocks. The treatment of the several topics is now, I think, more justly proportioned to their place in the context of the work as a whole.

The lecture on 'Self-activity' is in some respects a special case. On this neglected topic I was painfully conscious how much more ought to be said than I could contrive to pack into my scheduled time, if anything approaching justice was to be done to it. Accordingly, when invited to contribute an article to the new (3rd) series of *Contemporary British Philosophy*, I asked, and obtained, permission to make this consist of a rewritten and greatly enlarged version of the lecture I had prepared for delivery. Lecture VIII in the present volume is substantially the article which appeared in *Contemporary British Philosophy*, reproduced by kind permission of the Publishers.

In the third place, in a work that is now addressed not only to those for whom Lord Gifford desired that his Foundation should primarily cater, but also to academic philosophers, I have judged it desirable to make a certain number of additions, relating mostly to matters of current, and somewhat technical, philosophic controversy that bear upon the general theme. These additions are not numerous, and the lengthier ones have been relegated to appendices, where they need trouble no one.

So far as the main body of the work is concerned, I have assumed throughout that the clientèle whom Lord Gifford had in mind neither needs nor desires philosophy of the 'processed' variety; and I have made no attempt to 'write down'. Gifford audiences (and Gifford readers), I take it, consist for the most part of reflective members of the educated public who have an especially keen interest in problems concerning the nature and justification of religious belief. The pursuit of this interest has already led them to acquire some familiarity with, and some skill in manipulating, fundamental philosophical ideas. Naturally, their acquaintance with the more specialised problems of philosophy is unlikely to be extensive; but with the broader questions that fall within the field of their choice they are, I believe, well able to cope. I shall not pretend that they will find the going other than tough in some parts of this study—it may be doubted whether philosophy that is 'popular' in the sense that it wears its meaning on its face is worth the trouble, slight though it be, either of writing or of reading. But I have done everything in my power to ensure that the reader will not suffer needless provocation from the kind of obscurity that has no better excuse than the author's insufficient care to say what he wants to say in the clearest possible language. I have also taken some pains to make the Analytical Table of Contents detailed enough to serve as a real index to the general argument, and I hope that this will be found helpful by readers (and not *too* helpful by reviewers !).

I should add that, despite the revisions and additions to which I have alluded, there is in the book no change from the lectures as delivered on any point of substance. On that account, and on account of the book's general provenance, it has seemed to me appropriate that the original lecture format should be retained.

A word ought perhaps to be said here about the relationship to one another of the two Parts into which the book is divided. A Gifford Lecturer normally gives two courses in successive sessions; and he cannot assume that all, or even a majority of, those who attend his second course will have been present at the first. Accordingly, while it is obviously desirable that the two courses together should constitute some kind of a unity, equally obviously it is desirable that the argument of the later course should not lean at all heavily upon that of the earlier. The plan I eventually came to adopt seemed to me to reconcile reasonably well these two legitimate, but slightly conflicting, demands. Nevertheless, the reader whose interest is primarily theological ought perhaps to be warned that for some of the conclusions arrived at in the course on Godhood a fairly important part of the grounds belongs to the course on Selfhood (in particular, to Lectures I, II, IX, and X). It was, in fact, increasingly brought home to me during my preliminary deliberations how impossible it is to discuss the deeper problems of religion with any adequacy save on the basis of a carefully considered theory about the essential nature of the human self.

I might also, at this point, draw the reader's attention to the saving word 'On' in the title of the book. I have, indeed, done my best to give constructive answers to what seem to me the most fundamental questions concerning 'Selfhood' and 'Godhood' respectively; but in both fields there are questions of considerable philosophic interest, though not, I think, of comparable philosophic importance, which I have had to leave more or less untouched. To some of these I hope one day to return.

Readers of this book will not be long in discovering my inability to do obeisance to the twin gods of so much recent British philosophy—empiricism and linguisticism.[1] On the other hand, since I have already written perhaps more than enough elsewhere in a polemical vein, I have felt myself at liberty here to concentrate entirely upon my constructive purpose, and not to engage in explicit criticism of modernist doctrines save where these directly impugn fundamental positions which I am concerned to establish. In any event, where the cleavage is as deep

[1] Unsatisfactory as these labels are, at least they are less liable to mislead than ' analysis ', which has not yet succeeded in acquiring such definiteness of connotation as would enable one to distinguish by its means any particular philosophy from any other. There never has been a philosopher who did not devote a large part of his energy to ' analysis ' in some sense of that term.

as it is between proponents and opponents of the modernist way of philosophising, sporadic skirmishes on the frontiers seem to me somewhat futile. If effective contact between the adversaries is to be achieved at all, it can only be on the basis of a mutual readiness to re-examine first principles. I have therefore been at some pains in the present work to make clear my own first principles, and my reasons for holding them. It is my hope that the modernist will deem them worthy of his critical attention.

The readiness to re-examine first principles, however, pre-supposes the recognition that one's own first principles may conceivably be mistaken. Such a frame of mind is not common among pioneers of new philosophical movements, nor even among their immediate disciples. Perhaps it ought not to be expected. Perhaps it was a little naïve of the older generation of contemporary British philosophers to be so taken aback by its apparently total absence in logical positivists and later heralds of a new dawn. Perhaps also, however, it was pardonable that philosophers whose reflections upon the premises of latter-day empiricism and/of linguisticism left them profoundly sceptical of their validity should have been disquieted, incensed, or infuriated—according to temperament—by the practice that prevailed in most modernist quarters of automatically dismissing as worthless all writings which did not conform to modernist preconceptions (on the assumption, apparently, that their authors could only be philosophic Rip Van Winkles talking in their sleep).

Be that as it may, I hope I am not over-optimistic in thinking that in the course of the last few years, to the great benefit of philosophy, the modernist movement has entered upon a mellower phase, and is now evincing a far more hospitable temper. It may even be the case, as we have recently been informed by one well qualified to judge of contemporary trends, that 'it is foreign to the new way of doing philosophy to regard any other way as just a mistake' (Professor J. O. Urmson in *Philosophical Analysis*, p. 180). Not, of course, that the twentieth century 'revolution in philosophy' has petered out. It manifestly has not. But the past thirty years have seen the abandonment, one by one, of so many of the doctrines that seemed distinctive of it, and were certainly dear to it, that it has become hard to point to anything positive that now binds the revolutionaries together save a common enthusiasm (slightly abated) for linguistic analysis, and a common disposition to be as empirical as one can. Such being the situation, it would be surprising if there were not beginning to be visible today a more tolerant attitude towards the revolution's critics. After all, even a loyal friend of the revolution, once he has himself become persuaded that most of the leading propositions in which the revolution found earlier expression are untenable, can hardly, if he is a reasonable man, continue to take for granted that the chilly reception accorded to these same propositions by 'traditionalists' was based on nothing more worthy of respect than the typical reactionary's emotional attachment to the *status quo*. Without doubt there are still Jacobins of the revolution who are totally unmoved by such considerations, and for whom philosophers in another camp are, almost by definition, beyond the pale. But, by and large, philosophers are reasonable men. There is, I think, a steadily strengthening disposition to concede that there may be more than one profitable approach to philosophy, and to suspect that it may be no bad thing for the health of philosophy in this country if those who represent view-points other than the linguistic are granted a fair hearing.

Of course, inability to accept the claims, even the modified claims, explicitly or implicitly made for the linguistic approach by most British philosophers today, should not be taken to imply a refusal to ascribe any importance to this method of dealing with philosophical problems. That linguistic analysis is often not merely useful to, but indispensable to, effective philosophic enquiry, and that in point of fact it has been practised—though it may well be insufficiently and imperfectly—by almost every great philosopher of past times, is to my mind beyond question. But just how far it is capable of carrying the enquirer towards a solution (or dissolution) of what have commonly been accepted as the major philosophical problems is surely still wide open to debate. The conviction to which I have myself been forced is that seldom if ever can it take us to the heart of the matter, and that the current disposition to rely so largely upon it is proving a serious impediment to philosophical progress. There are good grounds, I think, for holding that in ethical philosophy the method of linguistic analysis has a wider field of profitable application than elsewhere; and it has certainly been exploited with brilliance by some contemporary British and American moralists. Yet even here, I should urge, excessive addiction to the method has led directly to errors of a very fundamental kind. I have argued this in Lecture X (and to some extent in Appendix B). If these arguments are unsound, I should be genuinely grateful to be so instructed.

Perhaps optimism should not go so far, however, as to suggest that the new hospitality extends in any appreciable measure to the practice of metaphysics. This does continue to excite angry passions in a great many philosophic breasts. Nevertheless, the revival of metaphysics in the foreseeable future may not be altogether a traditionalist's pipe-dream. Certainly the tabu upon it is much less strict than it was. Moreover, there must be *some* significance in the sturdy refusal of anti-metaphysicians to disclose just what the logical justification for hostility to metaphysics is supposed now to be (for the old anti-metaphysical props of twenty years ago offer feeble support today). But I have a little to say about this in my opening lecture, and I shall not enlarge upon it here.

Still, it is a great advance that controversy today no longer, save among the incurably doctrinaire, gives the appearance of presenting a clean-cut issue between philosophical salvation and philosophical damnation. In the highly charged atmosphere of the revolution's earlier phases, a great many foolish things were said, of which I do not suggest that either side enjoyed a monopoly. The more tranquil and judicial assessment of gains and losses which is now practicable, and of which there are some instructive examples already in being, must surely be welcomed by all who do not think it priggish to believe that philosophy is neither a word-game, nor a social accomplishment, nor a gladiatorial exhibition, but, quite simply, the rational pursuit of such truth as is attainable by human minds about the general character of the universe in which we find ourselves.

The agreeable duty remains of making acknowledgement of my obligations. My chief debt (a massive one) is to Professor W. G. Maclagan, whose counsel and criticism at every stage of the work's progress have been quite invaluable. I only hope that the heavy inroads he has allowed me to make upon his time have not unduly postponed the better book on these themes which he is so obviously able to write himself. I have also profited much from comments upon particular sections of the work by other friends and colleagues, notably Professor A. L. Macfie, Dr. W. D. Lamont, and Mr. George Brown, all of this University. Nor must I omit to mention a number of helpful suggestions, which I have been glad to put into effect, made to me by the Publishers' Reader. Professors Maclagan and Macfie have placed me further in their debt by generous assistance with the proof-reading. To all of these gentlemen I render grateful thanks; only adding, lest any reader be tempted to inculpate the innocent in the book's errors—a bêtise for which there are surprisingly many precedents—that sometimes, despite warnings, I have perversely gone on my own wilful way.

It is a pleasure also to express my thanks to Principal Knox and his St. Andrews colleagues for receiving me so hospitably into temporary membership of their community; and in particular to the Convener of the Gifford Lectureship Committee, Professor E. P. Dickie, and to Mrs. Dickie, who looked after their ward with such cheerful assiduity as entirely to conceal from him that, for such busy people, it must at times have been a burdensome assignment.

ANALYTICAL TABLE OF CONTENTS

xvi

LECTURE IV

IMPLICATIONS OF THE JUDGMENT-THEORY OF COGNITION

LECTURE V

SELF-CONSCIOUSNESS, SELF-IDENTITY AND PERSONAL IDENTITY

LECTURE VI

THE SELF'S RELATION TO ITS BODY

LECTURE VII

EMPIRICAL SELF-KNOWLEDGE: INTROSPECTION, AND THE INFERENCE TO DISPOSITIONS

LECTURE VIII

SELF-ACTIVITY AND ITS MODES

LECTURE X

MORAL EXPERIENCE AND ITS IMPLICATIONS FOR HUMAN SELFHOOD

PART TWO (SECOND COURSE)
ON GODHOOD

LECTURE XI

THE CONCEPT OF RELIGION

LECTURE XII

RELIGION AND THEISM

LECTURE XIII

THEISM AND THE PROBLEM OF EVIL: (I) SIN

LECTURE XIV

THEISM AND THE PROBLEM OF EVIL:
(2) SUFFERING

ANALYTICAL TABLE OF CONTENTS xxxi

page

5. The dilemma briefly debated; objections to 'Divine self-manifestation' theory serious, but do not seem insuperable, whereas 'Divine will' theory seems to involve a plain self-contradiction;   318

   not suggested that the notion of Divine creation as such imports contradiction into theistic position, as the notions of Divine will and thought, if literally interpreted—and *a fortiori* as the notions of goodness, wisdom, etc. that depend upon them—appear to do.   320

6. Review of argument of present course to stage now reached.   321

7. If literal theology of Rational theism unacceptable, must now go on to consider the possibility of a Supra-rational theism committed to a symbolic theology.   323

LECTURE XVI

OTTO AND THE NUMINOUS:
THE TRANSITION TO SUPRA-RATIONAL THEISM

1. Otto's doctrine of the numinous carries implication that it is *supra*-rational theism that is the authentic theoretical expression of religious experience; his doctrine (with the crucial, psychological side of which we agree) to be the main topic of this lecture.   325

2. The idea of the holy as including an 'over-plus' of meaning which transcends concepts—the 'numinous'; inadequate recognition of numinous element even in Schleiermacher's account of essence of religious experience; numinous epitomised as *mysterium tremendum et fascinans*; Otto's detailed elucidation of each of the three component terms here by comparing and contrasting what they stand for with their 'rational' counterparts.   327

3. Otto's epistemology of the numinous; the potentiality for numinous consciousness *a priori*; 'natural' experiences which incite this potentiality to become active; gradual unfolding of content of numinous in religious (and pre-religious) history; assertion, which we shall later call in question, that no empirical origin for numinous consciousness is conceivable.   333

4. Otto's account of the rational, as contrasted with the numinous, strand in the 'holy'; his insistence that this equally indispensable; question how God can be held to be at once supra-rational and the bearer of 'rational' qualities; Otto's answer that these rational qualities are conceptual 'schemata' of the numinous.   335

5. Meaning and basis of Otto's view that the schematisation proceeds from an 'inward necessity' of the mind; but though rational schemata thus indispensable, implication of doctrine is that the supra-rational is primary, and that the only theology possible is a symbolic theology.   338

LECTURE XVII

SUPRA-RATIONAL THEISM AND 'SYMBOLIC' KNOWLEDGE

LECTURE XVIII

THE OBJECTIVE VALIDITY OF RELIGION (I)

B

LECTURE XIX

THE OBJECTIVE VALIDITY OF RELIGION (II)

LECTURE XX

THE OBJECTIVE VALIDITY OF RELIGION (III)

PART ONE
(FIRST COURSE)

ON SELFHOOD

LECTURE I

PROLEGOMENA
RELIGION AND THE ARBITRAMENT
OF REASON

1. I should wish my first words to express my deep sense of the honour you have done me in inviting me to become your Gifford Lecturer. I am keenly conscious of the privilege, though at the same time of the responsibility, of discoursing, within these walls particularly, on the high themes prescribed by Lord Gifford. When I recall the names of those who have preceded me here in this office, and when I reflect upon the remarkable succession of philosophical thinkers and scholars who have taught in this University and have made the name of St. Andrews illustrious in philosophy as in so much else, I confess to feeling hardly less terrified than gratified by the charge you have entrusted to me. I can but promise to do my utmost not to be too grossly unworthy of the company to which, with so little desert, I have been admitted.

There is, however, one qualification for my present assignment to which I can fairly, and without immodesty, lay some claim. My interest in the kind of philosophical problems most relevant to the Gifford Foundation—problems within the general domain of natural theology—is of very old standing; stretching back, indeed, to long before my student days. As with so many of my contemporaries, it was this interest which acted as the chief inducement to me to embark upon formal philosophical study. In the early years of the twentieth century there was probably not much more religious belief among reflective Scotsmen than is to be found today. But there was certainly much less religious apathy.

The doubts plentifully expressed were real doubts; not just a disguise for indifference. No one then supposed that the question of the truth or falsity of the religious interpretation of the universe was of less than paramount importance to a man; and very few supposed that any enduring solvent of religious doubt was attainable save through the further exercise of that same 'reason' whose critical analysis had provoked it. 'The wounds inflicted by reason' (as my old teacher Sir Henry Jones never tired of quoting) 'reason alone can heal.' It was natural, then, for the young men of this generation to turn in their perplexities to philosophy for guidance —and it might be for succour. For did not philosophy in that strangely remote era (as, for that matter throughout the previous 2500 years) seek rationally supported answers to just those questions about the general character of the universe with which the most fundamental religious doubts were concerned?

The youthful interest in the problems of philosophical theology which I shared with my generation has suffered no abatement with the passing of the years. Inevitably, however, in the philosophical climate of the last quarter-century, it has enjoyed fewer opportunities for constructive expression than I could have wished. After all, the professional philosopher is only in small degree his own master as regards the direction of his studies. He is constrained, for example, by the duty he owes to his pupils to prepare himself to satisfy their natural, and rightful, curiosity about whatever may be making a stir in the philosophical world of the moment; a duty no less binding, though certainly more irksome, if in his view the avenues of exploration which excite the keenest contemporary interest are for the most part blind alleys. Thus the professional philosopher of the present day who happens to remain (as I fear I remain) totally unpersuaded of the virtues of the 'new look' which fashion has imposed upon the matter and the manner of his science, is likely to find himself free to devote only a poor fraction of his working hours to systematic thinking about the very problems which, as he understands philosophy, ought to be the life-long preoccupation of the philosophic mind.

To anyone so circumstanced, what could be more fortunate than a commission such as that with which you have so kindly charged me, which not merely permits but requires that one directs one's meditations to some of the great perennial problems of traditional philosophy, the problems which emerge as fundamental in the course of the effort of the human mind to gain the best understanding it can of the general nature of the universe and of man's place within it? I am grateful indeed that you should have provided me with so invincible an excuse for doing what I want to do.

2. The prescribed subject-matter of the Gifford Lectureship is 'Natural Theology'. This term is, of course, capable of being used in a wide variety of allied meanings; but it is unnecessary for my purpose to spend time over the niceties of its definition. I take it that there will be no serious dissent from the view I accept throughout these lectures of the main business of Natural Theology. Its main business, as I understand it, is to consider how much of certain or probable knowledge is obtainable, on grounds which approve themselves to reason, concerning the existence of God; and, in the event of an affirmative answer to the question of God's existence, concerning His nature, and His relationship to the world and to the human soul. Formulated in more rough and ready, but not, I think, fundamentally misleading fashion, Natural Theology seeks a rational answer to the question 'Is religion true? And if so, in what precise sense?' That is in fact the question which will determine the direction of these Lectures from start to finish.

We shall not, however, be plunging straightway into religious or theological topics. Indeed, the formal and systematic consideration of such topics will, for the most part, be deferred until our second course. For it seems to me that, in our present mid-twentieth-century climate of thought, there is a deal of patient work to be done by the natural theologian in clearing obstacles from the ground before he can gain right of entry to his own domain. To leap over these obstacles is tempting, but it is not a procedure open to the natural theologian. Committed as he is to the rule of reason, he is obliged to keep at least one foot on the ground or be disqualified.

Metaphor aside, let me explain briefly why there is today, in my judgment, a duty laid upon the natural theologian to undertake a rather extensive preliminary programme.

The obligation is imposed, as I see it, by the dominant trends
of contemporary philosophical thought. Whatever may be the case
with *Revealed* Theology, *Natural* Theology at any rate has no
claim to a respectful hearing if it does not take full account of
well-accredited movements of philosophic thought which have an
evident bearing upon its subject-matter. Now it may appear at
first sight that the concerns of present-day philosophers in this
country (the continent of Europe presents, of course, a very
different picture) are for the most part very remote indeed from
those of the theologian. About the concept of 'God', for example,
current philosophy has so far had little to say; though there are
undoubtedly signs of a growing interest and of a more sympathetic
effort to understand the context of experience from which this
concept derives its meaning for the believer.[1] One must agree also
that current philosophy has not much to say about the concept
of 'the world'; unless indeed, we count among the philosophers
(as I am afraid I do not) certain distinguished men of science, of
whose intrepidity in cosmic speculation one can only say 'c'est
magnifique, mais ce n'est pas la philosophie'. But what now about
the concept of 'the soul'? On *this* topic, so central in religious
thought, current philosophy has unquestionably something very
relevant to say; even though it be said, in most cases, only by
implication. And the essence of what it has to say is, to put it
bluntly, that the 'soul' is sheer myth. For current philosophy, in
its most characteristic British expressions, finds no room for a
'self', in the sense of an identical, perduring spiritual being; and
whatever may be the precise relationship between 'self' and 'soul',
it is at least certain that, where there are no 'selves' in this sense,
there can be no 'souls' in any sense that interests the theologian.
Scepticism about the self is a matter of course for philosophers
of Positivist leanings (I use this periphrastic mode of designation
because there seems to be nobody today willing to be labelled a
'Positivist' *simpliciter*). A like scepticism is implicit in the teachings
of Professor Ryle and those who share his quasi-Behaviourist

[1] This is evident in the useful collection of papers recently edited by Professor Flew under the title 'New Essays in Philosophical Theology'. The
contributors to this volume are, for the most part, plainly anxious that their
criticisms should be neither merely external nor merely destructive—though
they would perhaps agree that in the space they allow themselves constructive
suggestions cannot find more than a rather sketchy formulation.

concept of mind. And it lies little, if at all, below the surface in that large body of philosophers whose thinking, while relatively free from Positivist or Behaviourist influences, is yet infected with the characteristic revulsion of the age against anything that savours of substances—whether material or spiritual. One does not exaggerate, I think, in saying that, explicit or implicit in the writings of the vast majority of philosophers today who concern themselves at all about the human mind, is the conviction that the term 'self' stands, at most, only for particular mental states and events inter-related in a specific way, and perhaps stands only for some unique pattern of bodily behaviour.

Now *Psychology* without a soul is, of course, a phenomenon with which we have long been familiar: though one ought to add that this very lively (if at times somewhat brash) science has shown an inclination to become much more hospitable since the days, not so long ago, when there was point in the jest that Psychology had lost not only its soul but its mind, and was in imminent danger of losing consciousness as well. Again, *Philosophy* without a soul is, as we have just noticed, a commonplace in contemporary thought. But *Theology* without a soul would seem to amount to something very like a contradiction in terms.[1] If talk about the soul be forbidden to the theologian, he might as well retire from business altogether. The questions he is most interested in asking—let alone the answers to them—just don't make sense.

One must by no means take for granted, of course, that the

---

[1] To this generalisation it might seem at first sight as though Buddhist theology constituted a notable exception. But the Buddhism with which the doctrine of 'no-soul' is especially associated—the Buddhism which remains closely within the confines of its founder Gautama's teachings—has no place for a god or gods any more than it has for a soul. This form of Buddhism *has* no theology. The 'popular' Buddhism which developed in many forms, and with many glosses upon what appears to have been the original thought of Gautama, does recognise gods in plenty; and there is, of course, a corresponding theology. But it may be questioned whether for these popular variants the doctrine of 'no-soul', even where nominally retained, has much real significance. It would be foolish for the ignorant amateur to pronounce upon topics which the Buddhist scholar finds highly complicated and controversial, but one may just note in passing that there seems to be a growing scepticism in informed quarters about the alleged rejection of the 'individual ego' even by Gautama himself. (See e.g. Bouquet's *Comparative Religion*, pp. 162 ff., and Widgery's *Living Religions and Modern Thought*, pp. 61 ff.)

questions the theologian asks do make sense. About that I am at the moment expressing no opinion. At the moment I am concerned only to insist upon the uncompromising nature of the threat to theology that resides in current philosophical thinking about the soul. It is a threat which, in my opinion, the natural theologian dare not ignore. Nor, I think, will he meet it at all adequately if he be content with a counter-attack, however well mounted, at any single point of danger: e.g. against the notorious Verification theory of meaning. Admittedly that theory has been an important influence in generating the contemporary mistrust of all talk about entities not apprehensible through the senses. Admittedly also that theory has the signal merit, for the theologian, of being highly vulnerable. But the roots of scepticism about the soul in contemporary philosophy are far too deep and far too wide-spread for any such limited offensive to be satisfactory. If the natural theologian is to have any hope of vindicating to an audience familiar with current philosophical trends his right to employ the concept of soul in the manner in which, *qua* theologian, he must wish to employ it, he cannot content himself, I fear, with mere skirmishing, however successful. Something a good deal more like 'total war' is called for.

That brings me to the programme for this first course of lectures. The concept of the soul cannot be vindicated unless the concept of the self is vindicated. And I have found myself forced to the conclusion that, in the intellectual milieu of today, there can be no effective vindication of the self short of its constructive establishment from philosophic first principles. This involves, as I see it, an examination of our distinctively human experience in some of its more fundamental modes and manifestations. And it is to this examination that I propose to devote the greater part of this Session's lectures. It will occupy us, in fact, from the third lecture to the end of the course. Inevitably, some space will be given to criticism of contemporary views, but no more than seems necessary to pave the way for the constructive theory which will be our ultimate aim throughout. Our central questions will be, 'What kind of a being is man? Is he a "self" in any sense of that term which implies that he has, or may have, what is meant in religion by a "soul"? Is he, in fact, the kind of being he has got to be if religious language about him is to have any real meaning?'

It is my hope to show that there are in fact good grounds for returning to these questions answers not unsatisfactory to the theologian. If so—but only if so—it will be possible to enter upon the domain of natural theology proper in our second course with a reasonably clear philosophic conscience.

3. Within the domain of natural theology proper, however, the main questions are at bottom *metaphysical*; and some may feel that a due respect for the philosophical *Zeitgeist* requires that a vindication of metaphysics also be included in a satisfactory preface to natural theology. In a brilliant summing-up of British philosophy between the two World Wars, so temperate an historian as Professor Price could write: 'The word "metaphysical" is now almost a term of abuse.' [1] Many of the younger generation of philosophers would have described the situation in even stronger terms; like the candidate in an Honours examination who assured me a few years ago that ' "metaphysics" has now become a swear-word!' Those who regard metaphysics in this light—and I cannot pretend their number is, even now, negligible—must be warned that they will find parts of my second course in particular positively bristling with bad language! Nevertheless, in the light of the many hard blows which the philosophy of dogmatic empiricism has taken over the past couple of decades, I really cannot admit that there is any kind of propriety in the demand for yet another defence of the possibility of making significant metaphysical statements. I suggest that it will be time enough to defend this possibility all over again when our anti-metaphysicians have either attempted some reply to the criticisms that have been made of their standard objections so many times already in recent years by so many philosophers of repute, or, alternatively, when they have thought up some new arguments. The attitude of the more intransigeant anti-metaphysicians at the present day is surely very hard to defend. Their uncompromising hostility continues, but the source of its momentum would seem to lie in certain past theories which not even they themselves show any inclination now to sponsor. No longer is appeal made to some accredited general principle in the light of which the whole class of metaphysical

[1] *Horizon*, No. 109, p. 72.

statements can be summarily dismissed.[1] The presumption is that
the weakness of the theoretical basis for any wholesale condemnation of metaphysics has come to be recognised, and the implication
of that should be that in future, when metaphysical propositions
are rejected, it will be only after due consideration of each on its
own merits. This is what the logic of the situation would seem to
demand; and the metaphysician asks for nothing better. But
whether, or when, the metaphysician will get what the logic of the
situation demands is quite another question. There is little to
make him sanguine at the moment. I think, however, that in
default of anything new being said on the other side, he will
largely be wasting his time if he succumbs to the temptation to
indulge in an *apologia pro vita sua*. He will be better to get on
with his job. After all, though it is common for emotive attitudes
to linger a long time after the destruction of their original theoretical basis, they do eventually weaken and die: always provided,
of course, that they be not reinvigorated by some dose of fresh
theory.

Reverting for a moment to the relationship between our first
and our second course, I ought perhaps to add that while the first
is concerned primarily with the Self, and the second primarily
with God, the division between the two topics will not be too
pedantically observed. Any study of the self which aims at being
at all fundamental may be expected to cast some light upon the

---

[1] It is not now seriously claimed that the Verification Principle, in any form
of it at least in which it entails the rejection of metaphysical statements as
meaningless, has higher status than that of a useful working hypothesis. Nor
does much seem to survive of the hope, once so confidently entertained in
influential quarters, that metaphysical propositions could one and all be shown
to arise out of incorrect linguistic usage. Perhaps those who still denounce
metaphysical propositions as a class would be most inclined to base their
rejection on the alleged impossibility of synthetic *a priori* propositions. But
for obvious reasons this line of attack is not formally and publicly pursued.
For it is clear, in the first place, that the denial of the possibility of synthetic
a priori propositions is itself a synthetic *a priori* proposition, and thus involves
a self-contradiction; and it is clear, in the second place, that there are still
far too many defenders of synthetic *a priori* propositions among distinguished
philosophers of the present day for any pretence to be made that this type of
proposition is to all intents and purposes universally discredited. It is, unfortunately, much commoner for the impossibility of the synthetic *a priori*
proposition to be just taken for granted on the basis of general empiricist
presuppositions than to be carefully argued against the case made on the other
side by thinkers like e.g. Blanshard and Ewing.

general character of the universe to which the self belongs, and
thus to have some bearing upon metaphysics and theology. It is
equally obvious that the study of the self must for its part be
incomplete so long as abstraction is made (as it is in the first
course) from the phenomena of religious experience. The division
of territory between the two courses I have found to be convenient
for many purposes; but I should find it a good deal less convenient
if I were to consider myself debarred by any law of trespass from
occasional sallies across the border.

4. But now there is, I fear, a further preliminary obligation
imposed upon the natural theologian of today; one to which,
moreover, it seems necessary to give an even higher priority than
to that of vindicating the concept of soul. This is an obligation
imposed not by the climate of technical philosophy, but by the
climate of ideas generally, and of religious ideas in particular.
I have in mind that disposition to denigrate the human reason
which is so notorious a feature in so many fields of contemporary
culture. In the field of religion the 'revolt against reason' is
virtually a revolt against philosophy; and it is common knowledge
with what bitterness, and indeed violence, certain eminent
theologians of our age assail the competence of philosophy to
make, through its accepted organ reason, any significant contribution to problems of religious truth. That this religious misology
strikes at the very roots of natural theology is self-evident. For
natural theology—at any rate as I am understanding it in these
lectures—is philosophical and rational or it is nothing.

It goes without saying that this challenge to natural theology,
with all the weight of religious authority that lies behind it, cannot
be disregarded. On the other hand, I must take account here of
the fact that a comparatively short time has elapsed since my
immediate predecessor, Professor Brand Blanshard, devoted his
first course to a particularly systematic and comprehensive
examination of the modern critics of reason. I propose, therefore,
to limit rather closely the range of my own discussion. My chief
object will be to make clear that the urge to exclude philosophy
from the field of religion rests to a great extent upon misunderstanding. I shall argue, in what remains of this and in the following

lecture, that there are certain procedures entailed in every responsible search after religious truth which cannot conceivably be assigned to anything *but* philosophy.

5.   Our first step—and it is not quite so simple as it looks—is to try to get clear about the precise nature of the claim which the philosopher, *qua* philosopher, actually makes for the competence of reason. For it seems to me that the attack from the side of religion upon philosophy's alleged aggrandisement of reason is very often in practice an attack upon the (no doubt) overweening claims which *certain philosophers* (or schools of philosophy) have made for reason—not upon any claim that can be said to be inherent in the character of philosophy as such. The real point that is at issue, which is important, thus tends to be befogged for the ordinary religious enquirer not widely versed in philosophical literature. Persuaded, for example (as he very well may be), of the unanswerable force of such criticisms as those which Kierkegaard brings against the claims for reason implicit in the Hegelian philosophy, he is apt to imagine, and he is sometimes encouraged to believe, that it is the pretensions of philosophy itself that have been exposed and annihilated. I think there is great need, therefore, that the claim for reason inherent in philosophy itself be set out with care. When that is done, objection will, without a doubt, still be taken to the claim in some religious quarters. But it will no longer seem plausible, I think, to dismiss the claim as preposterous.

We need not linger long over a definition of reason sufficient for the purpose in hand. Within the framework of the dispute about the competence of reason in religion, reason can, I think, be taken with fair safety as denoting for all parties the kind of thinking which is directed to the attainment of truth under the sole guidance and control of thought's own internal standards. That is 'reason' in the sense in which reason is the characteristic instrument of philosophy. And obviously the philosopher *qua* philosopher must make *some* claim for the competence of his instrument. Our immediate question is, just how much must the philosopher claim for it, if he is not to stultify his very choice of it *as* his instrument?

Now it is clear at once that the competence claimed for it is not *omni*-competence; that is to say, it is certainly not the ability of reason to develop from its own internal resources the whole system of truths about the universe. So much *has*, of course, on occasion been claimed; in a downright way by some seventeenth-century Rationalists, and in a more qualified way by Hegelians. But there are no Rationalists today; and even those who believe—rightly in my view—that Hegel has at least as much to teach contemporary philosophy as contemporary philosophy has to teach him are not, as a rule, prepared to follow him closely in his constructive Panlogism. Today almost all philosophers are agreed that data for reason's search after truth, data for the construction of a philosophy, come from many sides of experience that cannot possibly be identified (even in 'the last resort') with reason. Almost all, e.g. acknowledge sense experience as an indispensable source of data: the vast majority would add introspection: a great many would add moral experience; and at least some important philosophers would add either aesthetic experience or religious experience or both.[1] Moreover, even those philosophers who, because they favour a subjectivist interpretation of moral or aesthetic or religious experience, do not regard such modes of experience as contributing positively to a theory of the nature of objective reality, would certainly allow that they are all of them 'data' for the philosopher, in the sense that they have at least got to be taken account of by reason in the course of any serious attempt at philosophical construction. Evidently, then, any criticism of the 'reason' of the philosophers on the ground that it ignores sides of experience other than the purely rational has no substance whatever in relation to philosophy of the present age.

But there is a more important, if perhaps less obvious, concession which can willingly be made to the critic of reason's powers without in any way prejudicing the claim for reason that is inherent in philosophy. The philosopher is not committed by his occupational loyalty to reason to the position that God can be known only if He can be apprehended as an 'object' of reason. A philosopher might come (and some philosophers have come) to the considered conclusion that reality is supra-rational, that it is not in its ultimate nature amenable to conceptual understanding: and he might combine with this the view, also on evidence that

[1] I do not, of course, suggest that this list of 'data' is exhaustive.

approves itself to his reason, that *putative* religious insights are, *sometimes*, authentic religious insights, i.e. genuine revelations of the ultimate reality that is God. In that case he would in effect be contending that God is known, but is known only in the immediacy of religious experience and not as an object of reason. Such a philosophical position may or may not be finally tenable. But that is not the point at present. The point is that it *is* a *philosophical* position, and is so regarded even by those who reject it. It follows that the very significant limitation of the competence of reason which this position entails is not taken by philosophers to be inconsistent with the claims for reason that are inherent in philosophy as such.

Now I have little doubt that a good deal of the animus towards philosophy which one remarks in so many religious circles today rests on the erroneous assumption that the philosopher does, *qua* philosopher, conceive of his instrument reason as an organ competent to apprehend God, if any God there be: and I should agree that against such a claim for reason it is possible to bring very formidable arguments indeed. On the other hand, it is certain that some of the religious critics of philosophy, and these not the least influential nor the least articulate, know perfectly well that this is not a claim that is intrinsic to philosophy, and that there are many philosophers who would not make it. Presumably, therefore, these critics must have in mind some *other* claim for reason which, rightly or wrongly, they ascribe to the philosopher, and which they feel to be offensive to religious faith. What is this claim?

I think it is as follows. And I think the critics are right in believing that it belongs to philosophy as such, but wrong in believing that it is an invalid claim, and wrong also in believing it to be somehow derogatory to religion.

The philosopher *must* claim, I think, that wherever the question of objective truth arises, whether it be the truth of religion or of anything else, it is for reason, and for reason *alone*, to carry out the assessment of the evidence, and to make the final adjudication upon it. The evidence may come from many quarters, including, unquestionably, what is called 'religious experience'. But how far, e.g. (if at all) a putative instance of religious experience can be regarded as an authentic instance of religious experience, involving the actual revelation of Deity that it is taken by the experiencing subject to involve; and how far, accordingly, (if at all) weight is to be attached to it in the construction of a theory about the ultimate nature of things—these are surely not matters that settle themselves. They are matters to be reflectively determined in the light of a variety of relevant considerations. And what is there save *reason*, the philosopher asks, to perform this office? That reason is the ultimate arbiter in the sphere of truth: that no proposition, no matter whence it springs, has in the end a valid title to acceptance except in so far as it approves itself to reason; such is the claim for reason which, it seems to me, the philosopher is bound to make if he is not to betray his own calling. He is not bound as a philosopher, I think, to claim anything more. But he is, I think, defaulting as a philosopher if he claims anything less.

Is this, then, the claim for reason inherent in philosophy which induces so many religious thinkers to repudiate and disparage philosophy? I believe that it is. To exalt philosophy, or its organ reason, to the status of supreme judge in matters even of *religious* truth seems to them shocking; an irreligious assault upon the supremacy of faith. 'If philosophy must make this claim or perish', they would say, 'then so much the worse for philosophy '.

Nevertheless, it does seem to me that the validity of this 'philosophic' claim for reason is, in the end, inescapable. And I think we can best see that it is so by directing our attention to a simple, but surely very significant, fact. No one, so far as I am aware, is prepared to admit that his own religious beliefs are unreasonable. If that were imputed against him, on the ground, perhaps, that he is putting his trust in some non-rational mode of apprehension, he is ready to argue in defence of his so doing. He will say, perhaps, that 'mere reason' is out of its depth in the realm of religion, and that a God who is truly God can be apprehended only through His own Self-revelation, not by any processes initiated and controlled by the human reason. But then, notice well, he *is arguing*. He is contending that it is reasonable, in view of certain relevant considerations, to put one's trust in a non-rational (or supra-rational) mode of apprehension. And what can this appeal to reason mean save the acceptance of reason as the ultimate court of appeal, even in matters of religion, which is just what the philosopher claims it to be?

Incidentally, it should be observed that the believer's argument is not self-contradictory in thus tacitly appealing to reason to show that it is not by reason that we can apprehend God. For his appeal is to reason as ultimate arbiter, not to show that reason is not the *ultimate arbiter*, but to show that reason is not an appropriate organ for the apprehension of God.

On the other hand, it *is* self-contradictory to appeal to reason as ultimate arbiter to show that reason is not the ultimate arbiter. And that, I am suggesting, is precisely what the religious critic of philosophy's claim for reason is committed to doing, if he is going to try to justify his attitude at all. He may, of course, simply *assert* that not reason, but Authority, or the Inner Light, or what you will, is the ultimate arbiter: but as soon as he commits himself to *defending* the proposition, to arguing in its support, he presupposes the truth of the very proposition he is aiming to disprove. 'Argument' has no meaning if it does not invite decision in accordance with the evidence as it approves itself to *reason*.

I cannot persuade myself, therefore, that there is any real alternative to acknowledging reason as the ultimate arbiter in the field of truth—religious truth or any other sort of truth—except silence, a dogged refusal even to begin to argue in defence of one's beliefs. It need hardly be pointed out that this alternative is not one that has much commended itself to the leading apostles of anti-reason in the religious world of today.

6.   Such, as I see it, is the logic of the situation. Logical analysis apart, however, it seems a little surprising that familiar facts of history and of social anthropology should not in themselves have sufficed to convince almost everyone of the overwhelming case for allowing the writ of reason to run freely in matters of religious truth. Looking back at the course of religious development since its crude beginnings, or, alternatively, looking at contemporary manifestations of religion in different communities at different cultural levels, no one, I should have thought, could plausibly deny that in large measure the content of what is there taken to be revelation is a function of prevailing cultural ideas. It is suffused with ideas whose ordinary human origination is unmistakable; with intellectual ideas concerning the nature of man and his

physical and social environment, and with ethical ideas concerning the nature of the good life. Now is it seriously open to question that the main causative factor in the progress of religion from the mumbo-jumbo stage of fantastic and repellent beliefs and practices to what we all regard as the infinitely superior level of the great historic religions of today, has been precisely the play of rational criticism upon the intellectual and ethical ideas incorporated in so-called revelations? If 'presumptuous reason' had in the past allowed itself to be warned off the premises of religious faith, as many would warn it off at the present time, does anyone in his sober senses doubt that the ill consequences would have been incalculably great? Let me quote the words of a recent, studiously fair-minded critic of the 'religious revolt against reason'— Professor H. de Wolf:

'. . . Many millions of men have devoted themselves with passionate completeness to the worship of such fiendish deities as never existed save in the imagination. There has been no lack of existential faith in them. In obedience to their supposed commands thousands have fasted, burned themselves, cast themselves from precipices, endured shame, fought fanatically, and offered their own children as bloody sacrifices. Will we condemn the use of reason by which great multitudes have learned that such gods did not exist, and hence have been freed from their tyranny?' [1]

Of course the religious critic of reason (as Professor de Wolf is well aware) does not really want to condemn the use of reason in the appraisal of *all* religious beliefs and practices. So far as I can judge, what a great many devout Christians really want is to say to Reason 'Thus far and no further! By all means subject the superstitions of the benighted heathen to reason's criticism, but *not* the one true religion. Hands off the word of God!' The trouble is that there can be no case for suddenly drawing the line at the Christian religion unless it be that we already *know* that religion to be true; and there can be no way of knowing that religion to be true, it seems to me, unless we subject it to critical examination by reason. 'Hands off the Word of God!' is a fine-sounding slogan; but it means just nothing at all unless we know, first, that there *is* a 'Word of God', and secondly, if there is, what it has to say to us.

[1] *The Religious Revolt against Reason*, p. 115.

LECTURE II

PROLEGOMENA
THE RÔLE OF REASON *VIS À VIS* REVELATION

1. In the course of my last lecture I suggested that some part at least of the hostility of so much contemporary religious thought towards philosophy was due to a failure to keep the distinction clear between two possible offices of reason in religion: between reason as an organ for the apprehension of the Divine, and reason as the ultimate arbiter upon claims to such apprehension. It is only in the latter office, I argued, that philosophy is bound by its inherent nature to insist upon reason's competence. If it were more generally appreciated that for philosophy it is an entirely open question, not a question to which the answer is pre-determined, whether God (if there be a God) is apprehensible by reason, the gulf between the attitudes of religion and philosophy would not, I think, appear as unbridgeable as it is taken to be in many religious quarters today.

At the same time, it is only fair to observe that the confusion between these two possible offices of reason is by no means confined to reason's critics. The Rationalist too is often deceived. Profoundly convinced that reason must be held to be supreme in determining religious truth no less than in determining truth elsewhere, he slips easily into an interpretation of this which implies that if there is a God to be apprehended at all, reason is competent to apprehend Him. Now the latter proposition may, of course, be perfectly sound. But it does not follow as a mere corollary of the former proposition, as the Rationalist is apt to assume. There is no *prima facie* contradiction in holding that reason is not a competent organ for the apprehension of the Divine, while also insisting upon reason's supremacy in the determination of religious truth in the sense that it, and it alone, can adjudicate upon conflicting claims to an apprehension of the Divine.

In the present lecture I want to develop and illustrate the thesis that reason is ultimate arbiter by considering, more *in concreto*, the kind of attitude which it seems proper for reason to adopt towards claims to religious 'revelation', and the principles or criteria which it seems proper for reason to apply in carrying out its task of appraisal. The need for such appraisal arises primarily from the simple fact that 'revelations' are not self-certifying. They carry with them no native hall-mark of authenticity, no internal characteristic by which we can confidently distinguish the genuine article from the spurious counterfeit. There is great point in Hobbes's observation that for a man to say that God 'hath spoken to him in a dream, is no more than to say that he dreamed that God spake to him'.[1] The strength of a man's own conviction is, of course, almost worthless as a criterion; for mutually contradictory 'revelations' can be accompanied by equally strong subjective conviction. The authenticity or otherwise of an ostensibly revelational experience has to be determined by quite other considerations which I now wish to discuss.

2. Among the first tasks of reason in this field will be, I suggest, to reflect critically upon the general notion of 'revelational' experience in religion, in the light, more especially, of the vast increase of knowledge about the workings of the human mind that has been made available in the last half-century. Ostensible revelations have certain typical characteristics which can be, and often have been, described, and about which there is substantial agreement. Now it would be absurd to ignore the fact that there are reputable and competent students of the mind who, after a careful survey of ostensibly revelational experience, have reached the considered conclusion that there is nothing in that experience which cannot be explained 'subjectively' or 'psychologically'. The content of the experience, so it is held, is not as it appears to the

[1] *Leviathan* (Everyman edn.), p. 200.

subject to be, viz. an object disclosed to him. It is an object *projected by* him. It is a 'fantasy' whose function it is to give fulfilment to certain wishes, hopes, etc., of whose very existence in his mind the subject may be unaware. Such fantasy projection—not always, of course, simulating a 'religious' experience—is now admitted to be a fairly common occurrence in the maladjusted mind, and a good deal is known about the inner tensions which occasion it. It is also admitted, even by those most sympathetic towards the general notion of religious revelation, that at least some, and probably very many, of the experiences which seem to the subject of them to be religious revelations must be interpreted as falling in fact into the category of wish-fulfilments. Inevitably the question arises, if this be true of some, may it not be true of all?

The formal discussion of this and allied problems concerning the nature of religious experience I must defer until our second course. I introduce the topic now merely by way of illustrating what seems to me an obvious office of reason as arbiter in the sphere of religious truths. That the psychological facts relating to ostensible revelations do have a bearing upon questions of religious truth seems undeniable. It seems equally undeniable that only reason can appraise their significance.

But perhaps we are going too fast. *Do* facts about the psychological origins of revelational experience have a bearing upon the question of the validity of the experience? Are we not, in suggesting that this is so, falling into the ancient error of confounding questions of origin with questions of validity?

Now I agree that there *is* an 'ancient error' to be detected here; but I also think there is a good deal of confusion about wherein precisely it lies. It is this confusion, perhaps, which is responsible for the curiously ambivalent attitude on the part of so many ethical and religious writers towards it. On the one hand they are very ready with their retort to their Naturalistic critics that 'an account of the origin of a concept tells us nothing about its validity'. On the other hand they almost all seem extraordinarily eager to prove that as a matter of fact such concepts as 'God' and 'Duty' do *not* originate subjectively.

As I see it, everything turns here upon what sort of 'origination' we are thinking of. The term can be understood in either of two broad ways. Understood in one of these ways, the question

of origin does not affect the question of validity. Understood in
the other way, it does. If we fail to lay firm hold of the distinction,
we naturally oscillate in attitude according as one or the other
meaning is before our minds.

The distinction in meaning may perhaps be conveniently
described as that between 'explanatory' origination and 'factual'
origination. The antecedent mental processes which are the
alleged subjective origin of an idea may be called its 'explanatory'
origin if, in terms of them alone (plus, of course, the operation of
independently established laws of psychology), we are able to
understand how the idea comes to be formed; they may be called
its 'factual' origin, on the other hand, if we are not able to understand *how*, but merely find *that*, the idea in question follows
regularly upon their occurrence. To illustrate. Freud would
contend that the subjective origin to which he ascribes the idea of
God is an explanatory origin, in that, as he believes, given the
antecedents he specifies, the generation in the mind of the idea of
God is fully intelligible. An instance of subjective origination
claimed to be no more than factual would be the sort of account
which the non-naturalistic moralist gives of the emergence of the
idea of 'duty' in the mind of primitive man, or in the mind of the
ordinary child, where (so it is insisted) the idea when it does
emerge contains something genuinely new, something quite
incapable of being understood in terms of its psychical antecedents
whether taken separately or in conjunction.

Let us, then, look at the relation of origin to validity in the
light of this distinction. It seems obvious that in the case of the
merely factual origination of an idea no inference is admissible
concerning its objective validity. The idea is, *ex hypothesi*, not
accounted for by the subjective processes, and there is therefore
nothing, so far, to set against the natural presumption that we
apprehend the object because it is there to be apprehended. But
if, on the other hand, the origin does really explain the idea, it
seems to me that we are bound to accept this as casting some
shadow of doubt upon the idea's objective validity. Of course it
does not *disprove* the independent existence of an object corresponding to the idea as conceived. But it does entail that we are
no longer in a position to appeal to what is normally taken as an
important part of the evidence for the independent existence of

an object, namely, the fact that we have an idea of it which we apparently cannot explain as arising from within our own minds.

To repeat. To exhibit the merely factual origination of an idea in subjective processes raises no presumption against its objective validity. To exhibit its explanatory origin does. Even then, the object *may* have independent existence. But our having an idea of it can no longer be taken as establishing any presumption to that effect.

I suggest, therefore, that it is by no means true without qualification that the question of the origin of an idea has no bearing upon the question of its validity. It all depends upon whether the origin specified can or can not be regarded as 'explanatory'. It follows that psychological accounts of the subjective origination of 'revelational' ideas may be very relevant indeed to the attempt to determine the truth of religion: and it is, I submit, one of the functions of reason as arbiter, and thus of the philosopher as conducting reason's arbitration, to determine just how much (or how little) relevance they have.

3.   Let us assume, however, that reason's examination of ostensibly revelational experience in general leaves it as at least an open question whether or not some instances of it are authentic revelations, disclosures of the nature of an objectively real being. The task remains for reason as arbiter to discriminate, with the highest measure of probability that the nature of the case permits, between the authentic and the spurious among the ostensible revelations. What, then, are the criteria which it is proper for reason to adopt in the execution of this task? I make no claim in what follows to be listing the criteria exhaustively, much less to be saying all that requires to be said about any one of them. But I shall deal in some detail with those criteria which seem to me to be the most important.

The criteria may be conveniently divided into (*a*) psychological criteria and (*b*) logical criteria. First, then, as to the psychological criteria.

4.   These are applicable, of course, only where we have a good deal of information about the individual who claims the revela-

tional experience. We require to know something of his personality, of his mental history, of his mode of life, and of the circumstances immediately preceding the alleged revelation. Sometimes we are not in a position to learn much about these matters; but where, as is not infrequent, fairly detailed knowledge is available, it can, I think, give legitimate aid in determining the authenticity or objectivity of the experience. For example, religious revelation, if it is anything, is revelation *of* a spirit *to* a spirit. We should therefore expect it to occur only in persons whose normal lives indicate that they are, in some measure, 'spiritually oriented'. *Some* degree of spiritual preparedness, we presume, must precede spiritual discernment. It seems unlikely that—to take an extreme case—a drunken profligate engrossed throughout most of his waking hours in fleshly pleasures should have the capacity for attaining exalted visions of the Divine nature. In a similar way it offends our sense of the fitness of things to suppose that the taking of drugs, e.g. the inhalation of nitrous oxide, can yield, as it does sometimes seem to the person concerned to be yielding, profound insights into the very heart of being (the 'anaesthetic revelation', as it has been called). We cannot, of course, rule out *a priori* the possibility of God revealing Himself for purposes of His own through what may appear to us rather surprising and improbable media. Nevertheless we do seem justified in taking it as evidence, so far, for the authenticity of an ostensible revelation that it occurs in a person whom we have reason to believe to be attuned to things of the spirit, and as evidence against where the experiencing subject is notoriously preoccupied with material concerns.

In the second place, in view of the virtual certainty that some ostensible revelations are fantasies unconsciously produced by the subject himself, psychological study of the experiencing subject can usefully be directed to ascertaining whether he appears to be the kind of inhibited and generally maladjusted person from whom, in accordance with the teachings of psychopathology, one might expect fantasy-projection as a means of effecting substitute satisfactions for unfulfilled desires; and more particularly to ascertaining whether, if a maladjustment *is* diagnosed, its specific character bears a discernible relationship to the specific content of the 'revelation'. The excesses in the way of forced interpretations which we find in over-enthusiastic practitioners of depth psychology may reasonably incline one to observe special caution in this line of enquiry; but few, I think, who have any considerable acquaintance with the strange forms which 'revelational' experience often takes would wish to discount the usefulness of such psychological techniques in discriminating the spurious from the authentic.

5. From these perhaps too cursory observations upon the psychological criteria I pass on to a somewhat closer consideration of the logical criteria.

By the 'logical' criteria I understand criteria relating directly to the *content* of the ostensible revelation; to the actual doctrines it incorporates or implies concerning God's nature and His relation to the world and to the human soul. Reason requires that the propositions affirmed explicitly or implicitly in the 'revelation' be propositions which reason can accept as true. This does *not* mean, be it noted, that they must be propositions which reason can see to be logically self-evident, or to be necessary implications of propositions that are logically self-evident. To require that would be to insist that reason is, after all, not merely the arbiter but also the organ of religious truth. What it does mean is that the propositions in question must, at the very least, not violate the principle of self-consistency. So understood, the logical criterion takes two main forms. We require that the propositions inherent in the revelation be consistent with one another. And we require also—although this is a condition which must be elaborated and in some degree qualified—that they be consistent with well-accredited propositions about reality got through other channels.

So far as the first form of the logical criterion is concerned—internal self-consistency—the demand of reason is absolute. If the content of the 'revelation' contains a definite self-contradiction, it cannot be a revelation of the truth. There are really only the two alternatives before reason. Either it declines the task of appraising ostensible revelations altogether; in which case the question arises—as unanswerable as it is inevitable—how then *are* we to distinguish between the authentic and the spurious?

Or, accepting the task, reason proceeds in accordance with its own inherent principles; in which case it must reject as untrue whatever contains a self-contradiction.

But there is an important *caveat* to be entered here. The criterion of internal self-consistency is absolute. But its application to religious utterances is very far from being always a simple matter. It must be remembered that religious utterances abound in deliberate paradox; in statements which at first glance are self-contradictions, and which if interpreted in a literal, everyday sense *are* self-contradictions, but which, in the meaning the words bear for the person uttering them, are not self-contradictory at all. When the mystic Tauler describes God as 'a rich naught', is he committing a self-contradiction? Is it enough to say that, since 'richness' and 'nothingness' are terms which negate one another, the proposition is just self-contradictory nonsense?

Surely not. An attempt must first be made to understand the proposition in the precise sense it had for its author. We see then that the significance of applying the term 'naught' to God lies for Tauler in the fact that, in the case of a Being who is (as Tauler takes God to be) all-inclusive, no determinate quality can fitly be predicated. For 'all determination is negation'. When Eckhart proclaims that 'God is neither this nor that', he is expressing virtually the same insight. To ascribe a particular predicate to God is thereby also to exclude something from Him, and therefore to limit from without that which is *ex hypothesi* all-inclusive, limited only by itself. In short, the real significance of the term 'naught' in Tauler's proposition consists not in lack of being, but rather in its very opposite, plenitude of being; and hence the prefixing to it of the term 'rich', while apparently contradictory, is in reality entirely apt.

Or take Eckhart's saying that 'the first day and the last are happening at the present instant yonder'. This too is easy enough to reduce to a *prima facie* contradiction. The 'present' instant has no meaning for us save through relation to 'past' and 'future' instants distinct from itself. But according to the words of the proposition there are *no* past or future instants 'yonder'—*sc.* 'in the Divine Reality'. 'First day' and 'last day' are declared to be comprehended in 'the present instant', which is thus the *only* instant. Accordingly, the proposition seems at once to be affirming a 'present instant', and denying the necessary condition of there *being* a present instant, viz. 'past' and 'future' instants.

But the reader of Eckhart knows very well that Eckhart does not mean these words to be understood as a literal expression of the truth. On the contrary, few thinkers have been more pertinacious than Eckhart in stressing that the category of Time, which he here takes for granted, is inadequate to the apprehension of God as He truly is. God's being is eternal—time-transcending. It seems clear that Eckhart would claim for his saying only a symbolic validity. The 'truth' that is being symbolised is that in God there are *no time-distinctions*. It is symbolised by the image of an all-embracing present—'the first day and the last are happening *at the present instant* yonder'; which is not a bad symbol, surely, as symbols go. Eckhart is not addressing the philosopher. He is addressing the ordinary devout man, and accommodating his language thereto; giving to the truth a symbolic form which might enable the ordinary man to come as near to grasping it as it is reasonable to expect.

I have been taking examples from the utterances of the mystics, who are intensely aware, and constantly reiterate, that their language for describing the Deity has no more than a symbolic significance. It is necessary to recognise, however, that there are countless religious utterances, purporting to give the content of revelation, in which the speaker does intend his words to be understood quite literally. Against these the claims of 'non-contradiction' must be satisfied in a plain straightforward way. At the same time one has to bear in mind that such utterances may have had for their original authors a purely, or largely, symbolic import, even although they are *now* proclaimed as literal truth by uninspired disciples. Where that is the case, the exposure by reason of a self-contradiction in their literal significance may still have a value. It may stimulate, or help to stimulate, a religious creed which has become arid and formal to recapture the original signification of the revelational experiences which were its living roots.

On the relationship of symbolism to religious truth I shall in the second course have a good deal to say. Indeed the second course might not be unsuitably sub-titled 'An Essay in Symbolic Theology'. But in the present context these few words must suffice.

6. Turning now to the second form of the logical criterion—consistency of the content of ostensible revelation with well-accredited knowledge got through other media—the great difficulty here is to decide when a piece of knowledge got through other media is *sufficiently* well-accredited to justify the rejection of a 'revelational' content inconsistent with it. Ideally, these other propositions should be so well-accredited as to be completely certain. If not, it is always possible that it is these other propositions that are in error, and that the religious utterances may be true. But most of us would agree that propositions about objective reality, got through ordinary channels, for which anything like complete certainty can be claimed, are very few indeed.

Nevertheless one is bound to hold, I think, that where an ostensible revelation is in conflict with a rationally grounded proposition for which the competent judges in the appropriate field claim a very high degree of probability, the likelihood that the ostensible revelation is authentic is, at the very least, sensibly weakened. It would be foolish to pretend, e.g. that confidence in a 'revelation', in terms of the Book of Genesis, about the historical origin of living things—as in George Fox's celebrated vision of the Creation—can remain unaffected by its contradiction of a biological proposition so amply evidenced as that which affirms the evolution of species. There are probably few professional biologists who would not regard a denial of the theory of evolution (as distinct, of course, from a denial of some theory concerning the mechanism by which evolution proceeds) as almost tantamount to a vote of 'no confidence' in the capacity of reason to achieve any sort of systematic knowledge about the natural world. And while there is a case for the view that reason is not a competent organ for the knowledge of the supernatural, the power over nature which science has enabled man to acquire seems sufficient answer to any suggestion that reason is not competent to deal even with the natural. The least that one could demand before agreeing that a 'revelation' of the simultaneous creation of all species should be taken seriously is a tolerably plausible alternative explanation of the vast multitude of facts enumerated by the biologist in support of his evolution theory. Of such plausible alternatives there seem to be none. I do not feel called upon to explain why I do not accept as 'tolerably plausible' the hypothesis

that the facts upon which the biologist relies—fossil remains and
the like—are deliberately deceitful evidence planted by God in
order to test the firmness of man's faith when it comes into
conflict with even the best founded deliverances of his reason.
I suppose it is in a sense inevitable that man should construe God
after the image of man; but there seems no need to construe Him
after the image of a rather disagreeable kind of man.

It is well to bear in mind, however, that the just claims of
scientific knowledge *vis à vis* the claims of religious revelation are
only its claims *as* scientific knowledge. The task of natural science
is to discover uniformities of sequence and coexistence between
physical events in the space-time order. Success in that undertaking entitles the scientist to make, with varying degrees of
confidence, retrospective judgments about the past course of
events in that order, and prospective judgments about the future
course of events. There is nothing whatever in his specialised
scientific training which qualifies him to talk about the *universe*;
which, at the lowest estimate, is something much more than a
space-time order of physical events. That the expert scientist is
somehow possessed of such qualifications is a myth which the
greater among them discourage by precept, and the less great by
awful example. Yet the myth dies hard. Presumably its rational
basis is the belief, plausible but quite untrue, that the scientist has
acquired an exceptional competence in the assessment of evidence.
He hasn't. He has probably acquired exceptional competence in
assessing a special kind of evidence—that relating to his own and
allied fields of specialist study. But competence in the assessment
of evidence is not transferable directly from one field to a quite
different field. Indeed it is hardly possible to know even what
constitutes evidence in a field markedly different from one's own
without the arduous preliminary of prolonged personal immersion
in its subject-matter. One may know very well what kind of
evidence to look for in order to evaluate the scientific proposition
that the mosquito *Anopheles* is a carrier of malaria, and yet have
not the faintest notion how to set about evaluating the philosophic
proposition that a unitary self-consciousness is a condition of the
possibility of significant experience. The singular naïveté which
so many eminent scientists display in their *obiter dicta* upon social,
economic, and political principles ought to be sufficient warning

that their pronouncements in the spheres of religion and meta-physics—where the relevant evidence is usually still less familiar to them than the relevant evidence for social, economic and political theory—are, to say the least of it, unlikely to be instructive.

Actually, since the primary concern of religion is with the ultimate ground of all being, and since this is in no way science's concern, it is not immediately obvious why the two should ever come into conflict at all. Conflicts do arise, however, and they are not wholly due to misunderstanding of the respective provinces of religion and science. The most important reason for this is, I think, that what goes on in the Space-Time world of Nature cannot be irrelevant to the view we take of Nature's ultimate ground. Conflict will occur—not necessarily, of course, irresolvable conflict—if science, in pursuit of her proper avocation, presents us with a picture of Nature which is, in some of its phases not easy to reconcile with the character which religion typically ascribes to Nature's ultimate ground; not easy to interpret in terms of an all-wise, all-powerful and supremely good Creator. Again, religious 'revelations' often enough extend (as we have seen in the case of George Fox's vision) to the manifestations of God's Will in the order of Nature, and may purport to give a comparatively detailed historical account of the course of events in certain important aspects. In so far as that is the case, a direct collision with science is in principle possible. I am inclined to think, however, that collisions induced in the latter manner are for the most part on the periphery of religion rather than at its centre. That is to say, not much of real consequence would be lost to religion if it were frankly to disavow all 'revelations' about the historical order that are clearly inconsistent with established scientific knowledge. For those 'revelations' whose religious significance is manifestly profound do not as a rule relate to occurrences about which there is well-accredited scientific knowledge. It could not be maintained, e.g. that the momentous religious proposition, founded upon revelation, that God was incarnated in the historical figure of Christ, conflicts with well-accredited scientific knowledge in the decisive way in which, e.g. the 'revelation' of the simultaneous creation of animal species does. I fancy that few of those who have arrived at a considered rejection of the proposition that God was incarnated in Christ, and hence of the authenticity of the 'revelation' on which it is based, would wish to support their denial by calling in evidence anything that would normally go by the name of 'scientific' knowledge at all.

But that very fact serves to remind us that the well-accredited knowledge from other sources with which reason demands that 'revelation' be consistent need not be confined to scientific knowledge. What, e.g. of the propositions of philosophy? It is obvious that where collision between philosophy and religion does occur, it must be of a peculiarly crucial character. For philosophy and religion are aiming, in their different ways, to do the same thing. Each of them, unlike science, aspires to apprehend the real in its *ultimate* nature, and in its *totality*. Potentially, therefore, religion would seem to have a great deal more to fear from philosophy than from science.

In actual practice, nevertheless, I think most religious people feel that they have a great deal less to fear from philosophy than from science; or at any rate from philosophy in its constructive, as distinct from its purely critical, manifestations. And the reason is not far to seek. It is simply that there are so very few, if indeed there be any, propositions of constructive philosophy which constitute 'well-accredited knowledge' in the sense in which a great many scientific propositions can claim that title, viz. as enjoying the assent of all competent judges. This lack of concord among the philosophers should not greatly surprise anyone who has reflected upon the nature of the philosopher's task and the kind of evidence that is appropriate to it. Still, the result is to leave the way open for a very obvious riposte from the defender of a religious view of the universe, if that should be challenged by some philosophical view. He can always say, with evident point, 'But aren't there any number of *philosophers* who reject this philosophical view? And if so, why should religion trouble itself over-much about it?'

At the same time it is easy to make too much, in the religious context, of these mutual disagreements of the philosophers. After all, are there so very many *religious* propositions that command the assent of all competent judges in the field of *religion*? We cannot deduce from the differences of opinion in philosophical theory that constructive philosophy is incapable in principle of achieving a metaphysic of reality, and may therefore be justly ignored by religion. Propositions of constructive philosophy that are opposed to an ostensible revelation *may* be true, even although thay have behind them no solid consensus of philosophic opinion. And it remains the case that, from the standpoint of the individual person reflecting upon the claim to validity of some ostensible revelation, that revelation must be accounted at least suspect if it contradicts any proposition which the individual himself is, on philosophical grounds, strongly disposed to believe. Awareness of the extent to which philosophers disagree among themselves in their constructive thinking ought certainly to discourage sharply any tendency to dogmatism on the part of the individual thinker. But it need not, and it clearly does not, prevent him from feeling at least considerable confidence about the truth of some philosophical propositions. This confidence is probably more often felt with regard to propositions in *moral* philosophy that have metaphysical bearings, than with regard to what are ordinarily called 'metaphysical' propositions. Many thinkers by no means inclined to dogmatism have arrived on grounds of reason at strong convictions about the truth of propositions concerning, e.g. the objective reality of duty, or the objective reality of moral responsibility. Where that is so, the individual thinker has no option but to require, with a degree of stringency proportionate to the degree of his certainty, that revelation be consistent with the proposition or propositions in question. Thus if reflection upon moral experience induces in a man a strong conviction of the reality of personal freedom in moral choice, he will rightly feel doubt about the authenticity of some 'revelation' which proclaims or implies that human choices are all preordained from the beginning of time.

There is, indeed, one alternative (if such it can be called) in which refuge may be sought by those who are fearful of letting their philosophical beliefs bear upon their religion. There is always the 'double-truth' hypothesis, according to which a proposition may be 'true for reason', and a proposition which directly contradicts it be 'true for religion'. I am afraid I can find nothing to commend in this endeavour to run with the hare and hunt with the hounds. To say that we can accept a proposition as true *qua* religious being, while rejecting it as false *qua* rational being, is to ignore the plain fact that we are for ourselves not two beings but one. We can acquiesce in our own self-diremption only if we fail to notice it. Admittedly this schizophrenic condition is not altogether rare. But where a man does notice his own 'double-think', where he does realise that he is subscribing to two mutually contradictory 'truths', the question surely forces itself upon him 'But which of the "truths" is really true?' And since it is the 'really true' that 'really matters', the 'not *really* true' must simply give way before it.

This lecture has been (so far) an attempt to reinforce the thesis of its predecessor by illustrating what I take to be the legitimate rôle of reason *vis à vis* the claims of revelation. In some measure, I confess, I have seemed to myself to be labouring the obvious. I do not find it easy to understand how anyone who has even a nodding acquaintance with comparative religion and modern psychology can seriously suppose an ostensible revelation—even where he is himself the experient—to be self-sufficient, in no need of support from any other quarter. On the other hand, it is hard not to interpret the anti-rational trend in much religious writing today as a direct encouragement to men to rest content with a faith that neither knows nor seeks any justification beyond itself. Perhaps, therefore, there may still be something to be gained by reasserting the ancient truth that the only faith that is fitting in a rational being is a faith that is buttressed by reason. As Socrates almost said, 'An unexamined faith is not worth having'. 'Child-like' faith is undoubtedly a beautiful thing; but only, I would suggest, in a child.

7. I have been speaking of the need that faith should be buttressed by reason, and I have been arguing throughout for reason as the ultimate arbiter. Before concluding this general justification of reason's claims, however, I feel bound to notice, on account of its considerable popularity among theologians, a line of thought which seeks to turn the tables upon the philosopher by showing that reason needs itself to be buttressed by faith. The argument is advanced in a variety of forms, and by many theologians who are also competent philosophers. I am not aware, however, of any version that adds appreciably to what is contained in Principal

Galloway's admirably fair-minded essay on 'Knowledge and Religious Faith'.[1] It should suffice if we take this as our text.

Scientists and philosophers, Galloway declares, are not 'free to object to faith as an attitude of mind to the object, for . . . faith enters into the attitude of the man of science as well as into that of the philosopher' (p. 52). How does it enter in? At least three ways are indicated.

(1) In respect of the ultimate criterion of truth, 'non-contradiction'. 'The principle of non-contradiction . . . rests, it seems to me, on a postulate of faith' (p. 51).

(2) In respect of the scientist's attitude to his hypotheses. 'Every fresh advance in science is won through belief or trust in a theory or hypothesis which goes beyond the immediate data of experience. The labour of verification is sustained by this trust' (p. 50).

(3) In respect of inductive arguments giving 'the empirical generalisations we call laws'. 'If we believe, and act on the belief, that these empirical generalisations will work in the future as they have done in the past, then our action is ultimately grounded on faith, not on proof' (p. 50).

Now it seems to me clear that the faith of the philosopher or scientist in each of these instances differs from religious faith in a manner that wholly invalidates the argument.

To begin with (1). The assumption is that the principle of non-contradiction is not capable of being proved. Now this is no doubt the case if we limit the term 'proof' to deductive demonstration from some higher principle. Clearly there is in this case no higher principle. But such a limitation has surely little to be said for it? The proof of the principle of non-contradiction is that it is a principle which we cannot help accepting if we are to think at all.[2] It cannot intelligibly be called in question, since the critic must himself assume it at every stage of his argument. But if a principle can be shown to be such that it cannot be significantly doubted, what stronger proof could anyone want of its validity? And if objection continues to be felt to this use of the term proof', let us, if it be preferred, speak of 'validation'. All that really matters is the recognition that here we have a principle doubt, of

---

[1] The opening essay in a volume entitled *Faith and Reason in Religion*.
[2] For a fuller discussion of this topic see Lecture XIX.

which is an absurdity. Where that is the case, to speak of it as, or as resting upon, a 'postulate of faith', is surely a misuse of language.

In respect of (2) and (3) there is indeed something in the scientist's attitude of mind more like what is ordinarily meant by 'faith'; but it is not, I think, very like what the religious man ordinarily means by faith. In both (2) and (3) the faith in question is a belief held provisionally; founded upon the evidence so far attained, but held in full consciousness of the possibility of fresh evidence accruing which will conflict with it and compel its revision or even total abandonment. 'Faith' is here in contrast with 'certainty'. But it would seem to be of the essence of faith as normally understood in religion that it does not stand in contrast with certainty, that it just is not a 'tentative' attitude of mind. In so far as the religious man admits a contrast of faith with knowledge, it is with knowledge not in respect of *certainty*, but rather in respect of the *foundations* of certainty. It is a contrast between a certainty gained by some form of non- or supra-rational insight, and a certainty gained by ordinary rational processes. The kind of 'belief' which constitutes religious faith is thus not, like (2) and (3), held merely provisionally. *Its* evidence is taken to be already adequate. There is no admission that further evidence may be forthcoming which will invalidate it.

Now this is an 'attitude of mind to the object' against which the scientist and philosopher *are* 'free to object'. No doubt their objections may be invalid; but they are not (as Galloway seems to suggest) self-stultifying, directed against an attitude of mind which they themselves adopt.

Oddly enough, Galloway himself recognises in an earlier part of his essay the difference to which we have been drawing attention between faith in its religious sense and the 'faith' referred to in (2) and (3) above. He tells us that 'to believe may merely mean to hold for true on satisfactory evidence', or again to 'suppose or opine something for which the evidence is not complete' (p. 25). But such belief, he goes on to point out, 'has a fluctuating character; the attitude is a provisional one, and differs essentially from the full assurance of faith' (p. 26). I entirely agree. But the author cannot, I suggest, have it both ways. If the faith of the scientist and philosopher is an attitude differing 'essentially' from religious faith, the scientist and philosopher cannot be prohibited from taking objection to religious faith on the score that they themselves evince the same attitude of mind in their own characteristic activities.

It is not to be denied, of course, that 'faith', even in its religious context, is sometimes used with a suggestion of imperfect certainty. But where this is so, there is no quarrel between philosophers and scientists on the one hand and the spokesmen for religion on the other. Philosophers and scientists, admittedly, are 'not free to object' to religious faith as so understood. But then they don't want to. What they take exception to is the faith that repudiates the possibility that it can be mistaken, and which in consequence refuses a fair hearing to all considerations hostile to it which might be advanced from the side of reason.

LECTURE III

THE ESSENCE OF COGNITION

1.   We shall be embarking in the present lecture upon the main project of our first course—the endeavour to show that, despite the contrary trend of so much contemporary philosophy, the rigorous application of reason does not compel a renunciation of the theologically indispensable concept of the soul. There are, however, certain preliminary observations of a methodological sort which it seems desirable to make.

As I indicated earlier, I do not think it possible to counter effectively a scepticism that is so widespread, and of such varied provenance, as present-day scepticism about the soul, by the method of rebutting piece-meal this, that and the other specific argument against the soul's reality. At bottom, this contemporary scepticism derives, I believe, from a whole way of approach to the problems of philosophy, and to the interpretation of the human mind in particular; a way of approach which has been gaining in popularity roughly since the turn of the century, and which at the present time may be said to claim the allegiance of the great majority of professional philosophers. It is given, very commonly, the general title of 'empiricism'; but this is not, perhaps, an entirely happy usage. For the great divide between philosophers in recent times is not, in my opinion, between those who appeal to 'experience' to provide evidence for their doctrines, and those who spin their theories out of something called 'pure reason'. Almost every philosopher today would at least claim to be basing his views on 'experience'. There is, however, a very real divide between those who understand by 'experience' merely *sensory* experience, and those who believe that experience as a source of evidence is far richer than is allowed for by its arbitrary limitation to the sensory.

So far as the study of the human mind is concerned, the least misleading term to designate the typical modern approach is, I think, 'naturalistic'. For the method of procedure now favoured is based throughout on the assumption that the human mind is just one among other objects in the 'natural' world. I need scarcely say that this is not the method I propose to adopt in these lectures. Criticism of particular manifestations of the naturalistic approach must await its proper occasion, but it is perhaps worth while indicating at once in general terms why I am convinced it can only lead to grave distortions. The naturalistic standpoint, the stand-point proper to, and indeed alone possible for, the study of physical objects, is the stand-point of the external observer. But that standpoint is bound to be inadequate to the study of that which is something not merely for an external observer, but also *for itself*. It will not afford us even a glimpse of this latter aspect of the thing's being; and in the degree that this latter aspect is important to the thing's being, any account which abstracts from it is bound to result in travesty. Now there can be no doubt that the human mind, whatever else it is, is at least 'something for itself'. And there can be very little doubt, I should have thought, that this aspect of it is of very great importance. Accordingly it seems to me clear that the naturalistic approach to the study of the mind, abstracting wholly from the standpoint of the experiencing subject, which can alone throw light upon what the mind is for itself, is in principle hopelessly incapable of revealing to us mental experience as it really is, and as, in our less doctrinaire moments, we all believe it to be.

I venture to suggest, therefore, even at the threshold of our enquiry, that people today who have a concern for religion are perhaps a little unduly disquieted by the inability of so many modern philosophers to discover in their investigations anything that could answer to the common notion of a 'self'—let alone of a 'soul'. Adopting, as these philosophers predominantly do, the naturalistic approach to human experience, the surprising thing would be if such a discovery *were* made. It does not follow, of course, that a conclusion satisfactory to the theologian will emerge from an enquiry conducted from the more adequate standpoint which takes due account of what our distinctively human experience is for the experiencing subject. But this standpoint does seem to be the only proper one; and it is one for which it is at least an open question whether or not the soul exists. I think that that question is in effect answered in advance by those who elect to adopt the naturalistic approach.

2.　In my first lecture I gave it as my view that 'in the intellectual milieu of today, there can be no effective vindication of the "self" short of its constructive establishment from philosophic first principles'; and that this involves 'an examination of our distinctively human experience in some of its more fundamental modes and manifestations'. Without prejudice to questions about the metaphysical primacy of one or another mode of experience, I shall, simply as a convenience of method, deal first with man as a *cognitive* being. What is characteristic of human, as distinct from merely animal, experience depends so vitally upon the presence of 'ideas' that not much of importance seems able to be said about human conation or human feeling without some prior understanding of human cognition. On the other hand, it is, I think, perfectly possible to elicit satisfactorily the essential character of human cognition with almost no reference to either conation or feeling. One does well to bear in mind, however, that there is probably no cognitive experience which has not a conative and a feeling aspect, and that it would be quite vain to try to understand a man's cognitive life as a whole, or even over any considerable span, without taking account of the manner in which all three sides of his nature interweave with and reciprocally determine one another.

Our problem in this lecture, then, will be to ascertain the essential nature of human cognition. I shall lead up to the answer in my own way; but I should like to make it clear that, to the best of my knowledge, it is only in mode of presentation, not in substance, that my answer differs from that given seventy odd years ago by F. H. Bradley and Bernard Bosanquet.

In inviting attention, as I am about to do, to one of the basic teachings of Absolute Idealism, a philosophy that has for some time been rumoured to be defunct, I am aware that many of you will feel that something in the way of an apology is called for. I fear, however, that any display of contrition on my part would be hypocritical. There is, indeed, much in the metaphysics, and hardly less in the ethics, of this school of philosophy which I should be most unhappy to have to defend; and of the imprecise and rhetorical language in which its doctrines have too often been presented, I think there *is* no defence. But that there are also to be found in it elements of very great value is doubted (so far as my experience goes) only by those who have contrived to remain in, or to return to, virtually a state of nature with respect to what the major representatives of this school have had to say. It is my own strong conviction that Idealism succeeded in laying hold of two outstandingly important truths, the neglect of which in recent philosophy has been nothing short of disastrous. Both of these truths, as it happens, are of the highest relevance to the subject of this course. The first is the centrality of the *judgment* in human cognition. The second is the centrality of *self-consciousness* in human experience generally. With the first we shall be concerned at once; for we have in the Idealist's 'judgment-theory' of cognition, I am persuaded, the one sound answer to the question with which the present lecture has to deal, viz. 'What is the essential nature of the fundamental mode of human experience we call "cognition"?'

Nevertheless, while I cannot bring myself to feel apologetic about asking your attention for a doctrine which I believe to be as true and as fruitful as it is now unfamiliar, I freely confess that I am a good deal troubled about how to expound it with reasonable brevity in terms that do not presuppose some acquaintance with the context of philosophic thought in which it arose. Yet the problem of the essential nature of cognition is, in my view, of such moment, not merely for an appreciation of what sort of thing a thinking mind is, but for philosophy in general, that the task must at least be attempted. I shall do what I can to avoid question-begging assumptions, and I shall hope to forestall some mis-understandings by taking note of such objections as appear in the rare references to the doctrine that I am able to discover in recent philosophical writings. (And for your comfort let me add that not until Lecture XIX do I propose again to tax your patience by involving the argument in a system of thought so uncongenial to contemporary philosophy as that of F. H. Bradley.)

3. Let us be quite clear what it is we are setting out to discover. We are looking for those characteristics in virtue of which we should be prepared, on reflection, to call an experience a *cognitive* experience; for those characteristics which are at once necessary to and sufficient for cognition. The procedure which may be expected to throw the required features into sharpest relief is, I think, to select some case in which what everyone would agree to call a cognitive experience supervenes upon what everyone would agree to call a non-cognitive experience, and to try to ascertain what happens in one's mind when the transition takes place. We want to concentrate attention upon the transition-point between non-cognition and cognition. And it will be better, I think, to take a case where the transition is not from total non-cognition to cognition (as in awaking from a profound and dreamless sleep), but rather from non-cognition in respect to a particular field to cognition in respect to that field. This latter type of case is preferable because instances of it are abundant, can be produced at will, and are much more amenable to intro-spective observation and analysis.

Here, then, is an instance [1] to serve as a basis for our analysis:

Let us suppose ourselves to be lying out on the open hillside on a fine summer day, completely absorbed in our private thoughts. All sorts of sights and sounds and smells assail our senses, but they 'mean nothing' to us. So far as awareness of our physical surroundings is concerned, we might as well be sitting before our study fire. Suddenly something occurs to arouse us abruptly from our reverie—perhaps the scream of a low-flying 'jet'. We 'come back to life' (as the saying is) and begin to notice what is before us and about us. What we were previously looking at, but without awareness, now 'registers' in our conscious mind. It has now, in sharp contrast with a moment ago, what it is natural to call a 'meaning' for us.

I take it that everyone will allow that we have here a case in which the mind passes from a non-cognitive to a cognitive state

---

[1] I take it more or less *verbatim* from my article 'Sense-data and Judgment in Sensory Cognition', in *Mind*, Vol. LVI, pp. 289-316. The treatment of it in the present lecture is in some parts more elaborate, in other parts much compressed, but does not differ, I think, on any point of substance.

with respect to our physical environment. Let us now select for special attention some particular item in the cognised field, for preference some very simple item like a patch of green; and let us consider what is involved in its thus becoming 'cognised'.

It will not have escaped notice that already, in what purported to be mere description, we have moved a little way towards an answer. The 'green', we suggested, in becoming cognised, acquires a 'meaning' for us. This step, I think, should offer no difficulty to anyone. The claim will hardly be made that there can be a state properly called 'cognitive' in which there is no awareness of meaning. It is, indeed, in complete accord with ordinary usage to say of an object when it first enters into our cognition that it 'takes on significance for us', or 'acquires a meaning for us'.

Nevertheless, 'meaning' is such a troublesome term in philosophy that it may be as well to protect our present use of it against misunderstanding. Be it noted, then, that the sense of the term 'meaning' in our present, quite familiar, usage is different from its sense in that still more familiar usage in which we speak of *symbols* (the most common of which are words) as having 'meaning'. 'Meaning' in our present usage is a much more ultimate notion than that. It has sometimes been asserted, I am aware, that 'only "symbols" mean'. But if 'mean' is here equivalent to 'have meaning', then the assertion involves an arbitrary and highly inconvenient limitation upon the meaning of the term. It is perfectly intelligible, and in some contexts important, to say 'In so far as an object is anything for a mind, it has a meaning for that mind'. That ultimate sense is the sense in which we are using the term 'meaning' here, and clearly it has nothing to do with *symbolic* reference as ordinarily understood.

In the passage, then, from the non-cognitive to the cognitive state in respect of the green patch, we pass from a state in which it has *no* meaning for us to a state in which it does have meaning. Let us concentrate upon this point of transition. Let us ask ourselves, introspecting with all possible care, what takes place in our experience when the 'green' we have been looking at, but have not 'cognised', is suddenly perceived *as* green.

The answer I propose to you, and shall go on to develop, is as follows. The green acquires a meaning for us, is cognised *as* green, when, and only when, we are aware of it as in some sense qualifying or characterising the objective world—and, accordingly, as related to other constituents of that world.

Now the term 'objective world' is here obviously of key importance. What it denotes cannot, strictly speaking, be defined. It stands, like 'meaning' in our present usage, for a quite ultimate notion. The notion of an objective world is not something *at* which cognition arrives, but something *from* which cognition starts, something necessarily presupposed in all cognition. We can best indicate its cognitive function by saying that 'objective world' denotes for us *that which in all cognition the cognising subject supposes himself to be knowing or seeking to know*. The life of cognition from beginning to end rests upon the presumption that there *is* an 'objective world', in this sense, to be known. If we try to dispense with the notion of it we find that *eo ipso* we are dispensing with the notion of cognition itself.

An equivalent of the expression 'objective world' would be 'objective reality'. And it is, I think, on the whole a preferable equivalent. For the expression 'objective *world*' has gathered about it in common speech certain limiting associations (e.g. with the merely physical realm of being). 'That which in all cognition we suppose ourselves to be knowing or seeking to know' clearly ought not to be identified in advance with purely physical entities (nor indeed even with these *plus* psychical entities). It is better designated by the more comprehensive expression 'objective reality'. We are justified in calling it 'objective', because in all cognition one takes for granted that what one is trying to get knowledge of exists independently of one's own knowing of it. And we are justified in calling it 'reality', because knowledge is and must be of *the real* if it is to be knowledge properly so called at all. (Apparent exceptions to this, such as knowledge of 'imaginary' entities like the isle of Prospero, could, I think, with very little trouble be shown to be merely apparent.)

With these linguistic explanations in mind, it can now be made clear, I think, what I meant by saying that the condition of the green being 'cognised', i.e. of its having meaning for us *as* green, is that it be apprehended as characterising the objective world— or, as we shall now say, the objective reality. If it were *not* apprehended thus as being a character of the objective reality, if it were for us (*per impossibile*) *just* 'green', then it would contribute nothing to, could in no way enter into, our cognitive experience. For the whole business of the cognitive life is to know the objective reality, i.e. to characterise it accurately and adequately. In other words, to be *just* 'green' is to be, for cognition, just *nothing*; it involves total isolation from the life of cognition. If, on the other hand, the green *is* apprehended as characterising the objective reality, then we can see at once how it enters significantly into the life of cognition and comes to play the part in that life which we find that a *cognised* 'green' does in fact play. If, and *only* if, what is 'cognised' is apprehended as characterising the objective reality, can we proceed to link it up with other constituents of the objective reality as characterised by us in other cognitions. It is thus and *only* thus, that that which, when it first enters into our cognition, may be, as in our example, no more than 'a green something', can develop for our cognition into, say, 'a green shrub in the middle of a stretch of moorland half a mile or so to the south-west'.

What I have been trying to do in this analysis is in effect to make explicit elements that are already implicit in any experience to which one is prepared, on reflection, to give the title 'cognitive'. Of course it is not immediately obvious that these elements *are* present. There would be no 'problem' about the essence of cognition if it were. That which is merely implicit is in the nature of the case never 'obvious'. I am convinced, however, that careful introspection, reinforced by consideration of what a cognition must involve if it is to make any contribution to the cognitive life in general—without which it can hardly qualify for the name 'cognition'—leaves no plausible alternative to the view I have been urging. I repeat the view once more, for it will be of much importance for our subsequent discussions. Unless and until an experience involves apprehension of something as characterising the objective reality, it cannot have the status of a 'cognition'. If, on the other hand, this minimal condition is satisfied, the experience in question at once becomes continuous with our cognitive life in general, and what is apprehended through it can be, and normally is, linked up with other characterisations of the objective reality. It is now in a position to contribute, as it could not possibly do before, to that progressive articulation of the nature of objective reality which is the specific function of the cognitive mode of experience.

We have now to notice that if the essence of cognition lies thus in the apprehension of something as characterising objective reality, cognition will in fact always involve what is commonly designated in philosophical discourse by the term 'judgment'. We have, quite clearly, the qualification of a subject by a predicate.[1] The *subject* is the objective reality that is being characterised. The *predicate* is that by which the objective reality is being characterised. The element of *affirmation* proper to the judgment —the mental affirmation that the predicate qualifies the subject— is perhaps less manifest. In many everyday cognitions, particularly in the field of sense-perception, we should feel it more natural to say that we 'mentally accept' that the predicate qualifies the subject rather than that we 'mentally affirm' it; as, e.g. when we 'cognise' that this room is warm. But on reflection it appears that 'acceptance' here is not different in principle from 'affirmation'. For if someone should say to us 'This room is rather cold', we should have no hesitation in taking this remark as contradicting our unexpressed thought. And it could not contradict our thought unless our thought involved affirming something, and was capable of being true or false; unless, in short, our thought involved *judgment*. Mental acceptance differs from mental affirmation, I think, only in that in the former the consciousness of affirmation is relatively inexplicit. For although there are no degrees in the affirmation characteristic of judgment, although we cannot affirm 'more or less', we can be more or less clearly conscious that we *are* affirming.

4. Cognition, then, always involves judgment. Shortly I shall go on to develop further what is involved in cognition by considering what precisely is entailed by its having the judgment-form. Only after that has been done shall we be fully prepared to appreciate the immensely important implications for philosophy which are (as I think) carried by the thesis that all cognition involves judgment. But it will be best to defer for a little this analysis of the judgment-form in its epistemological significance

[1] This manner of speaking will not be taken, I hope, as committing me to what, by a bad tradition, has come to be called 'the subject-predicate logic'. See Appendix A.

in order that we may consolidate our thesis as it has so far been propounded by a consideration of the kind of objections that tend to be raised against it.

I begin with a rather superficial objection which is, I think, just worth noticing, though not worth commenting on at length. It may be argued against the contention that all cognition involves judgment that certain utterances which undoubtedly express cognitions give no indication of the subject-predicate structure essential to judgment: as, e.g. when someone shouts out 'Fire!' The answer is simple. Overt utterance is only a clue, and often a most misleading clue, to the logical structure of the cognition it expresses. It is perfectly clear as soon as we reflect upon the actual cognition expressed by the single word 'Fire!' (though, of course, 'cognition' is not all that is expressed by the word) that subject and predicate are there, for thought though not in speech. Our actual awareness is of a house (or whatever else it may be) as *subject*, characterised by the state of being a-fire as *predicate*. The judgment is given abbreviated expression in utterance for practical purposes that are obvious.

5. What looks like a more formidable objection has been raised by Professor Price. He complains that 'judgment' as used by idealists is a sort of blanket term which covers indiscriminately different types of cognition which ought to be carefully distinguished. Idealist logicians, he says, 'used the ambiguous term "judgment" to cover knowledge, opinion and belief all at once, as if there was no difference between them'.[1] As a result of this linguistic solecism, he contends, idealist logicians implicitly deny certain truths so obvious as to have the standing of platitudes. By rejecting the distinction between believing and knowing, they implicitly deny, e.g. the following platitude: 'It is self-contradictory to say "X knows A is B but in fact A is not B"; whereas it is never self-contradictory (though it may be false) to say "X *believes* that A is B but in fact A is not B".'[2]

I fear it must be replied, however, with all respect to its

---

[1] *Horizon*, Vol. XIX, No. 109, p. 63.   [2] *Ibid.*

distinguished author, that this charge rests upon a misunderstanding of the idealist logician's teaching about judgment. The only sense in which idealist logicians can be said to use the term 'judgment' 'to cover knowledge, opinion and belief all at once' is a sense which is completely compatible with their recognising the mutual *distinctness* of knowledge, opinion, and belief. What they contend is that judgment is *common to* 'knowledge, opinion and belief' (and every other cognitive mode). Judgment may therefore be said to be, for the Idealist logician, an identical element *in* all three. But that is a totally different thing from saying, as Price is apparently saying, that for the idealist logician judgment is identical *with* all three, and that all three are therefore identical with one another!

To illustrate briefly. There is nothing in the judgment-theory of cognition to prevent our distinguishing 'opinion' from 'belief' in some such terms as these. *Opinion* that S is P is a state involving the judgment that it is in some degree probable that S is P. *Belief* that S is P is a state involving the judgment that S is certainly or almost certainly P. The case of Knowledge is trickier. We cannot define it, as we can define opinion and belief, without a reference, implicit if not explicit, to the truth-value of its 'content'; and even its psychological character is debatable. Perhaps the following might serve. *Knowledge* that S is P is a state involving the judgment that S is certainly P, where the evidence upon which the judgment is based is such as to justify logically the assertion of certainty.

But the precise terms in which the distinctions are made is unimportant. The point of substance is that there is no difficulty about making the distinctions compatibly with the doctrine that all cognition involves judgment. Price's charge that the idealist logician must implicitly deny the platitude he quotes is based on the premise that for the idealist logician 'believing' cannot be distinguished from 'knowing', since each is identical with 'judging'. With the collapse of that premise no case remains for the accused to answer.

6. I pass on to an objection that is really one of nomenclature. A good many philosophers who are not ill-disposed to the view that there is something at least closely resembling what the idealist

calls 'judgment' present in all cognition, nevertheless dislike the use of the term 'judgment' to refer to it. Admitting the thing—more or less—they are unhappy about the name. The complaint is lodged, I think, on two main counts.

(*a*) It is urged that the meaning idealists give to 'judgment' flouts traditional usage. According to Cook Wilson, 'judgment' as it is used in ordinary speech implies a *decision*, taken normally after doubt and deliberation.[1] Now it is as evident on the idealist account of cognition as on any other that very many cognitions cannot properly be so described. To use the term 'judgment', therefore, to signify something alleged to be common to all cognitions, involves a sharp conflict with traditional usage, and ought to be condemned as conducing to needless misunderstanding.

(*b*) It is complained that 'judgment' has the further inconvenience of *ambiguity*. It can mean either the act of judging or the content judged. Used indiscriminately for both, it breeds much avoidable confusion.

I cannot feel that there is really much substance in either of these objections. As regards the first, it has frequently in the history of thought been found expedient to pre-empt some term of common speech for a specialised technical usage. This is the alternative to inventing a completely new term in these situations where no term of common speech in its ordinary usage will satisfactorily fill the required rôle. If this specialised usage is announced at the outset, it should occasion no difficulty to the specialist reader for whom it is intended. The likelihood of the philosophical specialist being misled by a certain degree of divergence between the traditional use of the term 'judgment' in ordinary speech and its technical idealist usage seems remarkably slight. Idealist logicians commonly take the greatest care to explain how they propose to use the term. And after all, idealist logic was for so long predominant in the philosophical life of this country—roughly for forty years after the publication of Bradley's *Principles of Logic* in 1883—that it might fairly be argued that it has itself created for philosophers a 'traditional' usage.

As to (*b*), the ambiguity alleged seems to me to be greatly exaggerated. There is something of a fashion among philosophers

[1] *Statement and Inference*, Vol. I, pp. 92-3.

today of finding ambiguities in terms and expressions which, if read in their context as they are meant to be, ought to mislead nobody. (Incidentally, sentences that contain the word 'nobody' are a very good example.) It would surprise me to learn that any serious student of idealist logic has in practice been embarrassed by the ability of the term 'judgment' to mean either the judging or what is judged. My own experience has been that the context almost always makes it perfectly clear which of the two is meant; or whether, perhaps, as sometimes happens, it is the two sides as integrated in the unity of the concrete judgment to which the author is directing attention.

In some respects, moreover, it is a positive advantage in the term 'judgment' that it covers *both* the judging *and* the content judged. Normally, it is the side of 'content' in which the epistemologist is most interested. It is important, however, that he should not lose sight of the fact that 'content' is, after all, an abstraction, never to be found in and by itself. It is extremely easy to forget this if we do our epistemological thinking in terms of 'propositions'; almost impossible to forget it if we do it in terms of 'judgments'. Not so long ago a prodigious amount of philosophic ink was spilled over the pseudo-problem 'What kind of entities are "propositions"?'—as if propositions were *anything* in their own right, and not essentially relative to a mind that thinks them. Unhappily the remedy adopted by many philosophers, of going forward from propositions to 'sentences', instead of back to 'judgments', replaced a term which was apt to mislead in one way by a term that could hardly fail to mislead in another way.

7.   Finally, I want to refer at somewhat greater length to a recent criticism which comes 'nearer the bone', in as much as it impugns directly our view that the mental assertion characteristic of judgment is present in all cognition.

The author of this criticism, Professor G. E. Hughes, rightly points out that, in the last resort, the presence or absence of mental assertion is a matter to be settled by introspection, and that, as he puts it, 'if on introspection I cannot detect it in a particular case I do not think anyone has the right to tell me that it was there after all in spite of the fact that I couldn't detect it'.

He then proceeds to tell us what happens in his own introspecting.

> 'And when I try to introspect it seems to me that the answer is that in some cases I do detect such "mental assertions" but that in others I detect neither them nor any sub-vocal muttering of words; e.g. I think there is often a time-lag between seeing a shape in the darkness and the first tentative "perhaps it's a dog" or even "it's something on the other side of the road" (or their wordless analogues).' [1]

But the answer to this seems not very difficult. Certainly there often occurs a time-lag of the sort Hughes indicates. But this time-lag has point for Hughes' argument only if he is assuming that the *earlier* cognition—what he calls 'seeing a shape in the darkness'—does not itself contain the element of mental assertion. Hughes evidently thinks this is obvious. In point of fact it begs the very question at issue. For the idealist logician, the time-lag in the case cited is between two cognitions *each* of which involves the mental assertion of judgment. What difference is there, he would ask, between the cognition (if it really is a *cognition*) called 'seeing a shape in the darkness' and the mental assertion 'There is a shape in the darkness'? Seeing a shape in the darkness (like seeing the patch of green in the example I gave earlier of the transition from non-cognition to cognition) is every bit as much a judgment as the cognition expressed in the words 'Perhaps it's a dog'. The latter cognition, according to the idealist analysis, is just a further characterisation of that objective reality which has already been characterised in a more rudimentary way in the cognition of 'a shape in the darkness'. What Hughes *ought* to be trying to show, if his criticism is to be truly on the target, is that we can have an experience of a shape in the darkness which is genuinely cognitive and which yet does not involve mental assertion of a shape in the darkness. I have argued earlier that this is not possible. *Either* the shape in the darkness is nothing at all for cognition, *or* it is mentally asserted (or accepted) as characterising objective reality; i.e. either there is no cognition, or judgment is present.

Professor Hughes, who is, I am sure, sincerely anxious to be

[1] *Arist. Soc. Supp.*, Vol. XXIII, p. 104.

fair to idealism, goes on a little later in his article to suggest that there is both an important truth and an important mistake contained in the idealist argument that 'there cannot be perception without at least mental assertion of judgment':

'The truth it contains is this: that if we find we cannot answer *any* questions about a certain object, which we have reason to believe was in our presence recently, if we cannot even think of it in a context, then we do say "I couldn't have seen it" or (shifting the sense of "see") "I may have seen it but I wasn't aware of it". . . . But the mistake is this: what I have spoken of as involved in all perceiving (or all experiences properly described as "perceiving something") is an *ability* to say and/or do certain things. Now "ability" is a disposition word, and it is a mistake to conclude that because my seeing or hearing something gives rise to the ability to do or say certain things, this saying or doing or something like them was present *at the time of the seeing, hearing, etc.* This is, I think, a case of the failure to make that distinction between disposition-words and occurrent-words which it has been one of the most valuable achievements of recent philosophical work to clarify. And if we then ask the question "Is it possible for an experience which does not contain even a "mental assertion" to be a part-cause of our coming to make assertions, mental or verbal?" then the answer seems to me to be that there is no reason on earth why this should not happen.' [1]

Now I am not at all satisfied that it *is* a mistake to hold that my ability to say, e.g. 'That was a dog I saw' presupposes my mentally asserting 'That is a dog' at the moment of seeing. But it hardly seems worth while to dispute the matter, since the 'mistake' is not one which the idealist requires to make in order to establish his thesis; nor, so far as I am aware, is it a 'mistake' upon which any leading idealist writer has ever in fact based his view that perception involves the mental assertion of judgment. The idealist comes by his view not through inference from some external test of whether a given cognition has occurred (such as the ability to say or do certain things), but through the introspective study of actual cognition, and the answers which this yields when the appropriate questions are put. What was (I hope)

[1] *Loc. cit.* pp. 105-6.

a plain statement of the idealist argument along these lines was in fact offered in the article of mine [1] which was the occasion of Hughes's critical observations upon idealist epistemology. I venture to commend to his notice, in particular, pages 295-6, where (as in the present chapter) it is maintained that, while in the case of perception 'mental acceptance' is often a more fitting expression than 'mental assertion', the 'acceptance' of A as B is simply an inexplicit 'assertion' that A is B. I confess I am rather at a loss to understand why Professor Hughes should ignore this passage and prefer to father upon idealists an argument of his own devising.

I could wish also that Hughes had made more precise his charge of a failure by idealist epistemologists to make 'that distinction between disposition-words and occurrent-words which it has been one of the most valuable achievements of recent philosophical work to clarify'. Does he imagine that the idealist supposes 'ability' to be an occurrent-word? If the idealist did suppose that, he would suppose that one's ability to assert 'That was a dog I saw' entails that one is *now* asserting 'That was a dog I saw'. But even Professor Hughes has not, at any rate in the argument of his quoted above, accused the long-suffering idealist of this enormity. He has accused the idealists only of inferring, from the ability to assert, 'That was a dog I saw', that the assertion 'That is a dog' was present at the moment of seeing. It is possible that such an inference is, as Professor Hughes thinks, mistaken. But the mistake, if mistake it be, seems to me to be totally unconnected with a failure to distinguish between disposition-words and occurrent-words. Professor Hughes may well be right in his claim that the elucidation of the distinction between these two types of word is an achievement of very great philosophical value; I think he must look elsewhere, however, if he is to illustrate the justice of his claim.

8. The discussion of these typical criticisms will, I hope, have done something to clarify, as well as to justify, our contention that all cognition involves judgment. We have now to try to penetrate a little more deeply into cognition's essential character by analysing the judgment-form itself. I want to bring out, from

[1] See footnote to p. 40.

the epistemological point of view, the nature of the subject, of the predicate, and of the relation between them. And since again I have nothing to offer in the way of positive doctrine substantially different—in intention at least—from orthodox idealist teaching, I shall make my exegesis as brief as possible.

To begin with the *subject* of judgment. I earlier argued that cognition involves asserting something as characterising objective reality, and I pointed out that we have our subject of judgment in the reality which is being characterised. Looking at the matter now from the standpoint of the judgment-form, there are two simple ways in which it can be shown that the ultimate subject of judgment (from which we shall later have occasion to distinguish the immediate subject) is always 'Reality'.

1. The judgment, by its very form, claims to be *true*. Its inherent claim to truth is manifest from the consideration that if we make and utter a judgment—say, 'Glasgow is the oldest Scottish University'—and someone rejoins 'That's not true; St. Andrews is older', we at once recognise this rejoinder as the denial of a claim implicit in our judgment. But if the judgment does thus claim truth, what is there for it to be true *of* except Reality? Does not 'truth' imply 'reality' as its correlate? The claim of the judgment to be 'true' seems to make sense only if the judging mind distinguishes between the ideal content it is affirming on the one hand, and, on the other hand, an independent reality which it aims at characterising correctly by this ideal content. The essence of the truth-claim is that the ideal content correctly characterises, i.e. is true of, the independent reality. In short (however it may be proper to specify the *immediate* subject) the *ultimate* subject of judgment is always 'reality'.

2. The same result ensues from the consideration that there is no judgment 'S is P' which cannot be re-cast without change of meaning in the form 'Reality is such that S is P'. If that is the case (and surely it *is* the case?), how is it possible to deny that the ultimate subject about which we are asserting in the judgment is always Reality?

This doctrine about the ultimate subject of judgment has often been challenged, but always, in my opinion, through some misunderstanding of its essentially simple purport. Since it has, despite its simplicity, highly important philosophical implications (as I shall try to demonstrate in the next lecture), it will be expedient to pause here for a brief space in order to notice the kind of objection that is taken to it. Perhaps the article by Professor Hughes already referred to, which finds difficulties in this aspect of the judgment-theory also, may be accepted as sufficiently representative of modern criticism. Professor Hughes has very hard words indeed for the idealist formula 'Reality is such that . . .'. It will be instructive to consider what he thinks is wrong with it.

Hughes begins his complaint against it by urging that the word 'Reality' is used in the formula 'so all-embracingly' as to empty the assertions made in terms of the formula 'of all content whatsoever': and he ends it by expressly denying that the formula has any meaning. This, he thinks, can be shown from the very use the idealist makes of it:

'The idealist is anxious to point out that "any judgment 'S is P' whatsoever can be cast, without change of meaning, into the form 'Reality is such that S is P' ", but this . . . seems to me the clearest way of showing that "Reality is such that . . ." means nothing at all.' [1]

Now when Hughes speaks of the formula as using the term 'Reality' so all-embracingly as to empty the assertions of all content whatsoever, I presume he must be meaning that 'Reality is such that S is P' *adds* nothing in the way of content to mere 'S is P'. At any rate he can hardly mean anything so unplausible as that when one asserts that Reality is such that the leaves are brown one is asserting just nothing at all. But if all that Hughes means is that assertion in terms of the formula adds no fresh content, I see no reason why any idealist should wish to dissent. On the contrary, the idealist himself virtually says as much in declaring that assertions with and without the formula are mutually interchangeable so far as meaning is concerned. But from this fact that the formula adds no fresh content it does not follow, as Hughes apparently supposes, that the formula 'means nothing at all'. For the point of the formula is not to add fresh content. Its whole point is to make explicit *what the content of the judgment is asserted of* (i.e. 'Reality'). In our ordinary verbal expression of judgments this aspect does not appear. We say just 'The leaves

[1] *Loc. cit.* pp. 104-5.

are brown'. But that the aspect is nevertheless implicit in the judgment is clearly indicated by the fact that, once it is put to us, we recognise that when we substitute 'Reality is such that the leaves are brown' for plain 'The leaves are brown' we are not making a different judgment but merely re-stating the old one.

Professor Hughes' comments are somewhat tightly compressed, and I am not altogether sure whether he wants to deny not merely that the formula 'Reality is such that . . .' has meaning, but also that the word 'Reality' itself, when used thus all-embracingly, without specific determination, has meaning. On the whole the impression is left on me that the latter, no less than the former, is intended to fall under his axe. There is even some suggestion that the meaninglessness of the former is for him a consequence of the meaninglessness of the latter. It is desirable, therefore, that I should repeat here what I said earlier in this lecture; that what I at any rate mean by the word 'Reality' when used in this indeterminate way is 'that which in all cognition we are knowing or seeking to know'. If Hughes finds that these words convey nothing to his mind, I fear I can help him no further. I confess that the recent fashion among philosophers (now perhaps on the wane) of deriding all talk about 'Reality in general', or 'Reality with a capital R', is to me most perplexing; for it seems to myself quite clear that we cannot get rid of 'Reality in general' in our thought, whatever we may do in our talk. And indeed even our talk constantly implies it. It is nor usually considered a grave philosophic misdemeanour to talk of X as 'a specific determination of the real'. But it makes no sense that I can see for the critic to tell us 'We know what you mean all right when you speak of X as a specific determination of the real, but we have no idea what you can be after when you speak of a 'Reality' of which X is a specific determination'! [1]

9. I cannot find in Professor Hughes's difficulties, then—or elsewhere—any good reason to resile from the position that it is

[1] I regret that circumstances have obliged me, in this lecture, to shoot so exclusively at Professor Hughes, whose abilities I greatly respect; but a fairly intensive search has failed to discover informed criticism of the judgment-theory of cognition by any other writer representative of the contemporary movement in philosophy.

about Reality that we are asserting in all judgment. And it is, of course, a matter of complete indifference what kind of judgment it happens to be—attributive, relational, or any other kind.[1] If the arguments we have been advancing are sound, then the ultimate subject of judgment, whatever the judgment be, is 'Reality'.

Now given that this is the case, it follows that there is a legitimate sense in which the predicate of judgment, that which is asserted of the subject, can be described as the whole complex of terms-in-relation which constitute the ideal content of the judgment—*including* what we ordinarily distinguish within that content as the logical 'subject'. But what then happens, it may reasonably be asked, to this 'ordinarily' recognised distinction of logical subject from logical predicate?—e.g. the distinction of 'the leaves' as subject from 'brownness' as predicate in the judgment 'the leaves are brown'? It is surely an important distinction, which must be accorded some significance in any acceptable analysis of the judgment? Even if there is a legitimate sense in which the whole ideal content of the judgment falls on the side of the predicate, must we not admit another legitimate sense in which we can distinguish subject from predicate *within* the ideal content?

The point is a valid one; and its validity is recognised and allowed for by the idealist logic. As Bosanquet has put it, there is in the typical judgment 'a *starting-point or point of contact* with the ultimate subject' (i.e. Reality). Our interest in judging is normally focused upon some *aspect* of Reality which has already been partially characterised through past judgments, and which it is the business of the present judgment to characterise further. These past characterisations are accepted by the judging mind, provisionally at least, as correctly characterising Reality so far, and can therefore serve as bases for the progressive building of the fabric of knowledge. Now what is ordinarily distinguished as the 'subject' of the judgment is the partially characterised aspect of reality upon which our cognitive attention is focused; and what is ordinarily distinguished as the 'predicate' is the further characterisation which in the judgment we ascribe to it. It is convenient to have a name for this 'immediate' subject to mark it off from the ultimate subject, and the term 'immediate subject' will

---

[1] See Appendix A.

do as well as any. To illustrate. In the judgment 'This tree is a poplar', Reality is the *ultimate* subject, and the predicate is the whole ideal content 'the poplarity of this tree'. The *immediate* subject is the aspect of Reality already partially characterised to our satisfaction by what we mean by the words 'this tree'; and the corresponding predicate, by which in the judgment we now *further* characterise it, is what we mean by the words 'poplarity', or 'being a poplar'.

Judgment, then, and indeed knowledge generally, may be regarded as the characterisation of reality by the progressive articulation of the nature of specific or immediate subjects, which are already accepted as real by the judging mind in their nature as so far articulated. The situation has been happily and succinctly described by Joachim: 'In every judgment, when the logician reflects upon it, he must clearly distinguish (*a*) a certain extent and level of knowledge which it develops or expands—what Bosanquet somewhere calls the "growing-point" of knowledge; and (*b*) the "outgrowth"—i.e. the expansion or development effected in, and by, the judgment in question.' [1]

10. This very summary exegesis of the judgment-form is all that our limits of time will permit. But it provides a sufficient basis, I think, for me to explain in my next lecture just why I regard the judgment-theory of cognition to be of such palmary importance for philosophy, and just why I have ventured to describe the current neglect of it as a 'disaster'. If the judgment-theory should be valid (and I can hardly emphasise enough that, with rare exceptions, contemporary philosophers have not examined and rejected it, but simply ignored it), then it can be shown, I believe, that many of the problems that have been at, or near, the centre of philosophic controversy in the twentieth century are mere pseudo-problems. To make good these admittedly bold words will be the main task of the next lecture.

[1] *Logical Studies*, p. 219.

LECTURE IV

IMPLICATIONS OF THE
JUDGMENT-THEORY OF COGNITION

1. In this lecture I want to try to justify the rather large claims
for the importance of the judgment-theory of cognition made at
the close of my last lecture. To this end, I shall invite your attention to some examples of its impact upon controversies prominent
in the recent history of philosophy. My concluding example will
relate directly to the problem of the self, and this will naturally
receive very much fuller discussion.

Let us begin with the problem of the External World.

The problem of how, if at all, we can philosophically justify
belief in an External World has taken historically two main forms,
which we may distinguish as the seventeenth century form and the
twentieth century form respectively. The earlier calls in question
the legitimacy of any transcendence by the mind of its own 'ideas';
the later, the legitimacy of any transcendence by the mind of
'sensa' or ' sense-data'. The problem in either form loses all
meaning, I think, if one accepts the analysis of cognition involved
in the judgment-theory.

According to the seventeenth century formulation, I directly
apprehend in cognition my own ideas, and I directly apprehend
nothing else. These ideas, although both 'mental' and 'mine',
are not indeed, or not necessarily, *states* or *processes* of my mind,
like, e.g. desiring and perceiving. (And it is worth noting, in
parenthesis, that critics of the Representationalist epistemology
have sometimes made things much too easy for themselves by
forgetting this, as though the Representationalist were committed

to the absurd doctrine that all cognition is a kind of introspection.)
The ideas apprehended are mental 'objects', mental 'contents',
not mental states or processes. It remains true, however, that for
this view they *are* mental, and they *are* mine; and that is sufficient
to raise an acute problem as to how, if at all, I can legitimately
pass beyond them to the affirmation of an external world, a world
existing independently of my mind and its ideas.

Not many words are needed to show that, for the judgment-
theory of cognition which I have been advocating, the problem
has no existence. For on this view, cognition does not start with
apprehension of ideas or ideal contents. It is from the beginning,
and it continues to be, a process of ideally characterising an
independent objective reality. We have distinguished on the
judgment-theory, it is true, something that we called 'ideal
content'. But this ideal content is *not*, as it is for the Representationalist, an 'object' of cognition. It is just the meaning or complex
of meanings which we predicate of, and by which we seek to
characterise, the objective reality. Accordingly, if all cognition
involves judgment, an objective reality 'beyond' or independent
of our ideas is *presupposed* in all cognition. And it clearly does not
make sense to treat as problematic, and in need of independent
justification, something which in all our cognitions we presuppose.

The problem takes a somewhat different shape, but is resolv-
able in similar fashion, within the more modern 'sense-datum'
frame-work. According to the typical sense-datum view, sensing
gives us direct acquaintance with particular existents like 'this
red' or 'this sweet'; and we directly apprehend nothing else. But,
unlike the Representationalist, the believer in sense-data is not
committed to holding that these direct objects are either mental
or private in character. They may be or they may not be. That is
one of the problems that most actively engage his attention.
Hence the question that typically arises for him is not exactly that
of the reality of an external world; since sensa, if interpreted (with
whatever difficulty) as non-mental and public entities, may
intelligibly enough be said themselves to constitute an 'external
world'. *His* typical problem is rather that of the existence of the
kind of external world believed in by 'common-sense'; i.e. an
external world which is something more than just sensa in various
relationships and groupings, an external world which consists of

'things' that are in some way other than the sensory *qualia* which we normally take to 'belong' to them. Are we entitled to affirm the existence of 'things' which are not reducible to 'families' of actual and possible sensa, or is the so-called 'physical thing' merely a logical construction out of sensa and exhaustively definable in terms of sensa? Such in rather broad terms, seems to me to be the problem about the 'external world' that is most significant from the standpoint of sense-datum theory; the problem to which, e.g. (until its defects became too palpable) Phenomenalism was widely offered as the best solution.

But for us this problem too is just a pseudo-problem which arises out of, and gets all its point from, a false analysis of the fundamental nature of cognition. If our judgment-theory be valid, then the 'sensum', understood as a direct object of cognition, is sheer myth. There is *no* distinguishable cognitive activity of sensing of which the sensum is the direct object. The so-called 'sensum', like the 'idea' of the subjectivist, in so far as it is anything for, or enters in any way into, the life of cognition, is not an object, but just an ideal content or meaning by which we characterise objective reality in judgment. The perceived 'green', if it really is cognised *as* green, is a determinate shade of greenness affirmed as characterising a certain spatial expanse in the objective reality. It is an element intellectually distinguishable within the unity of the judgment, *not* an entity *per se*. No question can legitimately arise, therefore, as to whether there is or is not an external reality other than the so-called sensa in their several groupings. Such a question rests upon the hypostatisation of an abstraction: upon the imputing of an independent existential status to that which is, for cognition, always and only a character affirmed of objective reality in judgment. The acceptance of a real world 'beyond' so-called sensa is thus, on the judgment-theory of cognition, implied in all cognition, and cannot intelligibly be called in question.

What is perhaps most commonly regarded in philosophy today as the basic problem of perception—the problem of how we ought to understand the relationship between sensory *qualia* and the physical thing to which we normally take them to 'belong'—is not, of course, the same as the problem we have just been discussing. Nothing that has been said above is in any way intended to deny that genuine problems of perception remain. It is intended to deny only the propriety of formulating and discussing these problems in certain very familiar terms. So long as the problems are stated in terms of the relation to physical things of sensa which are supposed to be themselves distinct existences, their discussion is, in my view, hopelessly bedevilled from the start. It cannot be a 'real' problem to discover how an existent X is related to some other existent, if in fact X is not an existent at all, but is from the beginning and throughout apprehended as, and *only* as, characterising an existent. Hence any problem so posed is at bottom a pseudo-problem. Discussion of problems of perception in these terms may yield—indeed it clearly has yielded in the pages of philosophers like H. H. Price and A. J. Ayer— many by-products of an illuminating kind. But that is the most that can be expected. For the problems in the form in which they are stated just do not exist, and therefore cannot be 'solved'.

2.   It will be appropriate at this juncture to say a word or two about the impact of the judgment-theory upon the Verifiability theory of meaning. For I think that this theory, though it may not strictly depend upon, nevertheless owes a good deal of its appeal to, the belief that sensa, as directly apprehended in a cognitive process of sensing, have a special place of privilege and priority in the realm of knowledge.

The Verifiability Principle, as is well known, has undergone very substantial modifications since its first crude expression in the startling dictum that 'the meaning of a statement is the method of its verification'. And I am not going to flog dead horses by recapitulating the criticisms to which the earlier formulations were subjected. It can hardly, however, without losing its distinctive character altogether, retreat much beyond the point it has now reached. In so far as it is still a power in the land (and it is not altogether easy to judge how far that is the case) it can, I think, be formulated in some such terms as these—'a statement has (cognitive) meaning only if it is possible, at least in principle if not in fact, to point to sensory observations which are relevant to the determination of its truth or falsehood'. In this later formulation the principle is offered merely as a criterion, and not also as a definition, of meaning, and is at least not now (as might be argued of its earliest formulation) logically indefensible.

Even in so comparatively moderate a formulation, however, the Verifiability Principle must be uncompromisingly rejected if our judgment theory of cognition is valid. If cognition involves judgment, it involves, as we have seen, reference to an objective reality existing independently of the sensory *qualia* by which in judgment we attempt to characterise it. Now it can hardly be contended that there is 'no meaning' in the statement that there is an objective reality independent of these sensory *qualia*, if in fact every cognition presupposes that there is! Yet this statement is surely just the kind of 'metaphysical' statement about the supra-sensible which we are commanded in the name of the Verifiability Principle to abjure as meaningless. For no sensory observation can be pointed to which will be evidence towards either its confirmation or its rejection. On the judgment-theory of cognition the evidence in confirmation of this 'metaphysical' statement is simply the fact that we cannot think at all without accepting what the statement asserts. Can there be better 'evidence' for anything? I suggest that so far from its being the case that metaphysical statements are pseudo-statements, the real state of affairs is that the much canvassed 'problem' whether metaphysical statements can be meaningful is a pseudo-problem. It arises from the failure to notice that cognition involves elements of metaphysical meaning from the beginning.

One ought perhaps to remark in passing that although no further notable modification has occurred, or indeed is easily conceivable, in the *content* of the Verifiability Principle, there *has* occurred a modification which amounts almost to a revolution in the *status* which, on the whole, its champions now claim for it. It is now pretty generally agreed among those who still think the principle of some value that it is not a necessary truth, to which the philosopher is bound to submit, but should rather be regarded as a useful methodological postulate by which all philosophers will do well to be guided if they wish to philosophise with profit. But the reply to this, in the light of the criticisms we have just passed, is obvious. It can hardly be useful for *philosophy*—however useful it may be for other pursuits not concerned with ultimate

D

truth—to proceed upon a principle whose falsity is implied in every cognition.

3. Another vexatious problem from which we are happily delivered by the judgment-theory is the so-called 'Problem of Error'; which may be taken here as including the problem of 'unreal objects'. This problem has been a thorn in the very vitals of all Realist epistemologies. Modern Realism arose primarily as a reaction against the vast claims made by Idealism for the importance of 'mind' in the scheme of things, and in particular against what was believed to be the Idealist insistence upon the mind-dependent character of the 'object' of cognition. It is the very first article of the Realist creed that the object of cognition exists independently of the cognising mind. As the Realist fully appreciated, however, this epistemological premise at once raises troublesome questions about the object of *erroneous* cognition. If we believe that Charles I died in his bed, what we apprehend— our 'object'—cannot be said without most violent paradox to have real existence in any ordinary sense; and yet, according to the Realist premise, it must apparently have *some* kind of objective reality assigned to it. *What* kind? So too with cognised unicorns, centaurs, mirage lakes, the present King of France, and the like. As objects of cognition they have to be assigned to objective reality; but as unreal objects they cannot be assigned to objective reality in any ordinary sense. The puzzle is to find an extra-ordinary sense in which the curious notion of 'unreal reality' has intelligible meaning.

In a manner these matters are now *vieux jeux*; and I shall not weary you by describing the truly desperate intellectual contortions of the Realist philosophers, in the U.S.A. more particularly, as they struggled to invent some plausible account of error while still holding fast to their epistemological premise. More than any other factor it was the difficulties over error that brought about the early disintegration of the very vigorous and able school of American philosophers who assumed for themselves the title of 'New Realists'. All that I want to do here is to draw attention to, and comment briefly upon, two points. The first is that on the judgment-theory of cognition *no* epistemological problem of error arises. The second is that the *prima facie* plausibility of the Realist's premise concerning the independence of the object cognised arises from a confusion between two senses of the term 'object'; there is, as we shall see, a sense of 'object' in which the Realist premise does hold good; but in *that* sense our judgment-theory fully acknowledges its validity.

As regards the first point. What gives rise to the so-called problem, we saw, was the Realist assumption that unicorns, the proposition that Charles I died in his bed, and the rest, in so far as, and just because, they are objects of cognition, must have some sort of independent existence. But according to our judgment-analysis of cognition, the cognitive situation which the Realist postulates—of an apprehending mind on the one side and an object apprehended on the other—is a misleading simplification of what is in fact a much more complex state of affairs. Take the false proposition 'Charles I died in his bed'. On the judgment-theory, to cognise this proposition is to assert (mentally) that the ideal complex of terms-in-relation which is what we mean by 'Charles I having died in his bed' characterises the objective reality. Thus the proposition, as cognised, is not an object over against the mind. It is just the ideal content or meaning which the judging mind predicates of reality. As such it has, no more than 'ideas' or 'sensa', an existence independent of the cognising mind—which was the Realist postulate that gave rise to the whole problem. Considered by itself, the 'proposition' is a mere abstraction: and the only being which an abstraction has is as a constituent of that from which it has been abstracted—in this case the judgment.

Mutatis mutandis, the same is in principle true, I think, of all types of 'unreal object'. There is no way of cognising them except in judgment, and the so-called 'object' turns out, on analysis, to be an ideal content, or complex of meanings, by which the judging mind attempts to characterise objective reality. It is not an independent entity, and there is no problem, accordingly, about the sort of 'unreal reality' to be assigned to it.

I pass on to my second point. I strongly suspect that most of the troubles that afflict the Realist epistemology flow from an initial confusion between two senses of the term 'object'. In insisting upon the independent reality of the object of cognition, the Realist is insisting upon what is, in *one* sense of the term 'object', a perfectly genuine postulate of all cognition. The cognitive process would be self-stultifying if the character of the object which we seek to know were affected by the process of knowing it. But everything turns here upon what we understand by the 'object' that is thus independent of the cognising mind. It is crucial to recognise the distinction between the 'object' as *that which we are seeking to know*—the object 'as it really is'—and the object *in its character as actually cognised by us*. The *former* we do, and must, think of in all cognition as having its being independently of the cognising mind. And our judgment-theory of cognition takes due account of this through its contention that what we aim at characterising by our ideal content or meaning in judgment is always the independent *objective reality*. But the 'object' in the *latter* sense, the object *in its character as actually cognised*, is a totally different matter. The object as actually cognised is the object in the character we ascribe to it in the judgment. Why on earth should we suppose that the object as thus characterised by us is independent of the cognising mind? To suppose that the mind-independence of the 'object' in *this* sense is a postulate of cognition seems really to be nonsense.

Once this confusion between the two senses of 'object' is resolved, and we recognise that it is not the object in its character as cognised whose independence of the cognising mind is presupposed in the cognitive situation, the Realist's difficulties over 'false objects' disappear. For *these* objects are merely 'objects-as-cognised', and thus do not have the independent existence which is for the Realist the cause of all the trouble.

4.   Perhaps I may be permitted to linger a moment or two longer over this confusion between the two senses of the 'object' of cognition; for it seems to me to be very fundamental, and to have had consequences as unhappy as they have been extensive. I have very little doubt that the main attraction of the twentieth-century Realist revolt against the Idealist epistemology lay for most people in the belief that the Realist, in insisting upon the mind-*inde*-pendence of the object of cognition, was introducing a much-needed rectification of a radical blunder committed by the

Idealist. And this, I respectfully submit, is a delusion. The Idealist fully acknowledges the object's independence in the only sense in which that *is* a postulate of cognition. When I cognise this ink-pot, certainly I postulate in my cognising that there is something there to be cognised independently of my cognising it. That is every bit as true for Idealist as for Realist epistemology. But for the former what is postulated as existing independently is the object in its character as I *seek* to cognise it, *not* in its character as I actually *do* cognise it. The Realist differs from the Idealist in that he apparently wants to hold it to be a postulate of cognition that the ink-pot in its character as we do cognise it is independent of the cognising mind. For the acceptance of that postulate I can see no justification whatever. On the other hand it has, I think, a fairly obvious psychological explanation in the confusion between two different senses of the term 'object'.

It would not be difficult to supplement these samples of much-debated philosophical problems which lose all point if the judgment-theory of cognition should happen to be true. I venture to hope, however, that enough has been said to make good my claim that this theory has philosophical implications of the most fundamental kind. If this be granted, I think it ought also to be granted that there is an obligation upon philosophers to give some study to the judgment-theory before deciding to dismiss it.

5. I turn now to a philosophical implication of the judgment-theory of a rather different kind, one which bears much more directly upon the central problem of the present course. I want to consider for the remainder of the lecture the implication of the judgment-theory in respect of the *cognising subject*.

The judgment-theory of cognition finds one of its sharpest contrasts with rival theories in the emphasis it places upon the *activity* aspect of cognition; and in thus emphasising the activity aspect it at the same time draws attention to something which is apt to become obscured in Empiricist accounts of cognition, viz. that there can be no cognition apart from a cognising *subject*.

On Empiricist theories of cognition, for which the dominant rôle is played by sense-experience, the cognising subject tends, at any rate in the earlier phases of cognition, to be no more than a passive spectator of what is 'given' in sense. Now it is difficult in any field of operations to overlook the presence of an active player; but not of a passive spectator. And the spectator is the more readily overlooked where, as is the case when we perceive simple sensory *qualia* like 'red', the 'spectating' aspect is by no means easy to distinguish and hold clearly before the mind. Hence a transition is often unconsciously made from treating the sensory cognition as the passive *reception* of a sensum by a subject mind, to treating it as just the *occurrence* of a sensum. The recipient, the subject mind, tends to drop out of the picture altogether.

Even on Empiricist premises, however, a subject mind is much less easily dispensed with when one passes from the more elementary to the more advanced phases of cognition. Here what at least looks like an activity aspect forces itself upon one's attention; e.g. in such functions as comparing, relating and inferring. But, though difficult, the task of eliminating the 'thinker' has not even here proved beyond the Empiricist's ingenuity. It has to be remembered that the Empiricist subscribes to a basic principle of methodology which strongly predisposes him to seek for an account of cognition free from any reference to a subject mind; the principle, namely, that nothing should be accepted as an authentic reality which is not an object of experience. Since the experienc*ing* subject cannot, as such, be an *object* of experience, the Empiricist thinker starts with a powerful initial bias in its disfavour.

The classic example of an Empiricism which keeps stubbornly to its aim of excluding from its theory of cognition all such 'unverifiable' entities as subject minds is to be found, of course, in the philosophy of David Hume. For Locke, and still more for Berkeley, the activity aspect of cognition in one shape or another seemed inexpugnable, and neither of these philosophers, in consequence, shows any inclination to deny the existence of a subject. But to Hume, in at least one prominent strand in his thinking, it appeared that the Law of Association of Ideas could plausibly be called upon to perform the duties for which less rigorous Empiricists supposed that they must invoke a subject mind. The attempt is boldly made to depict the whole cognitive life of man in terms of particular mental events—impressions and ideas—which enter into relations with one another in accordance with this impersonal, external 'Law of Association'—the 'gentle force of attraction' which was the counterpart in Hume's 'statics and dynamics of the mind' of Newton's 'Law of Gravitation' in the sphere of matter.[1] The individual mind becomes for Hume the mere theatre in which a set of particular mental events happen. And the spatial metaphor 'theatre' is not, of course, meant by Hume to be taken too seriously, as though it denoted some reality additional to what goes on 'in' it. It signifies no more, I think, than Hume's recognition that the happenings in what, in common parlance, is called a 'mind' are inter-related in some way which constitutes them a distinctive kind of unity. When we get behind the metaphor, the reality of the individual mind consists in nothing more than the reality of particular mental events and groups of mental events in their distinctive unity.

The *judgment*-theory, on the other hand, construes cognition as essentially an *active* process, because judgment is essentially an active process. This activity-aspect of judgment can perhaps best be brought out by contrasting the connection of ideas as we experience it in a case of mere association, with the connection of ideas as we experience it in a judgment. Consider, e.g. our experience when the perception of a frozen pond excites in our mind the image of one's self skating on its surface, as contrasted with our experience when the same perception is the occasion of our framing the judgment that the pond is 'bearing'. In the former, the connection is experienced as something that happens *in* or *to* our mind. *We* do nothing about it. The image of one's self skating just 'rises up' in our consciousness. But in the latter, in the *judgment*, we are aware, however dimly, that we *are* doing something about it. The idea represented by the term 'bearing' is not experienced as something that just 'happens' in our mind following upon our perception of the frozen pond. In a real sense it is we who make it happen in our mind, by our active cognitive interest in, and consequent attention to, the character of the pond.

6. But at this point it would be wise, I think, to indulge in a partial digression. The emphasis I have been laying upon the active aspect of cognition, coupled with my earlier refusal to allow

[1] *The Philosophy of David Hume*, by N. Kemp Smith, pp. 71 ff.

existence to so-called 'sense-data' or 'sensa', may have created a suspicion that I want to deny to 'mere sensation' any effective part in the cognitive life. I must make it clear that such is not in fact my view. On the contrary, I take sensation to be, though not itself a mode of cognition, a vital determining factor *in* cognition. Let me elaborate this point a little.

Although the mind is never, I think, in any judgment, a mere recipient of ideas; although it is always, in some degree, active in initiating the changes which characterise its cognitive field when a judgment is made; nevertheless, it is not to be denied that in some judgments there is an aspect of passivity which is a great deal more striking than the aspect of activity. I have in mind especially those elementary sensory judgments in which we affirm that some simple sensory *quale*—a colour, a sound, or a smell—characterises a part of our physical environment. On these occasions, while it is doubtless true that no judgment would take place but for the initiating activity of the mind, it is also true that, if the mind does judge at all, it feels compelled to judge in a certain determinate way. And this compulsion is felt as coming from a source *external* to the judging mind. There is, of course, a sense in which in all judgment the mind is conscious of a compulsion to judge in one way rather than another; for there is an obligation to observe logical consistency acknowledged, implicitly or explicitly, in all our judging. But this 'logical' compulsiveness is, as it were, internal to the mind, and is in that respect quite different from the special kind of compulsiveness of which we are conscious in simple sensory judgments. If a coloured patch is presented to me and I am asked what colour I see, I normally feel a compulsion which is not in the least like a logical compulsion to judge that the patch has *this* and not *that* determinate colour. And if I am asked what is the source of this compulsion, I do not see what answer I can well offer except just 'the given in sensation' or some similar expression. It seems to me, therefore, that not only must we recognise an element of passivity, as well as of activity, in many judgments, but that this element is most naturally identified with the function in experience of 'sensation'.

But we must, I think, pursue the matter a stage or two further. For on this question of the rôle of sensation in cognition the school of epistemologists with which I am in general well content to associate myself, the idealist school which insists upon the centrality of the judgment in cognition, does seem to me to have laid itself open to criticism. They have, in point of fact, very little of a direct character to say on the question—which is in itself a ground for complaint, since the question is obviously important. But the language they tend to use about sensory cognition implies the ascription to the intellect of functions which, in the case of basic sensory cognitions at any rate, can hardly be defended. They are ready enough to grant, as a rule, that in sensory cognition the activity from the side of the mind is not the whole story. There must be, they acknowledge, some kind of a 'datum'. But this datum, apparently, is for them something upon which thought 'gets to work' in the way of interpretation. So much seems implied by their frequent assertion that there is always 'interpretation' as well as 'datum', and that the object of sensory cognition is always an 'interpreted datum'.

But this formula, 'an interpreted datum', surely signifies a gross over-estimate of the part played by the intellect in basic sensory cognitions? Without doubt, in the higher reaches of sense-perception much goes on that can very properly be called 'interpreting data'. Presented with a small, brown, smooth, oval shape, we interpret these data as 'egg'. On the basis of our past experience we can say to ourselves, 'these signify "egg" '. But where is the interpretation, and what is it that is interpreted, in a basic sensory cognition where a blue patch, say, is first cognised *as* blue? Here there is no passage, such as 'interpretation' involves, from that which is initially apprehended to the interpretation of it. There *are* no initially apprehended characteristics to be interpreted. What is present, I have suggested, is a felt extra-logical compulsion to affirm blueness of the patch: but this is as different as well can be from an act of 'interpreting' the patch as blue.

Our basic sensory cognition, then, though a judgment, is very misleadingly described when it is said to involve 'interpreting a datum'. The determinate content the judgment affirms is due not to interpretation by the intellect but to the extra-logical compulsion exerted by pure sensation or pure sensing.

Can we say any more by way of characterising this elusive 'sensation', which is not a mode of cognition, and is yet a basis for and determinant of cognition? I think we can say a little, but

not very much. I think we must at least say that it is something
which falls within the general field of 'experience'. It is not a
physical process in the brain (or elsewhere)—though we are able,
on what appear very good grounds, to correlate it with such
processes. When we suppose ourselves compelled by 'sensation'
to judge in certain ways, we do not suppose that it is some brain
process that so compels us, and we may not even be aware that
a brain process is going on. But while it seems proper to regard
'pure' sensing as, in its intrinsic nature, an experience, it is an
experience for which the distinction of subject from object does
not exist; an experience in which sensing and sensed are in
indivisible unity. It thus falls into the general category of immediate experience, or feeling. I am inclined to believe that this
is the least misleading way to regard 'pure' sensation—viz. as a
specific sort of immediate experience—and I doubt if we can
profitably characterise it much further.

7.   In any event, it is rather more than time that we took up
again the main thread of our argument. I had been pointing out
how the judgment theory of cognition differs from other theories
in its emphasis upon the activity aspect. Now the implication of
that emphasis is that the cognising *subject* is thrown into sharp
relief. Subscription to the judgment theory relieves us of any
temptation to look upon the individual mind as just a sort of
mise en scène for particular cognitive events. 'Activity' implies a
subject that is active. And—though some philosophers have at
least talked as though they thought otherwise—*that which is*
active in activity cannot possibly be *the activity itself*. To suppose
that activities can themselves be active is surely to commit an
outsize example of what Professor Ryle would call a 'category
mistake', and of what Professor Moore a generation back would
have called, more picturesquely if less precisely, a plain 'howler'.
     The impossibility of dispensing with a cognitive subject
distinguishable from, though not of course separable from,
particular cognitions, seems to me, then, to be one of the plain
implications of the judgment-theory. At the same time I should
not wish to leave the impression that, in my belief, the need for
positing a cognitive subject vanishes if one does not happen to be

persuaded that the judgment-theory of cognition is the true one. That theory, by the stress it lays on the activity aspect, merely high-lights the absurdity of trying to get along without a cognitive subject. But the absurdity remains, I should contend, though it may be less conspicuous, on any theory of cognition; always provided that, unlike Behaviouristic and quasi-Behaviouristic theories, it really *is* a theory of *cognition*. There is in fact a simple enough argument (already hinted at) which seems to me conclusive against all attempts to exorcise from cognition a subject distinct from the actual cognising. It is as follows. Let X be the psychical operation of cognising or apprehending, and Y be the object that is cognised or apprehended. Now presumably the apprehend*ed* implies an apprehend*er* of *some* sort. What then is the apprehend*er* of Y? According to those who deny a distinguishable subject, it can only be X, the actual operation of apprehending. But this is surely absurd. An apprehend*ing* cannot be *that which* apprehends. What is 'known' cannot be known *to* the operation of knowing. It can be known only *to* a subject which, while *engaged in* the knowing, is not itself *identical with* the knowing. As Professor Bowman observes in concluding his own admirable statement of the argument, 'To represent a mental process as at once a psychical performance and a performer is out of the question'.[1]

It is hardly surprising, therefore, that even those theories for which cognition is never more than a mere passive awareness are not really able to proceed far in their epistemology without having recourse to language which tacitly presupposes the cognising subject which their official conclusions repudiate. One need only think of the intolerable paradoxes in, e.g. Hume's explanation of how the 'bundle of perceptions' that is the individual mind comes to frame the 'illusion' that it is something other than a mere bundle. It is odd how little Hume's modern disciples seem to have learnt from their master's own revealing confession of failure in the well-known Appendix to the *Treatise*, where he comes next-door to acknowledging the total shipwreck of his atomistic interpretation of the human mind. An atomic

[1] *A Sacramental Universe*, p. 196. This unduly neglected work seems to me one of the few masterpieces of constructive philosophy published in the last quarter-century. In particular, nowhere else to my knowledge is there so penetrating an analysis as in these pages of what it means to be a 'subject' of experience.

mind, he now strongly suspects, just could not perform those reflections upon its own experiences which (as he earlier supposed) delude it into supposing that it is *not* atomic. Dr. F. R. Tennant has well said that 'no one ever has really dispensed with the subject of consciousness, whatever terms he may have used to hush up its existence'. [1]

But it is still a far cry, of course, from the vindication of the 'cognitive subject' to the vindication of something that might reasonably claim to be called a 'self'. In the next Lecture I hope to make more appreciable headway towards this goal by examining the nature of the cognitive subject from the standpoint of its own experience of itself. Our topic will, in short, be what is commonly known as 'self-consciousness'.

[1] *Philosophical Theology*, Vol. I, p. 18.

SELF-CONSCIOUSNESS, SELF-IDENTITY, AND PERSONAL IDENTITY

1. In the closing stages of my last lecture I argued that the judgment-theory of cognition throws into relief the hopelessness of trying to dispense with a distinguishable cognising subject. Today I want to begin consideration of the nature of this 'subject'. The fundamental difficulty we have to deal with is very well known. There seem to be respectable reasons for describing the cognising subject as a 'substantival' entity in *some* sense of that term: and there seem to be equally respectable reasons for rejecting the 'substantival' description in *any* sense of the term.

It is reasons of the latter order which, as one would expect, have received much the greater prominence in recent philosophy. But finding objections to the substantival theory has proved a great deal easier than finding a plausible alternative to it. My own view is that, while there are certainly forms of the substantival theory that are indefensible, the objections taken to the substantival theory as such, or in general, are invalid; whereas against any alternative to the substantival theory which has so far been offered there seem to me to be objections of a completely conclusive character. That will be the main thesis to be argued in the present lecture; but I must introduce it somewhat gradually.

2. Let us begin with a proposition the truth of which seems to me easily demonstrable within the context of our recent discussions; the proposition that the cognising subject is always in some degree aware of itself, or 'self-conscious'.

This, I think, can be seen to be yet another implication of the judgment-theory of cognition. All cognition involves judgment. All judgment involves reference to an 'objective' reality which the judging mind is seeking to know. But an essential part of the meaning which 'objective reality' carries for the judging mind is its independence of that mind. Hence a mind that is aware of objective reality is always also in some degree aware of itself as subject. It follows that all cognition implies in the cognising subject some degree of self-awareness.

It goes without saying that in very many cognitions the degree of self-awareness present is exceedingly small. But so, for that matter, in many cognitions, is the degree of awareness of an independent objective reality; and yet, as we saw earlier, there are cogent reasons for presuming it present, in however inexplicit a fashion, wherever anything which can strictly be called a cognition occurs. Hence if it be the case that 'objectivity' defines itself, for the cognising mind, at least in part, by contrast with 'subjectivity', we must, I think, conclude that cognition always involves some awareness, however inexplicit, of the subject as subject.

3.   But now what kind of a being is this 'subject' of which there is consciousness in all cognition? Its most important, and at the same time its most perplexing, characteristic is that it is, for itself, somehow the *self-same* being throughout its different experiences; and the self-same being not merely in contemporaneous experiences, but in experiences far removed from one another in time. Thus I am conscious that I who am now thinking about a peculiarly intractable philosophical problem am the same being as I who am now feeling the room to be slightly on the warm side, and am *also* the same being as I who (as I remember) saw a rainbow yesterday. Indeed, 'remembering' brings out in an especially striking manner the self's identity in difference. When we say '*I* remember that *I* saw a rainbow yesterday', we imply that the being who now remembers is identical with the being who saw the rainbow. The claim of the memory situation, a claim in the absence of which the situation ceases to be one of memory at all, is that the remember*ing* subject and the remember*ed* subject

are somehow the *same* being in experiences that are different both temporally and qualitatively.

The difficulties in the way of attaching a clear meaning to the self-sameness of the subject in different apprehensions will engage us shortly. But we must first of all support by more formal argument the thesis that cognition of *any* kind—not merely in remembering—implies a subject conscious of its own identity in its different apprehensions.

4. The standard argument for this doctrine is so exceedingly well-worn as almost to require apology for its repetition, and I shall expound it in very summary fashion. It derives, of course, from Kant. What follows will perhaps serve as a sufficient reminder of its general character.

Cognition is never of an atomic simple. It is always of a related plurality *as* a related plurality. This is self-evident if all cognition involves judgment, for in all judgment there must be at least the differences of subject and predicate and the affirmation or denial of their union. But we need not invoke the judgment theory to establish our point. It is clear enough, on reflection, that an 'object' which stands in no apprehended relation to other objects of our experience—'an atomic simple'—can have no significance for us, and is thus not an object of cognition at all. Even a 'this' is, for cognition, a 'this-not-that'; apart from its apprehended distinction from, and therefore relation to, a 'that' it could not be cognised as 'this'. But it seems gratuitous to pursue further a point which has so often received classic expression in post-Kantian philosophy. The critic may be challenged to produce a single instance of cognition, or 'meaningful apprehension', where the object does *not* consist in a related plurality.

What is cognised, then, is never bare A, but always A in some sort of relationship to B (C, D, etc.). But unless the subject to which B (C, D, etc.) is present is the same subject as that to which A is present, no relationship, obviously, could be apprehended between B (C, D, etc.) and A. To take the very familiar example of our cognition of succession in time, perhaps the most basic of all cognitions. If event B is cognised as sequent upon event A, clearly A must, in some form, be present to the same subject as that to which B is present. Otherwise A and B would simply fall apart into separate worlds of experience, and no discerned relationship—not even that of apartness, let alone that of temporal sequence—would be possible.

Does cognition imply not merely a subject identical in different cognitions, but a subject *conscious* of its identity in different cognitions? Some philosophers who are firmly persuaded of the subject's self-identity show a certain diffidence about pressing for the subject's consciousness of that identity. Nevertheless I would suggest that this must be pressed. For let us suppose that the subject, though in *fact* identical in two different apprehensions, is in no wise aware of its own identity in them. This subject, let us further suppose, has an apprehension of A, and then an apprehension of B. Now for an outside observer apprised, if that were possible, of the two apprehensions, A and B could be seen to be related, inasmuch as they could be seen both to be objects to the same subject. But for the *subject himself*, unaware (according to our supposition) that the self to whom B is present is the same being as the self to whom A was formerly present, the two apprehensions must fall apart into separate 'worlds' just as surely and completely as though he, the self-same subject, were in fact *two different* subjects; and the discernment by him of any *relationship* between A and B (such as that of temporal sequence) must then become impossible. The *prius* of any discernment by the subject of a specific relation between A and B is surely that the subject is aware of A and B as having at least that general relationship to one another which consists in their both being objects for *him*, the one self. He must, in other words, be conscious of his own identity in the different apprehensions.

The point is apt to be as elusive as it is certainly important, and a further illustration may be helpful.

Suppose I hear Big Ben striking. A moment later I—the same subject—hear it striking again. Now is my being 'the same subject' sufficient in itself to enable me to apprehend the second stroke *as* the second stroke, as *sequent upon* the first? Not, surely, unless by 'the same subject' we *mean* a subject conscious of its self-sameness. I may be in so advanced a state of senility that my memory-span is no longer adequate to bridge the gulf between the two strokes, so that, having forgotten the first when I hear the second, I cannot relate the two to one another. It is a pre-condition of my apprehending the second stroke *as* the second stroke that I remember having heard the first. But then I do not 'remember' having heard the first (and here is the crucial point) unless I am aware that it was *I*, the being who now hears the second stroke, who heard the first stroke; unless, in other words, I am not merely the same subject, but also conscious of my self-sameness, in the two experiences.

It seems to me, therefore, that while the identity of the cognising subject is a necessary, it is not, without consciousness of that identity, a sufficient, condition of cognitive awareness.

5. The point we have now reached (re-tracing, for the most part, familiar lines of argument) is that all cognition implies a subject that is conscious of itself, and that this self of which we are conscious in cognition is a being which is identical with itself throughout—and in despite of—the diversity of its cognitions. But now our troubles begin. We are led by the argument, appar-ently, to posit a self which is something 'over and above' its particular experiences; something that *has*, rather than *is*, its experiences, since its experiences are all different, while *it* some-how remains the same. It is, in short, what would usually be called a 'substance', in some sense of that term, and as such it provokes in the modern mind an hostility which, to say truth, the history of philosophy has done much to justify. What, it will be asked, *is* this 'I' that is supposed to remain the same, and in what does its sameness consist? By universal admission we never have any acquaintance with it by itself, but only as manifested in particular changing experiences. What possible meaning can we attach to an 'I' as an identical 'something' over and above these experiences? And our perplexities, it will be urged, by no means end there. If we try to conceive the self as an identical substance, how are we to reconcile with this all the phenomena of radical disunity made familiar to us by abnormal psychology, such as sudden drastic transformations of a self's personal character, not to speak of these strange cases of 'multiple personality' in which the 'one' self seems to divide up into two or more separate selves?

The difficulty of returning satisfactory answers to such

questions has proved so formidable that the strong trend of philosophic opinion today is in the direction of relinquishing the notion of a 'substantival' self altogether. The notion of a self of *some* sort, it is conceded, must be retained. We do mean something by the word 'I'; and we do mean something when we refer to a variety of different experiences as all 'my' experiences. But an interpretation must be found, it is urged, in terms of the particular knowable experiences themselves, not in terms of an 'unknowable' something beyond them. Hence it has appeared to many to be the most promising procedure to search *within* the different experiences for some identical quality or, more hopefully, some common relationship, in virtue of which they come to be regarded as all experiences of 'one self'.

6. What then *is* this quality or relationship? That is just the trouble. I think it is fair to say that, while the great body of contemporary philosophical opinion favours the view that this is where the meaning of self-identity must be sought, there is no manner of agreement as to what the quality or relationship can be. Indeed, no one seems to have much confidence even in the theory he himself proposes, but rather to be putting it forward tentatively as an hypothesis that is not wholly incredible, and is at any rate more credible than any form of substantival theory. As already hinted, some kind of common relationship, rather than some kind of identical quality, has been very generally taken to be the most hopeful thing to look for. But all the types of relationship between different experiences that are known to us in other contexts—similarity, causality, and the rest—seem open to obvious and crushing objections if we try to regard them as the basis of the mind's self-identity. Any one of them can exist between particular experiences without our having the slightest tendency to take these particular experiences to be all experiences of a single self.[1] It is, I think, not easy to dissent from the conclusion reached by Dr. Ewing after a critical survey of the several

---

[1] Mr. D. G. C. McNabb, in what is otherwise a most penetrating discussion of Hume's treatment of personal identity, seems to think that while such relations as similarity, causality, and spatial and temporal conjunction of perceptions will obviously not account for the kind of identity that belongs to a self, the relational theory may perhaps still be saved if we supplement

types of relationship that have been, or conceivably might be, suggested, viz. that 'if we adopt a view of the self according to which its identity is constituted . . . by a relation between its experiences, it is probably best just to say that the relation is unique and indefinable.'[1]

I do not, however, propose to take up time rehearsing the various relational theories *seriatim*, for the following reason. It seems to me that the whole project of seeking for the identity of the self in a relation of *whatever* kind, definable *or* indefinable, between members of a series or group of experiences, is funda-mentally futile; indeed self-contradictory. For consider. What we are trying to account for is the identity of a self *not* for some *external observer*, but for the *self itself*; the identity of the self as *subject*, not its identity as an *object*—which the self, *qua* self, just is *not*. Now as a result of cognition of particular events and their inter-relationships we might come to regard as belonging to 'one and the same' *object* events which exhibited a certain form of inter-relationship. Applied to mental events, there is some sense in saying that we might thereby arrive at the notion of an object-mind as an identical *it*. But it is the *subject*-mind, the identical 'I' of *self*-consciousness, which we are trying to account for; and by the route suggested this is plainly impossible. For, as we have already seen, cognition of relationships, and indeed cognition of any kind whatsoever, *presupposes* an identical subject conscious of its own identity. It follows that the 'relational' way of explaining self-identity can only be in terms which presuppose the very thing it is purporting to explain.

these relations by another 'empirically given relation which we may call co-presentation, which holds between any two or more perceptions which I am in a position to compare with one another'. He confesses himself, indeed, not too happy about this solution, since 'it looks very much as if it were an empirical fact that this relation is at least a three-term relation, involving at least two perceptions and something else, the mind to which they are presented and which is able to compare them'. I suggest that 'looks very much as if' is, to put it mildly, an understatement. If 'co-presentation' is really 'co-*presentation*', it is surely an analytic proposition that there is this 'third term'; while if 'co-presentation' means something else (which it has no right to mean), like 'co-occurrence' of perceptions, it is plainly useless for the purpose in hand. It may be that the 'third term' is, in Mr. McNabb's words, 'a very curious kind of entity'; but this hardly seems adequate ground for denying an analytic proposition. (*David Hume, His Theory of Knowledge and Morality*, pp. 149-50.)

[1] *The Fundamental Questions of Philosophy*, p. 115. (Italics not in text.)

I suggest, then, that the attempt to find a form of relationship between different experiences which is sufficient to account for my regarding these experiences as 'mine' is doomed to failure from the outset. There *is*, indeed, an apprehended relationship in virtue of which I call experiences 'mine', but it is not a relationship of experiences to one another. It can, I think, only be stated as a relationship of experiences to *me*, an identical subject conscious of having or owning them; a relationship of 'belonging to' which is unique and indefinable, but the apprehension of which is ingredient in all self-conscious experience. It is clear, however, that this relationship presupposes, and in no way constitutes, the identity of the self.

Still, the problem remains on our hands, 'In what does self-identity consist?' The relational theory may be, and I think is, open to fatal objections; but so far nothing explicit has been said to show that the substantival account, the difficulties in which gave rise to the relational theory, is in any better case. Let us now look back, therefore, at the notion of the self as a substantival entity, distinguishable from its experiences, and, a little fortified by the apparent bankruptcy of the rival relational theory, consider whether it cannot be formulated in a way that escapes the objections usually thought to be conclusive against it.

7. Two preliminary points are worth making briefly. Critics of the substantival self seem to me a great deal too ready to assimilate it either to Locke's 'unknowable substratum' of material things, or to Kant's 'noumenal ego'. This is, I think, unfortunate. It is by no means the case that the doctrine of the substantival self need take a form that lays it open to the objections to which Locke's and Kant's doctrines are notoriously exposed.

To take first the assimilation to Locke's unknowable substratum of material things, Berkeley has said perhaps all that needs to be said on the ineptitude of supposing that spiritual substance and material substance must stand or fall together. When Philonous in the Third Dialogue points out to Hylas that whereas I have no apprehension whatsoever of material substance, I yet 'am conscious of my own being, and that I myself am not my ideas, but somewhat else, a thinking, active principle that perceives, knows, wills, and operates about ideas', he is indicating a *prima facie* difference in the epistemological status of spiritual substance and material substance respectively that is fundamental. Self-consciousness, it must be insisted, is a *fact*, a datum from which we have to *start*. And in self-consciousness the subject of which we are conscious is a subject which in some sense has, not is, its different experiences, and is identical with itself in its different experiences. Even if it were possible for self-consciousness to be illusory, its mere occurrence is enough to refute those who take the view that the notion of a substantival self is as 'meaningless' as the notion of an unknowable substratum of material things. It is idle to deny that the former of these notions has any meaning for us if that *is* in fact what the self is for itself in self-conscious experience.

Very little more reflection is needed to see that the substantival self cannot be straightway identified with Kant's noumenal ego.

For Kant, it will be remembered, the subject self has its reality beyond the space-time world of mere phenomena; and while we can know in self-consciousness *that* it is, we can say nothing at all about *what* it is. Cognition of the character, the 'what', of the self through introspection is not, for Kant, discernment of the nature of the self as *subject*—i.e. of its real nature *qua* self—but only of the self as *object*, which is a mere appearance in time of the timeless 'real' self. Kant's noumenal ego is, from the point of view of theoretical cognition at any rate, as character-less as Locke's substratum of material things.

But the defender of the substantival self is under no obligation to accept Kant's views either about time or about what introspection can and cannot reveal to us. One may perfectly well agree with the argument from self-conscious experience to a distinguishable subject-self without being committed to any of the special arguments which lead Kant to assert that we can have no theoretical knowledge of that self as it really is. I shall in a later lecture have to give some attention to the problem of the nature and status of introspection as a mode of knowledge, and I shall try to show there that it is a mistake to suppose that introspection cannot reveal real characteristics of the self *qua* self, that is to say, of the self in its functioning as a *subject*. Meantime I would merely point to the direct testimony of self-consciousness. When I am conscious that I who think *A* am the I who desires *B* and the I who feels the emotion *C*, I regard my 'I' as manifesting *itself* in these operations of thinking, desiring and feeling: and as thus, so far, 'characterised' by these operations. The subject self as apprehended in self-consciousness is in that sense always a determinate or characterised self. To deny that the self is *reducible to* its experiences is by no means to deny that the self manifests its real character (in whole or in part) *in and through* these experiences. The onus of proof lies upon those who wish to maintain that to the self as subject we can assign no determinate characters at all.

I attach a fair amount of importance to these two points; for there is nothing to be gained by making the problem of justifying a substantival self still more difficult than it already is through pejorative misconceptions as to what belief in a substantival self in fact entails. But the puzzle about this self's identity remains baffling enough and must now be directly confronted.

8.   I propose to work towards the view which seems to me in the end the most acceptable by raising in turn, and trying to answer, four distinct but closely related questions.

1. Can a *meaning* be given to the substantival description of the self; i.e. to the description of it as a being which is distinct from the states in which it manifests itself and is identical with itself throughout these manifestations?

2. Granted that the description is not 'meaningless', is there good reason to believe that beings answering to that description actually *exist*?

3. Given an identical self as so described, of *what* is it an identity? Is it an identity of spiritual being, of material being, of both, or of something else?

4. How is the identity of the self, so understood, related to what is called '*personal* identity'?

Now so far as the first question is concerned, the answer has already been given in principle in the reference we made to Berkeley. Self-consciousness is a fact of experience; and the self of which we are conscious in self-consciousness *is* a subject which in some sense has, rather than is, its different experiences, and is identical with itself throughout them. It must be a strangely doctrinaire theory of meaning that would oblige us to denounce as meaningless a description which describes what the self is for itself in all self-conscious experience.

It is sometimes said that the substantival self is meaningless because openly self-contradictory. If 'I' change with my changing experience—as I surely do, and as the substantival theory must allow if its ego is not to be something quite apart from the self which interests us, the self of our actual experience—how can it be said, as the substantival theory says, that 'I' remain the same?

But this charge of self-contradiction rests on the assumption that sameness totally excludes difference; and this is an assumption to which all self-conscious experience gives the lie direct. I as a self-conscious subject cannot doubt that I who now hear the clock strike a second time am the same being who a moment ago also heard the clock strike, even though I must have become different in some respects in the interval. It can hardly be accepted as an irrefutable principle of philosophic criticism that sameness excludes all difference, when it is a datum of self-conscious experience that it does not.

It may be desirable to add, in order to avert possible misapprehensions, that to be meaningful is by no means the same thing as to be intelligible, where 'intelligible' is a synonym for 'capable of being understood'. The self as we have described it would be intelligible (in this sense) only if it were possible to understand *how* it remains one amid the plurality of its changing experiences. No claim is made here that the self is, even in principle, capable of being 'understood'; and no such claim will be made at any point in these lectures. We are aware of our self *as* of such and such a nature, not of *how* it is what it is. But awareness of the former is all that is necessary for it to have 'meaning' for us.

9. The answer to the second question can again be given very briefly. Yes, there are excellent reasons for believing that selves so characterised do actually exist. And the evidence again comes from self-conscious experience. In self-conscious experience it is surely just not possible to doubt the self's existence. The consciousness of self in self-conscious experience is the consciousness

not of something as having hypothetical existence, but of something as having actual existence. As I write these words I am conscious that I am casting about in thought for a suitable illustration, and conscious also that I am hearing 'noises without' of a somewhat distracting character. Now, try as I will, I find that I cannot doubt, in the first place, that I am the same being in each of these different experiences and distinct from either of them. But I find it equally impossible to doubt, in the second place, that this I, this identical subject of the different experiences, does actually exist. And if the reader is (as of course he ought to be) unprepared to accept this report at second-hand, let him make a similar experiment for himself. If it be made without preconceptions, I do not fear for the result.

Conceivably it will be said 'But the witness of self-consciousness may, after all, be false witness, generating mere illusion'. I must confess, however, that I cannot see how this hypothesis can even be formulated without self-contradiction. It involves us in saying 'Though I am certain whenever I am aware of my self that I do exist, nevertheless perhaps I don't.' But what can 'Perhaps *I* don't' mean if I am not aware of my*self* when I say it? But if I *am* aware of myself when I say it, I must, according to the *first* clause, be *certain* that I exist; and I am therefore contradicting myself when I say 'Perhaps I don't'.

The real source of most of the scepticism about the existence of the substantival self is, I suspect, doubts about its meaningfulness. But with these doubts we have already dealt. It may very well, we have agreed, not be *intelligible*, in the sense of understandable; but that is irrelevant to the question of its meaningfulness.

10.   Let us move on to our third question, 'Of *what* is self-identity an identity?' The testimony of self-conscious experience (in any form, at any rate, in which we have so far considered it) is to the identity of the self as a *conscious* subject. I who *think* of A am aware of my identity with I who *feel* B and *desire* C—i.e. an I who has other *conscious* experiences. It is true that I who think of A may be aware of my identity with I who am walking about the room. But the second 'I' here is, and must be, an 'I' which

has the *conscious experience* of 'walking about the room'. If it happened that, while thinking of A, I was so deeply absorbed in that thought as to be totally unconscious that I was walking about the room, then I clearly could not be conscious of identity between the I who thinks of A and the owner of this walking body. This consideration, of course, has no tendency to rule out the possibility that in fact 'I' *am* a body as well as a mind. It is common ground to all theories of the self that recognise minds and bodies at all that there is some kind of extremely intimate relationship between the self as mind and a particular animal body: and those philosophers may be right who declare that the relationship in question is not merely intimate but *integral*. That, however, is a problem which must be treated at length if it is to be treated at all, and we shall postpone its discussion. Meantime, we are in a position to say only that the identity of the self, as revealed in self-conscious experience, is *at least* an identity of mind or spirit, though it may turn out to be more than that. 'I' am *at least* a 'spiritual substance'.

11. How is the identity of the self, as above understood, related to *personal* identity? That was our fourth question, and the attempt to answer it will involve us in a long and somewhat complicated discussion. But it seems to me of particular moment that a clear answer to it should be reached. Not a few of the perplexities to which discussion of the self and its identity commonly gives rise have their source, in my opinion, in a failure to appreciate that 'self' and 'person' cannot conveniently be treated as interchangeable expressions. An important distinction has got to be drawn within the general conception of selfhood; and if it be not drawn firmly, and marked by an appropriate and consistently employed nomenclature, serious confusion is well-nigh inevitable.

The general nature of the distinction I have in mind can perhaps be most clearly brought out by considering what is implied in such relatively common expressions as 'I was not myself when I did that'. Let us take the case of a man making this statement after being told of some violent act he has committed (and of which he has perhaps no recollection) during an epileptic seizure, or some other species of brain-storm. The term 'I' in the statement is certainly intended by the speaker to designate his 'self' in some sense of that term. Yet in saying 'I was not myself' he seems by implication to be denying that the term 'I' as used does designate his self. Presumably he must be regarding his self, when he makes the statement, in two different aspects.

Now as regards one of these aspects, that in which the self's participation in the violent deed is denied, there is, I think, no great difficulty in seeing what, in general, the self is taken by itself to be. The self here is being thought of as essentially the bearer of a specific 'character'. Every man comes in the course of experience to acquire a set of relatively stable dispositions to feel, think, and behave in more or less well-marked ways. He comes to regard himself, accordingly, and to be regarded by others, as the kind of man who, in such and such a sort of situation, can be depended upon to respond in such and such a sort of way. Naturally enough he will be moved to repudiate, as incapable of really issuing from his self, acts which he not merely may have no recollection of having performed, but which he simply cannot conceive himself, *qua* bearer of his specific character, as ever having performed. He does (in certain circumstances) feel constrained to admit that in *some* sense it was 'he' who acted—'I was not myself' he says 'when *I* did that'. But while thus allowing that in some sense his self-identity was retained in the act, he will vigorously dispute that it was his self-identity as a 'person'. For 'personal identity' seems to him to lose its essential meaning if there be not preserved the salient features of that relatively stable set of dispositions which constitutes a man's character and marks him off as a distinct individual. (The term 'person' has, admittedly, had a long and fluctuating history, and is even now of highly ambiguous import; but to associate it in this manner with the possession of a relatively definite character is a practice that has plenty of confirmation from ordinary linguistic usage. Thus we do not regard the young infant as having yet become a 'person'. Only later on, when it shows signs of 'characteristic' interests and likes and dislikes and modes of response, do we come to speak of it as 'now quite a little *person*'.)

But what, now, is the self taken by itself to be in the *other* aspect, the aspect in which the self's engagement in the act is acknowledged even though its engagement as a *person* is denied?

Why is it that in spite of the strong tendency to identify one's self with the 'personal' bearer of a specific character—a tendency so strong that a not uncommon form of words for repudiating an act in one's personal authorship of which one cannot believe is 'I was not my *real* self when I did that'—why is it that one does nevertheless refer to the author of the 'contra-personal' act as *I*?

The reason is apparent enough, I think, in those cases where, as sometimes happens, one remembers, or even *thinks* one remembers, having committed the act. For the ontological identity of the subject of the remember*ing* experience—the I who re-members—with the subject of the remember*ed* experience is part of the very meaning of what we call 'remembering'. Remembering may be an illusion; but for the man who even thinks he remembers, that ontological identity is implied, and finds its natural expression in the verbal form 'I remember that *I* did that'. Thus in the case of my remembering having performed a 'contra-personal' act, I cannot avoid regarding the author of it as 'I'—the being that now remembers—at the same time as I may indignantly reject any suggestion that the remembered 'I' and the remembering 'I' are the same *person*.

The implication is, I think, that the 'other aspect' in which the self is being regarded in the case before us is that of its *ontological* character. It is the same self 'ontologically', but not 'personally', that is acknowledged to have committed the contra-personal act. When a man says 'I was not myself when I did that', the self-identity that is being *accepted* is identity of the self as what, in the light of our earlier argument, we may perhaps venture to call the same spiritual entity; whereas the self-identity that is being *denied* is the identity of that same spiritual entity considered *only in respect of its manifestations as a 'person'*.

A distinction in such terms may be said to be virtually forced upon us in cases like the above, where we 'remember' having committed the contra-personal act. Where, as is probably more common, no recollection of the act remains, we may not be prepared to acknowledge that our self was engaged in it in any legitimate sense of the term 'self'. We may insist that the testimony of witnesses is only to the behaviour of our body, which we decline to accept as our self, however closely the two may be related. In that event we shall, of course, decline to use such words as 'I was not myself when I did that', but shall rather say something like 'It was not I, but only my body, that so acted'. And in many instances we may be well justified in taking this line. There are many instances falling within the general class of actions we are discussing which offer no good evidence that anything save one's bodily processes are concerned. But on the other hand, there are also many instances in which, despite the absence of recollection, it is a reasonable inference that the self—even if not the self as 'person'—was in fact engaged; and the individual concerned may himself be brought to acknowledge that the evidence is strong enough to compel this conclusion. For while the evidence can be directly only of bodily behaviour, it may well be of modes of bodily behaviour that strikingly suggest conscious purpose (e.g. 'intelligible' speech), and which it is consequently hard not to interpret as betokening a directing 'mind' of some sort. Where that is the case (and assuming, of course, adequate testimony by reliable witnesses), our choice would seem to lie between ascribing the 'directing mind' to some intruding spirit that has in some mysterious manner obtained temporary control of our body, or, on the other hand, ascribing it to one's *self*, and recognising that the self does, under certain conditions, function in an abnormal way discontinuously with its 'character'. If only in view of the unique intimacy of the union which every man feels to exist between himself and 'his' body, an intimacy so close that it is usual for a man to regard his body as virtually or actually a part of himself, the latter would seem much the more credible hypothesis.

The view to which we are being led, then, is that *self*-identity is a much wider conception that *personal* identity. But though 'self' and 'person' must be quite sharply distinguished, it is vital to bear in mind that they do not designate two different beings. They designate one and the same ontological entity in two different aspects. The self may function when the person does not, but the person cannot function when the self does not. The person *is* the self, *qua* functioning in terms of its definitive and normal character. Indeed the person, so far from being an entity different from the self, may be said to be something which the self tends gradually to become. The self starts upon its career with a variety of native instincts, impulses and capacities closely dependent upon its association with a particular animal body. Through the self's actions upon and reactions to its physical and social environment on the basis of these given propensities and powers, the relatively stable system of dispositions we call its 'character' is gradually built up, and the self grows into what we call a 'person'.

But the self's energies, even when the self becomes a person, are not (as it were) poured without remainder into its functioning as a person. As we have seen, even 'contra-personal' functioning must on occasion be attributed to the self; self-identity being retained though personal identity is interrupted. We have conceded, it is true, that it is not logically impossible to suppose that the contra-personal act is the work of some intruding spirit, some alien 'self'; but it seems a far-fetched and extravagant hypothesis.

Moreover, our preferred hypothesis that it is the same self that functions in the contra-personal act as functions in the normal, personal, act is not so very mysterious once we accept the primal mystery that the spiritual substance in man functions only through the medium of, and under the limitations imposed by, a particular animal body. That the state of this body, and in particular the state of its brain and nervous system, conditions most and perhaps all mental functioning, is more or less agreed by everyone; though the advocate of spiritual substance would certainly want to insist (with many other philosophers) that the causal relation between mind and brain is not unilateral but mutual. Now if the brain in its normal state conditions the way in which the mind functions, it will presumably continue to condition it, but with very different effects, when in an abnormal state. More or less violent disturbances of the normal physical organisation of the brain, temporary or permanent, may be brought about by disease, by external injury, or by the chemical action of certain drugs; and where this occurs it is only to be expected that the mental functioning of the self will be abnormal. The degree and kind of abnormality it evinces, which may or may not entail a sharp discontinuity with its 'characteristic' functioning, will depend upon the degree and kind and location of the physical disturbance—a matter upon which the researches of physiological psychologists throw great and constantly increasing light. The fundamental point, however, is that once we admit (and how can we deny?) that the self as mind, the spiritual substance in man, is at least partly in thrall to an animal body and functions subject to the conditions which that imposes, there is in principle no mystery about the *same* self functioning abnormally, and perhaps 'out of character' (with consequent loss of 'personal identity'), where the bodily conditions have undergone sudden and drastic modifications with which the self has nothing to do.

It is not to be supposed, however, that the circumstances which give rise to loss or interruption of personal identity are by any means always purely physical (though it may well be the case that there is always associated with that loss or interruption some disturbance of the central nervous system). The well-known phenomena of 'dissociation of personality' are, as a rule, more amenable to explanation in psychological than in physiological terms. It is worth while to say a word or two about this, though it must be with a brevity which will, I fear, make an appearance of dogmatism inevitable.

The key principle I take to be that, in an important sense, the developed human mind can be described as a system of sub-systems; each of these sub-systems being an organised group of tendencies oriented towards some specific interest in the life of the self. These sub-systems, in as much as it is the interests of the one self to which they minister, are developed in relatively close integration with one another—only on that account can the mind be described as a *system* of sub-systems—and normally they are maintained in relatively close integration. This integration is of two distinct kinds. In the first place, the different sub-systems are in substantial harmony with one another; they do not excite to mutually contradictory ways of behaving. In the second place, there is ease of transition from one sub-system to another; so that the self, when for the time being functioning in terms of one sub-system, is not debarred thereby from responding readily to stimuli appropriate to the evocation of other sub-systems. Integration, however, is never perfect in either of these forms, and the degree of *dis*integration may be great. It is disintegration with respect to the second form which in our present context most closely concerns us, but a chief factor in bringing it about is disintegration with respect to the first. Just because the self is one, incompatibility between its sub-systems engenders a distressing sense of conflict, and one of the many ways in which the self seeks relief from this conflict is 'dissociation'. We have, say, a group of sub-systems X in keenly felt conflict with another group of sub-systems Y. Each is able to be retained and indulged, and the inner tension nevertheless resolved, *if* the two can be so completely detached from one another that the self's conscious life in relation to X totally excludes its conscious life in relation to Y, and vice versa. Where that is successfully accomplished—we need not here consider the mechanisms—the conscious life of the self becomes broken into two mutually exclusive phases; one of them, very often, representing the dominant trend of the self's character, the other some group of sub-systems that is in sharp conflict with, per-haps, major ethical dispositions in the self's character. In extreme pathological cases, where a comprehensive group of sub-systems is maintained in complete detachment from the 'main-stream' over a long period, it is understandable that the self functioning in the detached group should gradually acquire a new, 'secondary' personality which may differ in startling respects from the 'primary' personality manifested in the dominant phase of conscious life (from which the group of sub-systems character-istic of the secondary phase has been totally excluded). Thus we get the phenomenon of dual (or it may be multiple) personality.

Now in the light of this general account of the processes involved it would seem really rather absurd to suggest that, because two 'persons' have emerged, we must posit two *selves*—two ontologically different spiritual entities. For the self which, by its actions upon and reactions to its environment on the basis of its native endowment of powers and propensities, built up the specific group of sub-systems that have now become detached, was the *same* self that built up the group of sub-systems that persist in the main stream. It is surely gratuitous to suppose that the self which *now* functions in the detached group is a different being from the self which functioned prior to their detachment, and which is still functioning in the 'main-stream'? The natural interpretation is surely that it is the *same* self that functions throughout, and that it is its functioning over a prolonged period in a detached group of sub-systems that accounts for the emergence of a personality distinct from the primary personality. This interpretation, it should be added, finds strong confirmation in the frequent success of a psycho-therapy aimed at 'restoring' integration of personality by breaking down the barriers that have been subconsciously erected to separate the detached groups from one another. It is certainly very hard to see how two personalities can be integrated if they belong to two independent spiritual entities! The successful therapy seems to presuppose that the 'two persons' are different manifestations of a single entity, the 'one self'.

12.   The main thesis I have been trying to establish in this somewhat prolonged consideration of our fourth question is that the conception of self-identity is a much wider one than that of personal identity. The self is a spiritual substance which can, and normally does, function in accordance with its personal character. But on occasion, for reasons not entirely obscure, it may function in a *contra*-personal way; and, on still rarer occasions, in a *secondary*-personal way. Nor do these two latter ways exhaust the self's modes of 'non-personal' functioning. If the self's 'personal' functioning is its functioning in terms of its character or personality, what are we to say, for example, of the self's functioning *prior to* the establishment of anything that can be called a 'character' or a 'personality'? It is no more contra-personal, *or* secondary-personal, than it is personal; and yet it is hard to say that it is not the 'self' that is engaged in the building up of its own character. This is a case in which it would seem that the self as something *less* than personal is engaged. Furthermore, I shall suggest later, when I come to deal with the practical life of the self, that there is also a very important group of cases in which the self as something *more* than personal is engaged—that it can function in, as it were, a *supra*-personal as well as an *infra*-personal way. But this must wait. It is unfortunately not practicable to say everything at once, though it would obviate many difficulties if we could.

Let me now sum up this long discussion by stating in formal terms the answers arrived at to the four questions that were propounded.

1. The answer to the first question is that certainly a meaning can be given to the substantival description of the self; for self-conscious experience is a fact, and the self of which we are

conscious in self-conscious experience *is* a self to which this description applies.

2. The answer to the second question is that there is very good reason for believing in the actual existence of such selves; for in self-conscious experience one finds it just not possible to doubt the existence of the self of which one is conscious; and the hypothesis that what is thus indubitable for self-conscious experience may yet be mistaken is incapable of being formulated without an implicit self-contradiction.

3. The answer to the third question is that the self's identity is *at least* an identity of spiritual being, but that this does not rule out the possibility, to be considered at length later, that the relationship between the self and a particular animal body may be intrinsic to self-hood, part of its very essence.

4. The answer to the fourth question is that self-identity is a much wider conception than that of personal identity. The 'person' is the self only in so far forth as the latter manifests itself in general accord with the relatively stable set of dispositions which it acquires in the course of its experience and which constitutes what is commonly called its 'character'. The functioning of the self cannot be exhaustively described in terms of its 'personal' functioning. We must recognise 'contra-personal' and 'secondary-personal' functioning of the same self, and also—we briefly suggested at the end—'infra-personal' and 'supra-personal' functioning as well.

13. I have no serious objection if it be said that what I have been doing, in answering the fourth question, is to make a verbal recommendation, to the effect that the words 'self' and 'person' be used in a particular way. Certainly I have been doing that. I would only add that the recommendation is made, for what it is worth, on the basis of an analysis of the facts of self-experience which seems to disclose the need of a distinction within selfhood which is widely, but very vaguely, recognised, and whose nature is most clearly indicated by using the terms 'self' and 'person' in the way proposed. The proposal involves no revolution in established linguistic usage—that would only make confusion worse confounded. There is *no* established usage of these terms. Ordinary

E

usage is confused and inconsistent, with the inevitable consequence of blurring a distinction that is of the utmost theoretical importance. But the usage here proposed has, for both terms, very considerable support from ordinary usage; and that (I suggest) is as much as anyone has a right to demand of the philosopher's use of language when—as is the rule rather than the exception in the discussion of major philosophical problems—distinctions emerge within the subject-matter which are not, and for the practical purposes of ordinary life need not be, clearly and consistently grasped by the layman.

The ancient problem of the self's relation to its body is one which in the present lecture I have striven, perhaps not altogether successfully, to leave a completely open question. But formal discussion of it can no longer conveniently be deferred, and will be the exclusive concern of our next lecture.

LECTURE VI

THE SELF'S RELATION TO ITS BODY

1. The problem that will engage us in the greater part of this lecture is the very old one of the relation of the self to its body. It is common ground that selves, as we know them in experience, in *some* sense have (or perhaps are) bodies as well as minds. The question is, in *what* sense? Over this question the history of modern philosophy records a great clash of opinion.

Among the many problems which the mind-body relationship raises, however, there is one that is peculiarly fundamental for the purpose of these lectures, which is to discover the general nature and structure of the human self. It is this. Is the union of body and mind within the self a merely *de facto* union, so that their separation is at least conceivable? Or is it an *essential* union, so that a self which is not body and mind in one, a self which is not an 'embodied mind', is not a thinkable conception at all? Since at this stage in our total argument it can (I hope) be taken for granted that mind at any rate belongs to the essence of the self, we may pose the question in the form, 'Does or does not body also belong to the essence of the self?'

It has sometimes been claimed that Common Sense opinion, for what it is worth, comes down heavily on the side of those who declare the self to be essentially body as well as mind. But I suggest that this claim is ill-founded. It is true that to the question 'Is a physical body essential to a self?' the plain man may be tempted to reply in the affirmative, under the impression that the 'self' that is being referred to in the question is the self in this earthly existence of ours. But the affirmative answer in that case comes near to being a mere tautology, since the very notion of 'earthly' existence carries with it an implication of 'bodily' existence. It is

95

quite evident, on the other hand, that the plain man is by no means prepared to limit the possible existence of the self to earthly existence. He talks freely about the possibility of 'a future life', of the self's 'survival of bodily death'. This is manifestly incompatible with his conceiving the self as essentially body as well as mind; unless, indeed, he is assuming (which seems unlikely) that some new kind of astral body will accrue to the self after it has lost its fleshly body.

And here we may notice a very significant point. Almost everyone—even those to whom a negative answer seems virtually certain—takes it to be in principle intelligible to ask whether the self can survive the destruction of its *body*. But it is taken by no one to be in principle intelligible to ask whether the self can survive the destruction of its *mind*. This can only mean, I suggest, that for our ordinary opinions a mind is conceived as belonging to the essence of the self in a sense in which a body is not. For it is implied that what survives might be a self even if it had lost its body, but that it could not conceivably be a self if it were deprived of its mind.

It is necessary, of course, to keep clear the question of the essential nature of the self from the question of the essential nature of *man*. Undoubtedly we think of body as belonging to the essential nature of man; since by 'man' we mean a certain biological species into whose definition (as into the definition of all biological species) mention of an organic body enters as a constituent. But when we are thinking of 'selves' we are not thinking of a biological species, and the assertion that every self has a body is not, like the assertion that every man has a body, an analytic proposition.

The views of the ordinary intelligent man on such matters as the self-body relationship are not, I think, wholly devoid of value. He has considerable experience of, and may well have reflected seriously upon, the entities which are under discussion; and he is entitled, accordingly, to have an attention paid to his views here which he could not sensibly claim if he were offering his opinions on, say, the constitution of the atom. But although he does here, in a real if limited sense, 'know what he is talking about', he may of course have arrived at a wrong conclusion: just as he often does, e.g. in the field of ethical controversy, where he also, in a real if limited sense, 'knows what he is talking about'. It may be that, if he reflected more deeply and more consistently upon what it means to be a self, he would come to take the view that it is, after all, unthinkable without a bodily component.

And that is, in fact, the conclusion to which certain modern philosophers of great distinction have come; notably the late Professor G. F. Stout, whose views, always entitled to respect, carry exceptional weight on problems on the border-line between philosophy and psychology. According to Stout, 'What self-consciousness reveals is not mere mind or "mental phenomena", but mind and body together in the inseparable unity of the embodied self'.[1] We must consider this contention at some length, for it has implications of the most far-reaching kind.

2.   The doctrine that there is no self but the 'embodied' self rests, if I understand it aright, upon two main premises. The first is that in every self-conscious experience, even in those cases where we should find it most natural to say that what we are aware of is a purely mental functioning of the self, it is possible by careful introspection to detect the presence of 'organic sensations' (under which general term we may here include 'kinaesthetic' sensations). The second premise is that in experiencing organic sensations we directly locate them in, or refer them to our 'body'—they are, as it were, experiences of the self *qua* body.

Given these two premises, the doctrine of the embodied self follows, I think, cogently enough. For it would then appear that we just do not have the kind of experience which would enable us to attach meaning to a self that is not body as well as mind. There is no such thing as an experience of a *merely* mental state. Descartes was wrong, on this view, in supposing that any greater certitude attaches to the existence of our mind than to the existence of our body. In point of fact (it is alleged) the 'I think' carries with it an assurance of our bodily existence every bit as indubitable as the assurance of our mental existence.

The doctrine fails to follow if *either* of these two premises is invalid. And it is my opinion that, in fact, *both* premises are invalid. I propose to concentrate, however, upon the second of them—i.e. the contention that in experiencing organic sensations

[1] *Mind and Matter*, p. 308.

we are directly aware of them as bodily—because the first, in the nature of the case, lends itself much less readily to demonstrative argument one way or the other.

3. Let us begin by getting quite clear about that which is common ground to our opponents and ourselves. I agree with the advocates of the embodied self that there are two radically distinct ways in which we apprehend our own bodies. The body is apprehended, first, in the same way as any other physical object is apprehended by the self, through external perception; chiefly, though not of course solely, visual and tactual perception. But it is apprehended, secondly, in a way in which *no* other physical object is apprehended, through what Stout calls 'internal perception'. The crucial feature of the latter mode of perception, as contrasted with the former, is that in it the body is not apprehended as *object* to, and in that sense *external* to, the subject, but as *itself subjective*, as actually *constituent of* the apprehending subject. Suppose, e.g. I want to examine some minute part of my own body, and require, because of its minuteness, a special focusing of my eyes in order to get the image as clearly defined as possible. In so focusing I have, or may have, certain organic and kinaesthetic sensations which I identify with movements of my eyes. I shall in that case be apparently apprehending the bodily process of focusing my eyes, as well as apprehending the bodily state upon which they are focused. But whereas in the *latter* my body is apprehended as *object* to my subject self, in the *former* my body is apprehended as participating in the process of apprehending, and as therefore a *constituent of* my *subject self*. This is one route along which we come to the recognition that our body and our mind are (in Descartes' phrase) 'so closely intermixed' with one another as to 'compose a certain unity'.

So much, then, is common ground. What I am going to deny is that this location of organic sensations in one's body is something that is intrinsic to the having of the organic sensations. If it is not, then, even should it be true that all our 'mental' experiences involve organic sensations, it will not follow that our 'mental' experiences necessarily involve a reference to our body.

It seems to me that this premise of the 'embodied mind'

theorists is wrecked upon one simple fact; the fact, namely, that young children experience organic sensations long before they are aware that they *have* a body—long before, therefore, they could possibly 'locate' them in their bodies. No one denies that for adult experience organic sensations carry with them this reference to one's body, and normally to some specific part of it. Nor is it to be denied that this reference, as we now make it, shows no trace of conscious inference. What has got to be maintained, however, if the premise is to be adequate to the 'embodied mind' conclusion, is that the reference to the body is *intrinsic* to organic sensation in the sense that we cannot have an organic sensation *without* referring it to our body. And this seems to be just false; unless, indeed, it be denied—as, so far as I am aware, no psychologist denies—that the child's discovery that it has a body is a gradual achievement, long ante-dated by its experience of organic sensations. If this latter proposition be admitted, then the reference of organic sensations to the body cannot be intrinsic. It must presumably be an *interpretation*, based ultimately on some sort of inference; though an interpretation, admittedly, which habit has rendered automatic at a comparatively early period in our lives.

Nor does it seem to me particularly difficult to understand how such an inference comes about. We need not attempt a detailed account of how the young child gradually comes to isolate a specifically bounded portion of what is at first the externally observed world as belonging to its *self* in that peculiarly intimate sense involved in the recognition of it as 'its body'. It is clearly an elaborate and complicated process, involving primarily, I think, the correlation of certain external perceptions of occurrences in this particular bit of the physical world with certain feeling and motor experiences. The infant discovers, e.g. that when *this* particular bit of the physical world, and *only* this particular bit of the physical world, undergoes certain observed physical effects from other bits of the physical world, *it* (the infant) experiences in *its self* certain feelings—predominantly of pleasure and pain. It discovers, further, that this particular bit of the physical world, in sharp contra-distinction to all *other* bits of the physical world, is in a measure responsive to *its* (the infant's) wishes; moving, within limits, under *its* control. In such ways as these the young child comes to realise that there is a definitive portion of the physical world with which its self is uniquely and intimately identified, and to think of that portion of body as *its own* 'body'. And it is to be especially noted that these ways, and I think all other ways, through which the child can come to identify a particular portion of body with itself, presuppose in the child a consciousness of the self which is, up till then, *not* a 'bodily' self.

Now once one has become aware of one's body as *one's own* body, the interpretation of organic sensations as being located in one's body seems to me in principle easily intelligible. Intrinsically, organic sensations are simply sensations with a certain *quale*. What gives rise to the interpretation of them as feelings 'of one's body' is the fact that the *quale* of certain organic sensations has for the subject of them a recognisable likeness to the *quale* of certain feelings which are excited in him by *externally observed* affections of part of his body, feelings which he has therefore quite naturally come to identify as 'body-feelings'. For example, an externally observed punch in the solar plexus excites, besides mere pain, a certain qualitative feeling; and it is natural (in view of its observed origin) to think of that feeling as a 'body-feeling'. Now when an organic sensation which has a similar *quale* occurs —as in the case of an ordinary stomach-ache—it would be odd if we did not interpret this qualitatively similar feeling as a 'body-feeling' likewise, even though we have not *here* observed that our body is affected in any way. Which specific feeling-*qualia* represent which specific parts of the body can of course be learned by experience alone. But in view of the great multitude of external affections of one's body that are open to one's inspection and are attended by feelings of distinctive *qualia*, it is not in the least surprising that a wide and fairly accurate knowledge of such correlations is built up in a comparatively short time.

We may note in passing that there are certain well-known facts concerning the apprehension of our bodies through organic sensation which seem much easier to account for on the view that the body-reference is an interpretation based on analogical inference than on the view that it is direct. I refer to the phenomena of mislocation. There are any number of instances in which our organic sensations are referred by us to the wrong part of our body

—not to speak of the familiar case in which a person who has suffered amputation of a member refers his sensation to a part of his body that no longer exists. There is nothing in the least infallible about the body-reference of organic sensations. Now such mis-location presents no special difficulty if the reference to the body is an interpretation of a felt *quale* based on inference. Suppose that after the surgeon has removed my foot I have a sensation which I identify as an itch in my big toe. If the ultimate ground of that identification is my past experience of correlation between this kind of sensation and observed affections of my big toe, I may feel perhaps, some surprise, but no serious intellectual shock, to discover that in the present case my judgment is mistaken. For I am perfectly well aware of the fallibility of all inductive inferences from particular cases to general laws. If on the other hand the reference of the sensation to my body is supposed to rest, not on inference, but upon some sort of direct apprehension of my body, as is suggested by the doctrine that organic sensation carries with it an *intrinsic* reference to my body, then my apprehension of a bit of my body that isn't there seems to be distinctly more puzzling.

To summarise—my contention is that while we do of course directly experience organic sensations, we do *not* directly experience them as *bodily*. The apprehension of them as body-feelings is an interpretation based on analogical inference. But the practice of so interpreting them speedily becomes habitual, so that the body-reference speedily acquires what F. R. Tennant has called a 'psychical' as distinct from a 'psychological' immediacy [1]—very much as in the case of our adult apprehension of spatial perspectives, where we seem to ourselves to apprehend directly what genetic psychology shows to have become a possible object of our present apprehension only through past inferential processes.

If I am right in this account of the matter, it follows that it is untrue that we have no experience of ourselves save as embodied; untrue that the self has the same direct assurance of its bodily as of its mental existence; and untrue, therefore, that we must regard the body no less than the mind as belonging to the 'essence' of the self. It will *not* follow, of course, that the self does ever as a matter of fact engage in activities in which the body plays no part.

[1] *Philosophical Theology*, Vol. I, p. 46.

This may or may not be the case for all that we have shown. All that we claim here is that self-consciousness does not, as has often been confidently alleged, reveal 'body' to be an intrinsic necessity of selfhood.

If seems to me, therefore, that Common Sense is correct in regarding it as at least an *intelligible* question whether the self can survive the destruction of its body. It may be the case that it is not possible to conceive of states of the conscious self that do not include organic sensations. But if what has been said above is sound, we can perfectly well conceive a self which has organic sensations but does *not* refer them to a body, or again a self which has such sensations and *mistakenly* refers them to a body.

And after all, is it quite certain that we cannot conceive a self which has no organic sensations at all? That in all self-conscious experience organic sensations are detectable was, it will be remembered, the first premise of the argument for the embodied self. But there seems to be some evidence of pathological conditions in which there is total suspension of organic sensation and in which the patient *is* self-conscious.[1] For the patient, apparently, then regards his body as a 'foreign object', and he clearly could not do that if he had no consciousness of self. Hence, if the facts are as reported, it is not true that the only self of which we can be aware is an embodied self. But the facts of the situation are elusive, and perhaps insufficiently established to constitute a firm basis for theory.

The problem of the immortality of the soul is not one that will be systematically debated in these lectures. The significance for it, however, of the point I have just been trying to make is obvious. If it be granted that the self, as known to itself, is not in essential, but only in *de facto* union with its body, then the continued existence of the self after the destruction of its body falls at least into the category of abstract possibilities. Admittedly an 'abstract possibility' does not take us very far. But it leaves the way open for discussing on their merits the various ethical and religious considerations bearing upon the problem of immortality, which,

---

[1] Dr. F. R. Tennant tells us, though unfortunately without quoting authority, that 'when, through disease, coenaesthesis is in abeyance, a patient will regard his body as a strange and inimical thing, not belonging to him' (*Philosophical Theology*, Vol. I, p. 71).

so far as I can see, we should be obliged to rule out of court *a priori* if it were indeed the case that any self to *be* a self must be an *embodied* self.

4.   So far in this lecture I have been concerned with only a single aspect of the mind-body problem; though manifestly a very fundamental aspect, and one that is of especial significance for philosophical theology. I have been asking whether it is possible in principle to conceive of a self apart from a body—as it is certainly *not* possible, even in principle, to conceive of a self apart from a mind. This question I have answered, with some confidence, in the affirmative. Now there are, of course, a great many other aspects of the mind-body problem which have been the subject of philosophical controversy. But about these, with a single exception, I propose here to say little or nothing. Not, indeed, that I consider it to be of no account what view we take about them. It merely happens that the view I myself take coincides with the view that is taken by the great majority of philosophers today; and it would be an unrewarding business to rehearse the old hackneyed arguments in support of doctrines which almost no one is seriously interested in disputing. I refrain from discussing, therefore, the Behaviouristic hypothesis that mental events are a species of bodily events, so that the mind-body unity in man is in fact just a unity of body. If anyone really cares to commit what the late Professor Bowman once aptly termed the 'Fallacy of Eccentric Identification', and say that he means the same thing when he speaks about thoughts as when he speaks about cerebral and laryngeal motions and the like, I am content here to leave him to it. The refutation of Behaviourism I regard as a purely academic exercise, and it seems wiser that we should spend our limited time upon hypotheses which have at least some initial plausibility. Nor shall I discuss the hypothesis that goes by the name of 'Neutral Monism': the hypothesis that body and mind are different arrangements of a common 'stuff'—usually identified with sensation—and that we call events 'mental' when constituents of this common stuff are in *one* kind of relation to one another, and call them 'bodily' when they are in *another* kind of relation to one another. It seems clear that this attempt to reach a unifying

concept for body and mind can appeal only to that small minority of philosophers who find themselves able to accept a Phenomenalist account of body and a Sensationalist account of mind. As earlier lectures have, I hope, made plain, both of these accounts are in my opinion distortions of the facts. I feel no compunction either about omitting here any critique of the Epiphenomenalist theory of the relation of mind to body, according to which mental events, though admitted to be irreducibly different in quality from bodily events, are yet derivative from these events as their 'by-product', and are in themselves without any effects whatsoever either in the sphere of mind or in the sphere of body. Epiphenomenalism, though it may still hold attractions for some scientists with philosophic leanings, is not, to the best of my knowledge, now held by any philosopher of standing; and I am bound to say that the reasons for its rejection seem to me a good deal more than adequate.

5.   Let us take for granted, then, that *these* suggestions at any rate about the mind-body relation in man can be brushed aside. It remains to consider an aspect of our general problem about which there cannot be said to be a solid consensus of opinion among philosophers one way or the other, and upon which I must therefore not merely state, but seek in some measure to justify, my own view. I refer to the seeming interaction of bodily and mental events within the self. I say 'seeming' interaction. But were it not for certain difficulties in understanding *how* mind and body can affect one another, their interaction would be regarded as plain matter of fact. Evidence of it confronts us every day of our lives; in, e.g. the regular sequence of the mental events we call 'perceptions' upon certain physical events in our sense organs and nervous system, and in the regular sequence of certain movements of our body upon the mental events we call 'volitions'. There is no doubt about the 'appearances'. Certain considerations, however, have led some philosophers to doubt, or even to deny outright, that the appearance of mind-body interaction can represent the real fact.

Historically speaking, there have been, I think, two major considerations inclining in this direction. One of them we may now discount. For it seems to have become a matter of pretty general agreement that the principle of the Conservation of Energy, in any sense of it, at least, in which it is a securely established principle of physical science, is not necessarily violated by the hypothesis of mind-body interaction. There seems today to be only one widely held objection to the interaction hypothesis; but this is felt sufficiently strongly by a number of philosophers (though perhaps a dwindling number) to induce them to cast about anxiously for some alternative hypothesis which might explain the appearance of interaction without admitting the fact.

The objection in question is based on the extreme unlikeness of 'cause' and 'effect' where the interaction is supposed to be between mental entities and physical entities. And the objector is neither satisfied nor silenced when he is reminded that even within the purely physical sphere, where he acknowledges causal interaction, cause and effect are often extremely unlike one another. He will admit this: and probably he will even admit that cause and effect are *always* to *some* extent unlike one another (otherwise they would be indistinguishable), and that the likeness between cause and effect can never be more than a matter of degree. What troubles him, and what seems to him to put mind-body interaction in a category of its own, is that mental and bodily events seem to have *no* degree of likeness to one another at all. That which is essentially inextended and indivisible seems to lack any sort of community of nature with that which is essentially extended and infinitely divisible. So long as things have at least *some* character in common, we can conceive them, in virtue of that common character, to belong to the same system; and there is no special mystery about members of the same system mutually influencing one another. But if (as their usual definitions tend to suggest) mind and body have no common character at all, their alleged interaction seems to confront us with the paradox of 'communication without community'.

Now I must admit to being rather sceptical about the logical, as distinct from the psychological force, of the postulate 'No communication without community'. So far as I can see, there is only *one* common character which entities *must* possess in order for it to be logically possible that they should influence one another; and *that* character is shared by literally everything that is. For everything that is *eo ipso* shares in the common character of *being*. I can see no *a priori* grounds whatsoever for demanding that entities should share in some more determinate character in order that their interaction be logically conceivable. In so far as they share in the character of being, they are fellow-members of the same universe. Just what *a priori* knowledge are we supposed to have of this universe that forbids us to believe in their mutual interaction unless they have some more *special* characters in common?

But in point of fact it does not seem to me that in the particular case here in question, the mutual influence between mind and body, we are forced to rely simply upon their common possession of this most general of all characters, the character of 'being'; nor even upon that *plus* the further character, which it would be hard to dispute that mind and body share, of 'temporality'. We know our mind and body, I think, to have a much closer community of nature than is implied in their common possession of 'being' and 'temporality'. For although I have been at pains to deny, as against Stout, that the unity of body and mind within the self is (for us) anything more than a *de facto* unity, it does not seem to me possible to deny, in the light more particularly of the phenomena of internal perception, that it is none the less a *unity*. The internal perception of our body, it will be recalled, yields an apprehension of our body not as object to, but as constituent of, the apprehending self. We thus become aware of certain bodily processes as at least sometimes, and indeed normally, characterising the 'I', just as we are aware of certain mental processes as characterising the same 'I'. But if the 'I' manifests itself in certain bodily processes and likewise manifests itself in certain mental processes, then these bodily and mental processes have the community of nature that consists in their being alike modes of the same entity.

Hence even if the postulate 'No communication without community' be granted, this will not serve to disprove body-mind interaction. Not only is there community between body and mind in respect of the very general characters of being and temporality. There is the more specific community implied in their being modes of the same determinate system, the 'body-mind' of the empirical self. For, however little we understand it, it does not really seem doubtful that, within the empirical self at any rate, body and mind do 'compose a certain unity'. If that unity be acknowledged, the only serious objection to body-mind interaction vanishes. There seems no difficulty in supposing that a body-mode of the body-mind system can have causal efficacy upon a mental mode of the body-mind system, and *vice versa*.

6.   Since I have now, I think for the first time, had occasion to use the expression 'empirical self', and since this expression implies a distinction from some sort of 'non-empirical self', it is proper that I should try to make clear in what sense precisely I take such a distinction to be called for.

A word, first, about what the distinction is not. It is not a distinction between two different ontological entities. There is only one self. Nor is it a distinction of Kantian lineage between the self as it really is (the non-empirical self) and that same self in the form in which our human minds apprehend it (the empirical self). In my view (which will receive later defence and development) it is false to suppose that the self in the form in which we apprehend it is not the self as it really is.

But it need not be the *whole* of the self as it really is. And that brings me to the positive point intended by the distinction between the empirical and the non-empirical self. What I mean by the empirical self is the self considered in respect of its functioning in human experience. And what I mean by the non-empirical self is that same self considered in respect of a possible functioning outside of human experience.

An obvious objection to this manner of speaking leaps to the mind at once. If we only know the self in so far as it functions in human experience (and how else *could* we know it?), what sense is there, it will be asked, in distinguishing from it the self as not so functioning? Why suppose that there is anything corresponding to the expression 'non-empirical self'? The answer is that we are *not* supposing that there is. All we are doing is to recognise and allow for the possibility that there *may* be. For although there obviously cannot be evidence in experience of the self's non-empirical functioning, it does not follow that there is no evidence in experience for believing in the possibility of such functioning.

It is only to leave room for this possible functioning that I deem it necessary to make the distinction in question.

What I have in mind in speaking of evidence in experience for believing in the possibility of the non-empirical functioning of the self is simply this. The self to which self-consciousness testifies, I have constantly urged, is a self which *has*, rather than *is*, its experiences. But given that the self is thus distinguishable from its experiences, we have no right to assume that that self manifests *all that it is* in the human experiences through which we know it —its 'empirical' manifestations. It may well be, for all we know, that there are latent in this spiritual substance capacities whose expression is inhibited under the conditions of human experience, and in particular under the condition of union with a physical body.

And here it is relevant to remember what was earlier argued, that the self's union with a physical body is for our intelligences a merely *de facto*, not a necessary, union. If we had to conceive that union as integral to the self, then it would of course be idle to posit a possible functioning of the self apart from its body. But if the union is, for us, merely contingent, it is mere dogmatism to assert that the self is limited to this way of functioning.

We do well to bear in mind also that, even apart from the mystery of the self's union with a physical body, the self as disclosed in self-conscious experience is not a being that we *understand*. We find as an immediate deliverance of self-consciousness that we are the self-same subject in different experiences, but this 'identity in difference' of ours is not intelligible to us. We do not know *how* we are *what* we are. And I may here confess to a good deal of doubt whether in the end it really makes sense for finite beings to ask how they are what they are. It may be that our philosophy will lead us to the view that for us finite beings there is no alternative to accepting as ultimate certain brute facts which we do not, and in the nature of things cannot, understand; facts which represent the basic conditions of finite experience, and could become intelligible to a finite being only if, *per impossibile*, he could transcend the conditions of his own finitude.

But the discussion of these large matters must await the metaphysical enquiries reserved for our second course of lectures. Here my point is just this: that in default of such understanding there can be no ground for asserting that our self expresses all that it is in the different forms of self-manifestation disclosed by human experience. The self as an ontological entity, as a spiritual substance, may be, for all we can say to the contrary, a being of far richer potency than is, or ever can be, revealed under the conditions of human life; in the guise, that is to say, of the 'empirical self'.

7. Nevertheless, it is in its empirical manifestations alone that we find our positive clues to the nature of the self: and we are a long way yet from having exhausted these resources of positive knowledge, even as regards the fundamental characteristics of our selfhood (which constitute the limits of our enquiry in these lectures). We have still to consider the empirical manifestations of the self as a *practical* being, and more particularly in its capacity as a moral agent. That will occupy us for the greater part of what remains of this course; and I am hopeful that we shall derive therefrom strong confirmation of our substantival interpretation of the self as well as important further information about its basic structure. But there is one topic which, I think, it would be well to clear out of the way before embarking on this project. It will not have escaped notice that in several passages in recent lectures I have virtually assumed without discussion that we have at our disposal valid methods of empirical self-knowledge. Thus I have implied that introspection can yield authentic information about the manifestations of the subject self. I have been unwilling to interrupt the main course of the argument before it was absolutely imperative, but I think we can no longer decently avoid attempting some formal justification of assumptions which are, after all, challenged in a good many quarters. I propose, therefore, to devote a considerable part of my next lecture to saying what seems to me necessary in order to defend the conception of empirical self-knowledge whose validity I have so far been taking for granted.

LECTURE VII

EMPIRICAL SELF-KNOWLEDGE: INTROSPECTION, AND THE INFERENCE TO DISPOSITIONS

1. It would be pretty generally agreed, I think, that the wave of hostility towards introspection in the early decades of this century, manifested most strikingly in the self-denying, and strangely paradoxical, ordinance of the Behaviourist psychologists, who proclaimed that the only effective way of studying the mind was to avert one's gaze from it and attend exclusively to the body, has now, even among psychologists, in large measure spent itself. As Professor and Mrs. Knight have written in their recent *Modern Introduction to Psychology:* '. . . the opposition between introspectionists and behaviourists is no longer a live issue. The pure introspectionist view has long been abandoned, and extreme behaviourism now has few adherents.'[1] The controversy has, however, in many respects been not unfruitful. On the one side the difficulties, dangers, and limitations of the introspective method have been more precisely determined, and have achieved a wider recognition. On the other side it has become increasingly clear that, however necessary it be to exercise caution in the practice of this method, and to supplement it and check it, wherever practicable, by various extro-spective techniques, it is, nevertheless, not only an important, but a strictly indispensable, instrument for the acquirement of knowledge of mental states and processes.

This *rapprochement* is very welcome, and relieves me of the tedious duty of traversing again much well-trodden ground. It

[1] P. 7.

will be sufficient, I think, if I make clear my position on one or two matters of importance that are still the subject of some controversy.

2. I take it that most people, if asked to define what it is that introspection studies, would reply, in effect, 'psychical states and processes'. Yet Samuel Alexander was surely right in maintaining that as ordinarily used the term covers a good deal more than this.[1] It covers the study not only of psychical states and processes, but also of the 'objects' towards which these are directed, *in so far as* such objects are presented through the said states or processes. Suppose, e.g. I say to someone 'I believe X', and he replies 'Are you sure you believe X?' His question may mean either of two things, which it means being generally made apparent by the relative stress laid on the words 'believe' and 'X'. He may mean 'Is your state of mind towards X one to which the term "belief" is really appropriate?' Or he may mean 'Is it really X towards which you are in a believing state, and not, perhaps, XY, or XYZ?' Now in either case it is natural to say that we seek to answer the question by 'looking into our minds' to see what was really 'there' when we said 'I believe X'. And it is also natural to call this 'introspection'. But it seems quite clear that whereas in the former case we are indeed concerned to study a psychical state, in the latter we are not. *There* we seek to ascertain not whether our psychical state was one of believing—that question is not being raised—but whether the proposition believed is correctly described as X.

Now whether Alexander is also right in insisting that it is only to the former case—the examination of psychical states and processes—that the term 'introspection' can legitimately be applied, does not here concern us. Not that this is by any means a merely verbal question. Anyone who accepts Alexander's particular brand of realist epistemology must, I think, admit the propriety of Alexander's restriction upon the usage of the term. But in the present context our interest is only to justify introspection in the sense in which Alexander agrees that the term is appropriate. How far can we get by introspection valid knowledge

[1] *Space, Time, and Deity*, Vol. I, p. 18.

of the self's psychical states and processes, of the experiences of a self as, in Alexander's terminology, actually 'enjoyed'?

It has sometimes been suggested that, whatever knowledge introspection may yield, it cannot be knowledge of the self proper. For in introspection the self, in the nature of the case, is turned into an experienced *object*, which is just what the self, *qua* self, is not. It is of the very essence of the self *qua* self to be an experien*cing subject*. We do not, therefore, in introspection ever apprehend the self as it really is.

It does not seem to me, however, that there is very much in this objection. No doubt the self in introspection is in some sense an 'object'. But it need not be so in any sense which precludes it from being also the self as subject, the self in its actual subjective functioning. We may agree that the introspected object can never be the subject in its subjective functioning at the moment of introspecting. We do not directly introspect our own introspecting. But why should it not be the subjective functioning of the introspecting subject at some previous moment? Reluctance to admit this seems to arise from some misunderstanding about what we actually do when we introspect. It is insufficiently appreciated that when we want to introspect we begin (and indeed continue) by *re-living*, through memory, the experience in which we are interested. In introspection, of course, we re-live it 'with a difference'. In the past experience there was, as in all conscious experience, some degree of self-awareness: but it was likely to be a very low degree—for in ordinary life attention is normally concentrated upon the 'object' experienced rather than upon the experience itself—and it was certainly not self-awareness controlled by any 'scientific interest'. In introspection the past experience is lived through again, but now with the difference that the self-awareness is both raised to a high degree and is also scientifically oriented. Alexander is surely near to the heart of the matter when he defines introspection (in so far as used for psychological purposes) as 'enjoyment lived through with a scientific interest'.[1]

3. Is it only the self in its *past* subjective functioning that can be introspected? Is all introspection really retrospection? I have

[1] *Space, Time, and Deity*, Vol. II, p. 89.

hinted at my own agreement with this view, but the question merits much closer consideration. For if all introspection is retrospection, certain disabilities must attach to it, and they may be of a kind to prejudice seriously its claim to give satisfactory knowledge of the self.

Since Auguste Comte's classic criticism more than a century ago, it has been widely acknowledged that, at least in the case of the mind's cognitive processes, introspection at the time of occurrence is not practicable. As Comte puts it, 'The thinker cannot divide himself into two, of whom one reasons and the other observes him reason. The organ observed and the organ observing being in this case identical, how could observation take place?' [1] To this objection I know of no effective answer. I think we must grant that the cognitive processes at any rate cannot be introspected at the moment of their occurrence, but only afterwards as revived in memory; and we must frankly accept whatever reduction of the certainty of introspection in this field is entailed by the need to put our trust in memory.

But do the objections to 'introspection of the present moment' hold of cognitive processes *only*? This has sometimes been claimed to be the case (and Comte has himself lent some countenance to the claim). It is held that we can retain unabated our confidence in the direct observations of feelings and conations, since here 'the organ observed and the organ observing' are *not* one and the same. To take an obvious instance—the instance presumably most favourable to the possibility of 'introspection of the present moment'—that of a persistent physical pain. The experience of the pain, it is contended, does not involve a cognitive process of the mind, and there is accordingly no reason why the cognitive process of observing the experience of the pain should not be carried on simultaneously with the occurrence of the experience itself. And as a matter of plain fact, is not something of the sort happening constantly? The doctor asks his patient to tell him just what kind of a pain he is suffering from, and the patient does not require to rely upon his memory in order to give the information. He concentrates his attention upon the pain as it is now occurring, and reports that it is dull or acute, continuous or intermittent, in his heart or in his head, and so on.

[1] Quoted by William James, *Principles of Psychology*, Vol. I, p. 188.

I suggest, nevertheless, that this view is plausible only at first sight. It seems on fuller consideration that even an experience like that of pain must to some extent undergo change by being reflected upon by the victim of it. We can readily agree that the experienced pain does not involve what would ordinarily be called a 'cognitive process'. But it *does* involve the subject's *attention* to it; *in*voluntary attention, no doubt, but still attention. It is a common-place that one of the most efficacious ways of relieving a patient's pain is to *distract his attention* from it. There is even good evidence that a man can train himself to become virtually impervious to pain by prolonged practice in the art of concentrating upon extraneous matters 'at will'. If, then, as happens when he sets out to introspect, a man's attention is directed away from the pain, it seems inevitable that the experience of the pain will be modified in some degree, however slight. Introspection of a present pain does not involve Comte's 'thinker' dividing himself into two, in the technical sense of the term 'thinker'. But it does involve an attending subject dividing himself into two; and this feat seems no easier of accomplishment.

I find myself therefore forced to take the view that introspection of the present moment must fail of its proper object even where the experience to be introspected is one so remote from the cognitive activity as that of pain. I think there is in fact no mental state or process that can remain unaffected by being reflected upon 'with a scientific interest'. We can, of course, in a sense introspect a present pain. But the point is that this 'present pain' is not the pain we set out to introspect. That pain has undergone modifications through the influence of the introspective activity directed upon it. The present pain is what it is, at least in part, through such influence.

If such be the case, it becomes very necessary to enquire just how serious are the disabilities entailed in our having to rely upon memory in introspection generally.

4.   On the whole I incline to the opinion that these disabilities have been much exaggerated. That memory is in principle fallible, everyone admits. But there is a great deal of past experience in respect to which no one believes that memory does in fact deceive

us. Where the experience to be remembered belongs to the very recent past, and also includes items of which the subject was vividly conscious at the time, accurate introspection (or retrospection) of such items seems well within human powers. I can be virtually certain that my experience of a moment ago was one of pain, and that the pain was severe in intensity, was of a throbbing character, and was located in my big toe. Introspection runs into difficulties only where the past experience to be introspected was either remote in time, or where, though recent, it included features some of which were only faintly apprehended. Thus I should find difficulty in introspecting the characteristics of the pain I suffered from an attack of lumbago fifteen years ago, even though these characteristics were doubtless vividly enough focused in my attention during the original experience. Thus too, if only a few moments ago I made a troublesome practical decision which required me to take into account a great variety of factors, I should find great difficulty in introspecting the more dimly apprehended ingredients in the complex experience of my motivation, despite the recency of their occurrence.

But granting that it is hard to be confident of the accuracy of our introspection either in the case of experiences long past or in the case of the finer details in even the most recent experiences, it is apparent, I think, that at least one of these difficulties— remoteness in time—can in practice be largely discounted. For almost all of the mental states and processes which one is likely to want to introspect with a scientific interest either occur frequently in the natural course of events or, if they do not, are capable of being produced readily, and as often as required, by an act of constructive imagination. Introspection immediately after their occurrence is therefore almost always possible. Introspection compares very favourably indeed with extrospection of material things in regard to the easy accessibility of its objects, and we may well agree with Stout that 'this may be set down as the grand advantage of introspection, which compensates in a high degree for its drawbacks'.[1]

The other difficulty, however, remains: and few who have seriously tried their hands at introspecting the more faintly experienced constituents of even the most recent complex mental

[1] *Manual of Psychology*, p. 45 (3rd edn.).

states and processes are likely to under-rate it. There is no good reason, indeed, to suppose the difficulty insurmountable. Very much can be done in the way of correcting initial errors and over-sights by frequent repetitions of the experience to be introspected, and by careful comparison of one's findings with the findings of other workers in the same field. Still, one must admit that even the most skilful and experienced practitioners of introspection would seldom venture to claim that their efforts, however per-tinacious, have yielded a completely comprehensive and impecc-ably accurate picture of all that there is in any really complex mental experience.

It is a matter for satisfaction, therefore, that this very real difficulty has, after all, not much bearing upon the particular sort of empirical self-knowledge which is our concern in these lectures. It is sufficient for our purposes if the possibility of accurate introspection of the broad, basic modes of experience is granted; and the possibility of this does not seem to be effectively impugned by any of the criticisms of introspection we have considered. One may fairly regard it as significant that there is virtually no dis-agreement about the classification of these basic modes by psycho-logists who do not deny themselves the use of introspection. The traditional psychological distinctions, under the general rubrics of feeling, conation, and cognition, have been arrived at by introspection, and I see no good reason for doubting that intro-spection tells us substantially the truth about them. Moreover, if I have been right in dismissing as unsound the contention that the states and processes which are the objects of introspection cannot, because *objects*, be states and process of the self *qua subject*, then the truths which introspection yields can be taken to be truths about the self 'proper'. The basic modes of experience disclosed by introspection will be real manifestations of the real self, and as such will furnish evidence for valid conclusions about that self's 'nature'.

Before we finally take leave of introspection there is just one further point to which I should like to draw attention. I have been talking almost exclusively about the alleged defects of introspec-tion, with only a casual reminder of the 'grand advantage' of introspection in regard to the ready accessibility of its objects of study. But there is another 'grand advantage' of introspection over extrospection of physical things which is at least as important; an advantage which might even be said to establish knowledge of the inner life as on an altogether superior plane to knowledge of the external world. The 'objects' we are trying to know in introspection are mental states and processes as they are for the experience of them. The 'objects' we are trying to know in observation of the external world, on the other hand, are physical states and processes, not merely as they are for the experience of them, but as they are *in themselves*. In the case of the external world we may be virtually certain that the object as experienced by us has the character X; but this certainly does not carry with it any certainty that X is a character of the physical object itself. Possibly X is only a subjectively conditioned 'appearance' of the real object. But in the case of internal observation or introspection, the situation is quite otherwise. Here the distinction between the 'object' as it is for the experience of it and the 'object' as it is in itself does not arise. There is no meaning in asking what a mental state or process might be as *not* experienced. As not experienced, it is not strictly a mental state or process at all. If, e.g. we are sure on the basis of introspection that the mental state we are concerned to know was *for our experience* a state of pain, then we are sure that the mental state just *was* a state of pain. If on the other hand we are interested in observing a physical object—say a tomato—we may be perfectly sure that the object *as experienced* was red, and yet properly regard it as open to legitimate doubt whether the object *in itself* was red.

Our general conclusion about introspection, then, is that while expertise in it certainly requires much practice and some natural talent, it is a far more competent instrument for the acquirement of empirical self-knowledge than is usually allowed, and that there is no reason in principle why it should fail us in the broad use we make of it in these lectures.

5. I remarked a few moments ago that the mental states and processes revealed to us by introspection furnish valid evidence for conclusions about the self's *nature*. And indeed there is no other way of acquiring knowledge about the different aspects of the self's nature than by inference from observed facts of this sort.

As Lotze has said, 'We have to conceive its [the self's] nature as it must be in order that it should pass through what we know in ourselves as its states, and perform what we find in ourselves as its actions'. And he proceeds, 'Hence we must start from a comparison between mental phenomena; putting together the like, and separating the unlike, we shall sort the heterogeneous multitude into groups, each of which includes all that have one common stamp, and excludes whatever is of a divergent kind. Mental phenomena differ sufficiently among themselves to make it probable that this comparison, if made steadily from one point of view, will end in discovering several separate groups, for whose peculiar distinctions no common expression can be found. . . . For the whole of each department of phenomena we must attribute to the soul a peculiar faculty to energise in that manner which predominates uniformly throughout all its component parts. Accordingly we must suppose the soul to possess as many separate faculties as there are groups of phenomena left unresolvable by observation; but we shall at the same time be left with the conviction that they are not imprinted in its nature as an unconnected assemblage of faculties, but that there is between them an affinity by which, as various manifestations of one and the same being, they are harmonised into the whole of its rational development.' [1]

Despite (or, as some may think, because of) its somewhat old-fashioned flavour, I should myself take little serious exception to this way of stating the situation; not even to the use of the term 'faculty'—which, after all, means simply 'power' or 'capacity'. Philosophers (who sometimes betray their common humanity, paradoxically enough, by curiously ovine propensities) have for a long time suffered from a sort of group- or flock-phobia about the use of this term. No doubt they are fearful lest they be identified with those earlier students of the mind who supposed that they had offered an explanation of some specific type of mental process when they had postulated in the mind a specific 'faculty' for its performance. But these earlier psychologists were not obviously wrong—indeed I should say they were obviously right—in holding that there *are* faculties; for, after all, whatever the mind does (as Locke said) there must be in it a 'power' of doing.

[1] *Microcosmus*, Book II, Chap. II, pp. 168-9. (English translation by E. Hamilton and E. E. C. Jones.)

What *is* wrong—or rather what is dangerous—about 'faculty' talk is, of course, that one can so easily be beguiled by it into supposing that when one has ascribed a process to a 'faculty' one has 'explained' it. It is not so much false, as just a pointless tautology, to say of a man who adds 2 and 2 and gets 4 for the answer that he has a 'faculty' of addition. Of course he has, in so far as 'faculty' means 'power'. But the 'explanation' of the additive or any other cognitive process only begins when we are able to exhibit the power in question as a specific differentiation, in a determinate set of circumstances, of some more *general* cognitive power. In other words, the 'faculty' explanation stops before explanation proper begins.

Yet it does not follow from this that there is no sense at all in talking about 'faculties'. For 'explanation' has always certain limits; and it is in order to *mark the limit of explanation* that ascription to a faculty is in point. When, in the course of explaining the less general by the more general, we arrive at a mental process which appears incapable of being subsumed under any power more general than its own, we may fitly signalise this *ne plus ultra* by saying that the process is the expression of an ultimate power, or faculty: intending thereby, of course, no implication that we are 'explaining' anything. But just because ascription to faculties is proper and valuable *only* as marking the *terminus ad quem* of explanation, it is best, I think, to confine the use of the word 'faculty' exclusively to ultimate and irreducible powers of the mind. Used in this way—and it is, I believe, Lotze's way—the reference of mental processes to faculties, e.g. to faculties of cognition, conation, and feeling, seems unexceptionable. And in point of fact a good many philosophers and psychologists who shudder at the very mention of the word, and broadly hint that to believe in faculties is as intellectually disreputable as to believe in fairies, show that they do not really take exception to the thing, but only to the name, by their own free use of terms like 'power' and 'capacity' which are fundamentally synonymous with the term they repudiate.

6. Now it is not to our purpose here to attempt any general inventory of the mind's ultimate powers or faculties. Broadly

speaking, there is virtual unanimity among psychologists about this: and certainly I have no original suggestions to offer. There is, however, one such power—a power which the observed facts apparently force us to postulate—with which we must, I fear, deal at some length. For much controversy has centred upon it. Moreover, this power has a function in human experience almost as central as the basic powers of cognition, conation and feeling, to the effective exercise of which, indeed, it is quite indispensable. I refer to the mind's power of retaining within it, in some form, its past experiences, and utilising them, on receipt of appropriate stimuli, in the course of its future experience.

The paramount importance for human life of this capacity is evident from the simple fact that, in its absence, there could be no such thing as 'learning from experience'. Our world would be completely new for us at every moment. The development in the individual person of a body of knowledge, of a character, of sentiments, could not even begin if cognitions, conations, and feelings passed out of existence as soon as they had occurred.

But note that mere 'retention' of past experiences is not enough. Past experiences might conceivably be retained, in unconscious form, in the mind, but without their *doing* anything —in which case, presumably, we should not guess that they *were* retained. In fact we do know that they are retained (or most plausibly infer it), because we find we can give no intelligible account of the actual growth of an individual's experience without postulating that they are constantly at work, exercising a determining influence upon the course of his future mental life in all its phases. The past experiences, it would seem, not merely survive, but survive as tendencies or abilities of the mind to react, on receipt of stimuli similar in character to the stimuli of the past experiences, in certain ways which bear the unmistakable impress of these past experiences. The meaning that a perceived object has for us in adult life, for instance, we read into it in the light of past experiences of this and cognate objects, even although these past objects have not persisted in the *conscious* mind during the interval since their occurrence, and indeed are probably not even revived consciously in the mind now.

It will be apparent that what we are here about to deal with are these highly elusive 'somethings' called 'dispositions'. Or, to speak more accurately, acquired dispositions; tendencies or abilities that are built up in the individual mind out of its past experiences. For these must be distinguished from congenital dispositions, such as musical ability, which there is good reason to suppose belong to the mind independently of its actual experience; though experience is, of course, necessary for their activation and development. To speak more accurately still, we are concerned here with *acquired mental* dispositions; abilities and tendencies which, *prima facie* at any rate, arise out of mental experiences, are excited into action by mental experiences, and issue in mental experiences. That there are also congenital and acquired physiological dispositions, bodily tendencies to specific patterns of bodily behaviour, no one, I think, doubts.

In the little I have so far said about dispositions I have to some slight extent been mixing together fact and interpretation; e.g. in assuming the common-sense view that past experiences do 'survive' in *some* form. I hope that this may be excused in a preliminary exegesis, whose object is no more than to indicate in general terms what it is that we are to discuss. But it is time now to disentangle fact and theory; for the true interpretation of the facts relating to so-called 'dispositions' has come in recent times to be a matter of lively debate.

7. The bare facts may for present purposes be outlined in a very few words.

1. Most, and perhaps all, conscious experiences do *somehow* exercise causal influence of one sort or another upon later experiences of the 'same' mind.

2. During the interval, which may be very long indeed, between the occurrence of a past experience and the occurrence of a later experience causally affected by it, observation yields no direct evidence that the past experience is still 'there', in any form, to exercise its influence. If there are 'traces' of some sort left in the mind by past experiences, these traces are not, apparently, of the nature of conscious states; for the most patient introspection will not reveal them.

This is where the question of *theory* comes in. Do the past experiences perhaps persist in some form of *un*conscious traces, filling the temporal gap between the past and the present experience, and thus enabling us to interpret the situation without breach of the commonly accepted principle that the cause must be temporally continuous with its effect? Or is it perhaps the case that traces are not empirically observed because there just aren't any; in which case, presumably, the past experience achieves its effect by some kind of 'action at a distance'—the 'distance' here being not spatial but temporal?

There would seem, broadly speaking, to have been three main theories put forward to account for the phenomena; one which does not assume traces, and two which do. The one which does not, we have just alluded to. It prefers the assumption of causal action at a (temporal) distance. Lord Russell calls it the *Mnemic Causation* theory. The two theories which assume that traces persist in the mind differ sharply according to their interpretation of the phrase 'in the mind'. If we find it not unreasonable to believe that the mind has a relatively enduring structure, we may conceive that traces are modifications of that structure brought about by past experiences, and that through these traces, which have thus become ingredient in the mind's structure, the past experiences of a mind affect its future functioning in respect of relevant experiential situations. I propose to call this the *Structure-Trace* theory. On the other hand, if we are determined to avoid any traffic with 'substances', we may hold that the traces persist, not as modifications of the hypothetical structure of a hypothetical mind, but as ingredients of actual mental events, being passed on from the initial mental state to its successor in the series, and thence to its successor, and so on without intermission throughout the whole course of an individual's mental life. This I shall call the *Event-Trace* theory.

We have, then, (1) the Mnemic Causation theory; (2) the Structure-Trace theory; and (3) the Event-Trace theory.

Now so far as (1) and (3) are concerned, a rather odd thing about them is that no one, not even their sponsors, really likes them very much. Formidable objections to them are freely admitted. Such appeal as they have they may be said to owe to an extrinsic consideration; the consideration, namely, that they would seem to be virtually the only theories open to us *if* we suppose ourselves obliged to reject the view that the mind is a *substantival* entity, a relatively permanent being of which mental states are manifestations, and adopt instead the 'serial' view, according to which 'mind' is just a name for a succession of particular mental events inter-related in certain ways.

If, on the other hand, one happens to be satisfied with the substantival view of the self, then the second of the three theories, the theory that the mind's relatively permanent structure bears the traces left by past experiences, seems obvious and natural. Once we accept the thesis that the mind is a relatively abiding entity not reducible to particular experiences, there is no manifest objection in principle to conceiving this entity as having a structure which undergoes continual modification from its experiences. Nor would one expect modifications of structure to lie open to intro-spective observation, as one might expect of traces supposed to be ingredient in actual mental states. And although admittedly one does not know *how*, it seems by no means incredible *that* these modifications of the mind's structure should be such that in its future experiences the mind functions in a manner which mani-fests the traces left by its past experiences.

Since I myself regard some form of the substantival view as inescapable, I do not find it easy to get greatly excited about theories of how we might interpret the influence of past upon later experiences on the assumption that the substantival view has to be repudiated. I should have been rather glad, nevertheless, had time permitted a closer examination of theories (1) and (3), for they seem to me to provide instructive illustration of the truly desperate straits to which those philosophers are reduced who conceive it their duty to try to account for the facts of human experience in terms of the Serial view. In the time at our disposal in these lectures, however, criticism is best reserved for doctrines which, though in my view mistaken, do have some plausibility, and I shall make only the briefest of comments on the Mnemic Causation and Event-Trace theories.

8. It is common ground to all theories that if I now have a memory X of a childhood experience Y, Y is part-cause of X. The peculiarity of the Mnemic Causation theory is to hold that Y does not exercise its causality through any chain of intermediaries

(whether in the form of mental traces in, or structural changes of, my mind) which bridge the temporal gap between Y and X. Y has ceased to exist perhaps 50 years ago. Yet according to the theory this past Y somehow functions now as part-cause of my present memory X.

It is hardly surprising that this theory seems to have been found attractive by no philosopher except, for a spell, by Lord Russell. Perhaps the chief objection to it is that it requires us to accept a totally new kind of causality with no analogues elsewhere in human experience. Everywhere else, in cases where the cause does not immediately precede its effect, we find intermediaries bridging the temporal gap. 'Mnemic Causation' is a purely *ad hoc* invention which has no support from other regions of experience; and the only support it has from this, the mental, region of experience is negative—the alleged absurdity of alternative accounts, which posit intermediary causes which are not empirically observable.

I should heartily agree with Russell, however, that *one* of the alternative accounts, viz. the Event-Trace Theory, *is* absurd. This is the theory that the initial state leaves traces of itself which are passed on successively from mental state to mental state through all the intermediate states between it and the specific state, perhaps fifty years later, which manifests its causal influence.

The merit of this theory is, of course, that it preserves temporal continuity between cause and effect. But at what a cost! It is hard to see how such a theory can be seriously held by anyone who has faced up to its implications. On either of the 'Trace' theories one has to suppose that all, or almost all, a man's conscious experiences leave traces of themselves, and that these traces persist throughout the whole course of his life. On the *Event*-Trace theory it therefore follows that at any moment in the experience of an adult the particular experience he then enjoys is somehow the bearer of literally millions upon millions of these 'traces'. Suppose my razor slips and I cut myself. All that I can find in my momentary experience is a feeling of sharp pain located in some part of my face. But according to the Event-Trace theory there must *also* be ingredient in that momentary experience, in unconscious form, the uncountable multitude of traces left in my mind by past experiences from my infancy onwards. It seems to me that if one can believe this one can believe anything. For, notice, it is not an experiencing *subject*, but the *momentary* experience itself, in which these traces must be supposed to reside. On the theory before us there *is* no enduring 'subject' to carry the traces. One can understand what is meant by the teeming subconscious depths of the Freudian Ego, or even of the Leibnizian Monad. For these are substantival entities. But the teeming subconscious depths of a particular momentary mental state is another matter. Indeed I cannot help suspecting that a good many of those who profess some sympathy with the Event-Trace theory do really, despite themselves, think of the unconscious traces not as constituents of the particular mental events themselves but of an enduring subject in which these occur.

9.   Let us now leave these highly artificial and barely credible theories about mental dispositions, begotten by misplaced fidelity to the Serial view of the self, and let us return for the few minutes that remain to the common sense doctrine which interprets dispositions in terms of the relatively permanent mental structure of the self. I can readily imagine objection being taken to the use of the term 'structure' in this context, and I ought to say a word or two in its defence.

It must be freely admitted that 'structure', as applied to the mind, is an analogical term, derived from our experience of material things. We think of a material thing as having a structure if it is a whole of relatively permanent parts in relatively permanent relations to one another. Of the spatial relations of such parts we have, generally, very clear ideas. But there are, of course, other, somewhat less clear, types of physical relation, e.g. dynamical relations, which we also accept as contributing to the structure of the material thing. The structure of the atom could not be adequately described by indicating merely the spatial relationships of its parts; and much less could the structure of an organism. Now in applying the notion of 'structure' to the *mind* we frankly recognise that none of the physical relationships constitutive of 'material' structure obtain. But the application will be justified analogically if there is good reason to believe that the mind has relatively permanent 'parts' which stand in relatively permanent relations to one another.

F

And this it does seem reasonable to believe. We cannot, to be sure, perceive directly either the 'parts' of a mind or the inter-relations of these parts. We perceive directly only the mind's manifestations. Knowledge of the mind's parts and relations can be got only by inference from the observed manifestations. But the inference seems fair enough, once it has been accepted that there *is* an enduring subject. If, from observation of these mani-festations, we find certain distinct and irreducible kinds of experiencing constantly recurrent, e.g. conation, cognition and feeling, we may reasonably infer that there are different, relatively permanent 'parts' or 'organs' of the mind in virtue of which the self strives, cognises and feels. Again, if we find that these basic experiences in which the self manifests itself stand in certain relatively permanent relationships to one another—as we surely do find, else our experiences would be chaotic, which they are not —we may reasonably infer that the parts of the self in virtue of which it so manifests itself stand also in orderly relationship to one another. No doubt the knowledge we so gain of the mind's parts and relationships is both indirect and highly indefinite. We can only say that they are what they *must* be in order that the mind's manifestations should be what we *observe* them to be. It is not to be denied that of much of the ultimate structure of the human mind we have vague ideas at best. But that the mind *has* a structure, in the sense of being a whole of relatively permanent parts in relatively permanent relationships, and that we can speak accordingly of 'modifications of the mind's structure' in the course of its experience, seems a legitimate inference from direct observa-tion of the mind's actual manifestations.

It will be clear, then, that in my view a disposition is a potentiality based on an actuality—the 'actuality' being the existent mental structure of the self as modified in a specific manner by the relevant past experiences of that self. This is, I think, in complete accord with what is ordinarily understood by the term 'disposition'. When we say that a man has an ability to play bridge, it is not the case that our meaning is exhausted by a set of hypothetical propositions stating how he is likely to respond if he is confronted with certain more or less determinate situations. Rightly or wrongly, we mean also that, as a result of his past experience, his mind is now so constituted that if such situations confront him he will so respond.

What is it that is supposed to be wrong with this common-sense interpretation? Why is it rejected as naïve by so many present-day philosophers? The rock of offence is, of course, that it implies the substantival view of the self. It implies a mind which is a relatively permanent entity with a constitution of its own. The common-sense interpretation is unintelligible on the Serial view of the self which, in one form or another, is held to be forced upon us by a rigorously empirical approach to human experience.

I believe myself that a 'rigorously empirical' approach, which, if it is to be properly so described, must take full account of the self's experience of itself in self-consciousness, forces us to a very different conclusion. But concerning this enough has been said already. Rather I should like now (though it must be very briefly) to raise a question about the right of anyone who denies the substantival character of the mind to talk about 'mental dispositions' at all. I take it as agreed that a disposition is or involves some kind of potentiality—certainly it is very hard to talk about it intelligibly without using this or some similar term. What is it, I want to ask, that, on the Serial view, is supposed to 'have' this potentiality?

For surely *something* must 'have' it? A potentiality, it seems clear, cannot be itself merely potential. If it does not actually exist *as* a potentiality, it is just another word for nothing. Again, while actually existing as a potentiality, it cannot exist in the void. A potentiality is a sheer abstraction unless thought of as characterising an actual someone or something. So much seems to myself beyond reasonable dispute. But in the case of mental dispositions what is the actual someone or something that has the potentiality? There is no problem here on the *substantival* theory of the self; but if we accept the Serial theory I can see no answer that does not make plain nonsense. Smith, we say, is 'able' to understand German. What is it that has this ability or potentiality? What conceivable meaning is there in speaking of a series of particular mental events, inter-related as one will, having the ability to understand German?—or, for that matter, having any other ability? If the series of particular mental events is all that there is to Smith's mind, then that is all there is to it, and there is no room for predicating of it an ability or potentiality.

Unless, of course, a potentiality is nothing actual, but is itself merely potential. Is it unjust, I wonder, to suggest that the readiness to dispense with a mental substance to 'carry' mental dispositions is not unconnected with the fallacious belief that because the actualisation of a potentiality belongs to the future, a potentiality itself has no actual existence now? If that belief were not a fallacy, but valid, there would be something to be said for an analysis of mental dispositions in terms solely of hypothetical propositions about future events. I must insist, however, that a potentiality that is not itself something actual is nothing at all—not even a potentiality; that as an actual characteristic an actual location must be found for it; and that the Serialist, being debarred from finding any actual location for it, ought to abandon the notion altogether. And when the notion of potentiality goes, so too, as I see it, must go any talk of 'dispositions'. It is fortunate, therefore, that this disagreeable situation imposes itself only upon those who choose to deny the thesis, the truth of which seems to me to be independently established, that there are relatively permanent selves with relatively permanent mental structures.

10.   One final point. The dispositions with which we have been concerned are dispositions which, so far as the evidence of observation goes, arise from mental experiences, are excited into activity by mental experiences, and issue in mental experiences. They are called, therefore, very properly, 'mental' or 'psychical' dispositions, and I think they must be accounted for, primarily at least, in terms of modifications of the *mind's* structure. But although it seems to me impossible to account for them, as some have tried to do, in terms of modifications of bodily structure alone, nevertheless I by no means wish to rule out the hypothesis that our psychical dispositions (so-called) involve modifications of bodily structure also. It is, I think, highly probable that the experiences which give rise to modifications of mental structure invariably give rise also to corresponding modifications on the brain. After all, it is never to be forgotten that in the empirical self (i.e. in the self *qua* manifested in human experience) mind and

body are so intermixed 'as to compose a certain unity'. If any one should care to contend that there is no such thing as a *purely* psychical disposition, that all so-called psychical dispositions are at bottom psycho-physical, I have no quarrel with him. On the contrary, I suspect that he is right.

LECTURE VIII

SELF-ACTIVITY AND ITS MODES

1. Today, and for the remainder of the lectures in the present course, we shall be concerned with the fundamental manifestations of the self as a practical rather than as a theoretical being. Here the key concept is that of *activity*; and I propose to devote today's lecture to the elucidation and defence of this concept and to the discrimination of its species.

'Activity' and its synonyms—agency, initiation, striving and the like—along with its correlative 'passivity' and its synonyms, are expressions that we use every day of our lives. How, first of all, do we get the idea to which these expressions correspond?

On at least the general provenance of the idea we are fortunately able to count upon a very large measure of agreement. It is almost a philosophical common-place that we do not get the idea from observation of anything in the external world. There we may observe changes of various sorts, but nothing that could of itself even suggest the notion of an agency or activity that brings about the changes. We do come, indeed, rightly or wrongly, to ascribe agency to certain external things. But this ascription, it is agreed, is not based on direct observation of the things. What happens is that we read into these things a character derived from experience of our selves. It is from perception of the inner world of the mind, not from perception of the outer world of matter, that the notion of activity arises for us.

So much is more or less common ground. Immediately, however, we have to take notice of the fact that many philosophers declare that this idea is a 'fiction'.

Now this is, on the face of it, a somewhat puzzling pronounce-ment. Evidently it cannot be meant, in calling it a fiction, that there just *is* no idea for which the term 'activity' stands. That there is such an idea is a datum of the whole discussion. What then is meant when people tell us that the idea of activity is a fiction?

Roughly the first half of the present lecture will be devoted to an examination of this question. If, as I believe, the outcome is to vindicate the objective validity of the idea in general, the way will be cleared for an attempt in the second half to reach a more precise understanding of activity by the discrimination of some of the main species within it.

Part I

2.   It seems to me that there are, in principle, only two things that can with any plausibility be meant in calling the idea of activity a fiction. I shall deal with each in turn.

The first, and less important, is as follows. It may be urged that when we analyse the idea of activity with care, observing what precisely it is that we actually experience in those experiences which we are accustomed to speak of as experiences of 'activity', the constituents that are then disclosed turn out to be of such a character that we are no longer prepared, on reflection, to label the experience one of 'activity' at all. Our analysis reveals, perhaps, a certain complex of ideas and images and body-feelings—of cephalic tension, muscular innervation, and the like. But when we reflect upon this product of our analysis we realise that if, as seems to us to be the case, there is nothing *else* present in our experiences of 'activity' so-called, we have been deluded in supposing that such experiences have anything in them which entitles us to call them experiences of 'activity'.

I think that this is, at least sometimes, what is meant by calling 'activity' a fictitious idea. But if so, surely the critic's logic is curiously perverse? For how can he judge that the constituents disclosed by his analysis of the experience are such that he is not really entitled to call the experience an experience of 'activity', except in the light of some *different* idea of activity already in his possession which he takes to be a *genuine* idea of activity, an idea of 'activity proper'? Otherwise he is using words without meaning when he says that the experience of these constituents (in conjunction) is not really an experience of 'activity'. And he will be in no better case if, belatedly discovering this implication of his procedure, he should now try to show that his 'different' idea of activity, which he had been using as criterion, is *itself* analysable into constituents which we can see not to warrant us in regarding it as 'really' activity. For he will only be able to condemn this *second* idea of activity in the light of a *further* idea of it in his possession which he takes to be genuine. And so on *ad infinitum*. The attempt to explain away the idea of activity as fictitious always presupposes some other idea of activity which is assumed *not* to be fictitious. The idea of activity, it would seem, cannot be shown to be a fiction along these lines at any rate.

Nevertheless we can, I think, cordially agree with the critic of activity at least to this extent, that none of the sets of constituents into which analysts have so far resolved the experience of it does in fact give us anything that we feel satisfied, on reflection, to call 'activity'. Why should this be? Is it just that the analyses are bad analyses? In a sense, yes, and in another sense, no. They are (or may be) excellent analyses of what we *objectively* experience when we experience activity. But they are all of them very bad analyses, or rather they are not analyses at all, of what we *subjectively* experience when we experience activity. Herein, I suggest, lies the real root of the trouble. The critic cannot find anything deserving of the name of 'activity', because he seeks for it where it cannot possibly be found. For activity, if it is anything, is a function of the subject *qua* subject. It cannot be 'objectified'. To attempt to analyse the experience of activity from the standpoint of the external observer, ignoring the standpoint of the subject *qua* subject, the subject in its subjective functioning, is—if I may borrow Stout's apt adaptation of Berkeley's phrase—to blindfold ourselves and then complain that we cannot see. If the critic pursued what I suggest is the proper course of *re-enacting*, *re-living*, the subjective experience to which the name of 'activity' is commonly ascribed, he would, I think, find what he is looking for: and, by the same token, he would find that which he is himself unwittingly using as a criterion, when he condemns as inadequate to anything one can properly mean by 'activity' the constituents he has analysed out from the standpoint of the external observer.

There are not, perhaps, many errors that bring in their train so extensive a series of philosophical disasters as that of supposing that 'experience' is reducible without remainder to consciousness of something before the mind, something presented to the subject. The error is in part explicable, no doubt, by the fact that it is not his subjective activity, but the objects to which it is directed, that commonly interests the experiencing subject, and that thus lies in the focus of his attention. The subject's consciousness of his own subjective functioning is, as a rule, very faint and inexplicit by comparison with his consciousness of his object. Yet it is a little surprising that the strenuous efforts of notable thinkers like Maine de Biran in the nineteenth century, and Alexander, Pringle-Pattison, and Bowman in our own day, who have laboured to show that awareness of the subjective side is in some degree present in all experience, should have borne so very little fruit. Even if we are a little hesitant about endorsing their thesis in its full universality, still there do seem to be at least some experiences, for example that of effortful willing, in which the direct awareness of subjective functioning can hardly be missed save by those who are determined on *a priori* grounds not to find it. When we have collated with meticulous care all the items 'objectively' apprehended in an experience of effortful volition, it remains perfectly clear that these items in their totality do not add up to what we in fact experience in making the volition. There is missing what one might call, in Bradley's phrase, 'the felt out-going of the self from the self', the inner experience of the subject in its subjective functioning. To this experience we can at least attach a meaning; for we can reproduce it whenever we set ourselves to re-live a volition, although in the nature of the case it cannot be presented to us as an 'object'. It is thus, and thus alone, that activity in general is to be known: and I ought perhaps to give warning that a good deal of what I have to say in this lecture will be incomprehensible to anyone unable to discover in his experience anything more than the presentation of 'objects' to a 'subject'.

3.   I pass on to the second thing that might, I think, be meant by calling 'activity' a fictitious idea. Even if it be granted that there is an unique kind of experience which is called experience of

'activity', an experience not amenable to any internal analysis which might incline us, on reflection, to wish to withhold from it the name of 'activity' after all; still, it may be urged, there are certain *external* facts which ought to persuade us that we are mistaken in calling it an experience of 'activity'. For a man cannot in strictness be said to be experiencing activity if he is not *really* active. If there are facts which show that, in the given situation, he is not really active, then his 'experience' or 'feeling' of activity must be a delusion. And there *are* facts (it is alleged) which very strongly suggest that a man may feel active and yet not really be active. The man who wills to move his arm feels active in so doing, even if in fact (as might occur through sudden paralysis) his arm remains stationary. Is it not evident that here at any rate his feeling of activity is illusory? His willing does not in fact bring about anything. But if the feeling of activity is illusory here, it is possible in principle that it is illusory everywhere. Perhaps even in normal cases where the bodily movement does follow on the willing the man is deceived in supposing that it is his activity in willing that brings this about. And has not David Hume produced a formidable battery of arguments to show that he *is* so deceived, and that there is no intrinsic connection whatsoever discoverable between the act of willing on the one hand, and, on the other hand, the bodily movement which does in the ordinary run of things ensue?

Hume's arguments do not in fact seem to me so very formidable; but as it is far from evident where one is to find better ones to the same purport, and as they have certainly exerted a great deal of influence upon subsequent philosophy, we shall be obliged to consider them at some length. There is, however, one thing that can be said about them quite briefly, and at once. In so far as they are directed to showing that activity of *any* kind is unreal, they are invalid. The fact that the paralysed man's arm does not move when he wills it to move does not in the least entail that he was wrong in his conviction that he was really active. All that it entails is that he was wrong in his expectation that his 'spiritual' activity in willing *would produce a certain bodily result*—an entirely different thing. The failure to achieve the end to which his activity was directed has no tendency to disprove that he *was* active—spiritually active—*in trying to achieve* that end. That the activity will achieve its objective (though only—if we may anticipate a little—in co-operation with other factors not under our control) is in the case of certain bodily movements our normal expectation. But even if this expectation were never fulfilled, the correct implication would be, not that our activity is unreal, but, at most, that it is futile.

In other words, on the question whether one is really active, in the sense of 'spiritually' active, the evidence of the subject's own direct experience is conclusive. Another man may *suggest* to me that I am not 'trying'—say, to move my palsied leg. But I, the subject, *know* whether or not I am trying. And if I do directly experience myself as trying, there can be no more point in asking whether I am *really* active, in the sense of 'spiritually' active, than there would be in asking whether, when I directly experience myself as in pain, I really am in pain.

4. It must be frankly admitted, however, that what we have gained so far (if we have gained it) against Hume is of only limited importance. Spiritual activity—'trying', 'willing'—is always directed to some objective. If there should be good reason to believe that this spiritual activity has no intrinsic connection with the coming to be of its objective, then even though its reality as such is established, it can hardly be regarded as a very valuable human possession. It is obviously something a great deal poorer than what we commonly mean when we think of ourselves as 'active' beings. We commonly think of our activity as an active *power*, capable of producing effects beyond itself. If in fact this supposed power is a myth, those who insist that 'activity' is a myth will not be so very far wrong after all.

And it is, of course, against activity in this sense of active power that Hume in his famous chapter in the *Enquiry* [1] chiefly directs his attack. His discussion is conducted within the ambit of his search for the original of our idea of necessary connection. The suggestion naturally arises that perhaps the original is to be found in our experience of volition, where we seem to be directly aware of ourselves as actively producing that which we will; e.g.

[1] *An Enquiry concerning the Human Understanding*, Section VII (Selby-Bigge's edn.).

the movement of a limb. Is there in fact this *intrinsic* connection between the act of willing and the movement of the limb, or are we deceived in supposing that we directly discern it? Hume takes the latter view. 'We learn the influence of our will from experience alone.' [1] We have no 'internal impression' of our will producing the bodily movement to which it is directed. And Hume thinks he can explain how the illusion that we do have such an impression comes about. What happens is that, after observing repeated instances of acts of will being followed by the bodily movements to which they are directed, 'the mind is caused by habit, upon appearance of the one event, to expect its usual attendant'. Hence 'a new sentiment or impression', a custom-bred expectation, that when we will a bodily movement that bodily movement will take place. This felt compulsion in our minds to pass from the one idea to the other is misinterpreted by us as a necessary connection between the things to which the ideas relate—here, the act of will and the bodily movement. Hence on the occasion of willing a bodily movement, we mistakenly suppose that we directly apprehend our volition bringing the bodily movement about.

That (very summarily stated) is how Hume thinks that the illusion comes about. But why is he so sure in the first place that it *is* an illusion?—so sure that we do *not* in volition discern an active power in ourselves? Hume advances a number of arguments. But it will suffice, for reasons that will appear shortly, if we concentrate upon one of them. I shall select the argument which is perhaps generally regarded as the most powerful.[2] The specific proposition which Hume is here out to disprove is that in willing a bodily movement we are directly conscious of our will actively producing the bodily movement. His disproof is based upon certain admitted physiological facts. It has been firmly established that when we will to move our leg (and succeed in doing so), the movement of the leg does not follow *immediately* upon our willing. What immediately follow are certain physiological changes. Intervening between our act of will and the bodily movement to which it is directed lies a whole series of cerebral, neural, and muscular movements. Now, in the act of volition we have, normally, no consciousness whatsoever of these intermediary

---

[1] *An Enquiry concerning the Human Understanding*, Section VII, p. 66.
[2] *Ibid.* pp. 66-7.

processes. We cannot, therefore, as we commonly suppose, directly discern the power of our will to move our leg, since this power, if it exists at all, is exercised only through intermediaries of which we are totally unaware. The causal relation, if any, between the act of willing and the movement of the leg is a *mediate* relation; and as we are unaware of the mediation, we clearly cannot be directly discerning that mediate relation. The causal relation as we *suppose* it to be, on the other hand, just isn't there; so we must be deluded in thinking that we directly discern it.

This argument of Hume's has often been attacked; and along very divergent lines. It seems to me, however, that none of the criticisms go quite to the heart of the matter. For, in my opinion, Hume and his critics alike assume a basic premise which, while it looks self-evident, is in fact false. This premise is that when, as we say, we 'will to move our leg', the *immediate* object of our will is the moving of our leg.

What I want to suggest is that the expression 'willing to move our leg' is in fact elliptical. If we attend carefully to what is actually in our minds when we 'will to move our leg' we find, it seems to me, that the immediate object of our willing is not the movement of our leg but certain kinaesthetic and other sensations upon which, we have learned from experience, the movement of our leg normally supervenes. No doubt this will appear at first sight a highly paradoxical suggestion; but I am inclined to think that anyone who makes the required introspective experiment with care will discover that it is none the less true. The ulterior object of my willing is the movement of my leg, but the proximate or immediate object is the producing of the appropriate sensations.

Perhaps the easiest way to satisfy one's self that this is the case is as follows. Everyone would agree, I take it, that there are certain sensations associated with the moving of one's leg, and also that, normally, we can produce an image of them at will. But now let us suppose that we have somehow *forgotten* what these specific sensations are—how far this is factually possible is beside the point. Can we, in such a predicament, *will* to move our leg? It seems clear to me that we can *not*—we just don't know how to set about it. We may, of course, *wish* to move our leg. But this is no more the willing to move our leg than the wish to move, say, our appendix is the willing to move our appendix. 'Willing' is always directed to something we conceive to be in our power. If we have forgotten the appropriate sensations, the wish to move our leg must remain a *mere* wish, totally impotent, incapable of passing into a 'willing' of the movement.

It might be objected, indeed, that our inability to will the bodily movement in the absence from our mind of the appropriate sensations does not formally establish the *priority* of the sensations to the bodily movement as object of our willing. Abstractly considered, it might be the case that the bodily movement and the kinaesthetic sensations are inseparable for us, so that we cannot will the one without the other. But a very little reflection shows that this will not do. It seems perfectly possible to think of, and to will the occurrence of, the kinaesthetic sensations by themselves. In fact one can easily enough imagine a case in which, if a man wills the occurrence of the kinaesthetic sensations at all, he *must* will them by themselves. If a man has a foot amputated but still retains the sensations associated with its movement, then, provided he knows his foot is missing, he cannot *will* (though he may of course *visualise*, and *want*) the movement of it; yet he surely may (possibly from sheer curiosity about an interesting psycho-physiological phenomenon) will to produce the appropriate sensations.

I submit, then, that when we will a bodily movement the proximate or immediate object of our willing is the producing of the appropriate sensations, in the conviction—based ultimately on experience—that the ulterior object we have in view, the bodily movement, will thereby come to pass. But since it is only in abnormal situations, where the customary connection of sensations with bodily movement fails us, that the intermediary condition of the achievement of the latter tends to force itself upon our notice, we readily lose sight of this intermediary, and both speak and think as though the bodily movement were the immediate, and indeed the only, object of our willing.

5. Now when the basic premise of Hume and his critics is re-stated in this way, it puts a very different complexion on the whole matter.

We may readily admit, first of all, that between the movement of the limb and the appropriate sensations we discern no necessary connection. The connection is something that we learn solely from experience. We learn in infancy or in very early childhood, through what are at first instinctive or merely random movements of our body, that as a matter of brute fact certain sensations are usually associated with certain bodily movements. This purely factual information is the pre-condition of the stage at which we can *will* a body-movement. Hume is thus perfectly correct in so far as all that he wants to maintain is that we do not in willing directly discern a necessary connection between our willing and the bodily movement willed. The contingent relationship between the (intermediate) kinaesthetic sensations and the bodily movement rules that out conclusively.

But what Hume requires to show, in order to prove that we do not directly discern real agency, active power, in our willing of a bodily movement is, if our re-statement of the basic premise is sound, something very different. He has to show not just that there is no necessary connection discernible between our willing and the bodily movement, but that there is none discernible between our willing and the appropriate kinaesthetic sensations. He has to show that the *latter* connection is one that we *also* learn from experience. Hume, naturally enough, makes no attempt to show this. Nor, so far as I can see, is it possible to adapt any of the arguments he advances against the necessary connection of the volition with the bodily movement willed to support the different thesis that there is no necessary connection between the volition and the kinaesthetic sensations willed. Thus we could not, e.g. adapt the particular Humean argument with which we have been dealing, by pointing to unperceived intermediaries between the act of will and the occurrence of the kinaesthetic sensations willed. There is no psychological evidence of psychical intermediaries corresponding to the anatomical and physiological evidence of physical intermediaries that seems so decisive in the other case.

We have agreed that it is only by experience that we learn that specific kinaesthetic sensations are associated with specific movements of our body. The question at the moment is whether a plausible case can be made for the view that it is also from experience that we learn that there is a connection between willing these kinaesthetic sensations and their occurrence. I do not think that it can. Any such view presupposes that there is a stage at which we will these sensations without any expectations whatsoever that they will ensue. What, then, could possibly induce us to will them in the first instance? Do we, as it were, say to ourselves 'I should like to move my leg, and I have reason to believe from experience that if certain sensations occurred my leg would move. I should very much like, therefore, that these sensations would occur. What am I to do about it? Let's see whether "willing" them is any use —good gracious! Here they come!' This seems to me implausible in the last degree. I do not see how the 'experiment' of willing a thing with a view to its coming into being could ever suggest itself to a mind which did not already regard willing as an act which tends to bring about that to which it is directed. Or do we perhaps discover the connection by sheer *accident—happening* to will these sensations, and then finding, to our surprise, that the sensations occur? But surely 'happening to will', or 'accidental willing', contradicts the very notion of willing. Willing is not the sort of thing we can do by accident; for the very essence of it is its aim to bring about a definite something. The earlier question therefore recurs, 'What makes us suppose that the act of willing will tend to bring the thing about if we do not already believe in the connection?' The notion that we could conceivably be *surprised* to find that willing produces what it aims to produce—a notion implied in the suggestion that we learn the connection from experience—seems really absurd. When we will X, we will it because, and only because, we believe that willing X tends to bring X about.

6.   There is one further point that must be dealt with, however, if our answer to Hume is to be reasonably complete.

It is clear enough that if the active power of which we are directly conscious in willing to move a limb relates to the production of certain sensations, not to the movement of the limb, the mere fact that the limb may not be there does not raise any difficulty about accepting the reality of this active power. But suppose, now, a case in which, though the limb may be there, there is total anaesthesia with respect to it. If we are still able to image the kinaesthetic sensations, we can seek by willing to produce them;

but they will fail in fact to ensue. Now there can be no doubt that in such a case, just as much as in 'successful' volition, we would seem to ourselves in the volition to be exerting an active power. But is it not evident that here at any rate we should be deceived, since nothing whatever is produced—not even the kinaesthetic sensations? And if we are deceived in supposing that we directly discern an active power in these unsuccessful volitions, must that not reflect back a doubt upon our supposed discernment of an active power in successful volitions?

The difficulty is an instructive one; for the solution of it serves to bring out an important point about the nature of activity which we have not yet had occasion to notice.

It is undeniable, I think, that in the case cited we are deceived on one matter. We are deceived in our expectation that certain kinaesthetic sensations will ensue. But the fact that these sensations do not ensue does not imply that we are deceived in our belief that we are exerting an active power in relation to their production. For it is enough, in order for the volition to be an active *power*, that the exercise of it intrinsically *tends* to bring about the sensations willed; even though the co-operation of other factors, which may or may not be present, is required to ensure a successful issue. The lack of a successful issue is thus perfectly compatible with our being correct in supposing that we directly discern in the volition an active power in relation to the issue. The significance of these unsuccessful cases of volition is to bring home to us that the co-operation of other factors *is* required if the end to which the active power of volition is directed is to be in fact achieved. Our being deceived in our expectation, in the case cited, is due simply to our being unaware that certain of the necessary co-operating factors are absent. Strictly speaking, the active power of volition seems best described in the terms used by Stout—'a tendency towards its own fulfilment'.[1] But no more than this is needed to enable us to maintain, as against Hume, that there is an intrinsic or necessary connection between volition and its 'object'.

But if volitional activity is no more than a *tendency* to its own fulfilment, is it really justifiable (it may be asked) to speak of a 'necessary' connection between volition and its object? When we speak of a 'necessary' connection between A and B, we usually

---

[1] *Mind and Matter*, p. 24.

mean that, given A, we *must* have B. Yet in the case before us it is admitted that, given the volition, we may not get its object.

It seems to me, however, that the point at issue here is at bottom verbal. The expression 'necessary connection' is no doubt most commonly used in the sense just mentioned. But it is also used on occasion merely to mark the contrast with *de facto* connection. It is in that wider sense of the term that we are claiming that the connection of volition with its immediate object is necessary. And this is the sense specially relevant within the Humean context. For Hume, seeking to undermine the credentials of the idea of necessary connection, has been arguing that we do not really discern in volition an active power exerting influence upon the coming to be of the object; that the connection is purely *de facto*, not necessary. This is the position we were concerned to refute. Nevertheless I should agree that the common associations of the expression 'necessary connection' make it somewhat misleading in the present case, and that it would be preferable to speak of the connection between volition and its (immediate) object as 'intrinsic' only. There can, I think, be no objection on linguistic grounds to describing this connection as 'intrinsic', if it be true that the volition even 'tends' to bring about its object.

7.   It is not possible here to say more than a supplementary word or two about Hume's criticism of the power of volition over *ideas*, which follows immediately upon his criticism of its power over bodily movements. But in truth there seems little need to say much. What Hume's arguments on this head boil down to is that we do not *understand how* our willing is connected with the coming to be of what is willed. We are not 'acquainted with the nature of the human soul and the nature of an idea, or the aptitude of the one to produce the other'.[1] The power of the will is 'unknown and incomprehensible'. But is there really anyone who holds the contrary? What is supposed to follow from this ignorance of the 'how'? To affirm that in volition we are directly conscious of an intrinsic connection between the act of willing and the coming to be of what we will does not in the least require us to affirm that in volition we understand how willing brings about, or tends

[1] *Enquiry* p. 68.

to bring about, what it wills. For finite knowledge at any rate, there must be some things that just *are*; and the basic facts of our own nature may reasonably be supposed to fall into this category. We do not know *how* we are *what* we are. If it be conceded that we cannot will at all save in the conviction that our willing tends to bring about what we will, the intrinsic connection between willing and what we will may fairly be accepted as just an ultimate fact about our natures. After all, we do not understand how it is that we even *have* a will. But no one, I take it, supposes that we must wait until we know how it is that we have a will before we can justifiably believe that we do have a will.

PART II

8. It has seemed to me obligatory, the more so in the present state of philosophical opinion, to preface any attempt at a constructive account of activity by a rather extensive consideration of the prior question of whether there really is any fact to which the name 'activity' corresponds. I hope it may now be agreed, even if only provisionally, that activity is some kind of a fact. On that assumption let us go on to enquire, as systematically as space will permit, into its diverse modes.

For its modes are, I think, highly diversified. There would appear to be several distinct species of activity, in each of which we recognise ourselves to be in a real sense active, and yet, on reflection, active in irreducibly different ways. A fully systematic treatment would require to distinguish and relate to one another all of these several species. But to undertake so much within the confines of this lecture would be palpably absurd, and we shall try to make our task manageable by narrowing our problem to that of placing in its proper perspective the specific mode of self-activity which is (or appears to be) involved in 'free will'. We shall ignore here even so important a mode of activity as aesthetic imagining, since this would appear to have no special relevance for our present limited objective.

9. We may take our start from a seeming inconsistency in common ways of talking about activity. It is often said that the

self is active, in some degree, throughout the whole course of its waking life. On the other hand, the self's activity in certain experiences—e.g. volition—is often sharply contrasted with its passivity in others—e.g. in suffering the onset of a sudden pain. *Prima facie* one of these two views must be mistaken. For how can the self be at times passive if it is always in some degree active?

The answer lies, I think, in recognising a somewhat important, if obvious, distinction between activity *of* the self, which is self-activity *proper*, and activities *within* the self, which can and frequently do go on even where the self regards itself as not active but passive in respect of them.

For evidence of this distinction there is no need to appeal to the shadowy realm of the sub-conscious; e.g. to the now fairly well-attested phenomenon of sub-conscious intellectual processes which, in some happily endowed individuals, seem able to function effectively while the conscious intellect is otherwise engaged, or even in complete abeyance, and to produce results at times which the conscious intellect would be proud to acknowledge as its own. To my regret, this enviable state of affairs, though I have no doubt of its enjoyment by many, is not one with which I have myself first-hand acquaintance. But in truth the *conscious* functioning of the intellect within the self, while the self itself remains inactive with respect to it, is a situation of which we have all had experience. For example. Often when we are trying to settle ourselves for sleep after a hard evening's brain work, ideas connected with the task we are struggling to lay aside keep surging up and 'milling about' in our minds. It is not to be denied that we have here activity in *some* sense, and activity of a faculty which we recognise as in *some* sense belonging to the 'self'. But though we think of the activity as going on *in* the self, we do not regard our *self* as active in their regard. What our *self* is doing is trying to go to sleep, and it is with *this* endeavour that we naturally identify whatever self-activity proper there is in the situation. The intrusive activity of our intellectual consciousness, so far from being a phase of, or a secondary consequence of, the self's endeavour to settle for sleep, is experienced as offering resistance to that endeavour. Evidently, then, there can be activity of the intellectual consciousness within the self which we decisively distinguish from 'self-activity'.

That bodily activity also—even where it involves somewhat intricate physical manoeuvres—can be a merely functional activity within the self, is apparent at once. The practised pianist can play a familiar piece, and the expert juggler can accomplish at least the less dazzling feats in his repertoire, as it were 'automatically', with little or no 'engagement' of the self in their performance. Bodily activity is here undeniable, but *self*-activity in respect of it is near to vanishing point. In the sufferer from St. Vitus' Dance the vanishing-point of self-activity has been actually reached. The unfortunate victim certainly supposes his body to be undergoing a variety of lively muscular contractions, but he does not regard him*self* as active. On the contrary, he feels himself passive; patient, rather than agent, in respect of the movements of his body. Evidently, then, bodily activity need not be an expression of self-activity; even though it is true that self-activity does exceedingly often find expression in bodily activity, just as it exceedingly often finds expression in intellectual activity.

Very obviously also the activities of our appetitive consciousness can be merely functional. It is not necessary to elaborate the truism that desires are often felt as 'irruptions' within the self which impede the self in its active pursuit of its chosen end.

But in most obvious contrast of all with self-activity proper are the functional activities of our *feeling*-consciousness—pleasure and pain. Indeed pleasure and pain are so patently *not* manifestations of *self*-activity that they are sometimes taken as prime exemplars of pure passivity. Yet they should, I think, be placed in the category of '*functional* activity'. We certainly do speak of pain, e.g. as present in different degrees of 'activity' (or 'quiescence'). If pain is present at all, we find it natural to speak of it as being in some measure 'active'. The inclination to regard these feelings as belonging to a merely passive side of our nature is not, however, surprising. For while the (functional) activities of our intellectual and appetitive consciousness resemble self-activity in having 'objectives', the 'activities' of pleasure and pain have no 'objectives'. Pleasure and pain may, of course, and normally do, *excite* self-activity towards objectives; usually the objectives of prolonging the pleasure or removing the pain. But in themselves they are directionless; and accordingly in much sharper contrast than intellectual and appetitive processes are with self-activity proper.

In the light of the above we may say, I think, that while it is difficult to suppose any experience of waking life in which activity in the sense of *functional* activity is not present, this is compatible with the complete absence, on occasion, of *self*-activity.

But although it is theoretically possible for activity *of* the self to be absent while functional activity *within* the self is present, this is, in practice, a somewhat rare phenomenon. Even in the type of case already alluded to, where intellectual or appetitive processes go on 'in despite of one's self', the self is almost always actively directing itself to *some* end; one may be active, e.g. in seeking to get to sleep, at the same time as one is passive in respect of the ideas which one's intellect may be 'churning out'. Nevertheless there *are* a few experiences in which it would be difficult to maintain that any trace of self-activity proper is discoverable. Upon the onset of a sudden, unexpected, and violent pain there seems to be an appreciable moment when the self is wholly absorbed by its feeling-consciousness; though almost at once self-activity is resumed in the conscious seeking for relief. Again, it is probably the case that a man can be so completely in the grip of some powerful emotion—'paralysed by fear', perhaps—that for a brief space his self is 'without aim or object'; self-activity is in absolute suspension. And 'action upon impulse', about which I shall be saying something shortly, is I think, still another example.

Apart from these very occasional interruptions, however, it seems true that the self in its waking life is always active in pursuit of some end or other. Not, of course, that we are always explicitly conscious of pursuing an end. We may seem to ourselves, as we sit in the sunshine enjoying the sights and the sounds and the perfumed air of a summer's day, to be in a state of sheer quiescence, with no 'aim' in mind whatsoever. But we would not be enjoying these sensations if we were not consciously experiencing them; and we would not be consciously experiencing them if we were not attending to them; and we would not be attending to them if we were not wanting to attend to them. Our attention to them is the expression of our self-direction to the end of securing these enjoyable experiences. Explicit consciousness that we are directing ourselves to this end will probably only ensue if our agreeable state happens to suffer disturbance. Then we feel vexed because, as we have come to realise, it was our will, our aim, to go on enjoying the delights that nature was so bountifully providing. So far as sense perception in general is concerned, it is safe to say that where there is in the self no active interest in what the senses may reveal, the senses will reveal nothing. There will be a physical affection of the sense organs, but there will be no sense *perception*.

There would seem, then, to be a genuine form of self-activity which, if not absolutely all-pervasive of normal waking life, is next door to being so. It is essentially conative in character, a seeking to achieve ends more or less clearly conceived. Although this self-activity is conative, however, not everything which custom includes under the general heading of 'conation' is a mode of self-activity. Thus 'desire' is usually so included; but (as we have already noted) desire is often felt to be in actual opposition to the end to which self-activity is directed. And even when it is *not*, desire is never, strictly speaking, a *mode* of self-activity. There is a significant felt difference between desiring something and actively setting one's self to obtain it. Only in the latter case do we feel ourself to be 'active'. It is true, of course, that if we are in a state of desire towards X we normally go on to busy ourself to obtain X. But the two states are manifestly distinct. Desire normally engenders self-activity, but it is not itself a mode of it.

Nor can it be said that self-activity is invariably present even when our appetitions excite to definite 'action'. We have to take account here of the distinction between 'impulsive' action and 'willed' action. Purely impulsive action is no doubt rare in self-conscious beings, with 'the power to look before and after', but it can hardly be said *never* to occur. What distinguishes it from willed action is that in it action follows upon the impulse 'automatically', as it were, with no moment of intervention in which the self considers and endorses the end of the impulse. The self is not conscious of 'taking charge of' the situation. Its felt rôle is that of spectator rather than of agent. Hence we must say, I think, that self-activity is absent from the merely impulsive action. Willed action, on the other hand, differs from impulsive action precisely in the fact that in it the self does adopt the end of the impulse as its own end, and directs itself to its achievement. Here self-activity *is* always present.

Indeed this self-activity of willing or volition is identical with the self-activity we have just been discussing; that self-activity which, we claimed, is an all-but universal feature of our normal waking life. And if it seems a little odd, at first glance, to speak thus of volition as an all-but universal feature of normal waking life, that is doubtless because we are so apt to think of volition in terms of the deliberate choice between alternatives, which is of course *not* an activity that is pervasive of normal waking experience. But deliberate choice between alternatives is only one particular species of volition. The *genus* is the self's identification of itself with a conceived end; and this, though present in very varying degrees of explicitness, it is not paradoxical to regard as 'pervasive of normal waking experience'.

10.   We have next to see, however, that this self-activity ingredient in volition, and characteristic of our normal waking life, is by no means the only kind even of *self*-activity. I want to draw attention now to a quite distinct, and (I think) uniquely important, kind. This is the self-activity which is exercised in what we can best call 'moral decision'. But as the term 'moral decision' has more than one usage even in philosophical contexts I must begin by explaining how I am using it here.

The two commonest usages are, I think, these. We may mean (1) the decision as to which of two or more courses, each of which has *prima facie* qualifications to be regarded as our duty, really is our duty. Moral decision here is primarily an intellectual matter. Or we may mean (2) not the decision as to what is our duty, but as to *whether we shall do* our duty. This is a decision which has to be taken in every situation in which there is for the agent a felt conflict between what he conceives to be his duty and what he most strongly desires; i.e. in the situation of 'moral temptation'. Moral decision here is wholly a moral matter, and may fairly be said to constitute the very core of the moral life. It is this sense of moral decision that is relevant to our present purpose. There is a distinctive kind of self-activity involved in moral decision so understood, and our business is to try to elucidate its nature.

A word first of all, however, about an alleged difficulty in the 'setting' of the situation of moral temptation as we have just described it—the conflict of strongest desire with duty.

It has sometimes been maintained that we can attach an intelligible meaning to the expression 'strongest desire' only after the event, when we know which course has actually been chosen; that there is no way of telling which of two or more competing desires is the strongest except by observing which of them finds expression in action. But this view is surely mistaken. We frequently know very well, in advance of our actual choice, that provided we allow our desiring nature *and nothing else* to dictate our choice, it is desire X and not desire Y or desire Z that will prevail. All we need do to measure the relative strength of competing desires is to ask ourselves, in the given situation, which of them would in fact issue in action if we allowed our desiring nature alone to determine our choice. Sometimes, of course, we shall find it difficult to return a confident answer. But the difficulty arises not because we have no valid principle of relative measurement to apply to the desires, but because when we do apply our principle to them we find that two or more of them are approximately equal.

Assuming then that the situation has been properly enough described, let us now directly examine it. The procedure must be (basically—or so it seems to me—there is no other way of proceeding, for we are trying to grasp what the mental act of moral decision is for the subject performing it) to imagine an experience of moral temptation and the taking of the moral decision between the rival ends that it presents, and thereupon to consider whether one does not find that the following characteristics are unmistakably present in one's moral decision as thus imaginatively experienced.

In the first place (I suggest) the agent experiences the decision as something which *he* makes. That is to say, it is for him a manifestation of *self*-activity. No demurral to this deliverance of our practical consciousness is easily conceivable, and I pass on at once to the far more important, indeed crucial, characteristic which marks off this specific kind of self-activity from that which occurs in the ordinary choices where there is no felt conflict between duty and desire.

The decision whether or not to rise to duty (I suggest) is experienced as something which, though (as we have seen) issuing from the self, does not issue from the self's *character* as so far formed. There is in every man at every stage of his life a developing, but relatively stable and relatively systematic, complex of emotive and conative dispositions which we call his 'character'. It is this inner system, this character, which determines what desires will emerge in response to a given situation, what will be the relative strengths of these desires (if more than one emerge), and what, in consequence will be his strongest desire. A man's strongest desire at any moment may in fact be regarded as a function of his character in relation to the given situation. But if that is so, moral decision cannot be experienced by the agent *as flowing from his character*. For it is of the very essence of the moral decision as experienced that it is a decision whether or not to combat his strongest desire, and hence to *oppose* his formed character; and presumably strongest desire or formed character cannot find expression in the decision whether or not to fight against itself. The self-activity of moral decision, then, as experienced, differs very significantly from the self-activity of ordinary choices in virtue of the fact that while in both cases it is the self that is active, in the former case it is not the self merely *qua* formed character that acts, but the self as somehow *transcending* its own formed character.

Now I admit at once that this is a somewhat paradoxical deliverance of our practical consciousness. But the important thing is not whether it is paradoxical, but whether, as a reading of what we find ourselves believing, and unable not to believe, in the situation of moral temptation, it answers to our experience. To myself it seems clear that it does. And I am not wholly without hope that self-interrogation by others will lead them to the same result. Philosophers, it seems to me, have been somewhat too prone to reject as self-evidently absurd any view which implies that there is a distinction between the self and its 'character', without pausing to ask themselves whether in fact they do not themselves implicitly accept this distinction every time they make a moral decision between duty and strongest desire.

It is worth pointing out, moreover, that the alleged paradox is not really so paradoxical as it seems on the surface. It entails, admittedly, some limitation of the function of character as a determinant of conduct. But it leaves character still an enormously important factor in the moral life. It is formed character, as we saw, that determines what in any given situation the relative strengths of the agent's desires will be; including, of course, in 'duty' situations, the strength of his desire for the end which enjoys the further, and quite different, recommendation of being conceived as his duty. Now in all those practical choices—and they comprise perhaps 99 per cent. of the choices in most men's lives—in which there is *no* felt conflict of duty with desire, it seems clear that the determinant of choice can only be the agent's strongest desire. But if that is the case, then since it is a man's formed character that determines what his strongest desire will be, it is entirely conformable with acceptance of the distinction between self and character to hold that, over by far the greater part of the practical life, it is a man's character that determines his choices.

There will, I fancy, be some reluctance to accept our contention that, save where strongest desire is in conflict with what duty ordains, choice can only be in accordance with strongest desire. But I would ask, what possible motive *could* there be for a man to choose something different from that to which his desiring nature most strongly inclines him, except the fact that he deems this most strongly desired end to be somehow incompatible with his duty? No possible motive, surely, is conceivable. The implication may perhaps be unwelcome, but I do not see how it is to be escaped, that there are, in an important sense, no 'real' alternatives before the agent save in those practical situations in which considerations of duty are present. Elsewhere choice follows strongest desire. On the other hand, this should not be supposed to entail that in the ordinary run of choices man is subject to a merely external determination. For a man's desires are not something external to his self. His 'strongest desire' at any moment is the expression, in relation to the given situation, of that developing, but relatively stable and relatively systematic, complex of conative and emotive tendencies which we call his 'character'. Moreover, willing or choosing involves on the part of the agent the formal act of *self*-identification with one of the competing ends. He must, in choosing, accept the end as his own end; and in that sense, for what it is worth, his choice is always 'self-determining'.

There is, indeed, one practical situation which looks as though it constituted an exception to the rule that, save where there is conflict of desire with duty, choice follows strongest desire. Suppose I find in a given situation which raises no moral issues for me that my strongest desire is for X; and suppose that, irritated by philosophical theorists telling me that I have no option but to follow my strongest desire, I feel moved to vindicate my freedom to do otherwise by choosing the end of a weaker desire Y. Surely I *can* so choose? And surely, if so, this is incompatible with the thesis that (moral issues apart) choice follows strongest desire?

But a moment's reflection makes it clear that we are not really in this case choosing what we don't most strongly desire. All that has happened is that, under the stimulus of the philosopher's challenge to our freedom, our strongest desire is now directed to the vindication of that freedom, which is to be effected (we think) by choosing Y. So that here too, after all, our choice follows strongest desire.

It is worth observing, however, that what has just been said does not imply that, in believing himself to have real alternatives before him even in a *non*-moral practical situation, the agent is subject to mere illusion. When, e.g. he debates with no thought but his own pleasure whether he will read a book or watch the television programme, there is no reason to suppose him deluded in believing that he can choose *whichever* of these courses *he most strongly desires*. In *that* sense we can agree that there are 'real alternatives' open to him. He is mistaken only if he believes that he can choose either course *irrespective of* which he most strongly desires. In *this* sense the alternatives are not open. If he believes that they are, his belief is due, as I have tried to show, to a removable confusion. It is not a belief intrinsic to the non-moral practical situation, as the belief that one can choose the course contrary to that to which strongest desire inclines is (I think) intrinsic to the situation of moral temptation.

Even on our view, then, formed character does determine conduct over by far the greater part of a man's life. But of course an element of paradox in the view inevitably remains. Unless moral decision is something quite different from what it is experienced as being, the self which makes the decision (we have to say) must be something 'beyond' its formed character. And it would be absurd to pretend that it is easy to make clear to one's self just how one ought to understand this 'something beyond'.

Strictly speaking, it does not fall within the scope of the present lecture to attempt an answer to this last question. But I may perhaps be permitted to throw out, in passing, the suggestion that the difficulty we have in conceiving an act as at once the *self's* act and yet not flowing from the self's *character* is at bottom the difficulty—in one sense the impossibility—of understanding anything that is genuinely *creative*. If an act is creative, then nothing can determine it save the agent's doing of it. Hence we ought not to expect to 'understand' it, in the sense of seeing how it follows from determinate elements of the self's character; for then it would just not be a 'creative' act. We can expect to 'understand' it only in the sense of being able to 'attach meaning' to it. Now that, I submit, we clearly can do in the case of moral decision, if we approach it in the way appropriate to the apprehension of any genuine 'activity'; i.e. from the inside, from the standpoint of the agent *qua* acting. Unless the analysis given above of what moral decision involves for the experient of it is totally mistaken, the agent himself knows very well what it is to perform an act which is his own act and which is yet not determined by his formed character. From the standpoint of the external observer the creative act is, inevitably, sheer mystery, or worse than mystery. But it is vital to bear in mind that only from the standpoint of living experience *could* anything of the nature of creative activity be grasped if it existed. And here, I am afraid, we must leave the matter so far as the present lecture is concerned.

11. We have not done yet, however, with necessary distinctions within the general concept of activity. We had occasion first, it will be remembered, to distinguish functional activity *within* the self from activity *of* the self—self-activity proper. We then went on to distinguish, as types of self-activity proper, what may be called the 'expressive' self-activity characteristic of ordinary willing, where our act is merely the expression of our character as so far formed, from the 'creative' self-activity involved in moral decision. We have now to draw attention to a further mode of creative self-activity. We shall call it 'moral-effort' activity.

This mode of self-activity is to be found in the sufficiently familiar experience which we commonly describe in some such terms as 'making an effort to overcome our inclinations and rise to duty'. The situation in which it is, or may be, evoked is the same as that in which moral decision is evoked, i.e. where strongest desire clashes with duty; and the procedure must be, as before, to envisage such a situation and observe what one experiences when imaginatively engaged in it.

In this situation the agent is aware that if he lets his purely desiring nature have its way it is not X, his duty, but Y, the object of his strongest desire, that he will choose. But since the moral decision to be taken is between rising to duty or yielding to desire, it is plain that he believes that he *can* rise to duty, despite the contrary pressure of desire. He can rise to duty, however—or so it seems to him—only by exerting an *effort*: an effort quite distinct in kind from physical effort or intellectual effort (although either or both of these may be required consequentially, since the dutiful course may obviously entail the exertion of physical effort or of intellectual effort or of both). This unique kind of effort may appropriately be named 'moral' effort; for its whole function is to enable us to resist the importunings of desire in obedience to duty.

Now this moral-effort activity has for the agent, I suggest—whether viewed by him in prospect or in actual performance—both of the characteristics noted in moral-decision activity. For the agent, it is *he himself* that makes the effort; and yet this effort is not, for him, determined by his character as so far formed, since he believes himself to be exerting it precisely in order to resist, in the given situation, the behaviour trend of his formed character; i.e. to enable him to act contrary to his strongest desire. Moral-effort activity, therefore, like moral-decision activity, is essentially creative, involving a causal discontinuity with formed character. But the discontinuity here is, in a sense, a sharper one. For while moral-decision activity *may* be exerted in favour of the end to which formed character inclines, moral-effort activity can in the nature of the case be exerted only in favour of what duty is deemed to ordain.

A further word is desirable on the relationship between the moral decision to rise to duty, the decision to make the moral effort, and the actual making of the moral effort.

So far as I can see, the decision to choose X, our duty, as against Y, which we most strongly desire, *is* the decision to put forth here and now the requisite moral effort. We cannot *really* decide to choose X unless we decide to make the moral effort; for we know, when we decide, that the choosing of X is possible only by our making the effort. Again, it seems to me clear that we cannot really 'decide' to make the effort and then in fact *not* make it. For moral decision (as we have agreed to use the expression) is the decision whether or not to make the effort to rise to duty *here and now*, in an actually present situation of moral temptation: and a supposed 'decision' to make a moral effort here and now, without in fact making it, seems to me something to which we can attach no meaning at all in terms of possible experience. Of course though we cannot 'decide', we can do that much weaker thing, 'resolve', to make an effort, and yet not make the effort; for mere 'resolve' may relate to action in the more or less distant future, in which case it costs us nothing now, and very possibly never will cost us anything. For example, we may resolve to make the effort to give up smoking, our resolve being made at a time when our craving for nicotine is temporarily sated, perhaps to the point of nausea, and immediate effort is not required. Tobacco is now, it may be, the object not of our strongest desire but of our strongest aversion. Perhaps this is the commonest kind of occasion upon which 'good resolutions' are made. But needless to say there is no difficulty whatever in conceiving ourselves failing to exert in fact the effort upon which we have earlier 'resolved'.

12. Here we must bring to a close our long—but, I am well aware, far from exhaustive—analysis of activity. Its general relevance to the question of the ontological status of the human self will have been obvious, but perhaps it will be permitted to add a few words on the special relevance of the distinction drawn between the 'expressive' and the 'creative' modes of self-activity.

If self-activity did not reach beyond the expressive mode, then, so far as I can see, man's power of self-determination would be of very limited significance indeed. His choices would, no doubt, still be self-determining, in the sense that whatever end a self-conscious subject chooses he accepts as his *own* end. But such self-determination is formal rather than real, and is consistent with the effective determination of his choices coming from factors external to him. This becomes clear if we ask ourselves why a man comes to choose the particular ends he does choose in those situations—the ordinary run of situations—in which the *creative* self-activity of moral decision is not called for. The answer can only be that these are the things he most strongly desires. And if we then ask, what determines the relative strength of his desires, we are in the last resort forced back, it seems to me, upon the man's inherited nature and environmental nurture; that is to say, upon two factors outwith his own control. It is true that, proximately, a man's desires are the expression of his 'character'. But his character has been built up by past acts of choice which—if we still abstract from the creative self-activity of moral decision— are themselves in accordance with strongest desire. And when we finally ask (as we must) about these original acts of choice, before anything stable enough to be called a 'character' has emerged, I cannot see to what else we can point as determinant of the man's strongest desires (and accordingly of these choices) save the particular kind and degree of his congenital impulses *plus* the environmental situation by which they are in varying degrees fostered or discouraged.

In other words, it seems to me futile—as Sidgwick so clearly showed in his polemic against T. H. Green [1]—to attempt to base an effective self-determinism upon the mere fact that a self-conscious being can be moved to act only for an end which he himself accepts or approves. If what he himself accepts or approves is a function of circumstances with which *he* has nothing to do; if in order to understand why he makes the specific choices he does make we must look in the last resort to the 'given' nature of the man and the kind of influences to which he has been subjected by his physical and social environment; then the self-determination in the case is surely, as I have said, 'formal rather than real'.

But when, on the other hand, we turn to the *creative* types of self-activity in moral decision and moral effort, the whole situation is radically transformed. Here the self is revealed to itself as a being capable of transcending its own 'formed character'; a being with a power, so far as these aspects of its conduct are concerned, of *absolute* self-origination. No man as actually engaged in making

[1] *Lectures on the Ethics of T. H. Green, Mr. Herbert Spencer, and J. Martineau*, pp. 15 ff.

a moral decision between rising to duty or yielding to desire can possibly, I make bold to assert, regard that decision as determined by anything whatsoever save his own making of it here and now.

13. One final word. It will have been evident that throughout the greater part of this lecture the propositions advanced depend for their verification upon an appeal to introspection. I have been describing what I seem to myself to find in and before my mind in certain experiential situations; and the implied assumption has been that, if I have described correctly, anyone who introspects carefully and without preconceptions will find that my reports hold good for his experience likewise. To some philosophers this may seem an assumption so large and so precarious as to vitiate the whole procedure; for introspection is, at the moment, much out of favour as an instrument of philosophical enquiry. Clearly I cannot now undertake a formal vindication of introspective method in philosophy, but I may be permitted to make one observation about its adoption in this lecture. Recourse to the evidence of introspection may be undesirable where there is any effective substitute. But what if it is a case of 'Hobson's choice'? That, as I see it, is the situation so far as the investigation of activity is concerned. If it be true, as it is generally admitted to be, that our idea of activity is got not from outer experience, but only from experience of our inner life, it is just not avoidable that we should have recourse to introspection for the appreciation of its character. Either we study activity through the medium of introspection, or we resign ourselves to not studying it at all. I cannot think that we should rest content with the latter alternative.

HAS THE SELF 'FREE WILL'?

1. During the greater part of the last lecture, which was concerned with the defence of the notion of self-activity and with the classification of its main species, we were operating on the very threshold of the problem of Free Will; and in its later stages, particularly in connection with the analysis of moral-decision activity, we may perhaps be judged to have passed beyond the threshold. The present lecture, in which we address ourselves formally to the Free Will problem, is in fact so closely continuous with its predecessor that I should wish the two lectures to be regarded as constituting, in a real sense, a single unit.

In the later, more constructive part of my programme today this intimate dependence upon what has gone before will become very apparent. My initial task, however, must be one of elucidation and definition. The general question I have to try to answer, a question which is very far indeed from admitting of a ready answer, is, What precisely *is* the Free Will problem?

It is something of a truism that in philosophic enquiry the exact formulation of a problem often takes one a long way on the road to its solution. In the case of the Free Will problem I think there is a rather special need of careful formulation. For there are many sorts of human freedom; and it can easily happen that one wastes a great deal of labour in proving or disproving a freedom which has almost nothing to do with the freedom which is at issue in the traditional problem of Free Will. The abortiveness of so much of the argument for and against Free Will in contemporary philosophical literature seems to me due in the main

to insufficient pains being taken over the preliminary definition
of the problem. There is, indeed, one outstanding exception, Professor Broad's brilliant inaugural lecture entitled, 'Determinism,
Indeterminism, and Libertarianism',[1] in which forty-three pages
are devoted to setting out the problem, as against seven to its
solution! I confess that the solution does not seem to myself to
follow upon the formulation quite as easily as all that:[2] but Professor Broad's eminent example fortifies me in my decision to give
here what may seem at first sight a disproportionate amount of
time to the business of determining the essential characteristics of
the kind of freedom with which the traditional problem is concerned.

Fortunately we can at least make a beginning with a certain
amount of confidence. It is not seriously disputable that the kind
of freedom in question is the freedom which is commonly recognised to be in some sense a precondition of moral responsibility.
Clearly, it is on account of this integral connection with moral
responsibility that such exceptional importance has always been
felt to attach to the Free Will problem. But in what precise sense
is free will a precondition of moral responsibility, and thus a
postulate of the moral life in general? This is an exceedingly
troublesome question; but until we have satisfied ourselves about
the answer to it, we are not in a position to state, let alone decide,
the question whether 'Free Will' in its traditional, ethical,
significance is a reality.

Our first business, then, is to ask, exactly what kind of freedom
is it which is required for moral responsibility? And as to method
of procedure in this inquiry, there seems to me to be no real
choice. I know of only one method that carries with it any hope
of success; viz. the critical comparison of those acts for which, on
due reflection, we deem it proper to attribute moral praise or
blame to the agents, with those acts for which, on due reflection,
we deem such judgments to be improper. The ultimate touch-
stone, as I see it, can only be our moral consciousness as it
manifests itself in our more critical and considered moral judgments. The 'linguistic' approach by way of the analysis of moral

---

[1] Reprinted in *Ethics and the History of Philosophy, Selected Essays.*
[2] I have explained the grounds for my dissent from Broad's final conclusions
on pp. 27 ff. of *In Defence of Free Will* (Jackson Son & Co., 1938).

sentences seems to me, despite its present popularity, to be an almost infallible method for reaching wrong results in the moral field; but I must reserve what I have to say about this for the next lecture.

2.   The first point to note is that the freedom at issue (as indeed the very name 'Free *Will* Problem' indicates) pertains primarily not to overt acts but to inner acts. The nature of things has decreed that, save in the case of one's self, it is only overt acts which one can directly observe. But a very little reflection serves to show that in our moral judgments upon others their overt acts are regarded as significant only in so far as they are the expression of inner acts. We do not consider the acts of a robot to be morally responsible acts; nor do we consider the acts of a man to be so save in so far as they are distinguishable from those of a robot by reflecting an inner life of choice. Similarly, from the other side, if we are satisfied (as we may on occasion be, at least in the case of ourselves) that a person has definitely elected to follow a course which he believes to be wrong, but has been prevented by external circumstances from translating his inner choice into an overt act, we still regard him as morally blameworthy. Moral freedom, then, pertains to *inner* acts.

The next point seems at first sight equally obvious and uncontroversial; but, as we shall see, it has awkward implications if we are in real earnest with it (as almost nobody is). It is the simple point that the act must be one of which the person judged can be regarded as the *sole* author. It seems plain enough that if there are any *other* determinants of the act, external to the self, to that extent the act is not an act which the *self* determines, and to that extent not an act for which the self can be held morally responsible. The self is only part-author of the act, and his moral responsibility can logically extend only to those elements within the act (assuming for the moment that these can be isolated) of which he is the *sole* author.

The awkward implications of this apparent truism will be readily appreciated. For, if we are mindful of the influences exerted by heredity and environment, we may well feel some doubt whether there is any act of will at all of which one can truly say that the self is sole author, sole determinant. No man has a voice in determining the raw material of impulses and capacities that constitute his hereditary endowment, and no man has more than a very partial control of the material and social environment in which he is destined to live his life. Yet it would be manifestly absurd to deny that these two factors do constantly and profoundly affect the nature of a man's choices. That this is so we all of us recognise in our moral judgments when we 'make allowances', as we say, for a bad heredity or a vicious environment, and acknowledge in the victim of them a diminished moral responsibility for evil courses. Evidently we do *try*, in our moral judgments, however crudely, to praise or blame a man only in respect of that of which we can regard him as *wholly* the author. And evidently we do recognise that, for a man to be the author of an act in the full sense required for moral responsibility, it is not enough merely that he 'wills' or 'chooses' the act: since even the most unfortunate victim of heredity or environment does, as a rule, 'will' what he does. It is significant, however, that the ordinary man, though well enough aware of the influence upon choices of heredity and environment, does not feel obliged thereby to give up his assumption that moral predicates *are* somehow applicable. Plainly he still believes that there is *something* for which a man is morally responsible, something of which we can fairly say that he is the sole author. *What is this something?* To that question common-sense is not ready with an explicit answer—though an answer is, I think, implicit in the line which its moral judgments take. I shall do what I can to give an explicit answer later in this lecture. Meantime it must suffice to observe that, if we are to be true to the deliverances of our moral consciousness, it is very difficult to deny that *sole* authorship is a necessary condition of the morally responsible act.

Thirdly we come to a point over which much recent controversy has raged. We may approach it by raising the following question. Granted an act of which the agent is sole author, does this 'sole authorship' suffice to make the act a morally free act? We may be inclined to think that it does, until we contemplate the possibility that an act of which the agent is sole author might conceivably occur as a necessary expression of the agent's nature; the way in which, e.g. some philosophers have supposed the

Divine act of creation to occur. This consideration excites a legitimate doubt; for it is far from easy to see how a person can be regarded as a proper subject for moral praise or blame in respect of an act which he *cannot help* performing—even if it be his own 'nature' which necessitates it. Must we not recognise it as a condition of the morally free act that the agent 'could have acted otherwise' than he in fact did? It is true, indeed, that we sometimes praise or blame a man for an act about which we are prepared to say, in the light of our knowledge of his established character, that he 'could no other'. But I think that a little reflection shows that in such cases we are not praising or blaming the man strictly for what he does *now* (or at any rate we ought not to be), but rather for those past acts of his which have generated the firm habit of mind from which his *present* act follows 'necessarily'. In other words, our praise and blame, so far as justified, are really retrospective, being directed not to the agent *qua* performing *this* act, but to the agent *qua* performing those past acts which have built up his present character, and in respect to which we presume that he *could* have acted otherwise, that there really *were* open possibilities before him. These cases, therefore, seem to me to constitute no valid exception to what I must take to be the rule, viz. that a man can be morally praised or blamed for an act only if he could have acted otherwise.

Now philosophers today are fairly well agreed that it is a postulate of the morally responsible act that the agent 'could have acted otherwise' in *some* sense of that phrase. But sharp differences of opinion have arisen over the way in which the phrase ought to be interpreted. There is a strong disposition to water down its apparent meaning by insisting that it is not (as a postulate of moral responsibility) to be understood as a straightforward categorical proposition, but rather as a disguised hypothetical proposition. All that we really require to be assured of, in order to justify our holding X morally responsible for an act, is, we are told, that X could have acted otherwise *if* he had *chosen* otherwise (Moore, Stevenson); or perhaps that X could have acted otherwise *if* he had had a different character, or *if* he had been placed in different circumstances.

I think it is easy to understand, and even, in a measure, to sympathise with, the motives which induce philosophers to offer these counter-interpretations. It is not just the fact that 'X could have acted otherwise', as a bald categorical statement, is incompatible with the universal sway of causal law—though this is, to some philosophers, a serious stone of stumbling. The more widespread objection is that it at least looks as though it were incompatible with that causal continuity of an agent's character with his conduct which is implied when we believe (surely with justice) that we can often tell the sort of thing a man will do from our knowledge of the sort of man he is.

We shall have to make our accounts with that particular difficulty later. At this stage I wish merely to show that neither of the hypothetical propositions suggested—and I think the same could be shown for *any* hypothetical alternative—is an acceptable substitute for the categorical proposition 'X could have acted otherwise' as the presupposition of moral responsibility.

Let us look first at the earlier suggestion—'X could have acted otherwise *if* he had chosen otherwise'. Now clearly there are a great many acts with regard to which we are entirely satisfied that the agent is thus situated. We are often perfectly sure that—for this is all it amounts to—if X had chosen otherwise, the circumstances presented no external obstacle to the translation of that choice into action. For example, we often have no doubt at all that X, who in point of fact told a lie, could have told the truth *if* he had so chosen. But does our confidence on this score allay all legitimate doubts about whether X is really blameworthy? Does it entail that X is free in the sense required for moral responsibility? Surely not. The obvious question immediately arises: 'But *could* X have *chosen* otherwise than he did?' It is doubt about the true answer to *that* question which leads most people to doubt the reality of moral responsibility. Yet on this crucial question the hypothetical proposition which is offered as a sufficient statement of the condition justifying the ascription of moral responsibility gives us no information whatsoever.

Indeed this hypothetical substitute for the categorical 'X could have acted otherwise' seems to me to lack all plausibility unless one contrives to forget why it is, after all, that we ever come to feel fundamental doubts about man's moral responsibility. Such doubts are born, surely, when one becomes aware of certain reputable world-views in religion or philosophy, or of certain reputable scientific beliefs, which in their several ways imply that man's actions are necessitated, and thus could not be otherwise than they in fact are. But clearly a doubt so based is not even touched by the recognition that a man could very often act otherwise *if* he so chose. That proposition is entirely compatible with the necessitarian theories which generate our doubt: indeed it is this very compatibility that has recommended it to some philosophers, who are reluctant to give up either moral responsibility or Determinism. The proposition which we *must* be able to affirm if moral praise or blame of X is to be justified is the categorical proposition that X could have acted otherwise because— not if—he could have chosen otherwise; or, since it is essentially the inner side of the act that matters, the proposition simply that X could have chosen otherwise.

For the second of the alternative formulae suggested we cannot spare more than a few moments. But its inability to meet the demands it is required to meet is almost transparent. 'X could have acted otherwise', as a statement of a precondition of X's moral responsibility, really means (we are told) 'X could have acted otherwise *if* he were differently constituted, or *if* he had been placed in different circumstances'. It seems a sufficient reply to this to point out that the person whose moral responsibility is at issue is *X*; a specific individual, in a specific set of circumstances. It is totally irrelevant to *X*'s moral responsibility that we should be able to say that some person differently constituted from X, or X in a different set of circumstances, could have done something different from what X did.

3. Let me, then, briefly sum up the answer at which we have arrived to our question about the kind of freedom required to justify moral responsibility. It is that a man can be said to exercise free will in a morally significant sense only in so far as his chosen act is one of which he is the sole cause or author, and only if—in the straightforward, categorical sense of the phrase—he 'could have chosen otherwise'.

I confess that this answer is in some ways a disconcerting one. disconcerting, because most of us, however objective we are in the actual conduct of our thinking, would *like* to be able to believe that moral responsibility is real: whereas the freedom required for moral responsibility, on the analysis we have given, is certainly far more difficult to establish than the freedom required on the analyses we found ourselves obliged to reject. If, e.g. moral freedom entails only that I could have acted otherwise *if* I had chosen otherwise, there is no real 'problem' about it at all. I am 'free' in the normal case where there is no external obstacle to prevent my translating the alternative choice into action, and not free in other cases. Still less is there a problem if all that moral freedom entails is that I could have acted otherwise *if* I had been a differently constituted person, or been in different circumstances. Clearly I am *always* free in *this* sense of freedom. But, as I have argued, these so-called 'freedoms' fail to give us the pre-conditions of moral responsibility, and hence leave the freedom of the traditional free-will problem, the freedom that people are really concerned about, precisely where it was.

4. Another interpretation of freedom which I am bound to reject on the same general ground, i.e. that it is just not the kind of freedom that is relevant to moral responsibility, is the old idealist view which identifies the *free* will with the *rational* will; the rational will in its turn being identified with the will which wills the moral law in whole-hearted, single-minded obedience to it. This view is still worth at least a passing mention, if only because it has recently been resurrected in an interesting work by Professor A. E. Teale.[1] Moreover, I cannot but feel a certain nostalgic tenderness for a view in which I myself was (so to speak) philosophically cradled. The almost apostolic fervour with which my revered nursing-mother, the late Sir Henry Jones, was wont to impart it to his charges, and, hardly less, his ill-concealed scorn for ignoble natures (like my own) which still hankered after a free will in the old 'vulgar' sense, are vividly recalled for me in Professor Teale's stirring pages.

The true interpretation of free will, according to Professor Teale, the interpretation to which Kant, despite occasional back-slidings, adhered in his better moments, is that 'the will is

---

[1] *Kantian Ethics.*

free in the degree that it is informed and disciplined by the moral principle'.[1]

Now this is a perfectly intelligible sense of the word 'free'—or at any rate it can be made so with a little explanatory comment which Professor Teale well supplies but for which there is here no space. But clearly it is a very different sort of freedom from that which is at issue in the traditional problem of free will. This idealist 'freedom' sponsored by Teale belongs, on his own showing, only to the self in respect of its *good* willing. The freedom with which the traditional problem is concerned, inasmuch as it is the freedom presupposed by moral responsibility, must belong to the self in respect of its *bad*, no less than its *good*, willing. It is, in fact, the freedom to decide between genuinely open alternatives of good and bad willing.

Professor Teale, of course, is not unaware that the freedom he favours differs from freedom as traditionally understood. He recognises the traditional concept under its Kantian title of 'elective' freedom. But he leaves the reader in no kind of doubt about his disbelief in both the reality and the value of this elective freedom to do, or forbear from doing, one's duty.

The question of the reality of elective freedom I shall be dealing with shortly; and it will occupy us to the end of the lecture. At the moment I am concerned only with its value, and with the rival view that all that matters for the moral life is the 'rational' freedom which a man has in the degree that his will is 'informed and disciplined by the moral principle'. I confess that to myself the verdict on the rival view seems plain and inescapable. No amount of verbal ingenuity or argumentative convolutions can obscure the fact that it is in flat contradiction to the implications of moral responsibility. The point at issue is really perfectly straightforward. If, as this idealist theory maintains, my acting in defiance of what I deem to be my duty is not a 'free' act in *any* sense, let alone in the sense that 'I could have acted otherwise', then I cannot be morally blameworthy, and that is all there is to it. Nor, for that matter, is the idealist entitled to say that I am morally praiseworthy if I act dutifully; for although that act *is* a 'free' act in the idealist sense, it is on his own avowal not free in the sense that 'I could have acted otherwise'.

[1] *Op. cit.* p. 261.

It seems to me idle, therefore, to pretend that if one has to give up freedom in the traditional elective sense one is not giving up anything important. What we are giving up is, quite simply, the reality of the moral life. I recognise that to a certain type of religious nature (as well as, by an odd meeting of extremes, to a certain type of secular nature) that does not appear to matter so very much; but, for myself, I still think it sufficiently important to make it well worth while enquiring seriously into the possibility that the elective freedom upon which it rests may be real after all.

5. That brings me to the second, and more constructive, part of this lecture. From now on I shall be considering whether it is reasonable to believe that man does in fact possess a free will of the kind specified in the first part of the lecture. If so, just how and where within the complex fabric of the volitional life are we to locate it?—for although free will must presumably belong (if anywhere) to the volitional side of human experience, it is pretty clear from the way in which we have been forced to define it that it does not pertain simply to volition as such; not even to all volitions that are commonly dignified with the name of 'choices'. It has been, I think, one of the more serious impediments to profitable discussion of the Free Will problem that Libertarians and Determinists alike have so often failed to appreciate the comparatively narrow area within which the free will that is necessary to 'save' morality is required to operate. It goes without saying that this failure has been gravely prejudicial to the case for Libertarianism. I attach a good deal of importance, therefore, to the problem of locating free will correctly within the volitional orbit. Its solution forestalls and annuls, I believe, some of the more tiresome clichés of Determinist criticism.

We saw earlier that Common Sense's practice of 'making allowances' in its moral judgments for the influence of heredity and environment indicates Common Sense's conviction, both that a just moral judgment must discount determinants of choice over which the agent has no control, and also (since it still accepts moral judgments as legitimate) that *something* of moral relevance survives which can be regarded as genuinely self-originated. We are now to try to discover what this 'something' is. And I think we may still usefully take Common Sense as our guide. Suppose one asks the ordinary intelligent citizen *why* he deems it proper to make allowances for X, whose heredity and/or environment are unfortunate. He will tend to reply, I think, in some such terms as these: that X has more and stronger temptations to deviate from what is right than Y or Z, who are normally circumstanced, so that he must put forth a *stronger moral effort* if he is to achieve the same level of external conduct. The intended implication seems to be that X is just as morally praiseworthy as Y or Z *if* he exerts an equivalent moral effort, even though he may not thereby achieve an equal success in conforming his will to the 'concrete' demands of duty. And this implies, again, Common Sense's belief that *in moral effort* we have something for which a man is responsible *without qualification*, something that is *not* affected by heredity and environment but depends *solely* upon the self itself.

Now in my opinion Common Sense has here, in principle, hit upon the one and only defensible answer. Here, and here alone, so far as I can see, in the act of deciding whether to put forth or withhold the moral effort required to resist temptation and rise to duty, is to be found an act which is free in the sense required for moral responsibility; an act of which the self is sole author, and of which it is true to say that 'it could be' (or, after the event, 'could have been') 'otherwise'. Such is the thesis which we shall now try to establish.

6.   The species of argument appropriate to the establishment of a thesis of this sort should fall, I think, into two phases. First, there should be a consideration of the evidence of the moral agent's own inner experience. What *is* the act of moral decision, and what does it imply, from the standpoint of the actual participant? Since there is no way of knowing the act of moral decision—or for that matter any other form of activity—except by actual participation in it, the evidence of the subject, or agent, is on an issue of this kind of palmary importance. It can hardly, however, be taken as in itself conclusive. For even if that evidence should be overwhelmingly to the effect that moral decision does have the characteristics required by moral freedom, the question is bound to be raised—and in view of considerations from other quarters

pointing in a contrary direction is *rightly* raised—Can we *trust* the evidence of inner experience? That brings us to what will be the second phase of the argument. We shall have to go on to show, if we are to make good our case, that the extraneous considerations so often supposed to be fatal to the belief in moral freedom are in fact innocuous to it.

In the light of what was said in the last lecture about the self's experience of moral decision as a *creative* activity, we may perhaps be absolved from developing the first phase of the argument at any great length. The appeal is throughout to one's own experience in the actual taking of the moral decision in the situation of moral temptation. 'Is it possible', we must ask, 'for anyone so circumstanced to *dis*believe that he could be deciding otherwise?' The answer is surely not in doubt. When we decide to exert moral effort to resist a temptation, we feel quite certain that we *could* withhold the effort; just as, if we decide to withhold the effort and yield to our desires, we feel quite certain that we *could* exert it—otherwise we should not blame ourselves afterwards for having succumbed. It may be, indeed, that this conviction is mere self-delusion. But that is not at the moment our concern. It is enough at present to establish that the act of deciding to exert or to withhold moral effort, as we know it from the inside in actual moral living, belongs to the category of acts which 'could have been otherwise'.

Mutatis mutandis, the same reply is forthcoming if we ask, 'Is it possible for the moral agent in the taking of his decision to *dis*believe that he is the *sole* author of that decision?' Clearly he cannot disbelieve that it is *he* who takes the decision. That, however, is not in itself sufficient to enable him, on reflection, to regard himself as *solely* responsible for the act. For his 'character' as so far formed might conceivably be a factor in determining it, and no one can suppose that the constitution of his 'character' is uninfluenced by circumstances of heredity and environment with which *he* has nothing to do. But as we pointed out in the last lecture, the very essence of the moral decision as it is experienced is that it is a decision whether or not to *combat* our strongest desire, and our strongest desire *is* the expression in the situation of our character as so far formed. Now clearly our character cannot be a factor in determining the decision whether or not to *oppose* our character. I think we are entitled to say, therefore, that the act of moral decision is one in which the self is for itself not merely 'author' but 'sole author'.

7. We may pass on, then, to the second phase of our constructive argument; and this will demand more elaborate treatment. Even if a moral agent *qua* making a moral decision in the situation of 'temptation' cannot help believing that he has free will in the sense at issue—a moral freedom between real alternatives, between genuinely open possibilities—are there, nevertheless, objections to a freedom of this kind so cogent that we are bound to distrust the evidence of 'inner experience'?

I begin by drawing attention to a simple point whose significance tends, I think, to be under-estimated. If the phenomenological analysis we have offered is substantially correct, no one while functioning as a moral agent can help believing that he enjoys free will. Theoretically he may be completely convinced by Determinist arguments, but when actually confronted with a personal situation of conflict between duty and desire he is quite certain that it lies with him here and now whether or not he will rise to duty. It follows that if Determinists could produce convincing theoretical arguments against a free will of this kind, the awkward predicament would ensue that man has to deny as a theoretical being what he has to assert as a practical being. Now I think the Determinist ought to be a good deal more worried about this than he usually is. He seems to imagine that a strong case on general theoretical grounds is enough to prove that the 'practical' belief in free will, even if inescapable for us as practical beings, is mere illusion. But in fact it proves nothing of the sort. There is no reason whatever why a belief that we find ourselves obliged to hold *qua* practical beings should be required to give way before a belief which we find ourselves obliged to hold *qua* theoretical beings; or, for that matter, *vice versa*. All that the theoretical arguments of Determinism can prove, unless they are reinforced by a refutation of the phenomenological analysis that supports Libertarianism, is that there is a radical conflict between the theoretical and the practical sides of man's nature, an antinomy at the very heart of the self. And this is a state of affairs with which no one can easily rest satisfied. I think therefore that the Determinist ought to concern himself a great deal more than he does with phenomenological analysis, in order to show, if he can, that the assurance of free will is not really an inexpugnable element in man's practical consciousness. There is just as much obligation upon him, convinced though he may be of the soundness of his theoretical arguments, to expose the errors of the Libertarian's phenomenological analysis, as there is upon us, convinced though we may be of the soundness of the Libertarian's phenomenological analysis, to expose the errors of the Determinist's theoretical arguments.

8. However, we must at once begin the discharge of our own obligation. The rest of this lecture will be devoted to trying to show that the arguments which seem to carry most weight with Determinists are, to say the least of it, very far from compulsive.

Fortunately a good many of the arguments which at an earlier time in the history of philosophy would have been strongly urged against us make almost no appeal to the bulk of philosophers today, and we may here pass them by. That applies to any criticism of 'open possibilities' based on a metaphysical theory about the nature of the universe as a whole. Nobody today *has* a metaphysical theory about the nature of the universe as a whole! It applies also, with almost equal force, to criticisms based upon the universality of causal law as a supposed postulate of science. There have always been, in my opinion, sound philosophic reasons for doubting the validity, as distinct from the convenience, of the causal postulate in its universal form, but at the present time, when scientists themselves are deeply divided about the need for postulating causality even within their own special field, we shall do better to concentrate our attention upon criticisms which are more confidently advanced. I propose to ignore also, on different grounds, the type of criticism of free will that is sometimes advanced from the side of religion, based upon religious postulates of Divine Omnipotence and Omniscience. So far as I can see, a postulate of human freedom is every bit as necessary to meet certain religious demands (e.g. to make sense of the 'conviction of sin'), as postulates of Divine Omniscience and Omnipotence are to meet certain other religious demands. If so, then it can hardly be argued that religious experience as such tells more strongly against than for the position we are defending; and we may be satisfied, in the present context, to leave the matter there. It will be more profitable to discuss certain arguments which contemporary philosophers do think important, and which recur with a somewhat monotonous regularity in the literature of anti-Libertarianism.

These arguments can, I think, be reduced in principle to no more than two: first, the argument from 'predictability'; second, the argument from the alleged meaninglessness of an act supposed to be the self's act and yet not an expression of the self's character. Contemporary criticism of free will seems to me to consist almost exclusively of variations on these two themes. I shall deal with each in turn.

9.   On the first we touched in passing at an earlier stage. Surely it is beyond question (the critic urges) that when we know a person intimately we can foretell with a high degree of accuracy how he will respond to at least a large number of practical situations. One feels safe in predicting that one's dog-loving friend will not use his boot to repel the little mongrel that comes yapping at his heels; or again that one's wife will not pass with incurious eyes (or indeed pass at all) the new hat-shop in the city. So to behave would not be (as we say) 'in character'. But, so the criticism runs, you with your doctrine of 'genuinely open possibilities', of a free will by which the self can diverge from its own character, remove all rational basis from such prediction. You require us to make the absurd supposition that the success of countless predictions of the sort in the past has been mere matter of chance. If you *really* believed in your theory, you would not be surprised if tomorrow your friend with the notorious horror of strong drink should suddenly exhibit a passion for whisky and soda, or if your friend whose taste for reading has hitherto been satisfied with the sporting columns of the newspapers should be discovered on a fine Saturday afternoon poring over the works of Hegel. But of course you *would* be surprised. Social life would be sheer chaos if there were not well-grounded social expectations; and social

life is not sheer chaos. Your theory is hopelessly wrecked upon obvious facts.

Now whether or not this criticism holds good against some versions of Libertarian theory I need not here discuss. It is sufficient if I can make it clear that against the version advanced in this lecture, according to which free will is localised in a relatively narrow field of operation, the criticism has no relevance whatsoever.

Let us remind ourselves briefly of the setting within which, on our view, free will functions. There is X, the course which we believe we ought to follow, and Y, the course towards which we feel our desire is strongest. The freedom which we ascribe to the agent is the freedom to put forth or refrain from putting forth the moral effort required to resist the pressure of desire and do what he thinks he ought to do.

But then there is surely an immense range of practical situations—covering by far the greater part of life—in which there is no question of a conflict within the self between what he most desires to do and what he thinks he ought to do? Indeed such conflict is a comparatively rare phenomenon for the majority of men. Yet over that whole vast range there is nothing whatever in our version of Libertarianism to prevent our agreeing that character determines conduct. In the absence, real or supposed, of any 'moral' issue, what a man chooses will be simply that course which, after such reflection as seems called for, he deems most likely to bring him what he most strongly desires; and that is the same as to say the course to which his present character inclines him.

Over by far the greater area of human choices, then, our theory offers no more barrier to successful prediction on the basis of character than any other theory. For where there is no clash of strongest desire with duty, the free will we are defending has no business. There is just nothing for it to do.

But what about the situations—rare enough though they may be—in which there *is* this clash and in which free will does therefore operate? Does our theory entail that there at any rate, as the critic seems to suppose, 'anything may happen'?

Not by any manner of means. In the first place, and by the very nature of the case, the range of the agent's possible choices is bounded by what he thinks he ought to do on the one hand, and what he most strongly desires on the other. The freedom claimed for him is a freedom of decision to make or withhold the effort required to do what he thinks he ought to do. There is no question of a freedom to act in some 'wild' fashion, out of all relation to his characteristic beliefs and desires. This so-called 'freedom of caprice', so often charged against the Libertarian, is, to put it bluntly, a sheer figment of the critic's imagination, with no *habitat* in serious Libertarian theory. Even in situations where free will does come into play it is perfectly possible, on a view like ours, given the appropriate knowledge of a man's character, to predict within certain limits how he will respond.

But 'probable' prediction in such situations can, I think, go further than this. It is obvious that where desire and duty are at odds, the felt 'gap' (as it were) between the two may vary enormously in breadth in different cases. The moderate drinker and the chronic tippler may each want another glass, and each deem it his duty to abstain, but the felt gap between desire and duty in the case of the former is trivial beside the great gulf which is felt to separate them in the case of the latter. Hence it will take a far harder moral effort for the tippler than for the moderate drinker to achieve the same external result of abstention. So much is matter of common agreement. And we are entitled, I think, to take it into account in prediction, on the simple principle that the harder the moral effort required to resist desire the less likely it is to occur. Thus in the example taken, most people would predict that the tippler will very probably succumb to his desires, whereas there is a reasonable likelihood that the moderate drinker will make the comparatively slight effort needed to resist them. So long as the prediction does not pretend to more than a measure of probability, there is nothing in our theory which would disallow it.

I claim, therefore, that the view of free will I have been putting forward is consistent with predictability of conduct on the basis of character over a very wide field indeed. And I make the further claim that that field will cover all the situations in life concerning which there is any empirical evidence that successful prediction is possible.

10. Let us pass on to consider the second main line of criticism. This is, I think, much the more illuminating of the two, if only

because it compels the Libertarian to make explicit certain concepts which are indispensable to him, but which, being desperately hard to state clearly, are apt not to be stated at all. The critic's fundamental point might be stated somewhat as follows:

'Free will as you describe it is completely unintelligible. On your own showing no *reason* can be given, because there just *is* no reason, why a man decides to exert rather than to withhold moral effort, or *vice versa*. But such an act—or more properly, such an "occurrence"—it is nonsense to speak of as an act of a *self*. If there is nothing in the self's character to which it is, even in principle, in any way traceable, the self has nothing to do with it. Your so-called "freedom", therefore, so far from supporting the self's moral responsibility, destroys it as surely as the crudest Determinism could do.'

If we are to discuss this criticism usefully, it is important, I think, to begin by getting clear about two different senses of the word 'intelligible'.

If, in the first place, we mean by an 'intelligible' act one whose occurrence is in principle capable of being inferred, since it follows necessarily from something (though we may not know in fact from what), then it is certainly true that the Libertarian's free will is unintelligible. But that is only saying, is it not, that the Libertarian's 'free' act is not an act which follows necessarily from something! This can hardly rank as a *criticism* of Libertarianism. It is just a description of it. That there can be nothing unintelligible in *this* sense is precisely what the Determinist has got to *prove*.

Yet it is surprising how often the critic of Libertarianism involves himself in this circular mode of argument. Repeatedly it is urged against the Libertarian, with a great air of triumph, that on his view he can't say *why* I now decide to rise to duty, or now decide to follow my strongest desire in defiance of duty. Of course he can't. If he could he wouldn't *be* a Libertarian. To 'account for' a 'free' act is a contradiction in terms. A free will is *ex hypothesi* the sort of thing of which the request for an *explanation* is absurd. The assumption that an explanation must be in principle possible for the act of moral decision deserves to rank as a classic example of the ancient fallacy of 'begging the question'.

But the critic usually has in mind another sense of the word 'unintelligible'. He is apt to take it for granted that an act which is unintelligible in the *above* sense (as the morally free act of the Libertarian undoubtedly is) is unintelligible in the *further* sense that we can attach no meaning to it. And this is an altogether more serious matter. If it could really be shown that the Libertarian's 'free will' were unintelligible in this sense of being meaningless, that, for myself at any rate, would be the end of the affair. Libertarianism would have been conclusively refuted.

But it seems to me manifest that this can *not* be shown. The critic has allowed himself, I submit, to become the victim of a widely accepted but fundamentally vicious assumption. He has assumed that whatever is meaningful must exhibit its meaningfulness to those who view it from the standpoint of external observation. Now if one chooses thus to limit one's self to the rôle of external observer, it is, I think, perfectly true that one can attach no meaning to an act which is the act of something we call a 'self' and yet follows from nothing in that self's character. But then *why should we* so limit ourselves, when what is under consideration is a subjective activity? For the apprehension of subjective acts there is *another* standpoint available, that of *inner experience*, of the practical consciousness in its actual functioning. If our free will should turn out to be something to which we can attach a meaning from *this* standpoint, no more is required. And no more ought to be expected. For I must repeat that only from the inner standpoint of living experience *could* anything of the nature of 'activity' be directly grasped. Observation from without is in the nature of the case impotent to apprehend the active *qua* active. We can from without observe sequences of states. If into these we read activity (as we sometimes do), this can only be on the basis of what we discern in ourselves from the inner standpoint. It follows that if anyone insists upon taking his criterion of the meaningful simply from the standpoint of external observation, he is really deciding in advance of the evidence that the notion of activity, and *a fortiori* the notion of a free will, is 'meaningless'. He looks for the free act through a medium which is in the nature of the case incapable of revealing it, and then, because inevitably he doesn't find it, he declares that it doesn't exist!

But if, as we surely ought in this context, we adopt the inner standpoint, then (I am suggesting) things appear in a totally different light. From the inner standpoint, it seems to me plain, there is no difficulty whatever in attaching meaning to an act which is the self's act and which nevertheless does not follow from the self's character. So much I claim has been established by the phenomenological analysis, in this and the previous lecture, of the act of moral decision in face of moral temptation. It is thrown into particularly clear relief where the moral decision is to make the moral effort required to rise to duty. For the very function of moral effort, as it appears to the agent engaged in the act, is to enable the self to act against the line of least resistance, against the line to which his character as so far formed most strongly inclines him. But if the self is thus conscious here of *combating* his formed character, he surely cannot possibly suppose that the act, although his own act, *issues from* his formed character? I submit, therefore, that the self knows very well indeed—from the inner standpoint—what is meant by an act which is the *self's* act and which nevertheless does not follow from the self's *character*.

What this implies—and it seems to me to be an implication of cardinal importance for any theory of the self that aims at being more than superficial—is that the nature of the self is for itself something more than just its character as so far formed. The 'nature' of the self and what we commonly call the 'character' of the self are by no means the same thing, and it is utterly vital that they should not be confused. The 'nature' of the self comprehends, but is not without remainder reducible to, its 'character'; it must, if we are to be true to the testimony of our experience of it, be taken as including *also* the authentic creative power of fashioning and re-fashioning 'character'.

The misguided, and as a rule quite uncritical, belittlement, of the evidence offered by inner experience has, I am convinced, been responsible for more bad argument by the opponents of Free Will than has any other single factor. How often, for example, do we find the Determinist critic saying, in effect, '*Either* the act follows necessarily upon precedent states, *or* it is a mere matter of chance and accordingly of no moral significance'. The disjunction is invalid, for it does not exhaust the possible alternatives. It seems to the critic to do so only because he *will* limit himself to the standpoint which is proper, and indeed alone possible, in dealing with the physical world, the standpoint of the external observer. If only he would allow himself to assume the standpoint which is not merely proper for, but necessary to, the apprehension of subjective activity, the inner standpoint of the practical consciousness in its actual functioning, he would find himself obliged to recognise the falsity of his disjunction. Reflection upon the act of moral decision as apprehended from the inner standpoint would force him to recognise a *third* possibility, as remote from chance as from necessity, that, namely, of *creative activity*, in which (as I have ventured to express it) nothing determines the act save the agent's doing of it.

11. There we must leave the matter. But as this lecture has been, I know, somewhat densely packed, it may be helpful if I conclude by reminding you, in bald summary, of the main things I have been trying to say. Let me set them out in so many successive theses.

1. The freedom which is at issue in the traditional Free Will problem is the freedom which is presupposed in moral responsibility.

2. Critical reflection upon carefully considered attributions of moral responsibility reveals that the only freedom that will do is a freedom which pertains to inner acts of choice, and that these acts must be acts (*a*) of which the self is *sole* author, and (*b*) which the self could have performed otherwise.

3. From phenomenological analysis of the situation of moral temptation we find that the self as engaged in this situation is inescapably convinced that it possesses a freedom of precisely the specified kind, located in the decision to exert or withhold the moral effort needed to rise to duty where the pressure of its desiring nature is felt to urge it in a contrary direction.

Passing to the question of the *reality* of this moral freedom which the moral agent believes himself to possess, we argued:

4. Of the two types of Determinist criticism which seem to have most influence today, that based on the predictability of much human behaviour fails to touch a Libertarianism which confines the area of free will as above indicated. Libertarianism

so understood is compatible with all the predictability that the empirical facts warrant. And:

5. The second main type of criticism, which alleges the 'meaninglessness' of an act which is the self's act and which is yet not determined by the self's character, is based on a failure to appreciate that the standpoint of inner experience is not only legitimate but indispensable where what is at issue is the reality and nature of a subjective activity. The creative act of moral decision is inevitably meaningless to the mere external observer; but from the inner standpoint it is as real, and as significant, as anything in human experience.[1]

---

[1] An earlier, but not in substance dissimilar, version of my views on the Free Will problem has been criticised at length in Mr. Nowell-Smith's *Ethics*. A detailed reply to these criticisms will be found in Appendix B.

MORAL EXPERIENCE AND ITS
IMPLICATIONS FOR HUMAN SELFHOOD

1. Today we conclude the examination of fundamental modes of human experience which we undertook with a view to elucidating the general nature of human selfhood. We are to study in this lecture experience in its *moral* mode.

As is well known, there are two sharply contrasting schools of thought, the Naturalistic and the Non-naturalistic, concerning the proper analysis of 'moral experience', or 'the moral consciousness'. According to the Naturalistic view (characterising it very broadly, but sufficiently for present purposes), there is nothing unique or ultimate about moral experience. Consciousness of the moral ought resolves itself on analysis into a complex whose components are all of the nature of the ideas, desires, hopes, fears, etc., found in the context of non-moral experience. According to the Non-naturalistic view, the moral ought is either ultimate and unanalysable, or, if analysable, can be analysed only in terms which include some other ethical concept, such as 'good', in a sense in which *that* is ultimate and unanalysable.

I think it is not easy to exaggerate the extent to which one's conception of the character and status of human selfhood is affected by the decision one comes to upon the relative merits of these two rival types of analysis. If the *Non*-naturalistic analysis be sound, there is, I believe (and shall later argue), a legitimate inference from the fact of moral experience to the objective reality of a moral order, and to a relationship of the human self to that order which confers upon the life of man a dignity and a cosmic significance of which the alternative, Naturalistic analysis affords no hint.

Now where the outcome of an investigation is so patently

fraught with momentous consequences for the value and destiny of the human individual, there is a danger that *either* wishful thinking, *or* the anxiety not to be a wishful thinker, may exert a distorting influence. Of the former danger philosophers of our present disillusioned age may be said to be constantly and acutely aware. But in a good deal of the modern literature of ethics there are at least undertones which suggest that the latter danger is not to be discounted either. Indeed I should myself doubt whether any greater bias has been imparted to the writings of moral philosophers by the desire of some to reach agreeable results, than by the ruthless determination of others to be what they call 'tough-minded' at all costs. Assuredly there is no duty laid upon the philosopher to 'think nobly of the soul'. But he has no duty to think *ig*nobly about it either. By all means let us be tough-minded. But it is well to remember that if one makes a fetish of tough-mindedness the result is apt to be not too easily distinguishable from thick-headedness!

Of the two concepts commonly regarded as the fundamental concepts of morals, the 'ought' and the 'good', it is the former which will be our concern in the present investigation. For whatever else the moral consciousness may be, it is at least a consciousness of oughtness or obligation. No analysis of the moral consciousness can possibly be adequate that does not include an analysis of the consciousness of obligation. In making the 'ought' the central thing in our study, however, I am by no means wishing to foreclose any of the issues about the relationship of the ought to the good, or of the right to the good, which have been the subject of so much intensive and profitable research in recent decades. It may be that our consciousness of moral obligation is always of an obligation to ensue certain ends because, and only because, they are independently approved as good, or as means to good; and that the concept of good has thus a logical priority. It may be, on the other hand, that our consciousness of moral obligation is, at least sometimes, of an obligation to ensue certain ends just because they are obligatory, independently of any thought of a good which may attach to, or result from, their achievement. For our present purpose all such questions are irrelevant. On *any* theory, I feel free to assume, the moral consciousness is at least a consciousness of obligation. In order that a good may approve itself to our moral consciousness, and thus be esteemed *morally* good, it must be apprehensible (as, of course, many 'goods' are not) as a good which ought to be ensued by someone.

This lecture, then, will be concerned to examine the nature and implications of moral experience, understanding by that the experience of moral obligation. I propose to lead up to my own (as usual, old-fashioned) view by way of a critical survey of the main types of analyses of that experience which have been competing for the philosopher's favour in recent ethical literature.

2.   These analyses are numerous, and it may seem as though we were embarking upon an impossibly large undertaking for a single lecture. Nevertheless, though a trifle more space would certainly not have come amiss, I am not so sure that any very remarkable feat of condensation is called for. Taking my courage in both hands, I venture the opinion that a good many of the ethical novelties that have been proposed for our instruction in recent years have been accorded much too solemn a reception. I shall submit to you at the outset three critical canons which, it seems to me, should guide us in appraising presented analyses of the moral ought. If they are accepted (and the first two at any rate seem to me to need no defence), we shall find, I believe, that their application to contemporary analyses causes a surprising number of these to collapse completely.

   1. The meaning of the moral ought is intrinsically the same in all moral judgments, whether they be in the 1st Person, 2nd Person, or 3rd Person; whether they be in the Singular or the Plural Number; whatever their tense; and whatever their mood. Any analysis must be rejected which fails to apply satisfactorily to even *one* acknowledged case of genuine moral judgment.

   2. The meaning of the moral ought is not the same thing as the *criterion* of the moral ought. This platitude is perhaps hardly worthy to rank as a canon of criticism. But analyses are not seldom suggested which are plausible enough as accounts of the latter but are so *im*plausible as accounts of the former that one is bound to suspect some confusion of meaning with criterion.

   3. The meaning of the moral ought is its meaning in moral

experience, which *need* not, and frequently does not, find overt expression in speech or writing. Let us (conveniently, if a little arbitrarily) use the term 'moral sentences' to denote the overt expression of moral experiences. We may then say that any analysis fails if, though apparently appropriate to all moral sentences, it will not apply to the 'silent', uncommunicated, moral judgment.

This does not imply, I hasten to add, that analysis should rely wholly upon introspection, and take no account at all of the 'public' evidence afforded by moral sentences. Introspection must be safeguarded against personal idiosyncrasies by constant reference to the moral experience of others as this is disclosed (however imperfectly) in the overt expression of moral sentences both written and uttered. What *is* implied is that the analysis of moral sentences can be of only ancillary value, and that in the last resort the test of validity for any analysis of the moral ought must be 'Is this really what I mean by "ought" when I judge that I (or he, or they, or you, etc.) morally "ought" to do something?' The study of overt moral expressions is not merely unhelpful, but positively harmful, unless it is steadily borne in mind that what we are ultimately concerned with is the moral experience that underlies the expression.

As the implications of our third canon are in manifest conflict with the linguistic method of ethical research in such high favour today, some elaboration and defence of it will rightly be expected. I welcome the opportunity, for it seems to me that ethical studies at the present time are suffering severely from failure to appreciate the palpable defects of moral sentences as an index to the nature of actual moral experience. Let me instance a few of these defects.

In the first place, moral words—'right', 'wrong', 'ought' and the rest—are very far from being univocal. In many sentences they are used with no moral import at all, and we should go wildly astray if we sought to elicit from the sentences as such truths about moral experience. If we did not go behind the sentences to the thought that informs them, we should not know whether what we were doing had any relevance to *ethics* at all.

In the second place, even when the words *are* being used with a moral intent, the sentences that embody them are often the vehicle of what can only by courtesy be called 'moral' judgments. Many, perhaps most, of the 'moral' utterances of everyday life are no more than the casual, uncritical application of the conventional moral rubrics of one's society. But it is surely clear that the analysis of moral sentences can help us to understand moral experience only if what these express really *is* a moral experience. Analysis of the moral sentences that embody the rough and ready, ill-considered, almost 'slap-happy' judgments that so often pass for 'moral' in everyday intercourse may have a certain interest of its own; but it is bound to be an exceedingly unreliable guide to the deliverances of the moral consciousness.

In the third place—and this I take to be the most serious, because the most frequently overlooked, defect in the approach to ethical research by way of moral sentences—as soon as moral judgment, even well-considered moral judgment, is given overt expression in a sentence, new and extraneous elements enter into the situation. Overt expression—save in abnormal cases like 'talking aloud to one's self'—differs from the silent judgment in having an ulterior purpose, viz. communication to others. And we make communication to others only because we wish to affect in some way their future states or actions. This is true even of plain indicative sentences, which are normally uttered only because we want the persons addressed to be in possession of certain information. It is conspicuously true of *moral* sentences, and above all of 2nd person imperatives relating directly to future action. The analysis of moral *sentences*, therefore, is virtually bound to issue in the discovery that an important function of many of them is to influence future action in one way or another. But what has this got to do with the question of the import of moral *judgment?* The 'social purpose' of moral sentences is clearly extraneous to the moral judgment. For nothing seems plainer than that there are 'silent' moral judgments, judgments which we make mentally but to which we give no overt expression, and that these have no purpose beyond themselves—social or otherwise.

3.   The point we have just been making seems very obvious. Yet it is precisely the failure to distinguish clearly between the import of the moral judgment on the one hand, and the function of the

moral sentence through which the moral judgment may or may not find overt expression on the other hand, that has led to the modish view that moral judgments are wholly or partly of the nature of recommendation, or advice, or persuasion, or advocacy, or command. If our 'third canon of criticism' be sound, and the moral ought of whose import we are in search is the ought of moral *experience*, then we can reject almost out of hand and *en masse* those theories which hold that the import of moral judgment lies wholly or partly in the desire of the judging subject to affect the mind, and thereby the future behaviour, of some person or persons. Let us call all such theories, for short, 'Hortatory' theories—a more convenient term, I think, than 'Command' theories, since very different types of theory from that which now engages us (including our own) recognise something at least *like* a command in the moral situation. These Hortatory theories have a slightly greater plausibility in the case of 2nd person imperatives than elsewhere, so let us look for a moment at the moral judgment 'You ought to repay that money'. If I *say* (aloud) 'You ought to repay that money', it is reasonably certain that there is a hortatory element present. Normally, at any rate, I speak in the hope that my words will increase the likelihood of your discharging your debt. But this hortatory element cannot possibly be part of the meaning that the moral 'ought' has for me, for the simple reason that I can refrain from uttering the sentence 'you ought to repay that money' while still *thinking* 'you ought to repay that money', and it would be nonsensical to look for a hortatory element in my 'silent' judgment. I am certainly not trying to persuade you, yet it is surely beyond question that I *am* making a moral judgment, I *am* apprehending moral obligation or oughtness, when I merely 'think' that you ought to repay the money.

There is, indeed, formally, a last refuge open to the Hortatory theory in face of this objection. The only person I can possibly be exhorting in the silent moral judgment is myself—since I alone am aware of what is being exhorted—and it might be suggested that the import of the moral judgment lies in such exhortation addressed to *one's self*. When I merely think, and do not communicate the thought, that you ought to have repaid that money, what I am really doing (according to this view) is telling myself to be sure that whenever I am in a like position I pay back what I have borrowed. Whether any theorist has in fact ever sponsored so fantastic a view, I do not know. I can only insist that there is a limit, even in moral philosophy, to the hypotheses that deserve discussion, and give my opinion that this one passes well beyond that limit.

If it were not so clear that the application of our third critical canon is in itself fatal to the Hortatory theory in all its forms, it would be worth while to examine the theory in the light of the first canon also, and to show how extremely implausible it is even for many moral judgments that do find overt expression— for all, indeed, save those that happen to be in the second person, and for some even of these. But to myself this seems a work of supererogation. I shall confine myself, therefore, to offering a single illustration of the sort of difficulty which the Hortatory theory has to try to meet. Suppose A is on what he knows to be his death-bed, and is sorrowfully reflecting upon some unworthy past action. Obviously in mental distress, he is asked by his Father Confessor if there is anything in particular that is troubling him, and he replies 'Yes, I ought not to have behaved in that shabby way to B'. To whom is the supposed 'exhortation' addressed? Is A exhorting *himself* not to act in that sort of way in future? No, for he is well aware that for him there is no future. Is he then exhorting his *audience*? No, for his sole audience is his Father Confessor; and it would stretch credulity too far to be asked to believe that the death-bed penitent is in effect saying to his Father Confessor 'Don't *you* ever behave in that sort of way!' Whom, then, *is* he exhorting? I leave it to the friends of the Hortatory theory to find an answer. I can supply none that has the faintest plausibility.

4.   I turn now to another type of theory that is perhaps still more popular today. The advocates of this type of theory (at any rate in its pure or unmixed form) are not misled by the social purpose that is inherent in the overt expression of moral experience, and in fact proclaim that the essential import of moral 'judgment' lies not in communicating anything to others, but in expressing a particular emotion of one's own. When I say 'You ought (or ought not) to do X', the significance of the 'ought', it is contended,

is to express a particular pro-emotion (and of the 'ought not' to express a particular anti-emotion) which I feel towards your doing X—or perhaps towards the kind of action designated by X.

This type of theory (and so far it resembles the pure Hortatory type) denies that the so-called moral 'judgment' is really a judgment. Its ethics is, in the expression made familiar by the title of an extremely stimulating paper [1] by Professor Barnes, an 'ethics without propositions'. There may, indeed, be *non*-ethical propositions involved. Thus if I say 'You ought not to be doing X', I may reasonably be taken to be implicitly affirming that you *are* doing X —a non-ethical proposition. But the whole significance of the 'moral' word—'ought'—lies in its expressing a particular emotion which I feel towards the conduct in question.

The Emotive theory—or the Emotive-Expressive theory, as we may better call it to distinguish it from the Emotive-Assertive theory which we shall later notice—has assumed a wide variety of forms in contemporary ethics; but it will not be necessary for our purpose to give to each of these separate consideration. For it seems to me that there is one conclusive criticism to which the theory lies open in every form it can assume; viz. that when one tries to give an account of the distinctive character of the emotion that is expressed in moral sentences, one finds that this can only be done in terms which imply that the 'emotion' in question is *also* a judgment. Let me explain.

It is evident that there are any number of experiences in which we feel pro- or anti-emotions towards ways of behaving and which we yet do not identify as 'moral' experiences. An Emotive theory is manifestly defective if it tells us nothing about the distinctive character of the emotion typical of *moral* experience. What then are we to say of it? It does not seem difficult to show that any combination of ordinary 'non-moral' emotions that may be offered fails in fact to yield the particular emotion we feel in any serious moral 'judgment'. Professor Barnes is right, as far as he goes, in insisting that the moral emotion is unique—a 'peculiarly moral feeling'. But it seems to me clear that he does not go far enough. That there always is an emotion present in moral experience, and that this emotion is unique, I believe to be true. But we cannot stop there. Persons who experience the moral emotion do think

[1] *Arist. Soc. Supp.* Vol. XXII.

that they can say *something* in description of its nature. Moreover (and this is important) they are in substantial agreement as to what it is that can be said. If the ordinary man is asked how he would distinguish his pro-emotion towards keeping promises from his pro-emotion towards playing golf, he would not surely, unless abnormally inarticulate, be wholly gravelled for a reply. He would not be reduced to saying that 'they just feel different'. He would probably tell us something like this: that the former emotion, in contrast with the latter, is felt not as a mere personal liking for the action in question, but as carrying with it a *claim* upon him, and a *rightful* claim, to perform the action. Indeed, the ordinary man's most natural way of putting it would be to say that what distinguished his *moral* pro-emotion towards an action is the feeling that he *ought* to act in this way.

Now that this is as a matter of fact what we feel when we experience the moral pro-emotion, it seems to me extremely difficult to dispute. It is simply not true that we find ourselves unable to describe the moral emotion in *any* way; and for myself I cannot conceive of any essentially different way of describing it appropriately. The ordinary man's description can, indeed, be challenged on the ground of defective phrasing. Thus it can be objected that 'a feeling that . . .' is not a mere feeling at all, but implies a judgment. The objection is technically correct. *But it brings out the very point I am trying to make*; viz. that moral experience is intrinsically incapable of being described adequately in terms of mere feeling. The specific feeling which characterises it is a feeling which is in essential integration with a *judgment*; a feeling which can be *itself*—can be a 'moral' feeling—only through its self-completion in a judgment. On this ground alone, the strictly 'emotive' theory of the ought breaks down. The 'peculiarly moral feeling' is there; but *only* in indiscerptible union with a 'peculiarly moral *judgment*' in a complex experience which requires *both* the feeling *and* the judgment for its proper characterisation.

On a previous occasion I had an opportunity of discussing this important point in greater detail. Perhaps I may be permitted, in amplification of the present brief treatment, to quote from the article in question a passage on the manner of integration of feeling and judgment in moral experience:

'My contention is that the peculiarly moral feeling towards keeping promises involves the judgment that promises ought to be kept. The moral feeling, I am suggesting, is not *itself* without the judgment—it requires the judgment for the completion of its own nature. Two opposite, but equally ruinous, errors of analysis must be carefully avoided. We must not say that our moral feeling towards promise-keeping *generates* the judgment that promises ought to be kept: for (we have urged) it is not the distinctively *moral* feeling at all unless the judgment of oughtness is already present. But neither must we say that the moral feeling is *generated by* the judgment of oughtness: for if this judgment is a moral judgment proper, and not the mere mechanical repetition of a conventional formula (if, in other words, the 'ought' of the judgment is before our minds in its intrinsically moral meaning), then the distinctively moral feeling towards promise-keeping is already present. Most of the moralists who have held that the moral feeling is prior, and the moral judgment sequent upon it, have held this, I think, largely because it appeared to them that the only alternative was to suppose that the moral judgment precedes the moral feeling; an alternative which they rightly reject. Similarly, most of the moralists who have held that the moral judgment is prior, and the moral feeling sequent, have held this largely because it appeared to them that the only alternative was to suppose that the moral feeling precedes the moral judgment; an alternative which they, too, are right to reject. The possibility which is missed by both parties is that feeling and judgment are *twin* aspects of a *single* experience, neither of which has precedence over the other. This I believe to represent the true state of the case.' [1]

5. For the most part, philosophers who favour an 'ethics without propositions' have interpreted the 'ought' of moral judgment as expressing primarily either an exhortation or an emotion; though the *total* experience expressed would commonly be regarded by them as an 'attitude' in which both elements are present, and in which there may be present also something to which the names 'resolve' or 'intention' may be assigned. Only very recently, so far as I am aware, has the view been seriously put forward by any moralist that it is the *last* named of these elements that is the primary one. According to Professor Braithwaite, however, when

[1] *Mind*, Vol. LIX, pp. 91-2.

a man says 'I ought to do X', what is primary in his 'pro-attitude' towards X is 'his intention to perform the action when the occasion for it arises'.[1] It is not suggested that *all* expressions of intention are moral assertions. 'For the notion of morality to be applicable it is necessary that the policy of action intended by the asserter should be a general policy (e.g. the policy of utilitarianism) or that it should be subsumable under a general policy which the asserter intends to follow and which he would give as the reason for his more specific intention.' [2] But with that qualification Braithwaite is prepared to hold that 'when a man asserts that he ought to do so-and-so, he is using the assertion to declare that he resolves, to the best of his ability, to do so-and-so'.[3]

We shall, I hope, have from Professor Braithwaite before long a much fuller and more systematic exposition of his theory than was possible in his Eddington Memorial Lecture or in his earlier Critical Notice of R. M. Hare's *The Language of Morals* [4]—our only sources of information so far. As it stands, however, this 'conative' version (as Braithwaite calls it) of 'ethics without propositions' seems to me, I must confess, exceedingly unplausible. I shall briefly develop two major difficulties which are likely to give pause to most of Braithwaite's readers.

The type of case that is most favourable to Braithwaite's theory is, of course, the 1st person moral judgment relating to the future, 'I ought to do X'. But even here the difficulties seem to me fatal.

1. May not a man 'resolve, to the best of his ability' to pursue a policy of action X even though he believes that he morally ought not to follow it? Granted that a man can, in a particular situation, choose to do what he believes to be morally wrong, it is surely possible in principle for him to resolve to pursue a policy, even a policy of the highest generality, where he believes that to be morally wrong? Indeed it seems likely that such resolves are not only possible in principle but have sometimes, if rarely, been made in fact. Instances at least seem to have occurred in which, for example, a man with a passion for power has resolved to devote all his talents and energies, and to subordinate every other claim, including the claim of morality, to the achievement of this objec-

---

[1] *An Empiricist's View of the Nature of Religious Belief* (Eddington Memorial Lecture), p. 12.

[2] *Ibid.* p. 13.   [3] *Ibid.* pp. 13-14.   [4] *Mind*, April 1954.

tive. It is enough, however, that such a resolve should be possible in principle. If it is, then 'I ought to do so-and-so' cannot mean the same as 'I resolve, to the best of my ability to do so-and-so'.

If at first sight there is a faintly unrealistic look about this objection, that is only because ordinary linguistic usage has accustomed us to give to the word 'resolve' a certain moral, or quasi-moral significance. We tend to think of 'resolve' as the kind of thing which, if not always directed towards what the agent believes he ought to do, is at least never directed towards what he believes he ought not to do. We talk freely of 'good resolutions'; seldom if ever of 'bad resolutions'. And 'bad resolutions' are implied in the objection I have been raising. But of course Braithwaite is not entitled, and would not claim to be, to a usage of the word 'resolve' which contained a covert reference to 'oughtness', since his whole object is to explain 'oughtness' in terms of 'resolve'. In some contexts, as we have seen, he substitutes for 'resolve' the normally neutral word 'intention'. When his view is formulated in terms of 'intention', our criticism of it is, I think, relieved of any appearance of 'unrealism'. For it does not conflict with ordinary usage to say that one *intends* to follow a policy of action even though one believes it to be morally wrong.

2. The second fundamental objection to this 'intentional' theory of oughtness may be summarily stated as follows. Whereas moral oughtness is in certain cases accepted as self-justifying, in *no* case is an *intention* accepted as self-justifying.

A moral principle is acknowledged as a valid moral principle either because it is believed to be valid in its own right or because it is supposed capable of derivation from some more general principle (or principles) believed to be valid in its (or their) own right. In the case of the second of these alternatives, the question 'Why ought I to observe the principle?' is obviously meaningful. The answer lies in exhibiting its relationship to the more general principle or principles from which it is derived. In the case of the first alternative, a 'Why?' is just as obviously not meaningful. If the principle is acknowledged as valid in its own right, its oughtness is accepted as self-justifying, and any question of 'Why?' is recognised to be inept.

So much must, I think, be agreed. Ultimate moral principles, ultimate 'oughts', are their own justification. In these cases of oughtness the question 'Why?' has no meaning. But must we not also agree that in no case whatsoever of an *intention* is the question 'Why?' meaningless—not even where it is an 'ultimate' intention (or 'resolve', or 'personal decision') to adopt some total plan of life?

This seems to me so evident, and yet to be so manifestly fatal to the intentional theory of the ought, that I find the absence from Braithwaite's exposition (brief as it is) of any serious attempt to grapple with the difficulty a little surprising. It would appear, however, from a late reference in his lecture,[1] that he would try to meet it along lines suggested by Mr. Hare. Mr. Hare argues that an 'ultimate personal decision' *can* be self-justifying, admitting of no question 'why?' that is not able to be answered within the ambit of the decision itself. According to Hare, it will be 'a complete justification of a decision' if we give 'a complete specification of the way of life of which it is a part'—'a complete account of its effects, together with a complete account of the principles which it observed, and the effects of observing these principles'. 'If the inquirer still goes on asking "But why *should* I live like that?" then there is no further answer to give him, because we have already, *ex hypothesi*, said everything that could be included in this further answer.' [2]

This is ingenious, but I cannot think that it will really do. *Has* everything already been said that is relevant to a further answer? To suppose that it has seems to me to involve a *petitio principii*.

Consider how the ordinary moral man would react to Hare's claim. 'You have given me' he might say 'a complete specification of a way of life to which you are evidently prepared to commit yourself. But one thing that specification does *not* include which is extremely relevant, indeed fundamental, to the question why you or I or anybody else *should* adopt such a way of life, viz. any reference to its *obligatoriness*. To me at any rate this omission renders the 'answer' essentially *in*complete.'

The retort, no doubt, would be 'Of course I make no separate reference to obligatoriness or oughtness. For the essence of my view is that the "oughtness" of an ultimate principle is nothing

---

[1] p. 34.

[2] *The Language of Morals*, p. 69, for each citation in this paragraph.

other than its acceptance as a total way of life. To ask me to justify that way of life in terms of an "ought" that means anything else is just to betray that you do not understand my theory.'

But is there not here, as I have suggested, a *petitio principii?* The contention that no question can arise concerning the oughtness of the said way of life which is not already covered by the specification of it, is defended on the ground that its oughtness just *means* its ultimate adoption as a way of life. But the very point at issue is whether the meaning of the moral ought *is* thus reducible to a resolve, or personal decision. To the man who does not already so regard the ought, the argument can have no force whatever. For him the simple objection stands, that the specification of the way of life lacks one thing relevant and fundamental to the question why anyone should adopt that way of life, viz. any reason to suppose it morally obligatory. To allege, as Hare expresses it in one passage, that the decision to adopt such a fully specified way of life 'would be the most well-founded of decisions, because it would be based upon a consideration of *everything upon which it could possibly be founded*' [1] is merely to *assume* that a decision could not possibly be founded upon 'moral obligation' in its ordinary sense.

6.   Let us pass on now to theories of moral experience which do admit that judgment is involved—'assertive' theories, as they are often called, by contrast with 'expressive' theories. Characteristic of the forms of assertive theory that have had a vogue in recent times is the contention that the 'ought' in moral judgment is not ultimate and unique. As to what precisely it is that we affirm when we judge that X 'ought' to be done, there is much diversity of opinion, but it is a matter of common agreement that at least this 'ought' is something capable of analysis without remainder in terms that do not include or imply itself. It is these forms of assertive theory that I wish now to consider.

I do not propose to consider them, however, at any very great length. For two reasons. Firstly, because it is the Hortatory and Expressive types of analysis upon which by far the greater part of contemporary interest has centred. Secondly, because the

---

[1] *Op. cit.* p. 69. (Italics not in text.)

standard objections—to which I have little to add—against the Assertive type of theory are both well known and, I think, widely accepted as cogent. I shall do little more here than remind you, in regard to each of the Assertive theory's main varieties, of certain criticisms which to myself seem fatal. If they should appear to you equally conclusive, I venture to hope that in their light, and in the light of what has earlier been said in criticism of the Hortatory and Expressive types of theory, you may be sympathetically disposed to reconsider the claims of the once common view that the moral ought is ultimate and unanalysable.

The Assertive types of theory can be most conveniently classified, I think, under three heads; the *Emotion*-assertive, the *Command*-assertive, and the *Production*-assertive. We shall begin with the Emotion-assertive; and we shall look first at that form of it which holds that what is asserted when anyone makes the moral judgment 'You ought to do X' is the presence in the person judging of a pro-emotion towards your doing X.

The most obvious objection to which this theory lies open is that it becomes impossible in terms of it to allow that there can ever be real disagreement between two or more moral judgments. When I assert 'You ought to do X', and you reply 'No, I ought to do Y', what, on this theory, can you possibly mean by your prefatory 'No'? For all *I* am doing, if the theory is correct, is to assert the presence of a certain pro-emotion in *my* mind, and all *you* are doing is to assert the presence of a differently directed pro-emotion in *your* mind; and there is nothing incompatible in these two assertions. Both may be, and probably are, correct. Yet we do all in fact believe (as the prefatory 'No' indicates) that the two moral judgments do contradict one another. Apparently, then, we cannot really be meaning in our moral judgment what this theory declares that we mean.

We might also, of course, apply to this theory what we said earlier about the peculiar character of the moral 'emotion'. When we try to distinguish the *kind* of pro- or anti-emotion whose presence in ourselves we are supposed by this theory to be asserting in our moral judgment, we find that it is not *merely* an emotion. We find that it is the specifically moral emotion only if it is *also* a *judgment*. Hence this form of the assertive theory reduces to the absurd contention that moral judgment asserts the presence in the person judging of the moral judgment itself.

A second, perhaps commoner, form of the Emotion-Assertive theory is that what is asserted when I say 'I ought to do X' is that my doing of X evokes, or tends to evoke, a certain pro-emotion in the minds of some other person or persons or groups of persons; e.g. of most members of one's society, or of the majority of mankind.

This form of the theory is superior to the first form in not making disagreement between different moral judgments a logical impossibility. But it is difficult to see what other virtues it possesses. The simplest way of appreciating its inadequacy is to consider whether it is, or is not, a meaningful question to ask 'Ought I to do that which evokes, or tends to evoke, a certain pro-emotion in P?'—where 'P' denotes the particular person or persons or group of persons named in the theory. Everyone would agree that the question is meaningful.[1] But it could not *be* meaningful if 'I ought to do X' meant 'My doing of X evokes, or tends to evoke, a certain pro-emotion in P'. For in that case what I should be asking would be 'Ought I to do what I ought to do?'

The same general line of criticism—which has, of course, been fully exploited by Ross and (in relation to analysis of the 'good' rather than of the 'ought') by Moore—applies with equal force to *Command*-Assertive theories of the ought. According to this type of theory, the moral judgment 'I ought to do X' means 'My doing X is commanded by (or is in accordance with the will of) P', where P denotes whatever person or group of persons the theory accepts as having authority. This theory of the ought (so far at any rate as secular 'authorities' are concerned) is perhaps the implicit theory of certain 'plain men' rather than an explicit theory of philosophers. One might suppose it to have been the implicit theory of most citizens of, e.g. Nazi Germany and pre-War Japan. But again it *does* make sense, and on the theory it *should not* make sense, to ask 'Ought I to do what Hitler (or the Emperor) commands?' If 'I ought to do X' simply means 'My doing X is commanded by Hitler (or the Emperor)', the question reduces here also to the tautologous 'Ought I to do what I ought to do?'

The main responsibility for this theory, as for several other false theories, lies in a failure to distinguish clearly between the

[1] But see qualification below, pp. 197 ff.

meaning of ought and the *criterion* of ought. Many people have come, at all times in history, to accept as a belief not open to question that what they morally ought to do is whatever some specific 'authority' commands or wills; and this is apt to be taken as implying that for these people the moral ought has no meaning independently of the command of their authority. In fact it only implies that the command of their authority is for them the *criterion* or *norm* by which morally obligatory acts are determinable: not that even for them, this is the *meaning* of the ought. No doubt such persons often enough talk as though for them moral oughtness and the command of their favoured authority were identical. But this way of talking probably means no more than that the distinction between them is not one of which they have become explicitly conscious. For wherever there is unquestioning belief in the validity of a given criterion of the ought, wherever people have therefore ceased to ask (because the answer seems to them self-evident) 'What ought I to do?' there is little or no occasion for the explicit emergence in their minds of the notion of a criterion of the ought as something distinct from its meaning. Yet the distinction is surely latent in their minds all the same? Even the most fanatical Hitlerite would have deemed it significant —even if he regarded it as merely stating the obvious—to say, 'I ought to do whatever the Führer wills', He would not think he was merely saying 'I ought to do what I ought to do'. But this is how the sentence would have to be translated *if* he in fact takes what the Führer wills to be the meaning, and not merely the criterion, of the moral ought.

The same criticism naturally applies, *mutatis mutandis*, to the Command-assertive theory where it takes a *religious* form, in which case the assertion is (roughly) that 'ought' means 'commanded by God': and I mention it separately only because it makes so much wider an appeal than any secular variety of the theory. To some religious men it may, indeed, seem a rather silly question to ask 'Ought I to do what God commands?' It may seem to them that the reasons for an affirmative answer are so compelling that no one ought to be in any doubt about it. But that they do not regard it as a *meaningless* question is obvious from the very fact that they are ready with their reasons to show that the affirmative answer *is* the right one. Yet if 'I ought to do X' *means* 'I am

commanded by God to do X', the question 'Ought I to do what
I am commanded by God to do?' becomes the purely tautologous
'Ought I to do what I ought to do?' 'Divine Command' may or
may not be the criterion of the moral ought, but it certainly is
not its meaning.

At the same time it must be conceded that there is, formally,
a line of defence open to the last-ditch champion of these Assertive
theories of the meaning of 'ought' against the objections we have
been raising in terms of our second critical canon. He may deny
that there is any confusion in his mind between 'meaning' and
'criterion'. If he favours the Emotion-assertive theory, he may
boldly avow that the question 'Ought I to do what evokes or
tends to evoke a pro-feeling in P?' *is* for him a tautology, and
that he finds no difference between the statement 'This morally
ought to be done' and the statement 'This evokes or tends to
evoke a pro-feeling in P.' A corresponding line of defence (or act
of defiance?) is of course open to the Command-assertive theorist.

I must confess, however, that (as in the case of the last-ditch
defence of the Hortatory type of theory against the objection from
the side of the 'silent' moral judgment) this seems to me the sort
of desperate refuge to which no moralist would have resort unless
to save a theory at all costs. I think it reasonable to believe that
most sponsors of the Emotion-assertive or of the Command-
Assertive theory, once it is appreciated by them that their account
of the meaning of 'ought' has the consequence of rendering
tautologous the question 'Ought I to do . . . ?', will recognise
that their account is mistaken, and that they have in fact only
been led to adopt it by permitting themselves to slip into the
fallacy of identifying meaning with criterion. Still, it *is* logically
open to them to continue to hold their theory if they are prepared
to accept the consequence of the tautologous character of the
above question. If they are so prepared, if they insist that the
meaning conveyed by the words 'this morally ought to be done'
is for them precisely identical with that conveyed by the words
'This evokes or tends to evoke a pro-feeling in P', or 'This is
what P commands', there is not much one can do about it; though
one may speculate with justifiable curiosity about the genesis in
their minds of so eccentric a linguistic usage. One can be confident,

however, that they will make few converts. For most people it will
be more than sufficient to discredit the alleged identity of meaning
that in *their* experience the word 'ought' has always connoted
essentially a relation of acts to possible *doers* [1]—a relationship
about which the equivalents suggested by the Emotive-assertive
and the Command-assertive theories have nothing to say.

It is worth noting, however, that if the problem before us
concerned the definition of 'good' rather than of 'ought', we could
not quite so easily rest content with the 'argument from tautology'.
In his extremely able little book *Logic and the Basis of Ethics*
Professor A. N. Prior suggests that it is not beyond the power of
the Naturalistic moralist to explain, consistently with there being
no non-naturalistic quality of goodness, how it might come about
that, whatever naturalistic meaning X is offered in definition, it is
felt to be still significant to say 'X is good'. The pages he devotes
to the topic deserve to be read in their entirety, but briefly his
argument is this. As Mill has pointed out, 'A name not infrequently passes by successive links of resemblance from one object
to another, until it becomes applied to things having nothing in
common with the first things to which the name was given; which,
however, do not for that reason drop the name; so that it at last
denotes a confused huddle of objects, having nothing whatever in
common; and connotes nothing, not even a vague and general
resemblance'. This, the naturalist may argue, has happened to the
word 'good'. Professor Prior states their case as follows:

'At present, when we call a thing good we may mean that it is
pleasant, or that it is commanded by someone, or that it is customary,
or that it promotes survival, or any one of a number of things;
and because we use the same term to connote all these characteristics,
we think there must be some other single characteristic which they
all entail; but in fact there is not. When it is said that being good
means promoting survival, we are dissatisfied; we feel that it is
still significant to say that promoting survival is good; and the
same thing happens with every identification that is suggested; but
this is just because, in each case, the other meanings are still hovering
in our minds—to say that promoting survival is good is significant
because it means that to promote survival is what we desire; to say
that what we desire is good is significant because it means that
what we desire promotes survival; and so on.' [2]

[1] Cf. Ross, *Foundations of Ethics*, p. 23.   [2] *Op. cit.* pp. 9-10.

It is quite clear, of course, that this naturalistic 'explanation' can support no one specific naturalistic definition of 'good'. On the contrary, the explanation rests upon the plurivocal character of the word 'good' in current usage, and the naturalist can do no more than recommend adherence to a specific usage as a useful linguistic convention. Hence even if a parallel 'explanation' were possible in the case of the word 'ought', the Emotion-Assertive and the Command-Assertive theories of the meaning of 'ought' could find therein no succour. It is much more important to notice, however, that a parallel explanation in the case of the word 'ought' has little or no plausibility. 'Good' is admittedly a word with a wide variety of current usages; but there is no comparable collection of naturalistic meanings of 'ought' in current usage by 'ringing the changes' upon which we might (analogously to the case of 'good') still find it significant to say 'X ought to be done' where 'X' stands for some one naturalistic meaning. One could perhaps allow that 'ought' is sometimes taken in current usage as equivalent to 'required, under penalties, by law', or to 'decreed by social custom', or to 'commanded by God'. But reflective persons can usually be quite easily brought to see that none of these meanings is really the meaning he attaches to the *moral* ought. The fact that a small number of exceedingly reflective persons—i.e. certain philosophers—have lately offered us some new meanings of oughtness besides these (and of *moral* oughtness at that) is beside the point. For these new meanings have certainly not acquired currency in ordinary linguistic usage, and cannot, therefore, function in the way that Prior suggests that the different meanings of 'good' 'hovering in our minds' might function.

The third variety we distinguished in the Assertive type of theory—the Productive-Assertive—holds that 'I ought to do X' means, broadly speaking, 'My doing of X will be productive of maximum good'. Its forms differ, often sharply, with the very different interpretations that can be given to the expression 'maximum good'. If this view were offered as a theory of the criterion, and not of the meaning, of the moral ought, we should obviously require to treat it, in some of its forms, seriously and at length. As it is, it can readily be seen to collapse on the application to it of our old canon of criticism, and I do not propose to weary you with yet another variation on the old theme. Suffice it to say that if the objections advanced against the two previous varieties of Assertive theory are accepted as valid, there seems no ground for denying the validity of similar objections to the present variety.

7. Now we have not, of course, attempted in the foregoing to examine all the permutations and combinations that occur in contemporary analyses of the moral ought in terms other than itself. That would be impracticable. But we have, to the best of our belief, considered the leading types; and our conclusion is that there are insurmountable objections to each of them. I want to put forward now, as a 'substantive motion', that those philosophers are right who maintain that the moral ought is ultimate and unanalysable, incapable of definition save in terms that imply the *definiendum* itself. According to this view, we can know what the ought means in, but *only* in, actual experience of it. That meaning is as incommunicable to a person who cannot enjoy the requisite experience (if such there be) as the sensory quality 'redness' is to a colour-blind person. We can, indeed, put a man on the road to grasping the meaning of the moral ought by drawing his attention to the kind of situation in which it is typically experienced, and to some extent by the use of analogy; but these are never more than, at best, devices for aiding him to enjoy at first hand the direct experience which will alone reveal its nature.

It is always, in a manner, unsatisfactory to have to say that one knows what a thing is, yet cannot by any description of it communicate that insight to others. But this is of course a misfortune by no means peculiar to the moral ought. It pertains to every indefinable notion; and *some* indefinable notions there *must* be. Besides, as in the case of other indefinables, we can (as I have just remarked) say something by way of a 'pointer' to its nature. For instance, it is not without reason that the moral ought is commonly spoken of as a 'command'. It is certainly *like* a command in certain respects; though not, even in 2nd person moral judgments, a command *issued* by the person judging—that was the mistake of the Hortatory theory—but rather a command *apprehended* by the person judging. But it is also *un*like a command in certain important respects. It differs from ordinary, non-moral commands, in the first place, in that it is not, for the experiencing subject, intrinsically connected with any specific imponent. We may indeed come, for extrinsic reasons, to associate it with God or with some other being as imponent. But a relationship to God or to some other being as imponent is not something intrinsic to the 'ought' as experienced. The moral ought can be experienced *as* the moral ought with no reference whatever to a Divine or any other imponent. And it differs from ordinary commands in this second respect, that it is experienced as having *absolute* authority for us. Of all ordinary, non-moral commands we may legitimately ask 'What justification is there, if any, for its claim to our obedience?' But in the case of the moral ought, as experienced, such a question has no point. '*Why* ought I to do what I morally ought to do?' is a question that, for the moral consciousness, does not make sense. The moral ought, in other words, is experienced as an *unconditional*, or *categorical*, imperative.

But we must not, of course, suppose that when we say (rightly, I think) that the moral ought is a 'categorical imperative', and that the moral judgment asserts that certain conduct is unconditionally binding in some or all contexts, we are giving a description which will, *per se*, convey to another person a positive notion of the moral ought. He will be able to attach no positive meaning to a 'categorical imperative' if he has no direct personal experience of the moral ought, for nowhere else is a categorical imperative to be found. The description may well be of help in preventing him from looking for the moral ought in the wrong quarter. It can be no substitute for his own direct experience.

But what if a man tells us that, search as he may, he just cannot find in himself anything corresponding to this categorical imperative, and that if this is what a 'moral consciousness' implies then he at least is lacking in that commodity? He may admit, with some reluctance no doubt, that there is good evidence that most other persons do have it: and he *should* admit this, since most other persons, when it is put to them, can be persuaded to agree that they do *not* mean by the ought of morality any kind of merely conditional 'ought'—'I ought to do X, *if* I want Y, to which X is a means'. But he may insist that *he* at any rate never thinks of the ought in terms which imply more than a conditional significance. He recognises that certain ways of behaving (e.g. keeping faith) are required for the attainment of certain ends (e.g. social stability) which he finds himself approving for one reason or another; but the reason for approving them, he avers, is never any intrinsic obligatoriness conceived as belonging to the end. To the moral ought as a 'categorical imperative' he frankly declares that he can attach no meaning whatsoever.

Now if this position is consistently maintained by anyone, there is very little one can do about it. On the other hand, it is questionable if it ever *is* consistently maintained. At least very often, professed a-moralists slip into ways of speaking which suggest that what they are really concerned to reject is the supposed absolute obligatoriness of certain norms of behaviour proclaimed by their society, or even perhaps (in the case of large scale iconoclasts) by their 'age'. The *new* standards they themselves propose, or which are implicit in their criticism of the old, seem to exact the same unconditional claim upon *their* allegiance as the old standards do upon the more conventionally minded. As with Nietzsche, 'a-moralism' sometimes signifies no more than the *transvaluation* of moral values—not their *abnegation*. A disguised 'moralism' may even reveal itself in a fervently felt 'duty' to preach 'amoralism'!—just the same old categorical imperative in a new dress.

Again, one might (though perhaps with no great confidence) appeal to the professed a-moralist's modesty. If he admits that, as seems to be the case, there is good evidence that the great bulk of mankind, not merely at the civilised level but in the most primitive communities, do possess an authentically moral consciousness,[1] then he has to make his choice between two alternatives. Either he may confess that there must be some defect in his analysis of his own experience, or he may claim the distinction of being differently constituted from almost all other members of the human race. It is uncertain which choice he would make. But it does not seem uncertain which choice we ought to make for him.

8. The *existence* in man of a moral consciousness—a consciousness of unconditional obligation, of a categorical imperative—I

[1] Attention may be drawn to the highly instructive study of the anthropological evidence in Professor A. Macbeath's *Experiments in Living*.

propose now to take as established. Is there a further question to be faced, the question of the *objective validity* of the moral consciousness? May it conceivably be the case that though we do have the idea of an unconditional obligation, the presence of that idea in us is of only subjective significance, and tells us nothing about the objective nature of things?

I take the view myself that there is no such further question; or, to be more precise, that the 'further question' virtually answers itself. The notion that moral experience may have only subjective significance arises primarily, I think, from the erroneous belief, already criticised, that the essence of moral experience lies in feeling or emotion. When the true nature of moral experience is appreciated, the objective validity of the ought can be seen to be little more than a corollary. But to justify this pronouncement I must insert here a brief reminder of what was earlier said about the essential nature of moral experience.

The crucial point I was concerned to make was that moral experience is never a mere feeling, but always includes *judgment*. It is, as I then expressed it, 'a complex experience which requires *both* feeling *and* judgment for its proper characterisation'. Each by itself is a mere abstraction from the actual experience. This is a matter which can, and in the end must, be decided for everyone by personal experiment. Let any man imagine in himself what he is prepared to call a 'moral' pro-feeling (as contrasted with any other type of pro-feeling) towards his doing X, and let him answer whether he does not find that the *judgment* 'I ought to do X' belongs intrinsically to the experience. And let him imagine in himself what he is prepared to call a 'moral' judgment 'I ought to do X', and answer whether he does not find that a moral *pro-feeling* towards X belongs intrinsically to the experience. I must assume that he will find, as I find, that an affirmative answer is inescapable in both cases.

Now if judgment belongs thus to the essence of moral experience, a subjectivist interpretation of the ought seems to me to be ruled out *eo ipso*. It belongs to the essence of judgment to claim *truth* for what it asserts; and truth is always 'of' objective reality. Hence my experience of X as morally obligatory involves a judgment which can be legitimately expressed in the form 'It is true of objective reality that I ought to do X'. In other words, the

consciousness of moral obligation is at the same time the consciousness of that obligation as objectively valid, as rooted in the
nature of reality.

It must be admitted, however, that there are certain considerations not directly connected with a false analysis of moral
experience which tend to make people sceptical about the objective
validity of the moral ought. I must say a few words about two of
the commoner sources of confusion.

(a) I may be genuinely doubtful about what I ought to do,
not merely in some particular, and perhaps rather complex,
situation, but in regard to the general conduct of life. And lacking
certainty about even the broadest principles of morality, my moral
consciousness may never be in a position to express itself in any
definite judgment 'I ought to do this specific thing X'. There is,
that is to say, a question in my mind about the objective validity
of *any* specific embodiment of the moral ought. Now it is extremely
easy, I think, to confuse the problematic objective validity of *any*
specific embodiment of the ought with the problematic objective
validity of the ought itself. But it *is*, surely, a confusion. The very
statement 'I do not know what my duty is' presupposes the
recognition that there *is* a duty for me, if only I could discern
where it lies. The moral consciousness in any form implies the
belief that there *is something* which I ought morally to do. And
no more than that is required for the objective validity of 'oughtness' or 'duty' in general.

(b) It is a commonplace that the moral codes of different
peoples, or even of the same people in different ages, show striking
divergences from one another, and in some respects contradict
one another. This is apt to suggest to the mind that there is not a
single moral consciousness common to all men, but *a number* of
moral consciousnesses operating according to different and to
some extent mutually conflicting, principles. Now if such be the
case, it is indeed very difficult to see what could be meant by the
'objective validity' of the moral consciousness. There will apparently be no *one* objective moral order. And to say that there are
several different objective moral orders seems tantamount to
admitting that there is no objective moral order at all.

It seems to me, however, that the inference from the plurality of
conflicting moral codes to a plurality of moral consciousnesses is,

to say the least of it, over-hasty. The inference would have some justification if it were clearly impossible to interpret the conflicting moral codes as compatible with an underlying identity of ultimate moral principle. But *is* this impossible? Let us suppose that there is a common moral consciousness, and let us further suppose, merely for the sake of the argument, that it is informed by a single ultimate principle which is the obligation to promote the well-being of one's community. It is surely obvious that such an ultimate principle will manifest itself in very different rules of conduct, or 'moral codes', in different societies, corresponding to their differing cultural beliefs and different material, economic and social backgrounds? It is not merely understandable, but inevitable, that differently circumstanced societies should take different views as to what modes of behaviour best promote communal well-being; not to speak of different views as to what constitutes one's *community*—e.g. the family, the clan, the tribe, the nation, or all mankind. Hence rules of conduct that are superficially in violent conflict may be in reality quite compatible with a common moral consciousness functioning in accordance with the same ultimate principle.

Nor is this mere idle speculation upon abstract possibilities. Modern social anthropology has, I suggest, succeeded in making intelligible, and even in a sense acceptable, to *our* moral consciousness what at one time seemed to be wild and mysteriously alien 'moralities' in primitive peoples. Even the most bizarre moral rules have turned out to make sense as 'instruments' for the promotion of communal well-being, when interpreted in the light of a sympathetic appreciation of the whole cultural and material milieu of the societies in question. Indeed I think it hardly too much to say that while the relatively external and superficial reports of moral customs supplied by early anthropologists provoked natural doubts about the unity, and therefore the objective validity, of the moral consciousness of man, the far more intensive studies of later anthropologists, who have taken infinite pains to get, as it were, 'inside the skins' of those whose customs they seek to understand, have worked in exactly the opposite direction, and have provided truly impressive evidence of a fundamental identity of moral principle throughout the whole human race.

9.　A final word about the metaphysical implications of accepting the moral consciousness as having objective validity. For these seem to me to be of enormous importance. If the moral ought is objectively valid, this means nothing less than that a 'moral order' is *somehow* ingredient in the very nature of things. To develop the 'somehow' into a definite and intelligible concept is, of course, a task of the most formidable character, which only metaphysics is competent to discharge—if even *it* be competent. But in order to know *that*, as distinct from *how*, a moral order is rooted in the nature of reality, there is no need to wait for a metaphysical theory. If we are prepared to grant the objective validity of the moral ought, the fact of an objective moral order follows as a direct implication. We have need of a metaphysical theory only to know (if we can know) the manner in which 'the nature of things' incorporates that moral order.

Indeed, it may well be doubted whether the achievement of a sound metaphysical theory of the universe is of quite such moment to humanity as philosophers have often liked to suppose. Not *quite* so much would now seem to hang upon it. Certainly to know that a moral order belongs to the very nature of things, and is no mere figment of man's imagination, is not to know everything we should like to know about this universe in which we find ourselves. But it *is* to know (or so it seems to me) that which effectively eliminates the most haunting of those ultimate fears that chill the heart of reflective man; the fear that human existence has no meaning or purpose beyond itself. For it is just not possible to believe that the moral order is objectively real—that there *really are* obligations unconditionally binding upon us as human beings to behave in certain ways—and to believe also that human existence has no meaning and purpose beyond itself. Perplexity about what in particular we ought to do may, and no doubt in some degree always must, remain with us. But the dejection of spirit that darkens and corrodes the inner life of so many men today has its primary source, surely, not in mere inability to discern wherein their duty lies, but in an inability to be sure that there really *is* any duty to discern. To banish this doubt is, as I believe, to emancipate the human soul at a stroke from by far the most tormenting and most spiritually debilitating of all its cosmic forebodings.

10. I have left little time for a summing-up of the general argument of this course. But perhaps, after all, little time is needed. Its object has been to find whether a view of the self could be rationally defended which makes intelligible the sort of language theology is constrained to use in talking about the human soul. Such language is clearly meaningless if the term 'self' stands for no more than some inter-related set of particular states and events; which is all that most modern empiricists are prepared to recognise by it. But it is otherwise if, as the argument of these lectures has sought to show, human experience is found to imply a unitary and relatively enduring subject, a being not reducible *to* experiences, but manifesting itself *in* experiences; a being in which, in the manifestations by which we know it, spirit and body are intermingled, and 'compose a certain unity', yet a being of which the essence is spiritual, in the sense that while we can conceive its existence as possible without *body*, we can attach no meaning at all to its existence without *spirit*; a being which, though subject to manifold influences from without, is nevertheless endowed with a creative power which suffices to constitute it a free and responsible agent, master, in a real sense, of its own destiny; a being, again, which is intrinsically related through its moral consciousness and moral will to an objective moral order, whereby there is imparted to the life of man on earth a no less than cosmic significance; and, finally (for religion, perhaps, most significantly of all) a being that is for itself, in the last resort, a *mystery*; knowing in some measure, indeed, *what* it is, but knowing not at all *how* it is what it is.

Does the human self as so characterised lack anything that could be claimed as indispensable to the theological conception of the soul? It seems to me that it does not. The soul is always, I think, conceived in theology as a *relatively abiding* entity which maintains its identity throughout changes; as a *spiritual* entity—however close may be its affiliations to an animal body; and as an *active* entity, which is no mere passive plaything of external forces. These are the minimal requirements, and a philosophical theory of the human self which is incompatible with any one of them logically entails the rejection of all theological talk about the human 'soul'. But each of these requirements, I submit, is adequately met by the theory of the self which has emerged from the analysis of human experience conducted in these lectures.

If this be so, our question whether the nature of the self as it discloses itself to philosophical investigation is such as to render nonsensical theological talk about the soul is answered in the negative. The still larger question, whether there is in reality anything corresponding to theological talk about 'God', and, if so, how the nature of this 'God' and His relationship to the human soul ought to be understood, is what we are to debate in our second course.

APPENDIX A

IDEALISM AND THE SO-CALLED 'SUBJECT-PREDICATE LOGIC'

For a good many years now—dating back at least to the period of the early Russell—unflattering references have abounded to something that is called 'the subject-predicate logic'.

Yet this is surely a very odd label to attach to *any* logic? It seems to imply the existence of another logic, or other logics, concerned (*inter alia*, no doubt) with propositions which contrive to dispense with a subject, or with a predicate, or perhaps with both. But in what would seem to be the ordinary, straightforward meanings of the terms 'subject' and 'predicate', there *are* no such propositions; and therefore no such logics. Russell describes the subject-predicate logic as the logic 'which holds that every proposition ascribes a predicate to a subject',[1] and he thinks it obvious that *relational* propositions do not do this. But there is a perfectly good and well-established sense of the terms in which it seems obvious that they *do*. Take the proposition (one of Russell's examples)[2] 'this thing is bigger than that'. Here, certainly, as Russell says, we are asserting 'a relation of "this" and "that" '. But are we not *also* asserting of 'this thing' as *subject* the relational property of 'being bigger than that' as *predicate*? It goes without saying that the fact of the predicate here being a relational property of the subject gives to the proposition a logical form importantly different in certain respects from that of propositions in which the predicate is an *attribute* of the subject. But it seems confusing, to say the least of it, in the light of ordinary usage, to

[1] *Our Knowledge of the External World*, p. 39.
[2] *Ibid.* p. 45.

say that it is a logical form in which there is not a predicate ascribed to a subject.

The confusion in which the subject-predicate terminology has become enveloped in modern times is well illustrated by the statement sometimes made that there are propositions that have *neither* subject *nor* predicate. Thus Miss Stebbing tells us that 'Fire!' is a proposition which 'has neither subject nor predicate'.[1] It is clear, of course, that a subject and a predicate do not find linguistic expression in the verbal utterance 'Fire!'. But if we are talking of *propositions*, we are not talking of verbal utterances as such, but of the mentally asserted content that is expressed— adequately or inadequately—through the verbal utterance. Looked at from this point of view it is surely evident that in so far as a proposition is finding expression in the word 'Fire!' the characteristic of being a-fire, as predicate, is asserted of some more or less specific feature of the immediate environment as subject? A proposition, one may presume, is something capable of being true or false. It is hard to conjecture what could be meant by the 'truth' or the 'falsity' of something wherein there is nothing about which an assertion is made, and wherein about this 'nothing' there is nothing asserted.

It looks, then, as if those philosophers who distinguish a 'subject-predicate' logic from other logics must be using their key words in a somewhat esoteric way. And, in general terms, it is not difficult to know what that way is. The prototype of the subject-predicate logic is taken by its critics to be the traditional formal logic of the schools, which, it is alleged, recognises only one kind of predicate, viz. that which is an attribute or quality of the subject. Against this the critics insist that there are *irreducibly different* kinds of predicate. Most conspicuously, and contrary to the assumptions of the traditional logic, relational properties cannot be reduced to mere attributes of the subject to which they may be ascribed. But then, these irreducibly different *kinds* of predicate are, after all, kinds of *predicate*. In what sense, one may reasonably ask, is the title 'subject-predicate logic' supposed to be more appropriate to a logic which admits only one kind of predicate than to a logic which admits irreducibly different kinds of predicate?

[1] *A Modern Introduction to Logic*, p. 37.

Confirmation that those who denounce a subject-predicate logic really have in mind a subject-*attribute* logic is plentiful; sometimes in explicit statement, more often by implication. Russell himself, in the course of arguing for the non-universality of the subject-predicate form of propositions, actually uses the term 'quality' as though it were a synonym for 'predicate'. He supposes it to be a proof that there are some propositions not of 'the form which ascribes a predicate to a subject' that, 'if we say "this thing is bigger than that", we are not assigning a *quality* of "this", but a relation of "this" and "that" ' [1] (italics mine). Clearly such an argument makes its point only if the term 'predicate' and the term 'quality' are to be regarded as identical.

In ordinary usage—even in ordinary philosophical usage—'predicate' is a much wider term than 'quality' or 'attribute'. It remains perfectly good English to say that a *relational property* is 'predicated' of a subject. Would it not therefore be wiser to *say* 'quality' or 'attribute' where that is what we mean? I suggest that it would minister appreciably to the clarity of logical discussion if that unhappy piece of nomenclature, 'the subject-predicate logic', were abandoned—despite such historical justification as can be offered for it—and the much less misleading practice generally adopted of calling the logic which treats all predicates as attributes of the subject 'the subject-attribute logic'.

When it is appreciated that by 'subject-predicate' logic is really meant, substantially, 'subject-attribute' logic, it must come as a shock to students of F. H. Bradley to find that the logic of this thinker is often referred to as being of the 'subject-predicate' type; [2] with the implication, of course, that it suffers from the defects which almost everyone would now agree to be rightly chargeable against a logic which treats relational properties as mere attributes of a subject. On the face of it, the charge in Bradley's case seems monstrous. For so far from there being in Bradley any hint that he thus interprets relational properties, the plain fact is that he roundly condemns the traditional logic precisely on the ground that its acceptance of a subject-attribute

---

[1] *Our Knowledge of the External World*, p. 43.

[2] A notable exception is Professor Ryle, who explicitly gives credit to Bradley for recognising with Frege 'that judgments or propositions are not all of the one hallowed subject-predicate pattern'. (*The Revolution in Philosophy*, p. 7.)

analysis of propositions imposes disastrous limits upon the proper province of logic, by excluding therefrom a whole host of valid inferences.

Nevertheless there must presumably be some ground for this apparently absurd designation of Bradley's logic; apart, of course, from the purely verbal ground that Bradley (blissfully ignorant of the ambiguity which the future course of logical writings would inject into the use of these terms) formally analyses the general nature of judgment into a 'subject', a 'predicate', and a relation between them. The ground lies, I think, in the doctrine, common to Bradley with other idealist logicians, that the *ultimate* subject of judgment is always 'Reality as a whole'. As we saw in Lecture III, the total 'ideal content' of judgment, including what is ordinarily distinguished in logic as the subject, can on the idealist view be legitimately (and for some purposes usefully) regarded as predicated of Reality as subject. Now it is clear that Reality as a whole cannot be thought of as standing in relation to something other than itself, since there is nothing other than itself. It follows that, in so far as the subject of all judgment is Reality, the predicate ascribed to the subject can in no case be a *relational* property. And granted that we accept as exhaustive the disjunction between relational properties and attributes as predicates in propositions, this may appear to afford a plausible justification of the view that the idealist logic is of the 'subject-predicate' (subject-attribute) type.

Plausible, but on deeper consideration surely most inadequate? The whole point of condemning the subject-attribute logic is that its analysis of propositions is of such a kind as to entail the restriction of valid inferences to those which have their source in the relation of an attribute to a subject. But this restriction is *not* entailed by the analysis of propositions offered by the idealist logic. To suppose that it is is to forget that in addition to the *ultimate* subject (which is normally only implicit), the idealist analysis of propositions recognises that in almost every case there is also a *proximate* or *immediate* (and, as a rule, explicit) subject, distinguishable within the total ideal content predicated of Reality from what is ordinarily called the predicate, and constituting 'the starting-point or point of contact with the ultimate subject' (i.e. Reality). For the sake of brevity I must here refer the reader to the exposition of this doctrine given towards the end of the third lecture. It should be plain therefrom that the proximate subject of the idealist logic and its corresponding predicate are the subject and predicate which logic ordinarily distinguishes within the judgment, and that there is not the faintest reason why, for idealist logic, what is predicated of this proximate subject should be an attribute rather than a relational property. The view that in judgment we are always 'characterising Reality' is wholly consistent with our characterising it on occasion by the presence within it of relational situations in which the proximate subject has ascribed to it relational properties not reducible to attributes (as in the judgment 'Reality is such that this thing is bigger than that'). Once this is understood, it seems to me that no plausible ground remains for calling the idealist logic what it so plainly is *not* as actually expounded in the works of its leading representatives, a 'subject-attribute logic'.

One further point is worth a brief mention. It is sometimes suggested that there is a close connection, if not indeed a relation of entailment, between the idealists' logical doctrine that the ultimate subject of the judgment is Reality and the acceptance by the same philosophers of a metaphysical monism. I can discover no good reason for supposing this. Those who hold the logical doctrine in question can surely, in full consistency with it, make the judgment 'Reality is such that there exist within it independent entities whose relation to other entities within it is wholly external'. Here Reality is taken as the ultimate subject, yet monism is implicitly denied. Admittedly idealist philosophers do as a rule adopt a monistic metaphysics. But nowhere, so far as I am aware, is this supposed to be a direct consequence of the view that the ultimate subject of judgment is Reality. Monism requires for its establishment at least the additional premise that all relations are internal; a premise which idealist philosophers have laboured to justify by a vast amount of difficult and quite independent argument.

APPENDIX B

A REPLY TO MR. NOWELL-SMITH

In his recent 'Pelican' book entitled *Ethics*, Mr. Nowell-Smith has subjected to courteous, but very extensive, criticisms the positive doctrine about free will which I briefly sketched at the close of a paper in *Mind* (October 1951), and which I set out more fully in a book written some twenty-five years ago (*Scepticism and Construction*). As in almost every instance these criticisms seem to me to arise, directly or indirectly, from a refusal to attach weight to the evidence of introspection—which to myself is not merely indispensable but central—I have not felt obliged by them to introduce into the version of the present work any modification of my general position. This by no means implies, however, that I regard Mr. Nowell-Smith's criticisms as unimportant. They seem to me an excellent example of how the problem of free will appears —I might almost say *must* appear—to an acute analyst whose ethical thinking is determined throughout by the linguistic approach. If, as I much hope, those who do me the honour of reading this book include some philosophers partial to the linguistic approach, the detailed reply to Mr. Nowell-Smith which I now offer is likely to deal with a number of points to which they also feel objection.

It will be simplest if I take up Mr. Nowell-Smith's criticisms more or less in the order of their occurrence in his text.

1. Having previously argued that the expression 'he could have acted otherwise' must ordinarily, in non-moral contexts, be interpreted not categorically but hypothetically, Nowell-Smith

begins his section on *Libertarianism* by observing that 'it would indeed be remarkable if modal forms which are normally used in a hypothetical way were used categorically in one type of case alone' (p. 278).

I am afraid I do not see anything 'remarkable' about this. Where two or more different types of situation have important features in common, we often use the same verbal expression to refer to them, even if the difference also is, in some contexts, important, *provided that* in the context of our discourse this difference is not one to which we have any particular interest in drawing attention. Now in the context of ordinary discourse about human behaviour we seldom have any particular interest in drawing attention to differences that are of importance to the moral philosopher. It would not be in the least surprising, therefore, if in ordinary discourse we used the identical expression 'he could have acted otherwise' to refer to situations which had not only an obvious identity but had also philosophically important differences. Whether in fact such differences exist is a matter that can be settled only by an ethically directed analysis and comparison of the situations to which the (identical) verbal expressions relate.

2. Nowell-Smith proceeds:

'It is essential to notice that the categorical interpretation is supposed to be necessary only in a very small, but very important part of the whole range of human choice. And this too is remarkable; for it implies that the words "free" and "choose" are logically different in moral and in non-moral cases.' (pp. 278-9).

I find this even less 'remarkable'. If there is one word of philosophical significance in the vocabulary of the English language that can beat 'feeling' in the diversity of its usages, it is the word 'free'. That is why it is of such paramount importance for any discussion of the problem of 'free will' to begin by carefully distinguishing the precise nature of the 'freedom' whose existence or non-existence is in dispute. To anyone who appreciates the distinctive character of our usage of the word 'free' when we are talking about freedom as a condition of moral responsibility, it will certainly not come as a shock to learn that the 'logic' of the word 'free' is different in moral and in non-moral cases.

3. 'Campbell insists that the question whether choice is "free" in a contra-causal sense must be settled by introspection' (p. 280).

This does not quite represent my position. What I have insisted upon is that introspection provides highly important evidence for the settlement of the question, not that it can *per se* settle it. I have always explicitly recognised it to be in principle possible that the subjective assurance of contra-causal freedom which, in my view, introspection reports, may be illusory (e.g. on page 463 of the *Mind* article), and that various objections to accepting that assurance as veridical must be independently considered. Metaphysics, science, epistemology, ethics, and religion have all, I think, something relevant to contribute to a 'settlement'.

4. The above misunderstanding has, I think, a connection with Nowell-Smith's doubts about the 'propriety of the language' I use in reporting the results of my own introspection. Contrary to what he apparently supposes to be my attitude, I thoroughly agree with him when he says 'That I know introspectively what it is like to choose may be true; but I cannot be said to know introspectively that my choice was contra-causal or unpredictable; and this is the point at issue' (p. 281). I think he has failed to appreciate that what I report as discerned in introspection is (to take the crucial case of moral decision between rising to duty and yielding to strongest desire) not a contra-causal activity, but a *belief*—seemingly ineradicable—that one is contra-causally active. That is to say, it is a report of 'what it is like' to make a moral decision. My introspective report may itself be at fault (I must refer to the main text for the justification of its detail), but it is surely of the *kind* of thing which introspection is competent to discern?

Why do I regard the introspective report as offering 'highly important evidence'? Briefly, for this reason. We are trying to ascertain the true nature of the activity of 'moral decision' (in the sense of that expression just specified—there is, of course, a very different sense of it to which reference will be made later). And not until we have satisfied ourselves about that, so far as I can see, can we possibly hope to determine the kind of *language* which is appropriate in talking about moral decision. Now just because moral decision is an *activity*, it can be directly apprehended only 'from the inside', by the agent actually engaged in it. But if that is so, the introspective report which tells us how the agent as actually engaged in moral decision understands his activity is surely very good *prima facie* evidence about the nature of this activity, and in consequence about the form of words best fitted to express it?

5. 'The issue between determinists and libertarians is an issue about the way in which expressions such as "choose", "can", and "alternative possibilities" are to be construed; and this is surely an issue which is to be settled not by self-observation but by logical analysis' (p. 281).

I take it that the question how these expressions 'are to be construed' is equivalent to the question 'In what sense or senses of these expressions do they represent truly the situations to which they refer?' Otherwise, the issue between the determinists and Libertarians would seem to be being regarded as a *purely* verbal one; and I do not think Nowell-Smith wishes to go so far as that. He does apparently believe, however, that something called 'logical analysis' of these expressions can settle the issue.

If we are to consider this claim, we must try to get clear at the outset just what the co-called 'logical analysis' is. What is meant by the 'logical analysis' of an *expression*? I suppose what must be meant is the examination of an expression with a view to eliciting its entailments, compatibilities, and incompatibilities *vis à vis* other expressions. It seems patent, however, that the entailments, etc. of *expressions*, as distinct from those of *concepts* and *propositions*, are not strictly of a 'logical' character. The words 'can', 'choose', 'alternative possibilities', merely as *words*, have no logical relations whatsoever. If we are to speak at all of the 'logic' of these expressions (or of any other expressions), we can do so only on the assumption—which is certainly valid within limits— that there exist certain rules for the use of these expressions, which rules, however, are not themselves logical rules. We can then legitimately enquire what 'logically' follows from these rules with regard to any of these expressions in the way of entailments, compatibilities, and incompatibilities *vis à vis* other expressions. But it is crucial to remember—what is apt to be disguised by the simple use of the term 'logical analysis'—that the rules for the use of these expressions have not themselves the binding force of 'logic'.

Bearing this in mind, let us then consider how such 'logical analysis' works in the kind of case that is now before us; and let us take as our example the expression 'alternative possibilities'. Is there a 'rule' that this expression never entails, and perhaps is always incompatible with, expressions to the effect that when one of the possibilities has become fact, the other *could not* have happened, in the categorical sense of 'could'? I am not aware of one. And if I am told that nevertheless it exists, it is a fair question to ask 'Who imposed it, and what is his authority for doing so?' It is obviously no use appealing to the authority of the dictionary. This does indeed give us certain general rules (which have a valid claim to our respect) for the use of the expression, but it very properly says nothing one way or the other on the special point before us. Nor can it be argued that 'custom' prescribes the rule. Apart from the very dubious nature of the 'authority' of custom, there *is* no such custom. The custom of libertarians is to use the expression, in the context of moral decision, as entailing the categorical statement that whichever of the 'alternative possi- bilities' is decided upon, the decision *could* have been for the other. The custom of determinists is to use it in a sense which denies this. So by this route we reach an impasse. And so far as I can see there is only one way out. If we want to know how the expression *ought* to be used, we must try to discover which use of it best conforms to the *facts* to which it refers—the special realm of fact about which the dispute here arises being that of 'moral decision'. That, as I have already urged, entails, among other things, our studying the actual experience of making a moral decision, which is the primary source of the libertarian's claim that his use of the expression is the proper one.

In short, 'logical analysis of expressions' just will not 'deliver the goods'. Sooner or later we must go to the *facts*; and among the relevant facts are those supplied by introspection.

6. 'The libertarian regards explanation in terms of character as incompatible with genuine freedom and must therefore draw a contrast between "the self" and "the character". But if "self-determined" is to mean "determined by the self", it is necessary to give some account of what the "self" is . . .' (p. 283).

I agree; though I am not sure that anything much less than the extensive treatment I give to this problem in the present work would really have been useful. It is one of the more intractable difficulties confronting the writer on free will who aims at being constructive as well as critical that a diversity of basic problems will be relevant to his theory, and he manifestly cannot defend, and often cannot even expound, his views on these without writing a book. I try to make some amends in the present work; and I would call attention especially to Lecture V, in which I discuss the relation of *self*-identity to *personal* identity (which Nowell-Smith, I think mistakenly, treats as indistinguishable). In view of the complexity of that discussion I would perhaps be better advised to say no more here in answer to Nowell-Smith's very proper demand. But I shall venture nevertheless to add a few words.

I argue in the lecture referred to that a man's *self*-identity can be retained even where there is loss or suspension of *personal* identity—which latter is for me tantamount to identity of *character*, of the self's dominant cognitive, conative and emotive dispositions. And I accept in principle the consequence that a man may be properly liable to moral praise and blame for his past acts even if these have been committed at a time when, through injury or disease, he was not the same 'person' as he was before, and perhaps became again after. But I must stress the words 'in principle'. It may well be the case that the abrupt change induced in the man's personal identity or character was of such a kind that, in the given situation, no conflict of 'duty' with 'strongest desire' was present to his mind—as it would have been in his 'normal' state. In that event a necessary condition for the ascription of moral praise or blame in respect of the act will have been absent. Or again, the change in personal identity might have been such that the conflict of desire with duty was a great deal more acute, the desires opposed to duty having become much stronger, with the result that a correspondingly greater effort is required of the man if he is to 'rise to duty'. In that event, though moral praise or blame will undoubtedly be in order, appropriate allowance will fall to be made in passing moral judgment. It will be manifestly improper to condemn the man for succumbing to temptation as severely as one would if he had retained his normal character and been faced with the need of a less difficult moral effort.

It goes without saying, however, that in these cases of abrupt and drastic changes in personal identity wrought through injury or disease, the onlooker is seldom in possession of the relevant information in a sufficiently accurate and detailed form to warrant a confident judgment on the man's moral merits and demerits in respect of particular actions. But there is nothing new about that. The practical obstacles in the way of passing confident moral judgment on others are formidable even in normal cases, though not always adequately appreciated. Nor has this fact any tendency to show that the criterion being used for passing judgment is unsound. A criterion is not theoretically invalidated because it proves difficult or even impossible of practical application.

7. 'If it is necessary to decide whether or not a man could have acted otherwise before ascribing responsibility, it is necessary that we should have some criterion for deciding this; and on the libertarian theory such a criterion is quite impossible. For, let us suppose that we know a great deal about his character and also that the temptation which he faced seems to be a fairly easy one for such a man to overcome. On the libertarian hypothesis this information will not be sufficient to enable us to conclude that he could have acted otherwise, . . .' (pp. 283-4).

It is possible that I have not fully understood the argument of this paragraph; for, as I at any rate interpret the libertarian view, nothing that Nowell-Smith says has any tendency to show that the question of a criterion presents any special difficulty for it. The libertarian view (based primarily upon the introspective report of the moral agent engaged in the act of moral decision) is that a man in the situation Nowell-Smith depicts could *always* have acted otherwise; though of course the effort required to rise to duty will be harder in proportion to the strength of the temptation, and corresponding allowances will have to be made in passing moral judgment on the man—a practice which accords perfectly with our more carefully pondered moral assessments of men in ordinary life. There are, indeed, a few exceptional cases like that of the drug addict, or the victim of some pathological obsession, in which it is very difficult to say whether it was even *possible* for the temptation to be resisted. That difficult problem does not arise, however, in relation to the example Nowell-Smith has chosen, and I do not propose to initiate a discussion of it here. I shall only say that, with diffidence, I incline to doubt whether even in pathological cases (always provided that the idea of a duty opposed to inclination is present to the man's mind at all) we ought to say more than that the effort required to vanquish desire is so extreme that it is *virtually* impossible for the man to rise to duty; or, more accurately, to rise to his *full* duty—the dipsomaniac for whom it is virtually impossible to desist altogether from alcohol within his reach may yet, by a not too prodigious effort, succeed in *limiting* his indulgence to a level far below that which would satisfy his inclinations. But whatever be the correct solution of this particular problem, it does not seem to me to have any vital bearing upon the fundamental issue between libertarian and determinist.

8. 'The libertarian theory involves putting a very special construction on the principle that "ought" implies "can", which it is very doubtful whether it can bear. If we take this principle in a common-sense way it is undoubtedly true. It is no longer my duty to keep a promise, if I literally *cannot* do so. But when we say this we have in mind such possibilities as my being detained by the police or having a railway accident or the death of the promisee; and it is possible to discover empirically whether any of these exonerating conditions obtained. But if "cannot" be construed in such a way that it covers my being too dishonest a person or not making the necessary effort,

I

it is no longer obvious that "ought" implies "can". These reasons for failure, so far from exonerating, are just what make a man culpable' (p. 284).

To me it seems about as obvious as anything can be that 'ought' implies 'can' in a sense of 'can' which goes far beyond the absence of external obstacles to the fulfilment of the duty, which is apparently all that Nowell-Smith (judging from his illustrations) is willing to allow. I do not even believe that any very adroit maieutic would be needed to deliver this truth from 'commonsense'. For if on any grounds whatsoever—scientific, psychological, metaphysical, or religious—one has come to believe that moral choices are all determined in the sense that there only appear to be, and never really are, genuinely open possibilities before a man, so that he *cannot* act otherwise than he does, then it seems every bit as evident nonsense to say that he morally 'ought to act otherwise' as it would be if there were external obstacles such as Nowell-Smith cites preventing his so acting. And of course the 'cannot' here *does* cover 'being too dishonest a person', since it is implied (in the determinist belief) that he is too dishonest a person because 'that's the way he's made'; and it covers similarly his 'not making the necessary effort', since it is implied that he *couldn't* make the necessary effort. These 'reasons for failure', unlike those mentioned earlier, *are* indeed 'just what make a man culpable'; but only on the assumption that 'reasons for failure' here means *'ways of* failing' and *not 'conditions necessitating* failure'. Surely we *must* all agree that a man cannot be held morally culpable for that which he can't help doing? It matters not a jot, ethically speaking, whether what prevents him acting otherwise is the strong arm of the law or the metaphysical structure of the universe.

9. Nowell-Smith turns next, to my mind a little belatedly, to *The Concept of 'Trying'*, in order to ask whether the libertarian can find in this concept a criterion of moral culpability, and rather surprisingly, in words which, if I may say so, I might have written myself, he tells us that

'Morally we blame people, not for failing to live up to a certain standard, but for not trying hard enough to do so; and this is because while we do not believe that they could always succeed, we do believe that they could always try' (p. 285).

So far so good. But when Nowell-Smith attempts to analyse the experience of trying, of exerting moral effort, he seems to me to say very odd things:

'We all know what it *feels* like to make an effort. These feelings are phenomena or occurrences that we experience in the same way that we experience aches, pains, qualms, and twinges. And, if we take the introspective language of the libertarian seriously, it would seem that the question "Did he try?" can be answered only by the man himself and that he answers it by observing whether or not one of these feelings occurred. The logical status of the question will be like that of "Did it hurt?" But on this view an effort is not something that a man *makes*; it is something that *happens* to (or inside) him; and it would be highly implausible to make the question of his responsibility turn on the occurrence or non-occurrence of such a feeling' (p. 285).

But surely it will not do thus to assimilate the 'feeling' of moral effort to the 'feeling' of aches and pains, and to conclude that since the latter are 'passive', so too must be the former? It is true that moral effort, like any other kind of activity, can be apprehended only in direct experience; and in that sense it is 'felt' as pains are 'felt'. But there the resemblance ends. It clearly does not make sense to say that what we directly experience in directly experiencing *activity* is 'something that *happens* to (or inside) us'. When a man asks 'Did I try?' he is asking about the occurrence or non-occurrence of certain 'feelings' only in the sense that he is asking whether or not he had the experience of exerting moral effort. There may, indeed, be certain 'passive' feelings that *accompany* the experience of exerting moral effort—cephalic tension and the like. But it is certainly not about the occurrence or non-occurrence of *these* that a man is asking when he asks, in the context of the moral situation, 'Did I try?' (It is not easy to make one's self as clear as one would wish on these matters in brief compass, and perhaps I may be permitted to refer the reader for a fuller discussion not only to Lecture VIII of the present work, but also to my paper—which may, I think, have escaped Nowell-Smith's notice—in the *Proceedings of the Aristotelian Society* for 1939-1940, entitled *The Psychology of Effort of Will*.)

Very rightly, Nowell-Smith goes on to insist (though, as we have seen, he strangely thinks it to be inconsistent with the introspective language of libertarian psychology) that 'if making an effort is to be relevant to responsibility, it must be thought of as something which a man chooses to do or not to do'. That is to say, in my language, that in the situation of moral temptation the making of the effort (or the withholding of it) must be thought of as the outcome of the man's moral decision. But so understood, he declares, 'unfortunately it is fatal to the categorical interpretation of "he could have acted otherwise" (p. 286).

Why is it fatal? If I understand him correctly, the argument he offers is as follows. On the libertarian view, a man who fails to act rightly (to 'rise to duty') is culpable if, and only if, he 'could have tried harder than he did'. Now of 'his failure to try harder', we are told, there are only three possible interpretations. Either his failure is inexplicable; or it is due to circumstances beyond his control; or it is due to 'his not having tried to try as hard as he could have tried to try'. On the first two of these interpretations the man is not blameworthy but blameless, so they won't do. The libertarian is thus forced back upon the third. But it can easily be shown that this won't do either, since it leads to an infinite regress. It follows that we cannot intelligibly use 'the failure to try harder' as a criterion of culpability.

Now it seems to me that Nowell-Smith's criticism here rests entirely on an assumption which the libertarian would not tolerate for a moment. This is the assumption that we cannot intelligibly hold a man blameworthy for an act that is 'inexplicable'. The assumption betokens, I think, a failure to appreciate that *if* the act of moral decision is a free act, it is bound to be 'inexplicable', but that this kind of inexplicability by no means entails that the agent is not responsible for the act. That depends on the nature of the activity itself; and, once again, our primary clue to that must be, as in all activity, what it is like for the agent who directly experiences it. What, in my view, it is like for the agent actually engaged in moral decision, I have perhaps too often already described. For him, his decision to exert or withhold the moral effort required to rise to duty is certainly 'inexplicable', in the sense that the decision is a creative act which nothing determines save his doing of it. But because this 'inexplicability' is just the inexplicability inseparable from any creative activity, it has no tendency to induce the man to disclaim responsibility for his decision, and to deny his blameworthiness if the decision was to withhold the effort required and yield to the importunings of desire. To demand an 'explanation' of moral decision in terms of factors external to it is simply to *assume* that determinism is true. The libertarian who knows his business will reject any such demand as involving a plain *petitio principii*.

10. None of the criticisms of myself which I have so far noticed occasion me much surprise. By and large they seem to me the natural outcome of a standpoint which deliberately precludes consideration of the only direct evidence there can be of moral-decision activity, viz. the evidence of the moral agent's own direct experience of it. Yet I must confess to being not altogether prepared for the final charge which Nowell-Smith brings against me. Complaining that I take as 'the only case of moral choice to which appraisals are relevant that of a man who knows what he ought to do but is tempted to do something else', he proceeds as follows:

'Now this, so far from being the only case, is not even the commonest or most important. For in the great majority of cases of moral difficulty what is difficult is not to decide to do what one knows he ought to do, but to decide what one ought to do. . . . Men who belong to a generation for whom the questioning of accepted principles has been no mere academic exercise and who have found themselves faced with momentous choices in situations not covered by their traditional rules will be less likely than their fathers were to suppose that the only sort of moral difficulty is that of resisting temptation' (pp. 288-9).

Now this does rather stagger me, on two distinct counts.

(*a*) I am indeed sorry if Nowell-Smith supposes me ignorant of the commonplace that there is often very great difficulty in deciding what one ought to do. But I must protest that there is nothing in my writings on ethics which could justify him in such a delusion. I presume there must have been a time when I enjoyed this state of innocence; but it was certainly long before I began to write—nay, even before I began to read—philosophy. Moreover, I do assure Nowell-Smith that my early awareness of the commonplace was no symptom of a singular precocity. Nowell-Smith, in this respect far from alone among philosophers of his school, seems to have curious ideas about the state of man prior to the Wittgensteinian revolution (or should I say 'revelation'?). It is hard to think of *any* time in the history of civilisation at which reflective individuals have not 'found themselves faced with momentous choices in situations not covered by their traditional rules', and have not been led thereby to appreciate that there are other kinds of 'moral difficulty' besides the difficulty of resisting temptation. So far as concerns the comparatively recent generation which Nowell-Smith has specially in mind, the suggestion that for them 'the questioning of accepted principles' was a 'mere academic exercise' must seem to the social historian to border on the ludicrous.

It is true, of course, that in discussing the problem of free will I have thought it proper to focus attention upon the type of moral difficulty which occurs in the situation of moral temptation. But the reason for that is very simple. Free will is commonly thought to be a pre-condition of legitimate moral praise and blame; and it is at least primarily in respect of a man's response to the situation of moral temptation that he is accounted by others (and most assuredly accounts himself) morally praiseworthy or blameworthy. A man's response to the *theoretical* difficulty of deciding *what* he ought to do is an utterly different sort of thing. It is a response of his intellect and knowledge, not of his will—and we do not normally judge a man to be morally blameworthy for a failure of intellect or knowledge as we do for a failure of will.

(*b*) This brings me to my second point. The decision in cases of difficulty about *what* we ought to do, which Nowell-Smith chides me for not seeing to be both a commoner and a more important case of moral choice than the decision whether or not to rise to duty in moments of temptation, is neither a less nor a more common, and neither a less nor a more important, case of moral choice, since it is not a case of moral choice at all. In order to be brief, I must be somewhat dogmatic in discussing this; but refinements of statement hardly seem necessary where the principle (as it seems to me) is so perspicuously clear.

In the most common case of such difficulty, where we are unsure whether in our given situation we ought to do X or Y, the routine procedure (I presume it will be agreed) is to subject to a much closer examination than we have yet given them the implications and consequences of each of these alternative courses of action. In the light of the fresh considerations which then appear, we are generally, though not always, in a position to decide which course best accords with the moral rules or principles we accept as binding. But in what conceivable sense can I be said to be thereby 'choosing'—let alone *morally* choosing—that X, or Y, is what I ought to do? My decision is the conclusion of an argument, determined by the relevant objective considerations as they appear to me, and I no more 'choose' that X, rather than Y, is my duty than I 'choose' that 2 plus 2 equals 4 rather than 5.

In the less common case, where it is seeming collisions or inadequacies within the accepted rules themselves that occasion the perplexity, reflection is again the natural route to a decision about 'what we ought to do'; though reflection now upon the credentials of the rules we have hitherto accepted more or less uncritically. This is the typical situation that gives rise to the kind of thinking we call 'moral philosophy'. Its most usual result is to place the supposed rules in a new perspective in which their authority is seen to be not absolute but derivative; and in the light of the principle or principles from which we now see their authority to be derived we assess their relative claims and solve our problem. Again, clearly, our decision is determined by what appear to us the relevant objective considerations, and 'choice' has no place whatsoever.

The one type of case (and it is comparatively rare) in which there seems to me any plausibility at all in assimilating a decision about what we ought to do to 'choice' is this. It may occur that after reflection has done its very best in the time available before action is required, we can still find no ground for judging the duty claim of any one of the two or more competing courses (or rules) to be superior to the other or others. In that event there is a sense in which a choice, though a wholly arbitrary one, not only *may* but *must* be made in favour of one or another. But it is very necessary to ask, What is the precise nature of this choice in favour of, let us say, X rather than Y or Z. Are we 'choosing' *that X has the highest duty claim* (as Nowell-Smith would appear to imply)? Surely not. It makes sense to speak of *wishing* that a certain proposition were true, but no sense that I can see to speak of *choosing* that it be true. Are we then, perhaps, choosing *to believe that* X has the highest duty claim? Again, surely not. How can we choose to believe what we in fact *don't* believe?—for *ex hypothesi* we are in possession of a belief, reached by reflection, that X has *not* a higher duty claim than Y or Z. What we *are* choosing, I suggest, is to *act as if* we believed X to have the highest duty claim, even though we don't in fact believe it. If that be so, our choice is not merely not a psychological monstrosity, but is, in the circumstances, the one rational procedure—rational, because it is the only way of escaping what we *do* believe to be wrong, namely, the futility of taking no action at all.

I must add one further word. Even if this wholly arbitrary choice should be whatever Nowell-Smith thinks that it is, it would still be impossible to speak of it as a 'moral choice' in any sense relevant to the present discussion. It is, in Nowell-Smith's phrase, 'a leap in the dark'; and he himself tells us that 'just because it is a leap in the dark I doubt if we should be inclined to blame him [the leaper] if he leapt in what turned out to be the wrong direction' (p. 288). Yet what Nowell-Smith, by his own profession, is supposed to be discussing are 'cases of moral choice to which appraisals are relevant'.

PART TWO (SECOND COURSE)

ON GODHOOD

LECTURE XI

THE CONCEPT OF RELIGION

1. In the prefatory remarks to my first course I indicated that what I took to be the central question for Natural Theology—the question which finds colloquial expression in the form 'Is religion true?'—would determine the direction of the whole series of lectures. It seemed to me desirable, however, to confine myself in the first course to certain prolegomena; and, in particular (moved by the strong contrary trend of so much recent philosophy), to attempt a systematic vindication of the human self as a genuinely substantival entity. For religion presupposes that there are human 'souls'. And if there are no *selves* in the sense of identical, per-during, spiritual beings, there are no *souls* in any sense that is relevant to religion. How far the vindication I offered was found satisfactory by my audience, I cannot say. I am venturing to assume, however, that this threat from the side of metaphysical philosophy to the meaningfulness of the question 'Is religion true?' need no longer detain us.

But there is another, and much more obvious, threat to the meaningfulness of our question. Although the expression 'the truth of religion' is so often on people's lips, one does not require to be a philosopher to feel some doubt whether, if taken strictly, any precise significance can be attached to it. For 'religion' is instantiated in a host of different 'religions', whose characteristic beliefs conflict with one another at many important points. How can we possibly enquire into the truth of something that comprises mutually contradictory sets of propositions? It would seem to make sense to ask 'Is religion true?' only if we arbitrarily choose to mean by the term 'religion' not religion as such, religion in its generic nature, but some specific religion (e.g. the Christian religion), or, at most, some specific group of religions (e.g. the theistic group) which closely approximate to one another in certain cardinal tenets.

And no doubt some such arbitrary meaning is in fact in most people's minds when they raise the question of 'the truth of religion'. Nevertheless it seems to me that the question *can* be intelligibly raised concerning religion as such, or in its generic nature. For the name 'religion' is, presumably, given to each of the different acknowledged religions on account of something taken to be common to them all. We imply, in naming them all 'religions', that there is some set of essential characteristics in virtue of which the term 'religion' is used, and that each of these religions does in fact exhibit this common essence. Now if this common essence includes (as it surely must) some body of *belief*. we may legitimately ask 'Is religion true?' meaning 'Are those beliefs which pertain to the common essence of religion true beliefs?'

Our question, then, would seem to be intelligible enough. But is it also a worth-while question? May it not be the case that when we have tracked down those residual elements of belief that are identical in everything that we recognise as 'religion', we shall find this common nucleus to be so minute that the question of its truth-value will excite nobody? That is, in the abstract, a genuine possibility. I do not myself believe, however, that it is the fact. It seems to me that the common essence of religious belief is both substantial and of the highest significance. But whether or not this claim is well-founded will depend upon the validity of the definition of the term 'religion' (or—what is the same thing from another angle—of the analysis of the general concept of religion) towards which I shall be gradually working my way in the course of today's lecture.

Now *prima facie* no enterprise would seem better suited to an opening lecture in the field of philosophy of religion than the attempt to give a *definition* of religion. Yet we have to recognise at once that objection may be taken to it precisely on the ground of its *un*suitability for an opening lecture. For are we not constantly being told by eminent scholars in this field that a definition of religion is something that can be given only at the *end*—that it is the *terminus ad quem* of the study of religion, not the *terminus a quo*, presupposing for its intelligent statement an extensive survey of, and intensive reflection upon, the phenomena of religion?

This is an extremely common view; but it seems to me to be mistaken, and to get such plausibility as it possesses from a confusion between two quite distinct senses of 'definition'. When we ask for the definition of anything we may be seeking to know simply the connotation of the term in ordinary educated usage. This is in the case of most terms easy enough to get, provided we are within reach of a good dictionary; for dictionaries exist to provide just such information. Or we may, on the other hand, be seeking to know what *the thing denoted by the term* really and essentially is. That is an entirely different story. The kind of knowledge sought here is the kind of knowledge which is the ultimate objective of all science and all philosophy. In the case of religion it is manifest that we could not even come within sight of the requisite knowledge until we have given the closest consideration to a whole host of difficult questions; about, e.g. the origins of religion in human experience; about the impact upon religion of social forces; about the manner of religion's development—if it does develop—and the apparent goal of that development; above all, about the justification of religion's claim to express an unique insight into the ultimate nature of reality. Without any doubt the definition of religion in this *second* sense can come, if at all, only at the end of 'extensive survey of and intense reflection upon the phenomena of religion'. But notice. Definition in this second sense *presupposes* definition in the first sense. The student of religion would not know what phenomena to survey and reflect upon in order to attain to a definition in the *second* sense if he did not already have a definition in the *first* sense to guide and control his enquiries. And in point of fact it is usually quite clear in the case of those writers on religion who insist that a definition is impossible at the beginning, that they themselves tacitly assume one from the beginning.[1] The working of an implicit definition in their minds reveals itself throughout in

[1] Cf. J. Laird, *Problems of the Self*, p. 8. 'The sage remark that a definition is the culmination rather than the starting-point of an enquiry is very properly disregarded even by those who make it.'

their selection of phenomena to be studied as phenomena of *religion*.

Definition in the first sense, then, *must* be possible at the beginning. Equally certainly, I think, it is desirable at the beginning; for it is always a good thing to make clear to one's self and others, as soon as convenient, what one is going to talk about. And though it may turn out to be no simple task (for not in *every* case is even the 'dictionary-type' definition easy of achievement), it will at least be nothing like so troublesome as the effort to frame a satisfactory definition in the second sense. Anyone beginning the philosophical study of religion might well be disconcerted by the discovery that Leuba [1] has listed no less than forty-eight different definitions of religion offered by reputable philosophers, and that Ducasse [2] claims to have noted a further twenty-seven. There would indeed be good cause for alarm and despondency if this chaos of opinion related to the kind of phenomena that it is correct to classify under the heading of 'religion'. In fact, however, these seventy-five definitions are, almost without exception, definitions in our *second* sense; definitions of what the *thing* denoted by the term really and essentially is. And in that sense great diversity of view is only to be expected, since definition here involves a man's whole philosophy. The task of definition we propose for ourselves, on the other hand, is at least relatively simple. The requirements of this kind of definition are merely that it should include all of the characteristics that must be present, and include no characteristic that may be absent, where the term 'religion' is being correctly used in English speech or writing.

I have described our task as a relatively simple one. I must now, however, lay some stress upon the qualifying word 'relatively'. Although we are looking for a dictionary-type definition of religion, our problem is not to be solved just by looking up a good dictionary. Even good dictionaries, we should find, differ among themselves quite significantly in the definitions they propose, and there is no way of escaping ultimate responsibility for our own preference. The trouble is that careless usages of the term 'religion' abound in common speech, and to determine the 'correct' usage among the variations that are current is very far

---

[1] *A Psychological Study of Religion* pp. 339-61.
[2] *A Philosophical Scrutiny of Religion*, p. 20.

from being an easy matter. Indeed there must, perhaps, remain some element of arbitrariness in whatever definition is finally decided upon. Nevertheless I am not without hope that if we keep steadily before us, as the criterion of correct usage, the usage of educated persons when they are choosing their words with critical care, the element of arbitrariness can be reduced to insignificant dimensions.

2. It will be helpful, I think, to begin by looking for a moment at two of the main sources of that loose and incorrect usage of the term 'religion' against which we have to be on our guard in our search for a definition.

The first is that 'religion' (if we may a little anticipate what will later be argued) is a term which stands for a complex pheno-menon with a considerable number of defining characteristics. Wherever that is the case, there is a temptation to use the term where only *some* of the defining characteristics are present, provided that the characteristics present are of a striking sort. It is on that account, no doubt, that one sometimes hears of a man 'making *science* his religion'—or perhaps even 'making a religion of *golf*'—where all that there is in common with the traditional exemplifications of religion is an all-absorbing devotion to a given object. I fancy that in fact those who so speak more than half realise that they are using the word 'religion' loosely; they are anxious merely to emphasise the 'religion-*like*' character of the devotion that some people have to science or to golf. On the other hand, I doubt if the same can be said of the growing tendency to speak, even in 'serious' contexts, of *Communism* as a 'religion', despite the fact that here too an 'all-absorbing devotion' seems to be about the only essential feature that Communism shares with what are usually called 'religions'. I am bound to say that it seems to me a considerable disservice to the English language to use 'religion' in the flattened-out sense of an all-absorbing devotion to X, irrespective of *what* X may be. Traditional usage has permitted the term 'religion' only where, broadly speaking, X denotes some supernatural being or beings believed to have real existence and to have rightful claims to human reverence. If the meaning of the term is to be gratuitously enfeebled so as to con-form to the practice of those who call Communism a religion—

or for that matter who call Humanism a religion—then it will become necessary to invent some new term for that highly distinctive and enormously important species of all-absorbing devotion which has for its object what is commonly meant by a 'god'. But it would be rather an absurd situation if we found ourselves forced by such inept linguistic practices to invent a new name for something for which the old name 'religion' has been deemed good enough for centuries.

The type of linguistic looseness of which I have been complaining has the effect of extending the denotation of the word 'religion' beyond all reasonable limits. We may note now a second type of linguistic looseness that has just the opposite effect. The word 'religion' denotes a genus which has a wide variety of species, and most people are familiar only with the species represented in their own native culture. There is a temptation in consequence to think of 'religion' in terms of this familiar species, and to use the word in a way which implies that illegitimate restriction. Thus people often say 'religion' where they are clearly thinking only of Christianity, or at the very most of the theistic type of religion. But that it is a loose and incorrect use, even those who are guilty of it could, as a rule, be readily induced to acknowledge. Were the question directly put to them, 'Do you mean to imply that there are no religions except Christianity?' they would almost certainly answer that of course this was not their intention and that in saying 'religion' when they meant 'the Christian religion' they were using inexact language.

These examples may serve to illustrate both certain common deviations from correct usage of the term religion, and also the general manner of establishing what the correct usage is. Always the appeal must be to what people *really* mean by the term when they are using it not just casually, but in a serious and considered way, with a due recognition of the implications of their usage. Throughout what follows it is by this criterion that we shall be guided.

3.   I begin with an assertion which, though one cannot say it has never been questioned, does not seem to me seriously disputable: viz. that 'religion' stands for something in which a certain state

or attitude of *mind* is fundamental. That this state or attitude of mind generally finds expression for itself in specific forms of bodily behaviour, which may, for short, be here summarised under the title 'ritual', no one would wish to deny. But to suppose —if indeed anyone really does suppose it—that *mere* ritual, with no awareness of its meaning, no awareness of any being in whose honour it is performed, can ever amount to even an elementary phase of religion, seems to me quite unwarranted. No doubt it may be the case (though I should myself accept it only with considerable reservations) that the mere performance of ritual dances and the like sometimes evokes in the performer for the first time the beliefs and emotions appropriate to religious worship. All that that implies, however, is that ritual performances may be a *stimulus* leading to religion, not that the performances were, prior to the emergence of the appropriate frame of mind, *themselves* religious acts. It does not imply, that is to say, that we can have an early phase of religion in which the worshipper has no notion of what it is all about, and then a later phase of the same thing in which the worshipper begins to appreciate the significance of what he is doing. On the contrary, there is so complete a break of continuity between the mechanical performance of the ritual and the performance of it as a conscious mode of worship that to speak of the two as earlier and later phases of *the same thing* is totally inadmissible. One might as well say of the small boy who is taken to church and 'goes through the motions' without a clue to their meaning, that he is, though in an elementary way, 'practising religion'. But of course sensible people don't say anything so absurd. I see no reason to suppose that, on reflection, they would be any more inclined to say it in the parallel case of the savage. They would agree, I think, that at least some tincture of an informing spirit has got to be present in ritual if it is to be an expression of 'religion' in any legitimate sense of that term.

It is not to be denied, of course, that when people speak of 'religion', and still more when they speak of 'a' religion, they have in mind a great deal more than just mental states and attitudes of a specified kind. They usually have in mind also the institutions and the systems of ritual observances and exercises in which the religious spirit commonly objectifies itself. But these are, after all, 'objectifications'. Their *source* lies in the religious spirit, which has a natural urge to seek expression for itself in outward forms. Moreover, not only is 'the spirit' *primary* in, as well as necessary to, religion. I think we must also grant that, strictly speaking, it is *self-sufficient* for religion, in the sense that we can have (though we rarely do have) what we should feel obliged to call 'religion' even where ritual expression of the 'spirit' is completely absent. No doubt we should be justly sceptical of the presence of a genuinely religious spirit in a man who gave no evidence of it whatever in the sphere of 'action'; for it is hard to see how a genuinely religious spirit could fail to make itself manifest in the practical conduct of life. But 'the practical conduct of life' can scarcely be identified with what is normally understood by 'ritual expression'; and provided we are satisfied that a man's conduct is not incompatible with the religious spirit, we should, I think, deem it improper to deny the presence in him of that spirit, and to withhold from him the right to be called 'religious', solely on the ground that he takes no part in those overt observances and ceremonies that constitute what is ordinarily meant by 'ritual'.

4.   I hope we may agree that religion is at least primarily a state of mind. But what *kind* of state of mind?

To a small, but very small, extent I have already anticipated the answer in speaking as though *beliefs* and *emotions* were certainly ingredient in it. But that assumption was not, perhaps, a very venturesome one. Only a few words seem necessary for its justification.

So far as emotion is concerned, I cannot conceive that anyone nowadays would dream of describing as 'religious' a state of mind that did not include certain characteristic emotions. Intellectual beliefs, even if they relate to the existence of supernatural beings, would certainly not be deemed enough. Religion is not religion at all, it would be said, unless there is present an attitude of *worship*. And the attitude of worship is conspicuously an emotive attitude.

On the other hand, the element of *belief* seems every bit as indispensable to the religious state. There is no need, to be sure, that belief should be articulated in any kind of formal creed. But the emotive attitude of worship is itself meaningless if there is not, at the very least, belief in the real existence of the being or beings towards whom the attitude is directed. One may remind one-self also that 'faith' is commonly accepted as a characteristic of the religious state, and that faith, whatever else it is, does at least involve some kind of belief. Or again, one might point to the general practice of using the terms 'believer' and 'unbeliever' as virtual synonyms for the religious and the irreligious man respectively. But it hardly seems necessary to defend further a thesis which is not likely to be denied save through some easily removable misapprehension.

We arrive at territory that admits of real debate, however—indeed we come to the crux of the whole matter—when we set about trying to determine the *common content* of religious belief. There is, in all religions, belief in the real existence of the object worshipped. What common characteristics can be assigned to this 'object'? The difficulties are obvious when we remember that the characteristics must be common to the objects of *everything* that we are prepared, in considered judgment, to describe as 'religion'. Our conclusions must be applicable to the primitive religion of the Australian Bushmen (if we are prepared to call it 'religion') and to the highly sophisticated religion of Liberal Christianity (if we are prepared to call *that* 'religion'). Remembering this, it is self-evident that the 'object' of religious worship must not be identified with the 'God' of Theism, and it is more than doubtful whether the term 'God' can properly be used of it at all.

Nevertheless there is, I think, a reasonably secure basis from which analysis may commence. In all religions the object that is believed in is an object that is *worshipped*, and therefore, presumably, is deemed 'worshipful'. We can say this at least, then, that religion involves belief in the existence of a being of supposedly *worshipful* character. Our immediate task must be to analyse this notion of the 'worshipful', to try to see what qualities a being must be taken to have in order to appear worthy of worship. In so far as we are successful, the qualities elicited can fairly be said to be qualities belonging generically to the object of religious belief; qualities which in any religion its 'object' is deemed to have—though it goes without saying that there may not in actual fact *be* any object that possesses such qualities.

Let us ask, then, what is involved in the notion of the worshipful.

5. I think it will be granted that there must always be, in the first place, a certain element of *mystery* about the worshipful object. It must be something quite out of the ordinary run of nature, animate or inanimate; something whose mode of being and functioning is not 'intelligible' to us in the way in which we suppose that the familiar processes in things and persons are 'intelligible'. However much of power and excellence a being may be supposed to have, still, if that excellence and power are conceived as merely the same in kind as these qualities as they are manifested in the natural order or the human order, one may admire, or love, or respect, or fear their owner, but an attitude of *worship* (I think we should agree) would be inappropriate. What is worshipful must always have, I think, something of *super*natural quality.

The term 'supernatural' would, of course, be open to objection in this context if it were the case that recognition of a supernatural element presupposes clear grasp of the abstract distinction between 'natural' and 'supernatural'; for it is plain that many primitive tribes which practise genuine worship cannot be supposed to have arrived at that level of intellectual sophistication. In point of fact, however, the recognition of particular instances of supernatural intervention would seem to presuppose nothing more than belief in a certain body of regularities of sequence and coexistence in one's environment. And so much one must presume to be present in any community, however primitive, if it is to live and survive at all. Its behaviour must be based upon definite habits of expectation corresponding to definite observed regularities in natural events. There is a 'natural' order for the savage no less than for his civilised brother, though it is much more precariously founded and covers a much narrower range of 'fact'. And when confronted by some striking deviation from his norm of the natural—some 'extra-ordinary' event—it is surely not beyond the capacity of the savage intelligence to frame the notion of some supernatural agency at work to account for its occurrence?

Moreover, there is an abundance of evidence that extremely primitive tribes, over many parts of the earth's surface, do recognise the supernatural in particular instances. The languages of many are known to include words of an unmistakably supernatural import; e.g. such roughly equivalent terms as *mana*, *orenda, wakanda,* and the like. Codrington (I quote here from Marett) has defined *mana,* in its Polynesian use, as 'a force altogether different from physical powers, which acts in all kinds of ways for good and evil',[1] and again as 'what works to effect everything which is beyond the ordinary powers of men, outside the common processes of nature'.[2] Recognition of the supernatural in this sense seems to be at least as primitive as anything we should ever want to describe as 'religion'. Indeed it is, almost certainly, a great deal *more* primitive.

6.   The worshipful, then, whatever else it may be, is something mysterious or supernatural. But of course the converse is not true. What is mysterious or supernatural need not be worshipful. The savage is no more moved to adopt an attitude of worship towards every entity that he conceives to be endowed with *mana* than the modern man feels moved to do obeisance to poltergeists. The supernatural, in and by itself, will evoke the emotion of wonder; though a wonder, admittedly, that differs in quality from, and is only analogous to, the wonder that may be occasioned in ordinary life by striking and not immediately intelligible events which we nevertheless take for granted are in principle capable of a natural explanation. But this 'supernatural' wonder is only one major strand in the complex emotive attitude of worship. Worship implies *adoration*; a supernatural rapture of which the natural emotions of admiration, joy, and love afford but a pale transcript. And with this second 'major strand' in the attitude of worship we are led to recognise a second major component of the worshipful. For 'adoration' is evoked only by that which is felt to be endued with a transcendent *worth* or *value*. We may safely take it, therefore, that in order for a supernatural being to qualify as a fit object of worship, this further condition at least must be fulfilled, namely that it be felt to be endued with transcendent value.

The presence of this 'value' element in the notion of the worshipful, and consequently in the generic object of religion, is, I think, beyond serious doubt. And it is a not uninstructive illustration of the grave confusion which is apt to result in

[1] *The Threshold of Religion,* by R. R. Marett, p. 104 (2nd edn.).
[2] *Op. cit.* p. 105.

philosophical and anthropological works on religion from the
failure to begin with a considered definition of the term 'religion',
that many writers have not hesitated to include, within the
category of religion, cults in which this 'value' element is totally
wanting. A notable example is the so-called 'apotropaic religions'.
The whole object of these cults is to mollify, by gifts and sacrifices,
certain supposed supernatural beings who are conceived to be
inherently hostile to man; to be, in fact, 'demons' rather than
'gods'. No doubt devotees of these cults go through elaborate
rituals that are externally not easily distinguishable from those of
religious worship. But the inner spirit is about as different as well
could be. It is one thing to make gifts and sacrifices to a supernatural being in a mood of reverence and love that delights to do
him honour. It is quite another thing to make them simply with
a view to buying from him immunity from malicious visitations.
Adhering to our criterion of correct usage, viz. the *duly considered*
linguistic usage of competent persons, I cannot think that the term
'religion' is properly applied to organised bribery on a vast scale,
even if it be supernatural powers to whom the bribes are offered.

The case is little better for regarding as primitive 'religions'
those cults which conceive their supernatural beings as favourably
disposed, or at worst neutral, towards the worshipper, and which
ply them with gifts and sacrifices in the hope that this will
encourage them to exercise their stupendous powers in beneficent
interventions. In so far as this, and this alone, is the motive that
inspires ritual acts, we come not a step nearer to religion proper.
Currying favour with gods is no more a 'religious' act than is
bribery of demons. Indeed it seems to me that both of these types
of ritual show a much closer approximation to magic than to
religion. In them as in magic, certain ceremonies are performed
whose object is to 'work upon' supernatural forces in the service
of natural human purposes. There are, of course, significant
differences also. One main difference is that, whereas the ritual of
the cults aims at making use of supernatural forces through the
agency of supernatural beings who are believed to have such forces
at their disposal, the ritual of magic is often designed to work
directly upon the supernatural forces, with no thought of supernatural beings as intermediary. In that respect, since religious
worship is normally, and perhaps always, directed to supernatural

beings, the cults may be said to come a little closer to religion than magic does. But if they come a little closer to religion, they must still be accounted leagues away from it, unless we are prepared to deny a proposition that to me at least seems indubitable, viz. that religion is fundamentally a matter not of overt acts, but of the inner spirit.

It is perhaps desirable to add, in order to avert possible misunderstanding, that what I have said is not intended to deny that the attitudes of propitiation and cajolement characteristic of these cults may linger on even after religion proper has emerged, and may be discernible ingredients in the state of mind that informs a ritual which is in other respects authentically religious. Obviously they can and often do so linger. There is no incompatibility—if there is also no organic connection—between desiring to do honour to a worshipful God, and desiring to enlist His good offices on one's own mundane behalf. Both motives can be present in the same ritual performance; and I think it must be admitted that in the actual practice of most religions both motives very often are present. But the fact that the attitudes of propitiation and cajolement are not incompatible with religion does not of course make them in any sense 'religious' attitudes. The externality of their relationship to religion is strikingly indicated by the acknowledged fact that, as religions develop in purity and realise more adequately their true nature as religion, these attitudes tend to lose their prominence, and ultimately to drop out altogether. Ritual acts once dominated by such attitudes may survive in the same, or almost the same, external form (for there are few more conservative institutions than the organised religious body); but when they do, a new interpretation is generally found for them which has nothing to do with attempts to propitiate or cajole.

Something must now be said about a phenomenon which, though no doubt as rare as it is strange, may well seem at first sight to cast doubt upon our contention that a value element is intrinsic to the 'worshipful'. What about *Devil*-worship? Certain very peculiar ceremonies, to which the name 'Devil-worship'—or alternatively 'Diabolism' or 'Satanism'—is commonly given, do undeniably take place even at the present day. Now is not the essence of Devil-worship the doing obeisance to the very principle of Evil? And how is this to be reconciled with the claim that nothing can be deemed worshipful that is not also deemed good or valuable?

The difficulty has, I think, a fairly simple solution; but it requires that two distinct points be made.

In the first place, it is extremely questionable whether much, if any, of what is called Devil-worship is really Devil-*worship*, or would continue to be so called if people had clearer views about the nature of the thing they were labelling and were exercising proper care in their choice of language. There is in all cases, admittedly, a ritual closely resembling in externals the ritual of genuine worship, and it is to the supposed 'Devil' that it is directed. But the frame of mind informing the ritual is probably, much more often than not, that of the pseudo-religious cults to which we have lately been referring. Certain stereotyped acts believed pleasing to the Devil are performed; not, however, out of *esteem* for the Prince of Darkness, but in order to induce him in return to exert his supernatural power in the interests of the 'worshippers', securing for them the dazzling array of earthly (and earthy) prizes which, it is supposed, the Devil can and will bestow upon those who formally commit themselves to him. The 'pacts with the Devil' of which we hear so much in medieval times seem to have been of this general character. But where such is the case, it is clear that so-called 'Devil-*worship*' is at bottom a mere bargaining transaction, aimed at the purchase of diabolical favours; and 'worship' is surely quite the wrong name to give to it. It seems to me that we have here another example of inept linguistic usage, where a word is applied to something which resembles in conspicuous respects that which the word primarily denotes, the important difference which makes the application of the word in this context grossly improper being carelessly overlooked.

Obviously, however, this answer will not suffice of itself so long as we admit the possibility of any case of genuine Devil-*worship*, any case in which the Devil is honoured, as it were, 'for his own sake'; and I do not think we can by any means rule out this possibility. The solution in that case must turn, I think, upon the distinction between *objective* and *subjective* value; between value in the sense of that which is *truly* valuable, and value in the sense of that which someone *deems to be* valuable. It would certainly be absurd if we had claimed that nothing can be deemed 'worshipful' except that which is *truly* valuable. All that in fact we have claimed is that nothing can be deemed 'worshipful' unless it be thought by the worshipper to have value. Now the honouring of the Devil 'for his own sake' implies the attribution to him by the worshipper of 'subjective' value. And modern developments in abnormal psychology have gone far to make intelligible to us how this can come about. The content of the subjectively good or valuable is based upon nothing more exalted than actual human desire, and there seems no assignable limit to the possible perversions of human desires. It is in principle possible for the human soul to be so perverted that a man will take his greatest satisfaction to lie in a programme for living that conflicts at every major point with the traditional values of Christendom—in a programme that exalts hatred and cruelty and lust and pride and avarice. If such a person also believes (as many people still do) in the actual existence of the Devil, as a supernatural being who is the very prototype of all 'fiendish' qualities, the stage is perfectly set for 'Devil-worship'. But then Devil-worship, so understood, is plainly *not* a case of the worship of evil *as evil*. It is the worship of evil (or of what most people consider evil) in the *belief* that it is supremely good. Hence there is nothing here that is inconsistent with the analysis of the worshipful which we have been proposing. 'Devil-worship', so understood, is a genuine enough species of religion; a very *bad* species, it is true, but the genus 'religion', I fear we must admit, does include some very bad species.

7. I turn now to the third and last of what I take to be the essential components of the worshipful. It is one which, fortunately, calls for less extensive treatment than the value component, since in this case we are little, if at all, troubled by instances of ostensible 'worship' which are incompatible with it. The worshipful being is always a being deemed by the worshipper to be not only supernatural, and not only endued with transcendent worth or value, but also to have transcendent *power*.

This is perhaps most easily seen by reminding ourselves of the fact (as I take it everyone will admit it to be) that no less indispensable to the attitude of genuine worship than wonder and rapture, and in close integration with these, is the emotion of *awe*. Now the objective correlate of awe is *power*, power that is at once mysterious and overwhelming. It is clearly not enough that the power be merely mysterious (in the sense of supernatural). The supernatural as such is no doubt always credited with a mysterious power which excites our dread and wonder, but this mysterious power need not be on any majestic scale; and where it is not (as in the case of the ordinary kind of 'spook'), it does not inspire *awe*. Ingredient in the emotion of awe is a certain deep humility and self-abasement before the sheer magnitude of the mysterious power that confronts us; and it is pretty evident that though we may be terrified, we do not feel ourselves humbled or abased, in the presence of the ordinary kind of spook. If the supernatural object is to inspire awe it must then, I think, be accredited with a power not merely mysterious but also overwhelming; a 'transcendent' power, if that term may be accepted as combining in its connotation the force of both adjectives.

A more debatable question, but one over which we need not linger too long here, is whether *all* awe is *religious* awe. The answer to that question turns, as I see it, on the character of the value aspect which is conceived to belong to the awe-inspiring object. McDougall seems to me right to insist that in the emotion of awe there is always present, in addition to fear and wonder, an element of 'admiration'; and in that case there must presumably be recognition of value of some sort in the awe-inspiring object as the correlate of the admiration. But granted that admiration is a necessary constituent of awe, it need be no more, I suggest, than admiration for the supernatural being in respect of such value as consists in its possession of overwhelming power—for power as such, especially if it be very great, does normally evoke admiration —and this is compatible with the actual *dis*valuation of the supernatural being in respect of other of its characteristics and as a whole. Now if this be so, all that one is committed to holding in the way of 'value' concerning a being that inspires awe is that value is ascribed to some particular feature of it; not necessarily that value belongs to the being itself, in its integrity as an individual. And it will then follow that not *all* awe is religious awe. For in the religious attitude it seems certain that the worshipful being is taken as admirable *in itself*, not merely in respect of some feature or features which may be offset (as in the case, perhaps, of the traditional Satan) by other features that are far from admirable.

8. Mystery, Power, Value—in all essentials Otto's *Mysterium Tremendum et Fascinans*—these, then, seem to me to be the basic characteristics of the worshipful. Of course their degree of emphasis, both absolute and relatively to one another, varies enormously in different concrete religious states, and likewise in different historical religions. Mystery and Power, e.g. tend to be paramount in primitive religions. The first impact of the supernatural upon the primitive mind is by way of *power* manifestations. *Mana*, as we saw, is little, if anything, more than 'supernatural power'. Even when religion proper emerges, and transcendent value is integrated with transcendent power in a supernatural being who for the first time becomes an object of *worship*, the power element as a rule remains for long the dominant one. In the later developments of religion the three elements appear in an almost infinite variety of emphases. But always, I think, all three are present in *some* degree.

Our purpose in undertaking an analysis of the 'worshipful', it will be remembered, was to enable us to supply filling for the common content of religious beliefs. Since in all religion the object that is believed in is an object of worship, and therefore (presumably) deemed worshipful, it seemed to follow that whatever characteristics could be shown to belong indispensably to the worshipful would thereby be shown also to be indispensable components of the object of religious belief. We have done what we could to elicit these characteristics of the worshipful, and in their light we infer that in all that is properly called 'religion' there is belief in a supernatural being, or in supernatural beings, of transcendent worth and power. Are there any further qualities that can legitimately be ascribed to the 'generic' object of religious belief? For my own part, I can detect none. I think, in fact, we are now in a position to complete our initial task in this course by offering a definition of the term 'religion'. But I shall defer its actual formulation until the next lecture, in order that I may have the opportunity of answering immediately certain objections which it may very easily, though I think mistakenly, provoke.

RELIGION AND THEISM

1. At the close of my last lecture I intimated that the stage was now set for attempting the formal definition of religion. I deemed it expedient, however, to postpone my definition until today, since it was apparent to me that, baldly stated, it would seem to some to be much too narrow, and to others to be much too broad; and I was anxious to be in a position to rally at once to my own defence, which I could hardly have done satisfactorily in a lecture's dying moments.

Reminding you that I am using 'definition' in the sense in which definition formulates what the term connotes in the careful and considered linguistic usage of competent persons, and reminding you also that it is religion in its basic form as an *experience*, not religion as the objectification of that experience in historic institutions, that we are concerned with, I suggest that religion may be defined as 'a state of mind comprising belief in the reality of a supernatural being or beings endued with transcendent power and worth, together with the complex emotive attitude of worship intrinsically appropriate thereto'.

So far as I can see, it makes no difference whether one chooses to put 'belief' first or 'emotion' first in the definition; for the character of the belief that is intrinsic to religion implies the emotive attitude, and the character of the emotive attitude that is intrinsic to religion implies the belief. If I have myself preferred to put 'belief' first, that is merely because it is the belief element that is directly relevant to the question at the origin of our whole enquiry; the question, 'Is religion true?'

But as I have admitted, the definition is likely to seem too narrow to some, too broad to others; some will feel that there are items in it which are not indispensable to what one means by 'religion', others that there are items *not* in it which *are* indispensable to what one means by 'religion'. Let me deal first with the charge that our definition is too narrow.

2.   This charge is most likely to be based, I think, on our requirement that the religious 'object' be a *supernatural* being or beings. To insist upon this, it will be said, is arbitrarily to disqualify from admission to the fold certain 'religions' whose claim to be so called seems really unexceptionable. Does it not disqualify Buddhism, for example, a religion of an antiquity greater by half a millenium than that of Christianity itself, a religion which today numbers among its professed disciples some hundreds of millions of human souls?

The answer to this question seems to me to depend entirely upon what is being meant by 'Buddhism'. Everyone is agreed that there are striking differences between the Buddhism of its founder Gautama—what may be called the 'pure milk of the gospel' —and the Buddhism of those popular versions of the original doctrine which emerged within a comparatively few years of the Buddha's death and rapidly spread through a great part of the Eastern hemisphere; versions in which the 'pure milk' is, to say the least of it, diluted. The most notable difference is with respect to supernatural objects of worship. It is commonly (though not universally) accepted that the original Buddhism gave no recognition to such beings. In the popular versions of Buddhism, on the other hand, the Buddhism which every traveller in the Orient will constantly encounter, they play a very conspicuous part. 'Buddhism as we know it' Professor John Baillie has remarked, 'so far from being godless, seems to be only too well off with deities'.[1]

Now it is this later Buddhism, replete with all the trappings of the supernatural, that is the spiritual faith of so many millions, and that, by the vast range of its appeal, can stake a good claim to be one of the great historical religions of the world. And obviously no definition of religion can come anywhere near to being satisfactory which does not find room for *it*. Equally obviously,

---

[1] *The Interpretation of Religion*, p. 387.

however, our own definition does find room for it. It is only the
original Buddhism which (on the assumption that this discoun-
tenances supernatural objects of worship) our definition would
exclude. And why should we *not* exclude it? The very fact that
it has at no time succeeded in attracting the allegiance of more
than a tiny minority even among those who profess themselves
Buddhists suggests strongly that the religious consciousness itself
finds it wanting. Nor can it be argued with any force that the
undeniable continuity of later Buddhism with original Buddhism,
in virtue of which the common name 'Buddhism' is given to both,
entails that if we call the one 'religion' we cannot with propriety
withhold that name from the other. For continuity in some
respects is compatible with *dis*continuity in others. If we take the
orthodox view of the content of the Buddha's teaching, the
continuity of later with original Buddhism would seem to be only
in respect of ethics, psychology, and (in a sense) metaphysics, and
there is *dis*continuity in so fundamental a respect as the recognition
of supernatural objects of worship. In so far as that is the case,
there is, I suggest, ample ground for refusing to attach the same
descriptive label to both of them.

In short, I cannot see that the case of Buddhism offers any
real difficulty for our definition of religion. It may well be that,
as certain scholars maintain, even the original Buddhism finds
some place for worship of supernatural beings. If so, then it, as
well as later Buddhism, will be accommodated within our definition. But if the other view is the correct one, and the original
Buddhism was rather a philosophy of life dominated by a
singularly noble and austere ethic, there really seems no good
reason why it should be called anything else.

So far as I can judge, the answer here made to the charge that
my definition of religion is too narrow to include Buddhism is
equally applicable, *mutatis mutandis*, to other cases of historic
religions (e.g. Jainism and Confucianism) which contain no
obvious reference to the supernatural.

3. Let us turn then to the opposite ground of complaint, i.e.
that our definition is too broad, omitting certain items that are
essential to anything that can properly be called 'religion'.

Two such omissions seem likely to be charged against me. On one of them I have already said something at an earlier stage of the argument, but it may be well to add a few words to the somewhat cursory justification then submitted. I refer to *ritual*, which many people find it difficult not to regard as an integral part of any genuine religion.

I have excluded ritual from my definition very deliberately, because in my view it is, though a normal, ultimately a dispensable, manifestation of religion. I do not doubt for a moment that carefully selected, formalised action-patterns and speech-forms, gestures and posturings, rhythms of colour and line and sound, and whatever else may be included within the wide ambit of the term 'ritual', are for many minds of inestimable aid in evoking, heightening, and giving outlet to the emotions intrinsic to religious worship. But I cannot doubt either that to some minds, differently constituted and with perhaps a different theological orientation, these *auxilia imaginationis* can seem superfluous—nay, even a positive barrier, which partially inhibits that pure communing of spirit with spirit at which their worship aims. Historically, of course, religions differ enormously from one to another in the amount of sensuous symbolism they include, and in the degree of importance they attach to it. I can see no inconsistency of principle in the concept of a religion which disavows it altogether. The attitude of worship, we have agreed, is indispensable to religion. But may there not be a worship of silent, awe-struck adoration, where the worshipper's whole spiritual being, mind and heart and soul, is utterly concentrated upon the Divine object, and where the intrusion of sensory stimuli of whatever kind seems well-nigh intolerable? Quakerism, though not Quakerism alone, comes very near to it. Rudolf Otto has described the Quaker worship of 'silent waiting upon God' as 'the most spiritual form of divine service that has ever been practised'.[1] And whether or not we can wholly acquiesce in this judgment, few of us, I think, would have much confidence in the spiritual discernment of anyone who was prepared to exclude Quakerism from the family of genuine religions.

It may be objected in the second place, on what I cannot but feel to be much stronger grounds, that my definition, while duly

[1] *The Idea of the Holy* (English trs. by J. W. Harvey), p. 216.

recognising that transcendence is a character that is intrinsic to the object of religious worship, has nothing to say of Divine *immanence*. Does it not belong to the essence of religion that God (if for convenience and without committing ourselves to anything, we may use this term for the object of religious worship) is conceived not merely as transcending the world of men but also as somehow operative within it? For the religious man, must we not say, God is a *living presence*, sustaining and vitalising through the workings of His Holy Spirit the hearts of those that put their trust in Him? And must not something to indicate this aspect be included in any satisfactory definition of what the term 'religion' means?

I have, in point of fact, felt a good deal tempted to include in my definition something to this effect. But in the end I have judged that to do so would be a mistake. For while I do not doubt that the personal religion of most people—whether they be devotees of very primitive religions or of advanced religions like Christianity—does involve belief in some kind of Divine immanence, it seems to me not really possible to ignore the claims of *Deism* to be accounted a type of religion. Yet the distinctive characteristic of Deism, as I understand it, is precisely its rejection of the concept of God as immanent in His creation. For Deism, God is a spiritual being of transcendent power and worth and wisdom, and the Creator of the universe. But, having created it, the Deistic God seeks to modify *ad hoc* neither the orderly processes of Nature (which, after all, are obeying laws which He deliberately instituted), nor the wills and purposes of men (whom, after all, He has deliberately made as beings endowed with the power of self-direction).

It is easy to scoff at the Deistic conception of a God reigning in lonely splendour aloof from His creation; and certainly no one could claim that such is the nature of the God that is worshipped according to the Christian faith. But the crucial point for us here is not that, but just whether a Being so conceived is a possible object of worship. If He is not, then certainly a definition of religion is unsatisfactory if it leaves room for Deism as one of its possible varieties, and our definition will require adjustment accordingly. I am bound to say, however, that I am unable to discover convincing reasons why the God of Deism should not be capable of evoking the attitude of worship, and it seems to me that, as a matter of plain historic fact, such a Being *has* sometimes been worshipped. Moreover, I find it hard to credit that even those who personally have an unshakable belief in the immanence of God would wish to go further in disparagement of Deism than to say that it is an inferior brand of religion. They would be reluctant to say, I think, that it is not a brand of religion at all.

These being, so far as I can see, the main, though doubtless not the only, sins of omission and commission likely to be charged against my definition of religion, I am venturing to leave that definition as it stands. Whatever its shortcomings, I hope and believe that it departs in no vital respect from what the generic term 'religion' means in the careful and considered linguistic usage of competent persons at the present day.

4. In the light of our definition, then, let us now proceed to consider the meaning of the question to which, in some sense of it, everyone wants the answer, the question 'Is religion true?'

It is quite clear, I think, what this question *ought* to mean. Religion in its generic nature entails, as we have seen, belief in the reality of at least one supernatural being of transcendent power and value. The question 'Is religion true?' ought to mean, therefore, 'Is it the case that there exists at least one supernatural being of transcendent power and value?'

Now that is, I think, a tolerably important question even as it stands. It has to be admitted at once, however, that *as it stands* it represents most inadequately what the ordinary enquirer really wants to know when he asks whether religion is true. Suppose it to be answered in the affirmative—that there does exist at least one such being. The answer says nothing at all about a great deal that is almost certainly in the enquirer's mind when he asks the question. It leaves wholly undecided such fundamental questions as whether there is a plurality of Gods or only one God; whether, if there is only one God, He is finite or infinite—that is to say, whether He is a Being subject to limitation from without, or a Being that is self-complete and in some sense the ground of all that is; whether this Being is to be conceived as personal, or as impersonal, or perhaps as supra-personal; whether, again (the

K

question upon which we touched a few minutes ago), He is or is not immanent in the world, affecting the course of events, natural and spiritual, here and now; and doubtless other important questions besides. In short, an affirmative answer to the question 'Is religion true?' in its strict meaning will be perfectly compatible with *either* the truth *or* the falsity of many propositions that almost certainly will seem to the enquirer of the utmost importance for answering the question as he understands it. He is not getting an answer to what he really wants to know. Of course, if the answer to the question in its strict meaning should be a straight negative, the further questions that are implicit in the questioner's mind *will* be answered; though the answers may not be very much to his liking. The negative answer, unlike the affirmative, leaves undecided none of the questions listed above. Or rather, to speak more accurately, it renders these questions meaningless.

Now if the answer to the question 'Is religion true?' in its strict 'generic' meaning cannot tell the ordinary enquirer more than a fraction of what he wants to know when he puts the question—unless the answer happens to be a straight negative—it looks very much as though we had been wrong in our claim at the beginning of this course that the question of the truth of religion as such, or in its generic nature, was one of the very highest significance. The plain fact would seem to be that, at least among most educated persons in the community to which we belong, and perhaps in the civilised world as a whole, what the man who asks 'Is religion true?' is really concerned about is whether *Theism* is true. He wants to know (if we may venture roughly to summarise the chief tenets characteristic of Theism) whether there are or are not good reasons for believing in the reality of a Single, Infinite and Eternal Spirit, Perfect in Power, Wisdom and Goodness, Who is the source of all that is, Who is the Moral Governor of the World, and Who is yet a living presence in the hearts of men. But between the truth of religion as such, and the truth of Theism as thus formulated, it at least looks as though the gap were one that could not easily be spanned.

But is the gap really as wide as it at first sight appears to be? That is just what I am going to call in question. If it were as wide as it appears to be, it would be difficult to censure too sharply the slovenly language of those who ask 'Is religion true?' when what they really mean is 'Is Theism true?' But I am by no means sure that their implicit identification of religion with theism is merely, or even mainly, a matter of linguistic ineptitude. Underlying this identification in their minds, and giving meaning to it, there is present, I think, a certain assumption; the assumption, namely, that theism is not just one species of religion among others, but rather the *proper culmination of the development that is intrinsic to religion as such*. It is dimly felt, that is to say, that the theistic conception of the object of religious worship only brings out explicitly what is already implied in the generic religious notion of a supernatural being of transcendent power and value. Given the presence of that assumption, we can readily understand how the question of the truth of religion should be taken as virtually equivalent to the question of the truth of theism. If the beliefs characteristic of theism are just what the beliefs intrinsic to the generic religious attitude become when fully and clearly thought out, then in so far as the beliefs of religion in its generic sense are true, so also will be the beliefs of theism.

I am of the opinion that some such assumption must be deemed to be operative if we are to explain the otherwise very surprising prevalence of the practice of identifying the question 'Is religion true?' with the question 'Is theism true?' But the important thing, of course, is whether there are good reasons for supposing the assumption to be sound. I think that there are good reasons. I believe that the identification of religion with theism in the manner indicated has solid foundations both of an empirical and of a logical order. I shall say something first of its empirical justification.

5. The empirical justification lies in the historical evidence of close correlation between theism and intellectual culture. By and large it would appear to be true that the only religions that have shown any power of sustained appeal to communities enjoying a high level of intellectual culture have been theistic religions. This may seem at first glance a somewhat rash statement; and of course anything like a rigorous demonstration of its truth would require a volume. Nevertheless I am not at all sure but that, on reflection, the statement may appear more open to objection on the score of platitude than on the score of over-boldness.

The easiest way to test the truth of the statement is, I think, to ask one's self the simple question, 'What sizeable community can one in fact name in which the general level of intellectual culture is high and the religion practised (if any is practised) is not dominantly theistic?'

It is perfectly true, of course, that many communities not at all high in the intellectual scale have *also* embraced some form of theistic religion. But that is no argument against the generalisation we are proposing, which is that *all* enlightened communities, but not necessarily *only* enlightened communities, tend to adopt theism. It is very evident that there are other determinants of theism besides the pressure of intellectual criticism upon the content of belief. A particular theistic religion might make a strong appeal to a people because it happens to contain features emotively congenial to that people, and not in the least because of any superior theoretic value in the theistic theology. Indeed I suppose it would be generally agreed that this is the rule rather than the exception, and that the intellectual consistency of a religion's theology has comparatively little to do with the hold of that religion upon the affections of the great mass of its devotees even in relatively civilised communities, let alone in those primitive communities that have been converted to some form of theism by missionary enterprise. But all this is entirely compatible with the principle that, given a tolerably high level of intellectual culture, the tendency is to be dissatisfied with a religion until it assumes the theistic form.

Let us look for a little, then, at the question we asked ourselves, 'What sizeable community can one name in which the general level of intellectual culture is high and the religion practised (if any is practised) is not dominantly theistic?'

It is no doubt rather an invidious proceeding to institute comparisons between the nations of the world in respect of their degree of intellectual culture. Its offensiveness is at least mitigated, however, by the fact that, bearing in mind that we are concerned with the cultural level of communities in general, irrespective of particular sections which may rise notably above (or fall notably below) the general level, there would really seem to be very little difference of opinion about the broad divisions that fall to be made. There would, I take it, be virtual unanimity about including in the upper reaches most European countries, the U.S.A., and the white populations of Australasia, Canada, South Africa, and Latin America: in all of which, it need scarcely be said, religion is overwhelmingly theistic in character. And if we steadily bear in mind that a sprinkling of brilliant invididuals, or even groups, does not suffice to constitute an intellectually enlightened *community*, we should surely be hard put to it to extend the list much further. We might be tempted at first to add such great countries as India and China; rather sentimentally, perhaps, on account of the great antiquity of their civilisations, more relevantly because we are all well aware that these countries include today among their nationals not only a great many highly educated men and women, but also not a few sages and savants who would be outstanding in any intellectual company in the world. But that the temptation should be resisted is evident as soon as we remember that the intellectual leaders of these nations are the very foremost to deplore the ignorance and illiteracy of the great mass of their fellow-nationals, and would never dream of claiming high cultural status for their countries in general.

Indeed, so far as contemporary civilisations are concerned, there seems to me only one nation which could stake a serious claim to be added to our list; viz. Japan. But the case of Japan must be admitted to constitute a *prima facie* difficulty for our thesis. For while modern Japan would certainly be reckoned by most people to be a highly educated community, its national religion— Shintoism—is emphatically not theistic. Nor does there seem to be the slightest evidence of serious movements for religious reform in that direction. It looks as though we might have to admit here a disturbing exception to our general principle that intellectual culture in its application to religion tends to beget theism.

Nevertheless I do not think that our thesis is really placed in jeopardy by the non-theistic religion of educated Japan, and I shall try to explain why.

In the first place, it must be understood that our principle does not claim more than that intellectual culture *tends* to beget theism. Like other tendencies, this tendency can be offset by contrary tendencies. And we are, of course, obliged to recognise, with everyone else, that in the complex web of historical process there are powerful agencies constantly at work opposing the critical application of the intellect to a nation's traditional religion. The inhibiting agencies vary greatly in force in different countries: but even in countries like our own, with a very high degree of religious freedom, countries where legal penalties for unorthodoxy are almost inconceivable, their effect is far from negligible. We need not elaborate, but merely indicate, what is, after all, a commonplace. The inhibitions in question are both external and internal. Thus there are in every religious community *social* sanctions against unorthodoxy, of a more or less formidable kind. The ordinary man deeply resents any challenge to his religion, and the religious pioneer will need, as a rule, considerable strength of character and conviction to bear with equanimity the manifest disapproval of the great bulk of his affronted fellow-citizens. The internal obstacles to the free play of intellectual criticism are hardly less strong. For where the early conditioning of belief is as zealous and as ubiquitous as is normally the case in a religious community, habits of thought are generated that are as difficult to break as habits of action. To dissociate one's self even in one's private thinking from the traditional religious beliefs embedded in childhood and consolidated in youth is for many persons an even harder task (though of course for different reasons) than dissociating one's self in public pronouncements. Examples abound of men of distinguished intellectual attainments who seem virtually stone-blind to damaging implications for their religious views of ideas in related fields of experience which they wholeheartedly accept *within these fields*. The enormous power of the early conditioning of belief to incapacitate a man from 'thinking straight' on matters affecting such belief we are all of us very ready to acknowledge where that early conditioning is secular in character. We could hardly escape acknowledging it in view of the recent history of Europe. I think there is a rather marked reluctance to acknowledge it where the early conditioning happens to be religious.

These inhibiting agencies, I have said, are always present, though in varying degrees. Where there is reason to suppose that they are present in some country in surpassing strength, we should naturally expect in that country an advance much slower than usual, and perhaps no advance at all, towards the theism that is, on our

hypothesis, the logical *terminus ad quem* of the religious consciousness when it functions in co-operation with an enlightened
intelligence. What we have to note now is that in the case of Japan
the inhibiting agencies are rendered almost uniquely strong by
the inclusion of a special factor. For in Japanese Shintoism (or,
to be quite precise, in Japanese State Shintoism) we have the
phenomenon of a traditional religion that is linked up in the most
intimate way with *national patriotism*; a religion in which reverence
for the gods is inseparably united with love for one's native land.
Inevitably the effect will be to intensify vastly the popular indigna-
tion against any radical expression of religious heresy. Moreover,
it is only to be expected that national statesmanship will exploit
such a situation to the full. Even in time of peace it will be much
to the advantage of the rulers to foster the traditional religious
spirit, so that the call for service to the nation will carry with it
the profound emotional force of a call to religious duty. In times
of national danger (real or supposed), or in times when territorial
aggrandisement is a matter of settled national policy and plans
for aggressive war are in process of incubation, the 'playing up'
of the identity of religion and patriotism will be more vigorous
than ever. What hope is there, in such circumstances, of even the
bolder spirits venturing upon pronouncements critical of the
traditional religion, since these pronouncements will also appear
as subversive of the state, and even (on account of the unique
place of the Emperor in Shintoism) as an expression of *lèse-
majesté?*

But now the plain fact of the matter is that since the time that
Japan did become an 'educated' nation (and that is, after all,
fairly recent—only in the 1880's was compulsory elementary
education introduced), its circumstances have been, almost
without intermission, precisely those that we have just described.
In consequence the sanctions operating against overt criticism of
traditional religion in Japan have been so powerful that it would
be totally unrealistic to expect over that period anything in the
nature of a movement of religious reform in the direction of
theism, or indeed in any direction other than that of a still closer
identification of religion and nationalism.

And there is yet another factor inimical to criticism of religion
in educated Japan that is worth a passing mention. I have followed

custom, rather than personal judgment, in speaking of Japan as an 'educated' nation. This is no place to debate the question of what criteria are proper for the description of a person or a community as 'educated'; but it is permissible to point out that what 'education' has meant for the Japanese is something far removed from that conception of a 'liberal education' which has been the guiding ideal (however defectively implemented) in countries like our own. We in Britain would hesitate to call a man really educated (and certainly we should not describe him as intellectually cultured) if he were virtually devoid of knowledge concerning the diversity of views that have been proposed by eminent world-thinkers upon the more fundamental problems of human life and destiny; or, again, if he had not had instilled into him the desirability of the habit of impartial appraisal of competing theories by the free exercise of his own reason. The spirit of Japanese education is utterly different. It is true that in science, in commerce, in economics, in technology, the student is exhorted to learn all that the West can teach him, and that he has no lack of freedom there to think for himself and to pioneer new tracts of country. But free-thinking in such matters as morals, politics, sociology, or philosophy is quite another story. The heavily censored Japanese educational programme, not to speak of the 'Ministry of Thought Guidance', ensures that in these realms there will be no encouragement to the youth of the nation to develop dangerous ideas of their own. *There* it is *authority*, backed by an age-old tradition, not the individual reason, that is the ultimate court of appeal.

This consideration ought, I think, to dispose of any last lingering doubts about the compatibility of the continued prevalence of non-theistic Shintoism in educated Japan with our principle that intellectual culture tends to beget theism. For it now appears that the Japanese community, despite the undoubted thoroughness and excellence of its education in many respects, is nevertheless in large measure debarred from precisely those elements in the culture of the intellect which provide the substance, and the impetus, for critical reflection upon one's traditional religious beliefs.

Finally, there is one further general point in connection with the empirical justification of our hypothesis which deserves a few moments' attention. It is evident that in some of the countries whose religion is non-theistic, and in which the masses are largely ignorant and illiterate, there are yet pockets of the population—sometimes very large pockets—in which the intellectual culture is of a very high order. India is a conspicuous example. If our hypothesis is sound, therefore, ought we not to be able to detect in these 'pockets of enlightenment' at least a tendency in the direction of theism? More particularly so, one might expect, in India, since Hinduism is distinguished from almost all other religions in the generous tolerance it shows for diversity within its ranks. There, neither external nor internal sanctions should be strong enough to prevent the development of theistic beliefs, if theism is indeed the natural development of a religion that accepts the free co-operation of the intellect.

I think that this demand upon our hypothesis is a reasonable one; and I also think that in fact it is met. The case of India is very significant. Everyone knows that the Hindu Pantheon is thronged with a multitude of gods and goddesses of the most diverse attributes, some worshipped by one, others by another, of the many sects that Hinduism officially recognises. But polytheistic worship belongs to *popular* Hinduism, rather than to the Hinduism of the pundit or sage. The Hindu sage does not in any strict sense believe in, let alone worship, any of these finite and imperfect deities of the popular religion. He *tolerates* the worship of them—or at any rate of the best of them—because, in his view, with all their shortcomings they do represent for the crude imagination of the unlettered at least *some*thing of the many, faceted and many-splendoured Being that is the one true God. Better, he feels, that God be worshipped in these blurred and fragmentary images than that He be not worshipped at all. But he himself is under no illusions about their ultimate inadequacy as objects of worship. Moreover, he conceives it his duty to guide —though never to force—the unenlightened worshipper towards worthier conceptions of Godhood, and thus (as Radhakrishnan says) to 'further his spiritual growth by lending a sympathetic and helping hand wherever he stands'.[1] 'Hinduism', writes Radhakrishnan, 'requires every man to think steadily on life's meaning until he reaches the highest revelation. While the lower forms are

[1] *The Hindu View of Life*, p. 49.

tolerated in the interests of those who cannot suddenly transcend them, there is all through an insistence on the larger view and the purer worship.'[1] And this 'larger view and purer worship', there can be no doubt, is theistic. We have in Hinduism, I suggest, a first class empirical illustration of the general principle for which we are arguing, viz. that the religious consciousness that is intellectually enlightened moves naturally in the direction of theism.

6.　I turn now to the logical, as distinct from the empirical, justification of our thesis: but let us see first just what precisely the logical justification involves.

Religion in its generic character, it will be recalled, we came to define as 'belief in the reality of a supernatural being or beings of transcendent power and value, together with the complex emotive attitude of worship intrinsically appropriate thereto'. Theism we made no attempt to define in any rigorous way, but were content to accept as sufficient for our purpose what seemed to us to be fairly generally accepted as the common core of theistic doctrine: belief in 'One God, Perfect in Power, Wisdom, and Goodness, an Infinite and Eternal Spirit Who is the ultimate ground of all that is, Who is the Moral Governor of the world, and Who is at the same time a Living Presence in the hearts of men'. The logical justification of our thesis will consist in showing how the generic beliefs of religion, when their implications are reflected upon, turn out to entail the more specific set of beliefs characteristic of theism.

This 'logical nisus' of the religious consciousness has, of course, been *one* of the determinants of religion's historical development towards theism; though not always, and perhaps not often, a very powerful one. There have been occasions when it has had, apparently, almost nothing to do with a community's adoption of theism—one recalls how the official substitution of Christianity for Paganism in the Roman world, decreed by the Emperor Constantine, hung upon nothing more relevant to its theological validity than the outcome of a battle! On the other hand, from the standpoint of theological validity it is clearly the

[1] *The Hindu View of Life*, p. 49.

logical nisus that matters; for we have here the development of religion in so far forth as that is determined by no considerations whatsoever save the truth-value of its beliefs.

But in speaking thus of a 'logical' development towards theism we perhaps run the risk of some misunderstanding. Let me emphasise, therefore, that what we are here referring to is a logical development *of the religious consciousness*. The new doctrinal elements that we shall find emerging in that development are not the product of the 'abstract intellect'—whatever that may be. They are the product of the intellect functioning within the framework of the religious consciousness. If this is forgotten, the paramount importance that properly attaches to the logical development of religion is bound to be completely missed.

7. Let us then make a beginning with the identification of the worshipful being of religion with *spirit*. This we may, I think, deal with very briefly: the more so since, according to some schools of thought, there *is* no 'pre-animistic' stage of religion. There never was a time, it is held, at which the object of worship was *not* identified with spirit. Be this as it may, it at least seems clear that once man *has* come to distinguish his spirit from his body, and to conceive this spirit as the active, directing agency within him, and as that within him in virtue of which he is good or bad, wise or foolish, he can hardly help locating in 'spirit' the mysterious power and value that is felt to belong to his object of worship. For the notion of power finds its original exemplar in spirit, and only from the experience of spiritual agency in ourselves can we give it any positive content. And as to the transcendent value ascribed to the worshipful being, if this is to be given any concrete meaning at all it must be in terms of the highest values we know, such as Wisdom, and Justice, and Love: and these are qualities only thinkable, we may presume, as attributes of a *spiritual* being.

The real interest lies in the logical development beyond this stage, to the attributes and mode of being of the Divine Spirit or God.

The master-key to that development lies, I think, in the religious consciousness's refusal to tolerate any shadow of *defect* in the being before which it bows down in worship and adoration.

A being who is conceived, as his God is conceived by the worshipper, to be endued with transcendent or 'numinous' power and value, cannot at the same time be conceived as marred by what are recognised even at the human level to be imperfections. To recognise an imperfection in anything is in principle to adopt towards it an attitude of *criticism*. But the attitude of criticism is as remote as well can be from the adoration and awe that characterise the attitude of worship. The worshipful *qua* worshipful is, in short, without blemish—perfect.

The dynamic of what we may perhaps call the religio-logical spirit, then, leads gradually to the explicit recognition of that which is at first only implicitly recognised by the worshipper, the worshipful being's freedom from all imperfection. And it is an easy step from the explicit recognition of God's freedom from all imperfection to the doctrine that God is infinite. For to be finite is to be limited from without, and so to be conditioned in existence by something beyond one's self. But a being thus externally conditioned is to that extent deficient in power, and this defect is inconsistent with the Divine Perfection. God, if Perfect, can be limited by nothing outside Himself. He must be self-complete, self-limited; in a word, Infinite.

That there is only *one* God follows as another simple corollary from God's Perfection. There cannot be more than one Perfect Being. For if there are more than one, they must differ from one another. But in what could they differ? Presumably it would have to be in the *kinds* of powers and excellences they possess. But if they so differ, each must lack some kind or kinds of powers or excellences possessed by another. But to lack *any* kind of power or excellence is to be to that extent imperfect. Hence no one of these beings can be perfect. The conception of a plurality of perfect beings is self-contradictory. If to be God is to be Perfect, therefore, there can be but *one* God.

Next, a Being that is Perfect cannot be supposed to have a merely *transitory* existence. To be liable to death or decay is a symptom of imperfection. And indeed there is almost no quality more consistently ascribed to the worshipful being by its worshippers than the quality of 'deathlessness'. The gods of all religions are 'immortal' beings, endowed with everlasting life. On the other hand, deeper reflection reveals that 'everlastingness', if interpreted as unending duration in time, is not a mode of being that is adequate to a God Who is Perfect. For it is of the very essence of time as we know it to be incomplete. Every conceived time is of necessity conceived as part of a larger time, which is itself part of a larger time, and so on *ad infinitum*. Hence to conceive God as existing, even everlastingly, *in* time, is incompatible with the conception of Him as a being that is self-complete. Furthermore, to conceive God as existing in time is to conceive Him as conditioned in existence by something beyond Himself; and that again is inconsistent with His Perfection and self-completeness. Nor is there any escape by way of the suggestion that this time-conditioning of God's existence need not be external to Him, since God may Himself be the creator of the time-order in which He exists. For if God *creates* time, this Divine act of creation cannot itself have been an act *in* time. God may indeed create the time-order: but only if He Himself transcends the time-order. To say that He *creates* time and also exists *in* it is self-contradictory.

Where, then, do these considerations about time lead us? God's Perfection is incompatible with transitory existence in time, but it is also incompatible with unending existence in time. Apparently the only solution, if God exists at all, is to interpret His mode of existence as *time-transcending*. He is beyond death and decay, because His essential mode of being is not temporal at all, so that no temporal predicates, or implicates of them, are relevant to Him.

But further, the time-transcendence of God must not be interpreted in any sense of that term that would *exclude* time. If God's mode of being were simply outside of time, time-*less*, so that He stood in no positive relationship to the temporal order or, consequently, to the world of men, this would be a derogation from His power inconsistent with the Perfection *ex hypothesi* ascribed to Him; and a derogation, incidentally, of a kind peculiarly fitted to make nonsense of the religious life. If God is Perfect in Power, 'all-powerful', the time-order must be dependent upon Him, and His mode of being must be so understood that it not merely transcends but also somehow includes Time.

And that gives us, I think, in essence, what is usually meant by the theistic attribution to God of 'Eternal' being. Eternity is not just everlastingness in time. Nor is it a transcendence of the time order in the sense of sheer timelessness, which would leave the time-order as something external to it. It is a mode of being that at once transcends and includes time. And indeed only in so far as Eternity includes as well as transcends Time can there be any significance in the symbol (it can be no more than a symbol) of 'Everlastingness' which is so constantly applied in religion to the Divine Being. If the 'Eternity' of God meant that He was 'time-*less*', there could not be even symbolic truth in speaking of the 'everlasting God'. It would have no less, if also no more, truth to speak of Him as a 'transitory' God; for either adjective is completely irrelevant as applied to a Being that exists *out of* time. But if Eternity, or God in His Eternal Being, comprehends or encompasses the time-order, then 'everlastingness' does become a significant symbol, in as much as it directs our minds to the truth that though God is not in time, Time—*all* Time—is in God, so that there is *no* time in which God is *not*.

The question of God's relation to time leads on naturally to the question of God's relation to the world in general; His relation, as we might say, to all that is *not*-God. We may perhaps best approach this from the standpoint of God's perfection of *Power*, His Omnipotence. If God is Omnipotent, all that is in the world must be subject *absolutely* to His control. But it cannot be subject absolutely to His control unless it derives its very being from God. If things in the world have an independent nature of their own, a nature that is not 'God-given', then God's power over them is conditioned by that independent nature, and cannot be 'absolute'; very much as the range of what an artificer can do with some given material is conditioned by the independent nature of the material as well as by his own capacity. Hence if God is indeed Omnipotent we have to think all that is in the world, all that is not-God, as ultimately deriving its being from Him. That is to say, God must be, as Theism declares Him to be, the ultimate ground of all that is.

But again, if God is the ultimate source of all that is, He must, presumably, be the author of that Moral Law which men find written in their hearts. Once the level of ethical reflection has been reached at which moral law is clearly distinguished from man-made law, and both its objectivity and its universal application to mankind have come to be acknowledged, the recognition of God as the Moral Governor of the world is a natural consequence.

One last component of the theistic *credo* remains for logical justification—the doctrine that God is a 'Living Presence' in the hearts of men. It will be recalled that, while fully recognising that devotees of almost all religions believe in the immanence of their god or gods, I felt obliged to decide against incorporating any reference to immanence in the generic definition of religion; for Deism does not accept Divine Immanence, and it did not appear to me easy to deny altogether Deism's right to the title 'religion'. It does not follow, however, that the Immanence of God cannot now be introduced as a logical implication of the generic religious consciousness; as one of the items that are unfolded when we reflect carefully on all that is involved in the character of the object of religious worship. Actually, I think that it can be thus unfolded; though the Divine Immanence we arrive at can only be stated in very general terms. The argument might run somewhat as follows. A Being to whom transcendent value is ascribed we are bound to envisage, in so far as we give concrete meaning to the term 'value' at all, as endued with the highest excellences we know. Among the highest excellences we know Love must certainly be included; if indeed we do not accord it a rank above all others. Now a God of Love, we may infer, will have solicitude for the well-being of the creatures He has brought into being; and since He is all-powerful as well as all-loving, we may further infer that He will give practical expression to that solicitude, vouchsafing Divine aid to man in times of trouble to the extent, and in the manner, that seems best to Himself and in accordance with the purpose of His creation.

An Immanence more closely defined than this, so far as I can see, we have no grounds for inferring simply on the basis of the generic character of the object of religious worship. On the other hand, since Theism permits within its own ambit a very wide diversity of view concerning the manner and the extent of God's entrance into the lives of men, no more than this would seem to be required for the purposes of our present argument. The identity of the generic religious consciousness with Theism, once the implications of that consciousness are fully drawn out, is thus,

I think, sufficiently confirmed in respect of this last article of the theistic faith also.

8. I hope, though it may be with undue optimism, that even this inevitably brief sketch of the connection of theistic beliefs with the beliefs generic to religion may be enough to show that there is a strong case for the view that the 'logical nisus' of the religious consciousness presses forward to a theistic consummation, and that the ordinary religious man is, after all, obeying a sound instinct when he tacitly identifies the question of the truth of religion with the question of the truth of Theism. May we then accept this identification as a valid one, and in our future discussions replace the uncomfortably vague question 'Is religion true?' by the more determinate question 'Is Theism true?'? I think the answer is both 'Yes' and 'No'. But I must leave over the elucidation of this somewhat cryptic reply until next week.

THEISM AND THE PROBLEM OF EVIL:
(1) SIN

1. In last week's lecture I suggested that good reasons could be given, both empirical and logical, in support of the view that theism is what the beliefs essential to religion become when thoroughly thought out into their leading implications. Nevertheless, I ended the lecture by expressing some hesitation about giving an unqualified acceptance to this view; and I want to begin today's lecture by explaining why.

It will be remembered that when we set out to try to trace the logical development of religion—that is to say, the course which religious belief tends to take if permitted to develop in a milieu of full and free intellectual criticism—we were careful to emphasise that this development could only be correctly determined by an analysis which proceeded *within the framework of the religious consciousness*. Now is it, on reflection, quite certain that our exegesis of this development, with its cumulative characterisation of God by a group of more or less definite concepts —e.g. 'spirit', 'power', 'wisdom', and 'goodness'—took adequate account of the element of the *supernatural* in the object of the religious consciousness? Does the theistic creed as we defined it, and in a sense defended it as the true theoretical expression of religion, do full justice to the aura of *mystery* that envelops the Godhead in all known religions?

In my own view, the answer to that question depends upon the way in which one chooses to interpret the several conceptual terms in the theistic creed. Broadly speaking, two ways of interpretation are open to us; the literal and the non-literal. Thus we may understand by God's perfect power, wisdom and goodness, qualities identical in principle with those qualities as we know them in human experience; though premising that they have not in God the limitations which cling to them in even the highest human experience. On this, the literal way, it seems to me that there is room for a great deal of doubt as to whether, in the effort to make God meaningful, we have not made Him cease to be worshipful. According to the other, non-literal way, qualities like power and wisdom and goodness are not ascribable to God in the precise meaning they have for us in finite life, and our use of them has validity only as a *symbolic* expression of the Divine Nature. The doubts which this view provokes are the converse of the doubts provoked by the first view. It is by no means clear now whether in the effort to make God worshipful we have not made Him cease to be meaningful.

I shall not attempt to disguise in which direction my own sympathies lie. I believe that only in its symbolic interpretation is theism the logically developed expression of the religious consciousness; and the second half of the present course of lectures will be devoted, first, to defending that conviction, and secondly, to trying to answer the question whether theism, thus understood, is not only the proper theoretical expression of religion but is also (a very different matter) objectively true. But it is to the other, literal interpretation that we must first of all give our attention; for there can be little doubt that it is in this sense that most people have understood theism.

It may seem at first sight unfair to suggest that it is in this sense also that most theistic theologians have understood theism; nothing would be easier than to cite many utterances by many theistic theologians which openly acknowledge the ultimate incomprehensibility of God. But the trend of a theology is surely to be judged not by the detached utterances of individual theologians but by the operative principles of the systematic theology to which they subscribe. I shall return to this matter on a later occasion; but is it really doubtful that almost all systems of theology, in working out their conceptual account of the relation of God to the world and to man, presuppose that power and wisdom and goodness are ascribable to God in their literal meaning (though of course in a perfected form)? And indeed the theist could argue with a good deal of plausibility that we cannot have what would ordinarily be called a 'theology' at all if it is not 'rational' at least in the sense of accepting the conceivability in principle of the attributes of God. I think one ought to begin, therefore, by considering the truth-claims of theism in its literal version, and by considering in particular the ability or inability of theism so understood to return satisfactory answers to the fundamental difficulties which critics have constantly pressed upon it, and which theists themselves are as a rule very ready to recognise as genuine difficulties. This orthodox theism of the theologians I shall, for the present, often refer to simply as 'theism'. But I hope it will not be felt to be tendentious if on occasion, where some risk of confusion might thereby be averted, I give it the title of 'Rational Theism' in order to distinguish it from the 'Supra-rational Theism' which holds that the Divine Nature in principle transcends all human conception and is capable of apprehension only in symbols.

It will be generally agreed, I take it, that theism cannot be true if it is inconsistent *either* with itself *or* with the actual facts of experience as we are compelled to regard them. In today's lecture, and also in my lecture next week, I shall be concerned with its alleged inconsistency with certain facts of experience. My conclusion will be that no such inconsistency has been established, although there are undoubtedly certain facts of experience which subject the theistic faith to a strain that brings it uncomfortably near to breaking-point. Thereafter I shall take up the charge that theism is inconsistent with *itself*. And to this charge, I may as well say at once, I cannot persuade myself that there is any effective answer. If religion really stands or falls with the truth of Rational Theism then, in my judgment, religion falls. But as I have already hinted, I do not myself believe that religion stands or falls with the truth of Rational Theism, for in my view not Rational, but Supra-rational, Theism is the authentic theoretical expression of religion. From Lecture XVI onwards, accordingly, I shall be concerned almost solely with the nature and claims of Supra-rational Theism, a faith which seems to me capable of being formulated in a way which escapes the objections to Rational Theism while incurring no loss of anything that is really vital to a religious interpretation of the universe. These are bold words, and I am acutely conscious how presumptuous they may sound. I can only plead in extenuation that what I shall have to say about Supra-rational Theism represents a conviction of over thirty years' standing which I have been unable throughout that period to find any compelling reason to abandon.

2. Let us, then, address ourselves to the alleged inconsistency of theism with the actual facts of human experience.

Now the specific facts of human experience which have always been regarded as constituting the gravest problem for the theistic position are, of course, those that are epitomised by the word 'evil'. This 'Problem of Evil' (as it is called) falls naturally into two distinct parts: (1) the problem of *moral* evil, or, as it appears from the religious standpoint, of *sin*; and (2) the problem of *natural* evil, which it is customary to identify, more or less accurately, with the problem of *suffering*. Moral evil and natural evil both seem to be indisputable facts. The question is, how are these facts to be reconciled with the theistic hypothesis of a God Who is at once all-powerful and absolutely good?

Very strangely (as I cannot help thinking), it is the problem of moral evil that seems often to be regarded by theists as the more troublesome of the two. In my own view, so far from its being the more troublesome, the problem of moral evil is in a theistic context virtually non-existent. It will be the main business of today's lecture to try to explain and defend this judgment.

We must begin by getting clear about our terms. Basically, moral evil pertains to acts of will—only derivatively to dispositions, overt actions, and states of affairs. It can be defined sufficiently for present purposes, I think, as the willing of some course which the agent himself deems to be contrary to his duty. No doubt a man may be mistaken as to what course of action *is* in fact his duty; but whether he is mistaken or not, and whether or not, if mistaken, the mistake is one which he could have avoided if he had been a better man in the past, it remains incontrovertibly true, I think, that his present act of willing is morally evil if it is directed to an end which he himself deems to be contrary to his duty. And in no other conditions, so far as I can see, can an act of will *as such* be morally evil. It must be conceded that we do sometimes speak of an act as morally evil even when we have reason to believe that the agent does not at the time of acting regard it as contrary to his duty; but such a judgment is, in my opinion, legitimate only where it is believed that the agent morally ought to have known better, and that his present mistaken view of what constitutes his duty is the consequence of blameworthy negligence or some other moral fault in his past. In that case, however, what we are judging to be morally evil is not really his *present* act of will, but certain of his *past* acts of will. That is to say, our ascription to him of moral evil is a retrospective judgment, applicable to the man now only in the sense that he is presumably now the self-same person as he who willed badly in the past.

Sin I take to be morally evil willing where the willing is contrary not merely to what the agent deems to be his moral duty but also to what he deems to be the Will of God. For the religious man it is almost impossible not to identify God, as the ultimate source of all that is, with the imponent of that moral law which seems objectively to confront, and to claim unconditional obedience from, every rational being; and in that event moral evil becomes tantamount to sin. For the atheist, on the other hand, while moral evil can be as real as anything in the universe, 'sin' must be accounted a mere myth. Clearly there can be no disobeying a God that doesn't exist, let alone issue commands to rational beings.

Now granting the religious premises according to which moral evil is to be identified with sin, it is all too evident that sin exists as a fact of experience. But why should it be supposed that the sinning of the creature is difficult to reconcile with the Perfection of his Creator?

It is easy enough to see how sin (or 'the evil will' as we should call it in this context) presents a thorny problem to a certain metaphysic which has much in common with theism, the metaphysic of Absolute Idealism. According to this world-theory, everything that is (including of course each finite mind) is a mode of expression of the one ultimate reality, Absolute Mind or Spirit, which is also Absolute Perfection—the very norm of all 'goodness'. It is indeed pertinent to ask of this theory how the evil will, the will that deliberately opposes itself to goodness, can possibly be conceived as expressing (with whatever degree of inadequacy) the nature of a Being who is *ex hypothesi* supremely good. It seems quite futile to try to interpret good willing and bad willing, utterly opposed to one another as they are in their basic spiritual direction, as somehow expressive, though in different degrees, of the same spiritual principle. Bad willing is not an 'inadequate expression of goodness'. It is just a more or less adequate expression of badness. Proponents of Absolute Idealism have had some success in dodging, but, I think, none at all in meeting, this simple but fundamental objection to their system.

But surely this difficulty has no relevance for the metaphysic of *theism*. Here too, certainly, we have a Perfect Spirit Who is the source of all that is. But on the *theistic* doctrine finite selves are not *expressions* of, or *differentiations* of, but *creations* of, the one Perfect Spirit; and what is more, creations that are endowed by their Creator with a real measure of individual self-determination. Now this makes all the difference in the world. If it be agreed that finite selves receive from God a genuine power of initiative, that is as much as to say that finite selves do not *necessarily* align themselves with the principle of goodness—or, in religious language, with the Will of God. The possibility of evil willing is implied in the metaphysic of theism. Where then is the problem? Surely the real problem would be if human beings, despite the bestowal upon them of the freedom which theism postulates, were nevertheless always to will what is good!

Let us look at the matter further from a slightly different angle. Although the Divine purpose of creation is, no doubt, for theism as for other religious philosophies, something not fully comprehensible to the finite understanding, all theists would, I take it, agree that it accords with the Divine purpose for man on earth that he should set himself to realise the highest moral values. There is little demur among theists, I think, to the Keatsian interpretation of the world as at least 'a vale of soul-making'—though it may also be more than that. Now an indispensable condition of the achievement of moral values is 'free will'. And free will is meaningless if it is not a freedom to choose *wrongly* as well as to choose *rightly*. Would it not be rather absurd then, for theism to accept it as entirely conformable with God's goodness that He should create beings with the free will which is

the condition of their realising moral values, and at the same time
to find a difficulty in reconciling with God's goodness the fact
that these 'free' beings sometimes will wrongly?

In the last resort, perhaps the best answer to those who are
troubled about the compatibility of human sin with a God who is
supremely good (as well as omnipotent) is to ask a question. Would
it have been a *better* world if man had been created *without* the
power of self-determination; *without*, therefore, the opportunity
of realising moral values?—for it is only on that condition that
the complete absence of human sinning is conceivable. I fancy
that very few people, or at any rate very few Christians, would be
prepared to answer this question in the affirmative. To most of
us human life would seem to lose not only all its dignity but its
very meaning if men were not endowed with the freedom of choice
which makes their realisation of moral values possible. Indeed,
I can conceive of only one ground upon which it could be argued
with any force that a creation in which man was *not* vouchsafed
freedom would be a 'better' world, despite the consequence of
its being a world in which there could be no virtue any more than
there could be any vice. One might argue that the distress and
suffering that are inflicted upon innocent victims by human sin
are so extensive and so horrible that the bestowal upon man of
the freedom which makes sinning possible is on balance a bad
thing; in other words, that the price of a world in which moral
virtue is possible is too high; and that, accordingly, the created
order as we know it is incapable of being reconciled with the
theistic hypothesis of a Creator who is perfect in power, wisdom,
and goodness. Now I certainly do not regard this line of argument
as unworthy of serious notice. I would only point out here that it is
not, at bottom, an argument against the existence in a God-created
world of *moral* evil, or sin. It is an argument against the existence
in a God-created world of certain forms of distress and suffering;
i.e. of *natural* evil. We shall postpone our answer to it, therefore (in
so far as we can answer it), until the next lecture, when we shall be
attempting to deal systematically with the problem of suffering.

3. In what I have been saying up to the present, however,
I have been assuming the admission by the theist that while

human willing is sometimes sinful, it is also sometimes good; that we do at least sometimes choose what we believe to be our duty. This does not seem, on the face of it, a very outrageous assumption —it represents the belief of every man in his ordinary day to day life. But we must now recognise the fact that it is directly and vehemently challenged by a great many theistic theologians, who claim to know that the human will is *essentially* sinful. And this, if it were true, would put a very different complexion on the problem of evil. These theologians will allege that our discussions so far have been founded on a misconception of the nature of man, and consequently of his relationship to God. 'We do not deny' they may tell us 'that if man's will were only sometimes sinful, that would set no problem for theism. But the real situation is not that man's will is sometimes sinful but that it is always sinful. Human nature as we know it is intrinsically corrupt, so that man, where he depends on his own resources alone, cannot *but* will what is evil. The "problem of sin" is the problem of reconciling this "tainted nature" of man, his native bias towards evil, with the perfect goodness of the God Who created him. And the solution we theologians propound lies in our doctrine of the Fall of Man—a doctrine with the highest scriptural authority. Man has fallen from the original high estate in which the good God created him through a primal sin which implicates the whole of "Adam's seed" in a corruption of nature only redeemable through the operation of Divine grace'.

What are we to say of 'the problem of sin' in this altered guise?

With the very many variants of the doctrine of the Fall which have been offered by theologians in the effort to make the doctrine conflict a little less conspicuously with enlightened thought in history, psychology, ethics and metaphysics, there is fortunately no need for us here to concern ourselves. It will suffice for our purpose if we examine the premise which underlies and gives meaning to the doctrine (in so far, at any rate, as the doctrine is not taken simply to rest upon 'revelation'). We must examine, that is to say, the proposition that in human nature as we know it there is a native bias towards evil. If this premise is false, as I firmly believe it to be, the problem of sin to which the Fall is offered as a solution just does not arise.

I begin by dismissing as irrelevant the rather melodramatic

appeals often made today—understandably enough in a generation that has witnessed horrors on a scale that can have had few parallels in human history—to the enormous mass of wickedness that seems plainly to confront us in the world of men. The appeal is irrelevant, for the question at issue is not whether man's will is *often* evil but whether it is *always* evil. If we are to take our stand here upon externally observed facts at all, these facts must be permitted to include countless acts of noble self-sacrifice, and heroic devotion to duty on the part of a whole multitude of ordinary men and women, as well as the bestial cruelties of a Buchenwald or a Belsen; and the outcome then is to establish with at least as much certainty that human nature is sometimes almost incredibly *good* as that human nature is often almost incredibly *bad*.

But, in any event, evidence drawn from external observation is precarious at best where the subject of enquiry is moral good and evil. These are matters of the inner direction of the will towards or away from a conceived duty; and on this it is, in the last resort, only the agent himself who can tell us the truth.

In other words, 'inside' information is the only kind of information that can be at all decisive when our task is to judge the truth or falsity of such a proposition as that now under consideration; i.e. that the human will is inevitably sinful. It is imperative, therefore, that we look closely, and without preconceptions, at actual moral experience as we know it, and in particular at the situation which is the *mise en scène* for the more crucial of man's moral choices. I refer, of course, to the situation of 'moral temptation'. In my opinion introspective analysis of that situation makes it abundantly clear that we can make sense of the doctrine that man's will is essentially sinful only on pain of having to repudiate the most inescapable deliverances of our common moral consciousness.

The essence of the situation of moral temptation, as I understand it, is as follows.[1] We are conscious of X as our duty, and of Y, incompatible with X, as the object of strongest desire. There may be, and very often is, *some* desire for X, as well as the consciousness of moral obligation with respect to it; but we are aware of this desire as being weak relatively to the desire for Y, and we

[1] For a fuller account see previous lectures VIII and IX.

know that if we let our desiring nature have its way it is Y and not X that we shall choose. We feel quite certain, however, while actually engaged in the situation, that we *can* rise to our duty and choose X, though only by the exercise of moral effort; and that it lies with us here and now whether we make this effort or, alternatively, yield to the importunings of our strongest desire. So much, it seems to me, is not capable of being doubted by the moral agent *in the moral situation*. All sorts of doubts, engendered by scientific, psychological, philosophical, or theological theory, may assail us later concerning the trustworthiness of this testimony of our moral experience. But that this *is* the testimony of our moral experience in the crucial situation of moral temptation, anyone, it seems to me, can verify for himself by making with care the appropriate introspective experiment. Were there not in fact this conviction present that we have a personal choice between genuinely open alternatives of good and evil, it is hard to see how we should suppose ourselves, as we do, justly liable to moral censure if we choose what we deem to be evil.

Now how are we to fit into this picture the bias towards evil, which, we are assured, is intrinsic to human nature? Does it correspond to anything in actual moral experience?

It might be tempting at first sight to locate the alleged bias in our *desiring* nature, since, as we have seen, the main trend of our desires in the situation of moral temptation is always in opposition to the course ordained by duty. But this will clearly not do at all, for a variety of reasons. In the first place, situations of moral temptation are relatively rare episodes in the life of the normal man. In the great bulk of situations a man's desiring nature does not enter into conflict with 'duty' in any degree; and it is an ethical commonplace that in men of the highest virtue their desires have been brought into such substantial accord with duty that it would be sheer abuse of language to call their desiring nature anything but 'good'. In the second place (and the point here is crucial), the fact that man's desiring nature can and does *sometimes* incline him towards evil courses, so far from being an indication that man is essentially depraved, is actually an indispensable condition of his being morally good. If his desires always inclined man in the direction of what he deemed to be his duty, if man never felt tempted to do what he believes he ought not to do, there could be no moral life for him at all. The possibility of conflict between desire and duty is the precondition of his being *either* morally good *or* morally bad. And still a third reason why we cannot locate man's alleged natural bias towards evil in his desires is that desire, strictly speaking, is not a part of man's *natural* endowment at all. What is 'natural' are the instinctive impulses and appetites that constitute the 'raw material' of desires. But these instinctive impulses and appetites seem perfectly neutral with respect to good and evil. There is none, it would seem, that is incapable of being turned either to good or to ill account according to the manner in which it comes to be organised in the life policies of the individual agent after he has reached the level of self-conscious direction of his conduct.

On the other hand, it seems equally futile to look for the natural bias towards evil in some *other* factor. If, as I have argued, the pressure of 'desire' in the situation of moral temptation lends no support whatsoever to the 'natural depravity' thesis, to what else can we hopefully point as inclining the will towards evil? Is there the slightest hint to be found in actual moral experience—granted always that we approach it without prejudice from theological proconceptions—of the presence of any other impediment to the discharge of our duty? So far as I can see, none at all. Indeed it is extremely hard to understand, in terms of our moral experience, what the hypothesis of an inhibiting factor other than desire could even *mean*. And as for the claim that this hypothetical impediment intrinsic to man's nature so completely shackles the human will that it can be diverted from evil to good only by the operation of divine grace, its flat rejection is surely implicit in all moral experience. In the situation of moral temptation the agent, as we saw earlier, feels certain that he can *by his own moral effort* overcome the resistant elements in his nature and rise to his duty.[1]

The truth would seem to be that if we are to accept the natural depravity doctrine as valid we must be prepared to face the implication that the moral experience of man, with the conviction inseparable from it of personal responsibility for the choice between good and evil, is sheer delusion. Possibly some theists are prepared to accept this implication. But if they are, they

---

[1] Thereby, according to many neo-Calvinist critics, falling victim to the sin of 'spiritual pride'. On this confused and confusing charge see Appendix C.

should surely give up the pretence of appealing to the facts of experience in support of their doctrine. On the very kindest interpretation, the 'facts' they appeal to must be of a highly selective order.

4. I have been arguing that actual moral experience discloses no evidence whatever of a bias towards evil incapable of being overcome save by the miracle of *ad hoc* Divine assistance. This conclusion I should confidently expect to be confirmed by all those who do not bring with them to moral experience theological preconceptions which clash with the testimony of that experience. It would be too much to expect more than a partial confirmation from those who approach moral experience *with* such preconceptions. People who have been induced, from whatever causes, to accept as a religious truth that man is essentially vile, his nature so corrupt that only by Divine aid can he avoid choosing evil, will naturally try to interpret their moral experience in the light of those ideas. But try as they may, I doubt very much whether they ever at all fully succeed in doing so. A man may believe in his study that he has in himself no power to resist temptation. But set him in an actual moral situation and he can hardly prevent the intuition of personal freedom intrinsic to moral experience from giving the lie direct to his preconceptions. The usual outcome, I think, is a sort of muddled compromise state in which he believes that he can, and should, do something *himself* in the matter, but also believes that God's help is necessary for complete success.

I should agree, however, that on this particular matter it is hard to make confident pronouncements. The abnormal emotive force of religious beliefs must be allowed its full weight. Perhaps there *may* be cases in which preconceptions about man's inherent corruptness are held with such almost obsessional fervour that even in a 'live' situation of moral temptation the intuition of personal freedom is virtually suppressed, never emerging with sufficient explicitness to make an effective contribution to the complex mental state that accompanies the action. But if there are any such cases, they must be extremely rare. It is a familiar and noteworthy fact that even the most fanatical preachers of man's total impotence to resist temptation unaided often reveal by implication that they do not themselves whole-heartedly believe what they preach. For example, it is surely most unusual to find anyone, whatever his religious convictions, prepared to disavow completely personal responsibility for his failures to resist temptation? Yet if he really believed that he could not by his own unaided effort resist temptation, he ought surely to find it absurd to accept personal responsibility for succumbing to it. It is perfectly true, of course, that we often fail to detect certain of the logical implications of what we believe; but it is not easy to fail where the relevant situation is, as here, one that is constantly before our notice, and where the reasoning involved is of an extreme simplicity. There is nothing complicated or subtle, so far as I can see, about the intellectual process required to discern that a being who *cannot* by his own effort will other than evil is not to be blamed if in fact he *does* will nothing but evil. Or again, one might call in evidence those cases of moral temptation that are comparatively trivial in character but which are, of course, just as genuinely instances of the choice between good and evil as any other cases; e.g. the temptation to tell a seemingly harmless untruth in order to save one's self some petty inconvenience. I take leave to doubt whether those who are in theory uncompromising apostles of human depravity do in practice feel that they must call upon God's aid to enable them to resist temptation on such minor matters. Yet the principle is the same, whether the temptation be important and enduring, or unimportant and ephemeral. If it is admitted that one can by one's own efforts will the good even in the latter type of case, then the doctrine of the natural man's essential depravity is in principle abandoned.

5. I am well aware, of course, that efforts have by no means been lacking among theologians to do some kind of justice to the intuitions of moral experience, and in particular, to rescue for man some sort of moral responsibility, while still holding fast to the principle of man's natural depravity and his utter dependence upon Divine aid for the willing of any good thing. For example, a device to which theologians have frequently had recourse is to suggest that although man can will the good only by God's grace, nevertheless that grace is only *offered* to man. It lies in man's own

power whether he appropriates or repudiates the 'gift of grace' that God freely offers. But this suggestion, favoured by many theologians though hotly contested by others, surely contains a latent self-contradiction. The choice between appropriating and repudiating God's grace is just as much a choice between good and evil as is any straightforward choice between resisting a temptation to commit a wicked action and yielding to it. If a man can by his own 'human' power decide to accept rather than reject God's grace, how can we regard this decision as other than a manifestation of the man's will to *good*, and how then can we continue to retain the doctrine of man's 'natural' depravity? One may challenge the premises, but one must, I fear, respect the logic, of those more 'tough-minded' adherents of the natural depravity doctrine who insist that, even in respect of the reception of grace, the human being has nothing whatever to do with the matter. Whether or not the individual person receives grace, they declare, depends solely upon whether or not God elects to confer it upon him.

6.   I am bound to say that none of the feats of intellectual acrobatics which aim at reconciling man's moral responsibility with man's natural depravity seems to me to accomplish more than a certain obscuring of the inherent contradiction by enveloping it in a bewildering cloud of irrelevant subtleties. It seems to me that when the mists have been dispelled the simple truth stands out clearly that if man cannot will the good save by God's grace, there is no longer any point in talking about man's moral responsibility. There can be in man neither moral goodness nor moral badness. If the 'good' will never issues from the personal initiative of the agent, then it is not *he* that is morally 'good'. And if it is not open to him to be morally *good*, it is not open to him to be morally *bad* either. A man can only be morally bad if he fails to do what *he* could do; not if he fails to do what God alone could do for him.

To be perfectly candid, what has most troubled me in criticising the natural depravity doctrine is that the objections to it seem to me so obvious as hardly to be worth the stating. I should be glad to be able to believe that in fact there is no need to state them. In some respects, however, they would appear to stand in more urgent need of statement—or rather, of *re*-statement—today than for many generations. The powerful neo-Calvinist trend in recent theology is familiar to all. I do not for my own part have any doubt that there are elements of profound and permanent value in this trend. I should agree warmly that there was the most pressing need, as against certain forms of liberal theology that had much prevalence in my own youth, of the heavy stress that neo-Calvinists have laid upon the aspect of 'transcendence' in God; and again (a point which is of course closely connected) for their exposure of the vanity of the pretensions of human reason in aspiring to 'know' God. But I cannot for a moment admit that these important truths (as I believe them to be) can only be upheld at the cost of disparaging, and even of denouncing as fraudulent, the intuitions of personal responsibility that seem to be quite inseparable from man's moral experience. With the deplorable practical consequences that must follow upon teaching which, however unwillingly—and perhaps in some cases unwittingly —conveys the impression that ordinary moral experience is a tissue of delusions, I have here no concern. My business in this course of lectures is not with the practical value or disvalue of doctrines but with their claim to be true. And on the latter question I take my stand on this. No doctrine can be accounted true if it contradicts beliefs which are intrinsic to, ineradicable from, a mode of experience which belongs fundamentally to our common human nature. That moral experience, in the sense of experience of unconditional obligation, is a mode of experience that belongs fundamentally to our common human nature, and that the belief in personal freedom and responsibility is intrinsic to it, I have done my best to show in the concluding lectures of my previous course, and I must leave the matter there.

7. Clearly, however, there is one further question that *must* be raised, and, so far as may be, answered, before we can legitimately bring this discussion to a close. What lies behind this doctrine of the natural depravity of man? Wherein lies the immense force of its appeal?—for that it has the power to attract not merely great numbers of people whose religious zeal is uncontrolled by any noticeable exercise of a critical intelligence, but also many religious

thinkers of outstanding parts, and of the most enviable range of learning both sacred and secular, is beyond dispute. To put the question in somewhat tendentious form, what is it that makes men of evident spiritual discernment so firmly persuaded of the essentially corrupt nature of man that they are prepared to advance in support of it such remarkably unconvincing arguments? Until we have answered this question we have no right to feel wholly comfortable about our rejection of the doctrine.

Now it seems plain at least that the doctrine must have its ultimate roots somewhere in religious experience; for it is only in the religious mind that it secures any lodgment. It is as alien as anything well can be to the mind of the ordinary layman, who has no doubt at all that (within limits, of course) he is free to choose between good and evil. Is it possible that we have to do here with a conviction that is as intrinsic to the religious consciousness as the contrary conviction is to the moral consciousness? If so, we should indeed be confronted by a grave dilemma, since— or so it seems to me—there are at least as good, and very much more evident, grounds for insisting upon the objective validity of the *moral* consciousness as for insisting on the objective validity of the *religious* consciousness. We should be forced to admit a fundamental and irremovable cleavage within the very heart of human experience; and we should find ourselves oscillating between acceptance and rejection of the natural depravity doctrine according to whether the religious or the moral standpoint happened to be at the moment dominant in our minds.

I think that we can in fact find the roots of the doctrine in religious experience. I do not believe, however, that it is *intrinsic* thereto. On the contrary, I shall suggest that the facts of religious experience upon which the doctrine is based have been given a wrong significance, and have led to a false inference. In my judgment, there is a confusion here which it is extraordinarily easy to fall into, and, in a sense which will I hope become clear, is all the easier to fall into the more deeply religious the mind of the thinker.

An authentic element in religious experience, I think we should all agree, is the consciousness of an immeasurable and humanly unbridgeable gulf between the finite creature at his very best and the infinite perfection of his Creator. The more vivid and profound the consciousness of God, the more acutely realised is the contrast with mere man, and the keener in consequence is the sense of one's own, and of all men's, radical imperfection. Measured (if we may be permitted the paradox) by the immeasurable majesty and excellence of God, man must seem to himself utterly devoid of worth, mere 'dust and ashes'. But this is *not*, it is imperative to notice, the same thing as a conviction of *sin*. There is a clear distinction between consciousness of the gulf that separates one from God in virtue simply of man's creaturely nature, and consciousness of the far more terrible gulf that separates one in virtue of that deliberate self-alienation from God which is involved in evil willing; in the will that sets itself at once against moral law and Divine purpose. But though the two are distinguishable readily enough for abstract thought, in the impassioned consciousness of religion it is fatally easy for them to be fused and confused; and this confusion, I suggest, is the real root, in religious experience, of the belief in the essential depravity of human nature as such. The intrinsic, inevitable imperfection that belongs to man in virtue of his finite, creaturely status is falsely identified with the *different* mode of human imperfection which is sin; and *sin* accordingly comes to be regarded as something intrinsic and inevitable in human nature.

It seems to me that the doctrine of the natural depravity of man cannot survive a clear grasp of the distinction between these two different types of human imperfection. Common to our consciousness of imperfection in both cases, and the ground of the temptation to identify them, is the sense of profound estrangement from God, and limitless inferiority. What *distinguishes* the two—the consciousness of the imperfection that attaches to the creature *qua* creature from the consciousness of the imperfection that attaches to the creature *qua* sinful—is that in the latter we acknowledge in ourselves an act of deliberate defiance of God which has no place whatsoever in the former. It seems to me quite impossible to deny the reality of this distinction once it has been brought to one's notice. But to recognise the distinction is surely to recognise also that sin is not a universal but a special human state. It goes without saying that human nature is 'sinful' in the sense that man is so constituted that he can and does commit sins. But that human nature is 'sinful' in the sense that man is so constituted as not to be able of his own volition to do anything

L

but sin—that is a proposition which, in my judgment, is totally devoid of rational foundation. It is a proposition that wins assent from many religious minds only on account of a confusion between two similar, yet vitally different, kinds of human imperfection. The staggering paradox that all men are equally sinners is no more than a logical consequence of this proposition, but the fact that many theologians are prepared seriously to proclaim it seems to me to confirm up to the hilt the confusion I have alleged. For it makes good sense to say that all men are equally estranged from God, *if* we are thinking of the 'estrangement' that pertains to the creaturely status as such. It makes no sense at all that I can see if we are thinking of the 'estrangement' that pertains to *sin*, i.e. to deliberate defiance of the will of God.

8. I have, I fear, 'trailed my coat' a little in this lecture. I do most firmly believe everything I have said; but I am not so ingenuous as to suppose that in all quarters it will be cordially received. I shall be not too surprised, though I shall be sorry, if I am told that I have been talking about something which the devout understand but which I manifestly do not, and that my conclusions are in consequence mere nonsense. Possibly they are nonsense. Nevertheless it may not be altogether without profit even to the theologian to be made aware of the kind of nonsense that philosophers feel obliged to talk when they reflect, honestly if misguidedly, upon the kind of thing they are sometimes asked to believe by theologians.

Still, on the main question at issue in this lecture, viz. whether human sinfulness is compatible with the perfect goodness of God, I am glad to be able to range myself on the side of the theologian, even if it be, as he may think, for the wrong reasons. The affirmative answer seems to me open to no objections of any gravity once we rid ourselves of the self-contradictory premise that man is so constituted that he *can't help sinning*. For myself, indeed, the only problem of sin is the problem why sin should ever have been thought to be a 'problem'. The problem of *evil*, as I see it, is not the problem of sin but the problem of *suffering*. To that most formidable problem, though not without much misgiving, I shall address myself next week.

THEISM AND THE PROBLEM OF EVIL:
(2) SUFFERING

1. As we saw in the last lecture, the problem of reconciling the existence of evil with the omnipotence and perfect goodness of God assumes historically two distinct shapes, according as the kind of evil we have to deal with is *moral* evil or *natural* evil. In my last lecture I gave my reasons for believing that the problem of moral evil presents no real challenge to the theology of theism. But there is certainly no such easy way with the problem of natural evil. The question, briefly and broadly stated, is whether the goodness and omnipotence of God are consistent with the *prima facie* badness of so much of the suffering that exists in the world of His creation. I begin with some comment designed to specify the problem with greater precision.

It will be observed that I have spoken not of *all* the suffering, but of *so much of* the suffering, that exists in the world. The limitation was of course deliberate, and introduces us to the first point that must be made in closer definition of our problem. It is manifestly not suffering of every kind, wheresoever and howsoever it exists, that threatens the theistic creed. Suffering that is (as we say) 'deserved', and in the degree, approximately, that it is deserved, is not commonly regarded as in any objective sense bad. Very few people consider that there is any moral impropriety in the deliberate wrongdoer being made to suffer for his crimes. Indeed it is much more usual to see a threat to the moral government of the world in the fact that the wicked so often seem to get off scot-free, in this life at any rate.

Let us assume, then, that deserved suffering, in the degree (approximately) that it *is* deserved, constitutes no problem for the theist. *Un*deserved suffering, however, is another matter. Yet here too it is imperative to make qualifications when we are considering its compatibility or otherwise with the God of theism. Do we really regard a world in which there is undeserved suffering as *ipso facto* bad, or even as imperfect? I do not think so. It takes no very deep reflection to see that a world in which people could suffer only if they acted wickedly—a world without hazards or hardships for the virtuous—would be a world in which the soul could not develop its highest virtues. The moral achievements for which we hold men in highest honour would seem to be precisely those in which the path of duty as the individual has conceived it entails for him great personal suffering or the risk thereof. In so far as we approve of a world which serves as a theatre for moral endeavour, we cannot, I think, disapprove of a world in which there is at least some suffering that is undeserved. ,

Can we then specify the kind of undeserved suffering that really does trouble the theist—or that ought to trouble him if it doesn't? It seems to me that we can. No one is seriously troubled about undeserved suffering that is brief in duration, even though it be intense in degree; nor about undeserved suffering that is moderate in degree, even though it be of long duration. These are 'bearable' experiences. Pity for those who so suffer is natural; but we can see how such hardships, and the risk of such hardships, are necessary for the discipline and purification of character; they play an indispensable part in a world that is a 'vale of soul-making', and they cause us no moral offence. What does disquiet us is the occurrence of undeserved suffering that is both immoderate in degree—sometimes excruciating—and also long protracted. Here we do have a real problem. In this context it is unrealistic (and highly offensive) to talk about 'discipline and purification of character', or of any other valuable effects upon the spirit. What possible spiritual benefits can accrue to the man who is reduced by slow torture (as even the most heroic natures may be) to a state of mind in which he is no longer a rational being at all, but just one vast feeling-centre for devastating and all-enveloping pain? And if it be suggested that perhaps later recollection of his experience may somehow bring valuable spiritual effects, one must point out that in very many cases, so far as this life is concerned, there *is* no later recollection.

The assertion has, indeed, sometimes been ventured that in the nature of things suffering cannot be both very intense and prolonged; that when a certain degree of intensity is reached unconsciousness mercifully supervenes. Of course there is a modicum of truth in this. There *is* a point at which unconsciousness supervenes. But the 'threshold of unconsciousness' seems quite horrifyingly high. It is mere wishful thinking to suppose that when pain reaches the pitch of sheer agony, it is never long before insensibility sets in. Without doubt modern discoveries in the field of analgesics have done much to alleviate the human lot; but even if we forget the past (which we have no right to do), these have by no means removed the problem. Victims of the most painful diseases and wounds are not always, even yet, within reach of anodynes; and there is no drug in the pharmacopoeia that will make tolerable the mental anguish of, say, the wife and mother bereaved of her whole family in a single disaster.

It may be admitted that the incidence of suffering which is at once prolonged and very intense is comparatively rare. Not very many persons have had first-hand experience of it. That, perhaps, has something to do with the almost shockingly facile 'solutions' of the problem which are sometimes offered in apparent good faith. A strenuous effort of sympathetic imagination is necessary for most of us if we are to appreciate the problem of suffering in anything like its full poignancy. Logically, of course, the intense and prolonged suffering of others is no easier to reconcile with a God perfect in goodness, wisdom, and power, than similar suffering in one's self; psychologically, I fear, it is a great deal easier.

There are occasions, however, when even the least imaginative among us cannot remain blind to the spectacle of undeserved suffering of a well-nigh unbearable order. Two great wars have brought home the problem of suffering to many people who had somehow failed to realise that even in times of peace there are millions dying every year in acute distress from causes like hunger and disease that cannot plausibly be ascribed to any fault of their own. It is inevitable that the ordinary thoughtful man, confronted by so much undeserved misery, should ask himself 'Is this really compatible with the existence of a righteous and all-powerful God? Could not He, with whom "all things are possible", have created a world in which at least the more hideous kinds of suffering could not come about?' There can be no denying that many reflective and worthy men have felt themselves forced by their inability to return satisfactory answers to such questions as these to doubt, or even to disavow, their old belief in God, as the only alternative to the forfeiture of their intellectual integrity.

So much for the nature of the problem. Let us turn now to consider possible solutions.

2. The easiest solution, one which recurs fairly often in the history of theology and which earlier in the present century had a considerable vogue, is not, strictly speaking, a solution of the problem as we have formulated it, since it is based upon a modification of one of the premises. God's perfect goodness is a premise that obviously cannot be tampered with. But it is suggested that we do not need to think of God as *all*-powerful. It is enough that we think of Him as immensely more powerful than any conceivable human being. On that assumption, there will be no inconsistency in supposing that there is an independent 'material' upon which God works in His creation of the world, and that it may prove in some measure refractory; or even in supposing that there is some positive principle of Evil in the Universe, such as the Devil of so much early Christian theology, which opposes itself to God's beneficent purposes and may bring some of them to naught. Given this limitation of God's power, no religious difficulty arises from the incidence of so much undeserved suffering of an intense and prolonged character, for we are no longer obliged to conceive it as somehow in accord with the Divine will. On the contrary, we can fairly suppose that God would prevent it if He could, but that, limited as He is by opposing forces, He simply is not able.

The hypothesis of a Finite God—for that is what it amounts to—though it emerges periodically in theology, has a habit of vanishing again with curious rapidity. But perhaps its failure to survive for long is not so very curious. As suggested earlier in this course, the religious attitudes of worship and adoration are difficult to sustain in conjunction with an explicit recognition that the Being to whom they are directed is defective or imperfect in any way whatsoever. And we can hardly pretend to ourselves that limitation of power is not an imperfection. Or to look at the same point from a slightly different angle; it is generally accepted that one of the fruits of religious belief, where it is sincerely and deeply held, is a profound serenity of spirit—'the peace that passeth all understanding'—based on an absolute assurance that whatever ills and disasters may afflict the world all things are ultimately in God's hands and must, in obedience to His will, 'work together for good'. Now this religious peace of mind is just not possible, at any rate at a reflective level, once the infinitude of God has been compromised, and forces independent of God and either actually or potentially hostile to Him have been admitted. We may piously hope for, and even persuade ourselves to believe in, God's ultimate victory in some cosmic struggle against the Powers of Darkness; but we cannot logically have any assurance of such victory if these contrary forces are thought of as having their existence in complete independence of the Divine Will.

I am, of course, aware that the 'Devil' has (so to speak) an honourable tradition in Christian theology; but the postulate of a Devil is not *necessarily* incompatible with insistence upon the infinitude and omnipotence of God. Everything turns here upon how the ontological status of the alleged Devil is interpreted. Is the Devil a principle of Evil no less ultimate in nature than God Himself? Or is he rather to be thought of as 'a fallen angel', a being who is, in the last resort, a creature of God's own creation? If he is the latter (and this would seem the more orthodox theological interpretation), then no compromise of God's omnipotence is involved. Equally clearly, however, belief in this kind of Devil will not make the problem of suffering one whit easier of solution. For however much of the world's suffering we may feel disposed to attribute to the malignant machinations of the Evil One, we cannot blink the fact that, since God is *ex hypothesi* the author of the Devil's being, the ultimate responsibility for the Devil's work belongs to God. The problem of reconciling with the Divine goodness the suffering that offends our moral sentiments remains precisely where it was.

A somewhat similar reply would be pertinent against those who tell us that, after all, by far the greater part of human misery is due not to the world as God created it, but to the cruelties and follies of mankind. Waiving the objection that this view hardly appears to allow due weight to 'natural' catastrophies—earthquakes, floods, typhoons, pestilences and the like—as sources of human misery, the obvious retort is 'But didn't God create man as well as the rest of the world?' Nor does this retort seem adequately met by arguing that though God did create man, He conferred upon him free will, and that He cannot be held responsible for what men have done of their own free will. The responsibility for imparting free will to man remains with God. And if free will is a benefit that can accrue to man only at the risk of bringing in its train the horrifying sufferings which constitute our present problem, it cannot be deemed a proposition beyond all reasonable debate that a world *with* free will is better than a world *without* it. Moreover, as we shall have occasion to notice later, it seems a fair enough question to ask whether a truly omnipotent God could not have created conditions for human life that are compatible both with the exercise of free will by finite creatures and with the non-occurrence of the more morally objectionable kinds of human suffering.

3.   Let us pass on to attempted solutions which, whether or not they prove in the end any more satisfactory, have attracted more, and more authoritative, support from those seriously interested in our problem. I think that, ignoring minor variations, they reduce to *three*.

The first claims that there is no such thing as *un*deserved suffering; that man is so wicked a creature that he deserves whatever ills befall him. No human suffering, therefore, can legitimately cast doubt on the goodness of God.

The second frankly admits that there is much human suffering that is undeserved, that at least some of it cannot be justified in terms of the hazards and hardships necessary to spiritual progress, that, in short, some suffering must be acknowledged to be, *per se*, just *bad*, and therefore incapable of being directly willed by a good God; but it goes on to argue that we can see, on reflection, that the incidence of it is inevitable in a world-order which, taken as a whole, is the best world-order there could possibly be.

The third solution accepts the second solution as far as that goes, but regards it as insufficient without adding the postulate of the immortality of the soul. Given that postulate, we may suppose that due compensation will be made in a future life for miseries of the present life which, even if they be inevitable 'by-products' in the best possible world-order, nevertheless leave us with a bitter sense of injustice to the individual on the assumption that this is the only life man has. We shall examine each of these solutions in turn.

4. The first type of solution bases itself upon the premise of universal human wickedness. This premise I must confess I do not find it easy to take very seriously. It may be recalled that I tried to show in my last lecture how it originates in the main from an easily committed confusion; the confusion between, on the one hand, the universal imperfection that attaches to man merely in virtue of his finite, creaturely nature, and, on the other hand, the imperfection of (deliberate) sinning, which is a *specific* mode of human behaviour, not a *universal* mode at all, not something which pertains to human acts *as such*. I propose, therefore, to deal now very briefly indeed with the doctrine that all men are always wicked, in the main merely reminding you of certain points made before as they bear upon the present problem of man's 'deserts'.

In the first place, if universal human wickedness is taken as meaning that unaided man inevitably wills what is evil, then (*a*) this thesis (as was argued before) is in flat contradiction with the actual facts of moral experience as we know it; and (*b*) even if the thesis were sound, it would not establish that man 'deserves' whatever suffering befalls him, for the notion of 'desert' has no meaning at all in relation to a being without freedom of choice.

In the second place, if universal human wickedness is taken as meaning that, though man could choose good rather than evil, as a matter of fact all men always do choose evil, the thesis again conflicts hopelessly with the only direct evidence we have on the question, viz. our own moral experience. I doubt if there is any sane man who believes that, though he has the power to resist temptation, he has never in fact resisted it in the whole course of his life. And though it is only in the case of our own choices that we can be said strictly to *know* that man sometimes uses his freedom of choice for good as well as for evil, there is every reason to suppose that other men are in like case, and no reason to believe the contrary. It is apparently possible for those who have strong religious preconceptions about the inevitability of human sin to persuade themselves, sporadically at any rate, that even men and women who to the innocent eyes of the rest of the world have characters of rare nobility and beauty are nevertheless in reality sunk deep in iniquity. It would be very surprising to find that any normal human being had arrived at this odd view without such preconceptions.

If anything were needed to clinch the case against suffering being a just retribution for human wickedness, it is surely to be found in the acute suffering often undergone by little children, who are old enough to feel pain, but too young as yet to be miserable sinners. Most of us will resolutely decline to believe, no matter who tells us, that the toddler who plays too close to the fire and is burned to death in agony is merely receiving just punishment for its sins. It seems to me that anyone who can believe this is in need of a moral no less than an intellectual spring-cleaning: or, to change the metaphor, he ought to have his heart as well as his head examined.

I fear, however, that we cannot even yet quite leave behind us the type of solution of the problem of suffering that bases itself on the wickedness of man. There is a modified thesis about human wickedness which apparently seems to some minds to be capable of justifying all human suffering on the score of desert. This is the thesis that, though the human will is occasionally good, evil willing preponderates so vastly over good willing that 'mankind' as a whole can and must be stigmatised as 'wicked'. I do not myself believe that there is convincing evidence for this supposed over-plus of evil willing. On the other hand, I know of no way of actually disproving that thesis. Let us therefore admit its possibility, and ask whether, if true, it has anything to contribute to the problem before us.

The argument must be, I suppose, that since 'mankind' is

wicked, the sufferings of 'mankind' are deserved. Now on the face of it this seems too glaringly fallacious for anyone to hold. 'Mankind' in the premise simply means the vast majority of mankind, whereas in the conclusion (if the argument is to be relevant to the problem of suffering) it must mean all men individually. Do the proponents of this argument really mean that the minority of the human race, who are not wicked, deserve to suffer for the guilt of the majority, who are wicked?

Incredible as it may seem, there are eminent theologians who apparently want to say either this or something that is in principle indistinguishable from it. They acknowledge (almost reluctantly, one feels) that it is not really plausible to say that all men are wicked; but they are prepared to talk of what they call the 'collective guilt' of the human race, of 'mankind', and it is perfectly clear that they mean by 'collective' guilt a guilt in which *every* member of the human race is a sharer. Very often, no doubt, this involvement of the individual in a racial guilt is conceived as arising from the sin of Adam, man's common ancestor, rather than from the sins of the mass of mankind. But the principle is the same, in so far as in both cases guilt is imputed to individuals for crimes which they have not themselves committed, simply in virtue of their common membership of the human race.

This notion of collective guilt, taken as implying that the individual shares in the guilt for acts in which he played no part, seems to me to be nearer to undisguised self-contradiction than even the neo-Calvinist usually likes to approach. Either that, or else he is electing to use words, not just in an extension of their ordinary meaning, but in flat defiance of their ordinary meaning. For all ordinary usage of the term, to be 'guilty' of an act means (among other things) that one has been at the very least a contributory agent in its performance. If the neo-Calvinist is using words in their ordinary meanings, therefore, the self-contradiction of his doctrine seems unqualified. If, on the other hand, he is using the word 'guilty' in some new sense peculiar to himself, it is obvious that the word cannot have in its new sense the same implications as it had in its old sense; and in particular, there is no reason to suppose that it has the implication that is relevant to our problem, viz. that the 'guilty' deserve to suffer. In either case, therefore, his doctrine makes no contribution to the problem of suffering.

I am well aware, of course, that the protagonists of this strange notion of collective guilt are less worried about contradictions than ordinary mortals. The way to deal with them apparently (if they pertain to one's own doctrine), is to call them 'paradoxes', and then everything is all right. Collective guilt is declared to be one of the great 'paradoxes' of religion, of which the unregenerate can naturally make nothing, but the profound truth of which is revealed to the man of spiritual discernment. Unfortunately for this view, there are a great many persons whom there seems every reason to credit with spiritual discernment equal to that enjoyed by neo-Calvinists who also find themselves able to make nothing of the doctrine. Dare one suggest that what is really required in order to be able to see that a man can be guilty of an act in which he played no part whatsoever is not a rare spiritual discernment but a thoroughly muddled mind?—due chiefly, perhaps, to an inflexible determination to justify at any intellectual cost what is taken to be the authority of the scriptures in respect to certain aspects of the relationship between God and man.

The confusions that lie at the root of the doctrine of collective guilt have nowhere, to my knowledge, been so effectively exposed in brief compass as in Professor H. D. Lewis's *Morals and the New Theology*. I could wish that Chapters V, VI, and VII of this work were made compulsory reading for all who may be tempted to look to the said doctrine for an escape from their perplexities. Here I have room to touch upon only one of these confusions; the confusion involved in slipping from the proposition, which seems clearly true, that man is *nothing apart from* the social whole to which he belongs, to the different proposition, by no means clearly true, that man is *nothing but an element in* the social whole to which he belongs. If the latter proposition did happen to be true, then of course guilt could pertain to an individual man only derivatively from the social group, since he has no being save *as* an element in the group, and the 'collective guilt' doctrine could then claim some plausibility. But the two propositions are *not*, as is sometimes carelessly assumed, just alternative ways of stating the same fact. It may be the case that a man is nothing apart from society, in the sense that his existence as a man is inconceivable without certain social relationships; but it may be the case that his existence as a man is *also* inconceivable if he be not credited with an active initiative in responding to the social influences surrounding him which is not itself derivable from the social whole. We have no right to pass directly from the proposition that man is not an atomic individual, wholly self-contained, to the proposition that he is not an individual at all, but only a function of the social group. If the latter proposition is to be established, it must be by special argument: and the fate that has overtaken the various 'organic' theories of society that have from time to time been propounded by philosophers does not promise very well for any such argument.

It is not of course necessary to deny that there *are* types of whole conceivable in which the parts draw every bit of their significance from the whole to which they belong, so that to try to view the part as in any sense an individual unit is to try to view it as it is not. A living organism may be said to come fairly near to this peculiarly intimate sort of systematic unity; and a work of art, in proportion to its perfection, comes nearer still. But surely it is beyond doubt that no human society (let alone the human race) is conceivable as a unity of this kind? It is a commonplace, we agree, that in the life of primitive tribes, where the member of the tribe is (for cogent reasons) subjected from infancy to a host of influences designed to foster in him the maximum sense of community, the individual tends to have no clear consciousness of himself as distinct from the tribe, and in consequence does not demur (within limits) to sharing responsibility for acts committed by others of his tribe. But even in the most primitive societies the distinction is only obscured, not abolished. The primitive tribesman can think and act, and sometimes he does, in ways not sanctioned by the tribe, and he knows that he can; though by reason of a life-time of mental and moral conditioning he fails to draw explicitly the correct inference that, despite his dependence on the tribe for almost everything, he has a 'self' which is something more than just a manifestation of the tribal self, a 'self' which has rights and duties not exhaustively definable in terms of the tribal will. It is probably the case that man only discovers his 'private' self when a certain level of reflective analysis has been attained. But surely we are not going to say that the view which prevails on the relationship between man and society *before* the emergence of reflective analysis has better credentials than the

view which prevails *thereafter*? It is ironical indeed that representatives of a religion like Christianity, which justly prides itself on
the centrality it accords to the human person and the individual
soul, should today be aligning themselves with primitive notions
of man's relation to society which prevailed only because the
idea of an individual soul had not yet emerged into clear consciousness.

5.   The second type of solution we undertook to consider seems
to me very much more plausible. In it there is no pretence that
undeserved suffering prolonged and intense is other than evil.
But it is urged that, on reflection, we can see that a certain amount
of suffering of this sort is an *inevitable*, though an unfortunate,
incident in a world whose internal arrangements are such as to
constitute it, on the whole, the best conceivable world. If this can
be shown to be the case, God's Omnipotence and Goodness will
not be threatened. For it is a mistake to interpret 'omnipotence'
as a power to do absolutely anything, even the intrinsically
impossible, even the self-contradictory. As Professor C. S. Lewis
points out, we must distinguish between the *relatively* impossible
and the *absolutely* or *intrinsically* impossible. The relatively
impossible is impossible *unless* certain conditions, difficult, but
still possible of fulfilment, are in fact fulfilled. It is relatively
impossible to get from St. Andrews to Glasgow in three minutes;
but it is not intrinsically impossible, since conditions are conceivable (e.g. some revolution in aircraft design) under which it could
be managed. The intrinsically or absolutely impossible, on the
other hand, is impossible under any conditions whatsoever. Thus
it is intrinsically impossible for a man to get from St. Andrews to
Glasgow in no time at all. 'Omnipotence', says Dr. Lewis, 'means
power to do all that is intrinsically possible, not to do the intrinsically impossible.' [1] We can still legitimately say, he goes on,
that with God all things are possible, even though He cannot
do the intrinsically impossible; for 'intrinsic impossibilities are
not things but nonentities'.[2]

If this distinction (with its application to Omnipotence) be
granted, the existence in the world of the suffering that is so

[1] *The Problem of Pain*, p. 16.   [2] *Ibid.*

peculiarly distressing will be compatible with the Goodness and Omnipotence of God *provided that* we are able to show it to be logically bound up with the conditions of a world that is the best conceivable, so that the elimination of such suffering from the best conceivable world is an 'intrinsic impossibility'.

The argument that is intended to lead to this conclusion rests, I think, on three main propositions.

The first is that the best conceivable world should provide the opportunity for realising the highest moral values. This proposition, though we cannot perhaps call it self-evident, would, I think, be accepted by most people.

The second is that some suffering, even undeserved suffering, there must be in such a world. This proposition seems unexceptionable. We noticed earlier how hazards and hardships are indispensable to a world of moral achievement.

The third is that a world in which a moral agent can effectively operate must be an orderly world, in which events conform to objective laws. This proposition also seems to me to be true. 'Without such regularity in physical phenomena', writes Dr. F. R. Tennant (who has elaborated this proposition in most instructive fashion), 'there could be no probability to guide us: no prediction, no prudence, no accumulation of ordered experience, no formation of habit, no possibility of character or of culture.' [1]

The implications of this third proposition bring us to the heart of the matter. As Tennant proceeds to point out, 'We cannot have the advantages of a determinate order of things without its logically or its causally necessary disadvantages'.[2] The only way in which such disadvantages as we are here specially concerned with—viz. the incidence of sufferings which are *per se* evil— could be avoided would be if God were to intervene to suspend temporarily the operation of the 'natural' laws which govern the disposition of masses every time that their unimpeded operation would bring about such calamities. But when we try to think out what this would mean in practice, we can see that the interventions would have to be on such a vast scale as to undermine all confidence in the predictability of natural events. We could never, with our narrow knowledge, have reasonable assurance that any

[1] *Philosophical Theology*, Vol. II, pp. 199-200.
[2] *Op. cit.* p. 200.

particular natural sequence in which we happened to be prospectively interested would not be interrupted by Divine act because of some tragic consequence to human beings which God foresaw and of which we had no inkling. But confidence in the predictability of natural events is a necessary precondition of our undertaking purposive projects of any magnitude, including our moral and spiritual projects. We may reasonably conclude, therefore (Tennant and C. S. Lewis suggest), that it is intrinsically impossible for the sufferings we deplore to be absent from 'the best possible world'.

This seems to me a most interesting and carefully considered attempt to cope with our perplexing problem, and worthy of all respect. Nevertheless I cannot persuade myself that it will in the end really do. Granting all three of the basic propositions, and granting that *some* suffering not in itself desirable is an inevitable incident in even the best conceivable world-order, it still does not appear to me to follow that the *special kind* of undeserved suffering that constitutes our problem is an 'inevitable incident'. The question that seems to me to demand, and nowhere (as far as I know) to receive, an answer is this—'Why not a world in which all the conditions named in the basic propositions obtain, but in which the body-mind structure of beings with the capacity to suffer has been so determined by the Creator that agony at once intense and prolonged just cannot be experienced?' It is surely not obvious that it is *intrinsically* impossible for things to be so arranged by the Creator. Indeed, to put it rather crudely, it is hard to see why it should be any more troublesome for the Creator to determine the body-mind structure in this way than in the way that He has in fact chosen.

And there is a further question which, I think, one cannot altogether escape when one reflects upon the merits of this second type of solution. Suppose its advocates to be right, and us to be wrong, about the inevitability of even the more shocking kinds of suffering in a world that is a fit theatre for moral endeavour. Is it so certain that, *if* this is the price that has to be paid for such a world, the existence of such a world is better than its non-existence? Is it really established, therefore, that the creation of our world is consistent with the hypothesis of God's goodness as well as of His omnipotence? At the very least we are bound to recognise,

I think, that there have been many good and thoughtful men who have not felt it possible, 'on soul and conscience', to return an affirmative answer.

6.   Whatever its defects, however, the second type of solution does have the great merit of making clear that the problem of suffering must be considered in relation to the total conditions of the best conceivable world; and the third type of solution which we are to consider, that based on 'the hope of immortality', seems to me to gain in effectiveness if regarded as a supplement to the second type, rather than as standing by itself. Its special point is the suggestion that there is no sort of suffering, however 'cruel', that cannot be reconciled with the hypothesis of a supremely good and omnipotent God, *provided* we suppose the sufferer to be compensated in a future life by an equivalent or greater happiness.

This, I think, is the type of solution towards which the plain man most naturally leans when he reflects on the problem of suffering; just as the theologian tends towards the first type, and the philosopher towards the second. The plain man is not likely to be impressed by paradoxes like that of universal human wickedness, nor by abstract discussions about the distinction between absolute and relative impossibility. But he is well at home with the notion of joy compensating sorrow; and even though he would not always call himself 'religious', he is seldom prepared to rule out as impossible the hypothesis of an after life. Indeed this is probably to under-state the case. It would seem that most men find it difficult really to believe in their own final extinction. When, e.g. Stephen Leacock humorously confesses a dislike for life-assurance agents, because they always try to persuade him that he will one day die, 'which is not the case', the joke makes its point for us through our recognition that, despite its *prima facie* absurdity, something very like this disbelief in our own death lies deep down in the minds of most of us.

The immortality type of solution is, of course, devoid of value for those who are completely convinced that there is no after life. But it will have some value (assuming it has no fatal internal defect) for all who accept immortality as a possibility; and its value will be enhanced for those who deem immortality to be not merely possible but probable, and in proportion to the degree of probability they attach to it. This means, I think, that it has some value, though it may be slight, for most men, and even for most philosophers. For even among philosophers (a category which does not automatically include scientists, however eminent in their own field, who think fit to publish causeries upon philosophical questions) forthright denial of a future life has been comparatively rare. Moreover, philosophers who do deny it without qualification commonly do so on the basis of a doctrine about the self, and about the self's relation to its body, which, in my opinion at any rate, is radically false. It may be recalled that the upshot of our analysis of the self in last year's course of lectures, so far as our present question is concerned, was that our knowledge of the self and its relation to its body leaves it an entirely open question whether the soul does or does not survive the destruction of its earthly tenement.

For myself, therefore, holding as I do that a future life is a real possibility, the immortality type of solution is by no means one to be lightly dismissed. Let us then look at it more closely.

It must be conceded to it, I think, that within the ambit of our ordinary lives the principle of joy compensating sorrow is familiar, and readily accepted. A man who has experienced much severe suffering which seems to him undeserved does not as a rule rail against fate, does not complain that life has been 'unfair' to him, so long as he can call to mind much keen happiness which he feels to be no more merited than his misfortunes. He accepts the joys as counter-balancing and cancelling out the sorrows. Nor do I see on what ground it could be denied that this simple principle of compensation is equally applicable where the joys that are to balance the sorrows occur not in the individual's earthly life but in a life hereafter. The one proviso is that this future life must be such that the individual who enjoys its felicities is aware of being the same self who in earthly life suffered the excess of pain or sorrow. The retention of personal identity does seem to be a *sine qua non* of any immortality that can serve the purpose of compensating earthly suffering. This proviso, however, entails no more (though of course also no less) difficulty than the hypothesis of the immortality of the soul itself. For it is not the *soul* that is immortal on any hypothesis which does not allow to the future experiencing subject consciousness of his identity with the subject of the past experiences.

Yet there is one serious difficulty which the immortality solution must find some way of meeting. It can be stated as follows:

Let us agree that, granted the possibility of appropriate future compensation, even the worst abominations of suffering in this life do not necessarily entail injustice in the human situation taken as a whole. The world of God's creation may, after all, be at least a 'good' world. But can it be the 'best conceivable' world?—as it ought to be on the assumption that it is created by a Being perfect in power and goodness. If there was force in the objection we raised earlier to the second type of solution, the objection that there is no evident reason why such a Being should not have so deter-mined the mind-body structure of man as to make impossible the extravagant sufferings that appal our moral sensibilities, this seems very doubtful. For there seems in that case no difficulty in con-ceiving a world in which such sufferings do not occur, yet in which the joys of an after-life which it was suggested might compensate them *do* occur—not by way of compensation (which is no longer required) but simply as an act of grace. Such a world, other things being equal, would be a better world than one in which these same joys are compensations for past miseries. Happiness is a good, so that, other things being equal, one world is better than another if it contains more happiness; and obviously there is more happi-ness in a world in which the joys of an after-life are not just a 'plus' that cancels out with a previous 'minus'.

I think that this objection can be countered only by challenging an assumption which underlay our criticism of the second type of solution. While we agreed that the best conceivable world must be one which affords opportunity for the achievement of the highest moral values, and that a necessary condition of such a world is the occurrence of much suffering that is undeserved, it seemed to us that this condition could be adequately fulfilled without permitting the possibility of certain horrifying kinds of suffering that men and women are sometimes called upon to endure. But perhaps our assumption was over-hasty. An advocate of the immortality solution might retort with the pertinent question, 'On what principle do you presume to limit the degree of suffering in a world that is to be a theatre for the achievement of the highest moral values?' The difficulty of fixing a limit is apparent when one remembers that one's admiration for a man who follows the path of duty, in despite of the personal suffering it entails or may be expected to entail, is (other things being equal) roughly proportionate to the magnitude of the suffering entailed or expected. The implication would seem to be that the greater the suffering that can occur, the greater the moral value it is open to men to achieve. But if this is so, how can it be possible to put any limit to the degree of suffering that should be permitted in a world that is to be the best possible theatre for moral endeavour? And the 'immortality' advocate might complete his defence in some such terms as these. 'We are willing to grant you that the "best conceivable" world is not necessarily identical with that which is the best conceivable regarded solely from the standpoint of opportunities for moral achievement. If happiness is a good (and we do not deny it), *its* claim to inclusion in the best conceivable world cannot be ignored. You are fully entitled to insist that a Creator whom we can honestly esteem as supremely good must not show himself indifferent to the happiness of the creatures he calls into being. But that is just where our hypothesis of immortality comes in. *If* one knew that this earthly life was all, then there would be much point in arguing that man's Creator either was not omnipotent or, on the count of his inadequate concern for human happiness, was not perfect in goodness. But it is *not* known that this earthly life is all. An after-life is a real possibility; and if it is possible, it is also possible that it should be of such a kind as to satisfy completely the legitimate demand that a Creator who is perfect in goodness should have a concern for the happiness of his creatures. Hence your objection to the solution we propose breaks down.'

Is this defence a valid one? On the whole, I incline to accept it —a little tentatively perhaps, for I cannot feel as confident as I should like that there are not flaws in it which I have failed to detect. I conclude, accordingly, that the facts of human suffering are not demonstrably fatal to Rational Theism; though they do confront it with a formidable problem of which I can see no plausible solution that does not depend upon the hypothesis of appropriate compensation in a future life.

7. I have examined in this lecture what I take to be the three most important ways in which Rational Theists have sought to reconcile with their faith the grimmer facts of human suffering. Perhaps it will seem to some that there is a fourth way which has a comparable claim to consideration. I have in mind the view that the whole project of seeking to 'explain' or 'justify' the world which God creates is in principle absurd; indeed irreligious, since it implies that mere finite minds can plumb the depths of the Creative Mind, and thereby denies in effect the immensity of the gulf which for the truly religious man must always be humbly acknowledged as separating the creature from his Creator. The real solution of the problem of suffering, it is suggested, lies in seeing that it is not a problem that can have intelligible meaning for finite minds at all.

I have excluded this type of 'solution' quite deliberately, because it seems to me that, whatever its virtues 'in the abstract', it is not a type of solution open to Rational Theists. If we are Rational, as distinct from Supra-rational, Theists, we are committed to the view that the qualities of goodness, power, etc., ascribed to God are to be interpreted in their literal significance; i.e. in the meanings these qualities have for our experience. But this implies that the workings of the Divine Mind *are*, in principle, intelligible to the human mind. And to admit this is surely to deny one's self any right to plead man's impotence to fathom the 'inscrutable purposes' of God against those who argue that there are facts of experience incompatible with the purpose of a Creator who is perfect in goodness and power in the literal signification of these terms.

I am *not* saying, let it be noted, that it is *not* an absurdity for human minds to set out to 'justify the ways of God to men'. I am only saying that it should not be deemed absurd from the standpoint of Rational Theism. For myself, I believe that it *is* an absurdity. But that is because I take the element of 'mystery' in the Godhead in much fuller earnest than Rational Theism chooses to do. On the Supra-rationalist view that qualities like goodness and power cannot have more than a symbolic import when ascribed to God, any attempt to understand the manifestations of God in terms of these qualities as literally interpreted is *ex hypothesi* absurd. The question how we are to justify the ways of

God to man is not, for supra-rational Theism, a question that it is difficult to answer. It is a question that it is ridiculous to raise.

But this is to anticipate. We have not yet passed beyond 'Rational' Theism; and since I have admitted that Rational Theism is not disproved by the difficulties over human suffering, no need to pass beyond it has yet appeared. Rational Theism has survived the charge of being inconsistent with acknowledged facts of experience. Can it also survive the charge of being inconsistent with itself? That is the question to which we shall turn in the next lecture.

IS RATIONAL THEISM
SELF-CONTRADICTORY?

1. In this lecture we are to consider the tenability of Rational Theism from the point of view not of its consistency with acknowledged facts of experience but of its own internal consistency. Theism in general proclaims that God is wholly perfect; and, as is entirely natural, it interprets this Divine perfection in terms of 'the highest we know' in human experience; applying to God, accordingly, such concepts as those of goodness, wisdom and power in their highest conceivable manifestations. The trouble begins as soon as we set ourselves to think out just what such concepts can really mean when applied to an absolutely perfect being. If the concepts involved are to be used significantly of God at all, their meanings must, presumably, bear some intimate relation to the meanings they have in ordinary usage. But if that relation is taken, as it is by Rational Theism, to be one of literal identity, there is at least a strong *prima facie* case for the view that, so understood, these concepts actually *contradict* the very concept of Divine Perfection which it is their professed function to illustrate. There may be some sense (and I, for my part, believe, and shall later try to show, that there is) in which a Being acknowledged to be wholly perfect, and therefore infinite or self-complete, can at the same time be significantly described as good, wise, powerful, just, benevolent, merciful and the like. But if there is, it is not easy to see how it can be a *literal* sense. Such, at any rate, is to be the chief contention of today's lecture.

It need hardly be said that there is nothing original, or even unfamiliar, about such speculations. There are probably few serious theologians of any persuasion in whose writings there does not sooner or later come a point at which they say in effect 'But *of course* God's power, wisdom and goodness cannot be properly understood in terms of these qualities as we finite beings can alone envisage them. The finite mind is incompetent to frame a concept of the infinite power and wisdom and goodness of God. We must humbly recognise that the attributes of the Creator are in the last resort a mystery to the mere creature.' So far so good. What is not so good is that, to all appearances, this recognition of the mystery of the Godhead has for most theists exceedingly little effect upon their actual theology. Lip-service having been duly paid to it, they seem to feel themselves absolved from any further theoretical obligations in the matter. They proceed forthwith to debate refinements of theological doctrines which seem plainly to imply the concepts in question in their literal meaning; as though it could somehow just be taken for granted that the admitted differences of meaning that these concepts must bear in their application to God are of such a kind as not to undermine the theological doctrines themselves. Yet if it once be conceded that these concepts are applicable to God only 'with a difference', it is surely imperative to establish that this 'difference' is at least not so radical that the doctrines employing these concepts completely lose their old sense—and perhaps even gain no new one!

Whatever its professions, then, it seems to me hard to deny that the actual practice of orthodox or official theism identifies it with what I have called Rational theism. Let us now begin our enquiry into the internal consistency of Rational theism.

2. The simplest way of proceeding, I think, will be to examine two concepts that lie at the base of all the intellectual and moral qualities which theism ascribes to God; the concepts, namely, of *Thought* and *Will*. Wisdom, justice, love, benevolence, etc., all presuppose the activities either of thought, or of will, or of both. If thought and will cannot in any literal sense be predicated of a Perfect Being, *a fortiori* we cannot predicate of God in a literal sense any one of the intellectual and moral qualities that pre-suppose thought and will. Let us look first, then, at thought. Can

a Being who is *ex hypothesi* perfect be conceived as in any literal sense a 'thinking' being?

Now if the doctrine concerning thought which I expounded and defended at some length in my first series, the doctrine that all cognition involves *judgment*, is valid, the answer to our present question seems to be almost self-evidently in the negative. In judgment there must be a predicate distinct from the subject; and the function of the predicate in the judgment is that thereby we further characterise some feature of the objective reality which we take as already accurately characterised so far by the qualities implicit in our 'subject' term. Expansion and development of existing knowledge is thus of the very essence of the judgment. But expansion and development of existing knowledge have clearly no application to the mind of a perfect being. They presuppose defect for their very possibility. Accordingly thinking, if it be true that all cognition involves judging, is not conceivable as a function of the Divine nature.

Moreover, not only does judgment *presuppose* defect in knowledge, it is itself, even when 'completed', defective *as* knowledge. And this defect is inherent in its nature. Bradley's argument to this conclusion, in his famous (but, alas! not now familiar) chapter on 'Thought and Reality', seems to myself decisive. There is always, he points out, in the subject of judgment an aspect of existence, of 'thatness', which is not included in the thought-content of the judgment, and which thus leaves the judgment inevitably incomplete as 'knowledge' of the 'subject'. Make an actual judgment, he adjures us, and 'see if you do not discover, beyond the content of your thought, a subject *of* which it is true, and which it (your thought-content) does not comprehend'.[1] The subject is always, in some measure, 'beyond the predicated content'. But clearly the subject we are seeking to know cannot be perfectly known so long as there remains *any* aspect of it uncomprehended by the thought. We seem bound to say, therefore, that thought, in so far as it is judgment, implies some degree of defect of knowledge in its very constitution.

It will not do, however, to presume that the present audience was persuaded by, or now even recalls, or for that matter ever heard, the rather lengthy argument by which I sought in the first

---

[1] *Appearance and Reality*, p. 169 (7th impression). Italics mine.

series to recommend the old-fashioned—but, as I firmly believe, the almost incomparably important—doctrine that all thinking involves judging. And there is one kind of thinking, often contrasted with judging, which it would be particularly unwise of us to ignore merely on the strength of a general principle discussed a year ago. I refer to 'intuitive thinking', the special relevance of which to our question of the possibility of Divine thought is obvious.

Now not all intuitive thinking, of course, can be contrasted with judgment. Many philosophers believe that there is an intuitive thinking which grasps the truth of certain self-evident propositions: and here the 'intuition' is quite clearly an 'intuitive' *judgment*. The alleged intuitive thinking which might be placed in rivalry with judging is rather that to which Professor Price has given the name of 'totalistic thinking'. This kind of intuition has nothing to do with the discernment of self-evident truths. Its contents may very well be false. The essence of it lies in its contrast with discursive thinking; and the difference between these two Price explains in a passage that deserves to be transcribed *in toto*:

'In discursive consciousness (as the name suggests) there is a *passage of the mind* from one item to another related item, for instance, from a subject to a concept under which we classify it, or from premises to conclusion. There may also be that kind of passage which is characteristic of "wondering", when after developing the consequences of one alternative we pass to another alternative, and then to its consequences, and then to a third. And when we have discursive consciousness of a whole or complex of any sort (as in counting), although the whole may be vaguely present to the mind from the first, yet definite consciousness of the whole comes *after* consciousness of the parts. In intuitive consciousness, on the other hand, consciousness of the whole comes before definite consciousness of the parts. And there is no passage of the mind: whatever we intuit is present all at once. We might say that intuitive consciousness is "totalistic", not "progressive" or "additive".

'There is a further difference. In the discursive form of consciousness we seem to be active, to be, as it were, "seeking" or "following" something. But in the intuitive form, though there is an act of consciousness—in the sense of an *actus*, the actualising of a power at a certain moment,—yet there is no *activity*. The mind rests, as it were, on its object. (Not that it is passive either: it is just non-active.)' [1]

[1] Perception, pp. 150-1.

Price is concerned to exploit this important distinction in a context very different from ours, but its significance for the question of the possibility of thinking in a Perfect Being is manifest. 'Passage of the mind' implies defect of knowledge in the mind that 'passes'. But in this 'totalistic' thinking 'there is no passage of the mind: whatever we intuit is present all at once'. We do not even 'pass' from whole to part. We apprehend the whole *in* its differentiations, and we apprehend the parts *only as* differentiations of the whole. Is it not possible, then, that we have here a type of thinking which can legitimately be ascribed to a Perfect Being?

I think not. And the reason is, in a nut-shell, that totalistic intuition, despite appearances to the contrary, cannot at bottom escape being a judgment. The intuited content, it seems to me clear, is always implicitly predicated *of* a subject that is not itself comprehended within that content. Take, e.g. the totalistic intuition of an individual person—it is, of course, to the apprehension of such individual wholes as persons that this kind of intuition is especially adapted. Our intuition here is, I suggest, always of a being that *has*, not of a being that just *is*, the differentiated unity of qualities which constitutes the 'content' of the intuition. There is an aspect of 'thatness' in the person not comprehended in the 'what' of the intuited content. And the proof that this is so lies in the manner of our natural reaction in cases where, as sometimes happens, the person of whom we had this 'intuitive' apprehension goes on to behave in a way that conflicts with our intuition of him. When this occurs, we are doubtless surprised. But we are not *stupefied*, as we ought to be if we really supposed that *he*, this person, was wholly comprehended within, reduced without remainder to, the content of our intuition. Our natural reaction is just to say that 'he' did not after all have precisely the character we took him to have. But if, for our intuition, 'he' just *was* the individual whole intuited, that reaction would be absurd. There could then be no 'he' about whom a mistake was being made, no 'he' to be the bearer of the different character which we now recognise that 'he' has. We should be obliged to suppose that it is not really 'he' but some other person altogether that we now observe acting 'out of character' with the intuited person. But in fact, of course, we suppose nothing of the sort. As already remarked, we take for granted a 'he' of whom our intuited content was implicitly predicated. In short, 'totalistic thinking' involves *judgment*, with whatever disabilities as knowledge may attach thereto, and it cannot, accordingly, be ascribed to God, any more than 'discursive' thinking can.

I think we must say, then, that there always is, even in totalistic thinking, an aspect of 'thatness' in the intuited object not comprehended in the intuited content, and constituting, therefore, an 'other' over against thought. Our *desideratum* in the search for a thinking completely free from defect, and thus appropriate to a Perfect Being, is a kind of thinking in which this element of otherness is eliminated and thought becomes truly 'one with' its object. Is there any reasonably promising candidate for this office besides totalistic thinking?

One only, it seems to me—the kind of thinking (if indeed it qualifies for this name) which occurs in certain aesthetic experiences. Descriptions of such experiences are frequently offered which suggest an at least very close approximation to the actual identification of mind with its object. In contemplating the beauty of a great picture or a great poem, a man's mind, it is claimed, may be so absorbed by, so caught up into, the consummately satisfying unity of the object that for a brief but appreciable spell it is truer to say that he *is* the painting, or the poem, rather than that 'it' is an object of 'his' contemplation. The subject-object distinction would seem to be temporarily annulled. There is no longer awareness of self *over against* an other, but only of self *in* other. Thought has become 'one with its object'.

There is little doubt that this way of talking does point to an important truth about aesthetic appreciation. But it is, I think, as it stands, an over-statement of that truth. For even if it were the case that our mind became literally one with its object, it seems certain that we could never be *aware* that it was so. We could not be aware of it during the experience itself; for we could not frame the judgment 'I and my object are one', if we did not in our thought distinguish the 'I' from the 'object'—that is to say, the judgment presupposes the very distinction which it asserts to be non-existent. Nor could we be aware of it by means of memory; for one can only remember that of which one has once been aware; and (as has just been pointed out) we cannot have been aware during the supposed experience of being one with the object that we *were* one with the object.

I am not, let me make clear, contending that there cannot be an experience in which there is no sense of an 'other' beyond the self, an experience of genuine unity with the object. All that I am contending is that, if there is, it is not an experience of *knowing*. I do not see how there can be an experience properly called 'knowing' where we are not, and cannot be, aware that we are knowing. A unitary experience in which we have no awareness either of knowing or of an object known surely falls into the category of *feeling* rather than of thinking or knowing. No doubt many philosophers have offered descriptions of ideally perfect knowledge in which an essential factor is that this distinction between knower and known has been overcome; but it does not follow that there is any conceivable experience to which such descriptions correspond. Of course such descriptions are not just meaningless. But their significance is, I think, wholly negative. Those who offer them rightly see it to be a condition of perfect knowledge, in which there must be no inadequacy calling for supplementation by further knowledge, that there cannot remain any 'other' over against thought; and they accordingly formulate this ideal state as an experience in which the distinction of subject from object is transcended. The words of the description may be positive; but their significance, so far as I can see, is merely to indicate certain conditions of our ordinary knowledge that cannot be allowed to survive if perfect knowledge is to be achieved. That is to say, their significance lies wholly in what they negate.

It is time, moreover, that we reminded ourselves that even if such phrases as *noesis noeseos* did denote a conceivable kind of thinking, it would still not be the kind of thinking that any Theist would wish to ascribe to God. For Theism the created world is, and presumably is contemplated by God as, other than God's self. In God's apprehension of the created world that world must be in some sense a 'not-self' to God, if theistic accounts of God's relation to the world are to make sense. It seems quite hopeless, therefore, to try to accommodate the Divine thinking to any description of perfect thought which requires the annulment of the distinction of self from not-self.

3. But a question of some interest arises here. The not-self of God, i.e. the created world, is a quite unique sort of not-self. For it is a not-self that is nevertheless (for theism) a manifestation of the *self*. It would seem, therefore, that we have in this one unique instance, both the not-self which is necessary if the self is to have 'knowledge' in any sense of the term to which we finite beings can attach meaning, and at the same time a not-self which has within it no uncomprehended 'that' as distinct from its comprehended 'what' (since in this instance the not-self is created by the self, i.e. by God, and is thus presumably known to the self in every aspect of its being). If so, then we have here the possibility of knowing without the defects intrinsic to human knowing.

The suggestion is intriguing. But I fear it will not serve to remove our old difficulty. It is tempting to say that if God created the world he must 'know' it in its entirety, its 'that' as well as its 'what'. But it remains the case that we have no idea at all what it would be like to 'know' any existent thing in its 'thatness' as well as its 'whatness'. In the thinking to which we can alone attach positive meaning the divorce of 'that' from 'what' in the object apprehended seems inescapable. But if the Divine 'knowledge' of the created world is thus different in principle from any 'knowledge' with which we are acquainted, it can surely only mislead to talk and think of it as 'knowledge' at all.

The nearest analogy within human experience to knowledge of an entity in which there is no uncomprehended 'thatness' is probably to be found in the realm of 'factitious' ideas. If we frame the idea of a gold mountain, or of a parallelogram, we know everything there is to our object—in a sense, its 'that' as well as its 'what'; for there is nothing in the object which we have not ourselves put there. But this perfect knowledge is possible because, and only because, the existence of the 'object' here is a purely conceptual existence. If the world as the object of God's thought could be regarded in this light, as existing only for His *thought*, then we could certainly attach a clear meaning to His knowledge of it. But it is not a merely conceptual existence in God's mind that the created world is supposed to enjoy. No doubt, according to many accounts of Creation, the world did exist in God's mind conceptually as a precondition of His creating it. But the very essence of the act of Creation is that the world, whether or not previously existing in idea, is now given *actual* existence.

Before passing finally from the question of the possibility of a Perfect Being 'thinking', it is worth noticing, though of necessity very briefly, a special difficulty that relates to the apprehension of *time*. God's thinking of the world in time, if it is to be perfect knowledge, must be a thinking that completely comprehends the time-order in a single act. But can we really attach any meaning to such 'thinking'? The trouble is that it would seem to be of the very nature of time as we experience it to be *in*complete. Any time of which we can be conscious *as* a time points beyond itself both before and after. For our minds at any rate, a 'time' that has no further time beyond itself is not what we mean by 'time' at all. How then can we possibly attach meaning to a 'thinking' that comprehends 'the whole of time'?

It has sometimes been suggested that the analogy of 'the specious present' may help us here. It is pointed out that the 'present' for any single act of finite awareness is really a *duration*, a block or span of time that comprises a before and after within itself. Could not we think of God as apprehending time in a magnified specious present that comprises within itself *all* 'befores' and 'afters'?

I do not think so; for the simple reason that the specious present, to be a 'present' for us at all, is always apprehended as *itself* temporally after a past and temporally before a future. We are not helped in the least towards the conception of *completed* time by the notion of the specious present. Indeed I am inclined to think that those who find in the specious present a clue to the Divine apprehension of time are misconceiving the problem. The problem is not how a temporal span, a duration, can be apprehended in a single act. It is how a duration of any kind can be apprehended otherwise than within a time that extends beyond it. And to this problem, so far as I can see, the notion of the specious present is irrelevant.

4. We may now turn from the problem presented by Divine thinking to the problem presented by Divine willing. 'God's Will' is an expression than which there are few more common in the

religious life of man. Yet will, far more obviously than thought, presents apparently intractable difficulties when we try to conceive it as exercised by a Perfect Being.

For it seems almost self-evident that will (and the same holds good of other conative terms like desire and purpose) implies defect. In the typical conation the conative subject envisages a state of affairs not yet existing which he conceives to be better than the state of affairs that now exists. The imperfection of the subject's present state thus seems to be of conation's very essence. Sometimes, it is true, the object of our will (or desire, or purpose) is not a state different from our present state, but the prolongation into the future of our present state; and this looks at first sight like a special case of willing that implies no defect and is therefore applicable, for what it is worth, to a Perfect Being. But even this hope is incapable of being sustained. There can be no point in willing the prolongation of a state unless it is supposed that this state will, or at least may, cease to be if we do not take appropriate action. But this implies in the willing agent the consciousness of an at least *possible* imperfection. And a being cannot be 'perfect' if there is even a possibility of his becoming imperfect; still less if he is *mistaken* in supposing that he may possibly become imperfect. Moreover, willing the prolongation of a present state, like all other willing, presupposes the existence of the willing subject himself within a temporal order. And we have already seen in an earlier lecture the difficulty of reconciling perfect, self-complete being with a temporal order of existence.

The puzzles that beset the notion of Divine willing find very significant illustration in the intricate controversies of the theologians over the manner of God's creation of the world. From very early times theologians have been keenly alive to the difficulty of interpreting creation as an act of God's *will*; and at the same time to the apparently equal difficulty of interpreting it in any other way. Let us glance briefly at the two sides of the dilemma that here confronts theology.

In the first place, if the creation of the world be conceived as due to a specific act of the Divine will, this seems to imply a time at which the world as yet was not, and at which God was conscious of 'lack', of incomplete excellence; and this is inconsistent with the postulate of God's Perfection. Nor does the difficulty appear to be removable by supposing, with Augustine and many others, that the Divine Will brings the time-order itself into being along with 'the world'. The merit of this hypothesis is that if it be accepted we are no longer required—indeed we are no longer able —to conceive of God's existence (in a state of 'lack') prior to the creation of the world. For there was *no* 'time' at which the world did not exist. The *trouble* about this hypothesis is that it seems merely to shift the difficulty from one point to another. For we cannot intelligibly speak of God willing the creation of the time-order if it be the case, as it would appear to be, that 'willing' in any sense in which it has a meaning for us, implies that there is for the willing agent a contrast between the 'now' and the 'not yet'. In other words, the 'willing' of the existence of a time-order seems itself to presuppose the existence of a time-order.

Harassed by these and similar difficulties, many theologians have attempted a counter-interpretation of the creative activity. According to the alternative they suggest, the world comes into being not by a specific act of God's will, but as a *self-manifestation* of the Divine nature. On this view the world is, as it were, 'organic' to God. God could no more be without the world than the world could be without God. The world is as eternal as God Himself, and creation must be regarded as an 'eternal act'.

The most common objection to this view is that in abandoning the notion of a Divine act of will it seems to deny by implication anything of the nature of intelligent choice or purpose in the creation of the world. This is a deprivation which those nurtured in the tradition of a theistic religion can scarcely be expected to regard with equanimity. If they had to give up talking of God's 'purpose' for the world, of God's 'plan' for His creation, they would find it hard to believe that something is not being lost that belongs to the very core of theism. Moreover, it is felt by many that a view of the world as a 'self-manifestation' of God has pantheistic implications absent from the view of it as called into being by an act of Divine will. It is more difficult, it is felt, to conceive of beings in the created world as enjoying even a measure of independent initiative; and some measure of independent initiative it is important for theism to retain, at least in respect of those of God's creatures whom we think of as endowed with 'soul' or 'personality'.

M

Of these two doctrines of the relation of the created world to its source, the Divine Will doctrine and the Divine self-manifestation doctrine, the latter is, in my opinion, by far the less vulnerable. The objections to the former appear to me to admit of no really effective answer. An act of will on the part of a Perfect Being does seem to be a plain contradiction in terms. For this reason alone it will be worth our while to spend a little time over the objections to the 'self-manifestation' doctrine, with a view to seeing whether they are in fact insurmountable. The main objections have just been stated: first, that the doctrine apparently implies the rejection of purpose or plan for the created world; and secondly, that it apparently reduces the created world to a mere phase or mode of the Divine life, and is thus not easily distinguishable from Pantheism.

5.   The second of these objections at any rate does not appear insurmountable. On *any* theory of the relation of the world to its creator, the endowment of the creature with some real independence of its creator is a puzzling matter. It implies on the part of the creator an act of self-limitation of which it is hard to form any clear idea. But is there any *greater* difficulty in supposing that it is intrinsic to the Divine Nature to manifest itself in the creation of individual persons with a measure of genuine initiative, than there is in supposing that this situation comes about through a specific act of Divine Will? I cannot see that there is. Indeed I rather suspect that those who find a pantheistic threat in the 'self-manifestation' doctrine of creation may be guilty of a certain confusion between two different senses in which the term 'creation' in this context may be understood. We may be meaning by God's 'creation' *either* the *act* of creation, the bringing into being of the world; *or*, on the other hand, the *thing created, the world itself*. Now if the 'self-manifestation' doctrine holds that 'creation' in the *latter* sense is a self-manifestation of God, and if it understands by 'the thing created' (as is natural enough) all that happens, has happened, or will happen therein, I should agree that Pantheism is inescapable. No 'activity' on the part of the creature could then be regarded as more than a specific differentiation of the Divine activity. But if, on the other hand, it is 'creation' in

the *former* sense that is being meant, there is, so far as I can judge, no implication of Pantheism. For the act of creation in which God manifests His nature may well be (as traditional theism normally holds) a bringing into being of creatures some of whom are also, within limits, themselves creators; creatures whose activities cannot be regarded as just modes of the Divine activity since they have been granted, by an act of God which is at once a self-manifestation and a self-limitation, a real measure of freedom in the conduct of their lives.

It will be appreciated, I hope, that I am not suggesting for a moment that the notion of the creating of creators is one that is easy to understand on the doctrine that creation is a self-mani-festation of the Divine nature. Far from it. What I do suggest is that it is no harder to understand on this doctrine than on the alternative doctrine that creation comes about through an act of Divine will. And if this be so, the internal difficulties which beset the conception of a Perfect Being exercising 'will' are sufficient to make the 'self-manifestation' doctrine much the preferable.

The first objection to the doctrine is more formidable; namely, that only if we can regard the world as the product of Divine Will can we suppose it to have any purpose or plan. Yet I think that it too admits of at least partial solution.

The partial solution lies in seeing that, while it is true that on the 'self-manifestation' as contrasted with the 'Divine Will' doctrine of creation we are forbidden to suppose that God had a 'purpose' in His 'Mind' in creating the world, this does not necessarily have the disquieting implications it is commonly taken to have. We are apt to think (in our habitually anthropomorphic way) that if the world does not issue from a Divine purpose, it must be 'purposeless' in the sense of 'fortuitous', and thus a world without meaning or value. Now this would indeed be a disquieting thought. But a little reflection suffices to show that nothing of the kind is implied by the doctrine we are now considering. For according to this doctrine the creation of the world is the self-manifestation of a *Perfect* Being, a Being of transcendent excellence no less than of transcendent power. How can we consistently suppose a world which so originates to be devoid of meaning and value? Must we not rather agree that the very notion contradicts itself? No doubt the self-manifestation doctrine can of itself do no more than reassure us *that* the created world has meaning and value. It does not inform us wherein its meaning and value consist. But that would only be calamitous, I submit, if it entailed that we finite creatures are therefore left rudderless and helpless, with no means of knowing whither we should direct our course, no means of distinguishing good from evil in the conduct of life. And surely this is *not* our plight? We must not forget that there is, after all, such a thing as a 'moral consciousness' in man. The analysis of the moral consciousness belonged to our first series of lectures, and I cannot, of course, recapitulate it here. But if the argument of the final lecture of that series had any force, then we have in the moral consciousness something whose very essence it is to direct us to the objectively good, to the good 'in the nature of things'; something which, I argued, constitutes even in itself a sufficient guarantee of the meaning and value of human life.

I cannot see, therefore, that any vital interest of humanity, religious or otherwise, is threatened if we accept the Divine self-manifestation doctrine rather than the Divine Will doctrine concerning the relation of God to His creation. And I must again insist upon the fundamental theoretic superiority of the former. Mystery there is, on *any* showing, about the relation of God to His creation. How, for beings that themselves belong to the creaturely order, could it be otherwise? But mystery is one thing, self-contradiction is another. It is a mystery that the world should be a manifestation of the Divine Nature; but it is not, or at any rate not obviously, a self-contradiction. On the other hand, it seems no mere mystery, but sheer self-contradiction, that a Perfect Being should create the world by an act whose very nature implies defect, as is the case with the act of will.

The intrinsic interest of the topic of creation has led me to give to it perhaps more space than was strictly its due within the context of the present lecture; though it does serve to illustrate in a particularly fundamental way the difficulties inherent in the concept of 'God's Will', with which Rational or 'orthodox' Theism makes so much play. I should like to stress, however, that I am very far from wishing to suggest that the notion of Divine 'Creation' in itself brings contradiction into the theistic position —as the notion of Divine *Thought* and Divine *Will* appear to me to do. For theism is not committed to the specific doctrine that

God's creation proceeds from an act of will. What is essential to theism here (and essential, I think, to all developed religion) is simply that God is *somehow* the source of all that is. Trouble begins only when one tries to conceptualise this 'somehow'. There is in most minds of philosophic bent a powerful urge to deny in practice—while often accepting in formal theory—that there is a limit to the human mind's powers of explanation, even where what is to be explained is nothing less than the existence of the world itself and of our own souls. If one does succumb to the temptation of trying to offer a conceptual account of the Creative activity, nothing is more natural than that one should do so in terms of the highest forms of activity with which we are ourselves acquainted, those of thought and will. But that the temptation is one that must be resisted if we are not to fall into manifest absurdities, seems to myself beyond reasonable doubt. Even if the sole alternative to a theology which assumes Divine Thought and Divine Will should be just no theology at all, that would still, in my judgment, be an insufficient excuse for sponsoring doctrines that entail self-contradictions. And to call the self-contradictions 'paradoxes'—blessed word!—seems to me to aggravate rather than to mitigate the offence.

6. Destructive criticism such as is exemplified throughout the whole of the present lecture is, however, of little or no value save in so far as it paves the way for reconstruction. The latter immeasurably more difficult task is to be initiated in the next lecture, and it will occupy us to the end of the course. It will perhaps help to place in proper perspective the task ahead of us if I pause here to review briefly the movement of the argument in this second course up to the present juncture.

We began by trying to get a satisfactory definition of the term 'religion'; not of the 'thing' which the term denotes, but of the term 'religion' itself when it is being used in a critical and considered way in educated speech and writing. The conclusion we eventually arrived at was that 'religion' essentially connotes an experience comprising belief in a supernatural being or beings of transcendent power and value, along with the complex emotive attitudes intrinsically appropriate thereto. We then proceeded to argue, in Lecture XII, that there is much more than mere parochial prejudice behind the virtual identification, which is in practice so common, of the question 'Is religion true?' with the question 'Is *theism* true?' Theism we took as consisting essentially in 'belief in one God, Perfect in Power, Wisdom and Goodness, an Infinite and Eternal Spirit Who is the ground of all that is, Who is the Moral Governor of the world, and Who is yet a living presence in the hearts of men'. And theism so understood, we tried to show, can with much plausibility be regarded as not just one among other species of 'religion' as we defined it, but rather as the logical development of religion itself; or, more explicitly, as the theoretical form which religion tends to assume when its implications are freely and critically reflected upon by disciplined and know-ledgeable minds.

Since it appeared, then, that there was strong justification for the ordinary man's identification of the question of the truth of religion with the question of the truth of theism, the way seemed open for us to make a direct attack upon the fundamental problem of these lectures by a critical examination of the beliefs charac-teristic of theism. But we found that we could not do this without taking due account of a vital distinction between two ways of interpreting theistic beliefs. Are the qualities which theism predi-cates of God to be understood in their *literal* meaning, or only in some merely *symbolic* meaning? We confessed our personal doubts about whether a theism which gave them a literal meaning could really be regarded as doing justice to the element of transcendent mystery which religion recognises in its worshipful object, and our doubts, consequently, about such a theism's claim to be the true theoretical expression of the religious consciousness. At the same time we could not ignore that the manner in which theistic theologians in general articulate and develop their doctrines appeared to imply a large acceptance of these Divine qualities in their literal meaning. It seemed right, therefore, to ask the question 'Is theism true?' in the first place of theism in its orthodox, 'rational' form.

That enquiry has occupied us throughout the last three lectures. We examined Rational Theism from the standpoint, firstly, of the consistency of theism with the 'facts of experience' as we seem bound to regard them; and secondly, of the consistency of theism with itself—that is to say, the consistency of the attributes and qualities of the theistic God with one another. The first standpoint entailed a prolonged discussion of the problem of evil in its twin forms of the problem of sin and the problem of suffering. Our conclusion was that theism was not inconsistent with the existence of evil in either form; though hard put to it, without enlisting the postulate of immortality, to maintain itself in the face of certain facts of undeserved suffering of a prolonged and intense character. But the consistency of Rational theism with *itself*, examined in the present lecture, we found ourselves quite unable to defend. The acceptance of God as a Perfect Being, Infinite and Self-complete, seemed in irresoluble conflict with the conception of God as exercising thought and will in any straightforward meaning of these terms. Yet thought and will are the indispensable bases of all the moral and intellectual qualities that Rational Theism ascribes to the Divine Nature.

7. I am forced to the conclusion, then, that Rational Theism is untenable. And I must here repeat once more that, despite the periodic verbal acknowledgments of the unfathomable mystery of God made by so many theistic writers, I cannot see how the theism that inspires the theistic theologies can escape (even if it wants to) identification with 'Rational' Theism. The credal systems that are elaborated concerning the Divine Nature, and the relation of God to the world and to the souls of men, are surely intended, in very large part at any rate, to mean just what they say; and it is certain that they are so understood by the rank and file of believers. The theist, I must insist, cannot have it both ways. If he is really in earnest with the mystery of the Godhead to the extent of recognising the impropriety of applying to God terms like thought and will in any literal sense, he cannot logically go on to construct a 'literal' theology. To be in earnest with the mystery of the Godhead is, as I see it, to commit oneself to the disjunction 'Either *symbolic* theology or no theology at all'.

But is a 'symbolic' theology really practicable? Is it really possible to 'justify' in *any* way propositions that ascribe to God qualities like wisdom and goodness at the same time as we admit that these propositions in their literal meaning are nonsense?

I am convinced that it *is* possible; though very much less confident of my ability to demonstrate the possibility in practice. There *is* a middle path, I believe, between the region of pure unadulterated mystery, the sheerly unknowable, on the one hand, and the region of literal theology with its 'rational' concepts on the other. But it is a razor-edge; and to travel it without falling to one side or the other has defeated far more skilful theological equilibrists than the present lecturer. Among those who have sought to travel the middle path, there is only one who seems to me to have achieved any impressive measure of success—the late Rudolf Otto (though even he at times sways most perilously!). I propose, therefore, to make the transition from the rational or literal theism we have been studying, to the supra-rational or symbolic theism which it will be the aim of the rest of this course to expound and defend, by discussing at some length in my next lecture the views of this very remarkable religious thinker.

OTTO AND THE NUMINOUS:
THE TRANSITION TO SUPRA-RATIONAL
THEISM

1. Earlier in the present course, it will be remembered, we found it necessary to make a basic distinction between two different types of theism. According to Rational or Literal Theism, qualities like goodness, wisdom and power can be ascribed to God in their literal meaning. According to Supra-rational or Symbolic Theism, it is only in a symbolic significance that such qualities can be ascribed to a Being who is, *ex hypothesi*, completely perfect. So far, however, we have made no attempt to develop the concept of 'supra-rational theism'. Since it seemed to us that the orthodox or 'official' theism of the schools belonged fundamentally to the former type, we thought it best first of all to consider Rational Theism, and to ask whether its claim to truth could survive critical examination. Our conclusion has been that it can not—that it breaks down in self-contradiction. Goodness, wisdom and power, in the literal meanings we attach to them, presuppose either thought, or will, or both of these; and thought and will, we tried to show, are functions which in their very nature imply defect in the subject so functioning, and are therefore in contradiction with the absolute perfection that theism in all its forms ascribes to God.

It does not follow, of course, that supra-rational theism, to which we now turn, will fare any better. Though escaping, no doubt, the particular difficulty which seems to wreck rational theism, it may well founder from other causes. Thus it may, in the first place, fail to establish itself as the authentic theoretical expression of religious experience. Or, in the second place, it may be discovered, when we think it out with due care, to be not really meaningful—for the notion of a valid symbolic knowledge, where the thing symbolised is, strictly speaking, inconceivable, must be admitted to be a puzzling one. Or, in the third place, even if we should be satisfied that supra-rational theism is the authentic expression of religious experience, and also that it is meaningful, it may still turn out that there is no good reason to suppose it to be *true*; no good reason to suppose that the God of supra-rational theism has any objective reality.

In this lecture I shall be attempting to meet the first (which is in my opinion much the least formidable) of these three 'waves'. To this end I shall attempt an outline of the views of Rudolf Otto, more particularly as they find expression in his celebrated *Das Heilige*. For Otto seems to me to have shown, not indeed that supra-rational theism is *true*, but that it is the only form of theism that is in accord with the full complexity of actual religious experience. There is a natural tendency in theology (inasmuch as it is an intellectual discipline bent on conceptual formulations) to make formal acknowledgment of the supra-rational as an important element in religious experience, and then to allow it to recede far into the background; if not, indeed, to forget about it altogether. Against this tendency Otto's work is a sustained protest. It is, I shall suggest, Otto's major achievement to have reminded us that no theology can have any pretensions to validity that treats this element as less than central. But when the supra-rational element does receive due recognition, a reorientation of the orthodox attitude towards the use of rational concepts in theology seems really inescapable. It becomes very difficult indeed to see how more than a symbolic validity can be assigned to these concepts. They would seem to be appropriate ideograms (to use one of Otto's favourite terms) rather than literally true representations, of the Divine nature.

In the lecture that follows the present one I shall be engaged in elaborating the idea of a 'supra-rational theism', and in meeting what seem to me the most formidable objections to the view that it is in this, rather than in 'rational' theism, that the proper *terminus ad quem* of religious development is to be found. When that has been accomplished, our old question 'Is religion true?', having passed through the intermediate form 'Is theism true?', will have come to assume its final (and, as I think, its proper) form, 'Is supra-rational theism true?'. The answer to that question will be our sole concern thereafter.

Today, however, I aim at little more than to expound Otto, who is to myself, by a wide margin, the most illuminating religious thinker of modern times. This is a judgment which will, I fear, seem strange, and perhaps a little shocking, to many theologians in this country. British theologians, in common with British philosophers, have a strong common-sensical tradition. Though in the nature of the case they cannot wholly reject, they have a deep-rooted suspicion of, the mysterious, the supra-rational, the numinous. They like to pride themselves on keeping both feet firmly planted on the ground—which seems, after all, a rather unpromising way of reaching to Heaven! That it is possible, and undesirable, when soaring into the empyrean to lose all contact with the solid earth, no one would dream of denying. This is a temptation to which all forms of mystical religion are admittedly much exposed. But it is not, in my opinion, a temptation to which Rudolf Otto, despite his vigorous championship of the supra-rational, can fairly be said to succumb.

But enough of preamble. Let us try to see now, by attending to the argument of Otto's major work, what his doctrine of the supra-rational amounts to, and how he arrives at it.

2.   The leading aim of *Das Heilige* may be said to be to delineate, in as precise a manner as is possible, the characteristics possessed by the object of religious worship for the actual religious worshipper. Otto is undertaking, in fact, an analysis of religious experience. It is common ground that the distinctive *general* character of the object of religious experience, as experienced, is 'Holiness'. The holy, and only the holy, is genuinely 'worshipful'. It is common ground too that the holy as conceived in religion includes within itself the highest moral attributes known to man, and in the highest possible degree. It *ought* also to be common ground, Otto contends, though it is in fact a truth which has for a variety of reasons been heavily obscured in much traditional theistic thinking, that the Holy cannot be exhaustively described in terms of moral or any other attributes capable of conceptual

formulation. The historical manifestations of all the great religions bear constant witness, and careful introspection of one's own most deeply felt religious experiences abundantly confirms, that there is something more in the specifically religious valuation of the Holy Being than appreciation of powers and excellences of which we can form definite rational concepts. What is this 'something more'—the 'over-plus of meaning' essentially ingredient in the Holy for any experience that is truly religious?

The answer of *Das Heilige* is that it is what its author calls 'the numinous'. And while it would of course be absurd to claim for Otto the discovery of this constituent of religious experience, we can, I think, fairly claim for him that he has, in the first place, virtually forced general recognition of it by the brilliance of his presentation, and that he has, in the second place, distinguished its different facets by a psychological analysis of incomparable subtlety and delicacy; an analysis, moreover, reinforced at every vital point by a wealth of apt illustrative detail garnered from an encyclopaedic knowledge of the records of religion in many different quarters of the globe and at many different levels of development. Whatever the critics may have to say of Otto's religious epistemology and religious metaphysic (and I allow that for these my own admiration is well within bounds), few would wish to deny that as an essay in the psychology of religious experience *Das Heilige* is a *tour de force*.

From the outset Otto takes pains to impress upon his readers that they are not to expect from him a clean-cut conceptual definition of the numinous; for this is in the nature of the case impossible. The 'numen', like 'Duty', is an unique content of experience, not definable in terms of anything other than itself. But just as, in the case of Duty, much can be done towards evoking the unique moral experience in which alone duty can be apprehended by comparing it with, and disentangling it from, familiar experiences that in one way or another resemble it, so too there are experiences resembling the numinous in one aspect or another which can be helpfully used in guiding the mind towards the unique apprehension of the 'numen'. In both cases, however, the ultimate appeal must be to direct experience; to the moral experience of Duty in the one case, to the religious experience of the Holy in the other. Otto therefore enjoins the reader, if he wishes to make anything of the analysis that is to follow, to 'direct his mind to a moment of deeply-felt religious experience, as little as possible qualified by other forms of consciousness'; [1] and to pay special regard to what is unique in such a state of the soul rather than to that which it has in common with other similar states.

Close inspection of such states, Otto begins by claiming, should enable us to see the partial truth, and at the same time the inadequacy, of Schleiermacher's view that the most fundamental and distinctive feature of religious experience is the 'feeling of absolute dependence'. The 'feeling of absolute dependence' is an instructive description so far as it goes; but in Otto's opinion Schleiermacher's interpretative comments upon it betray that he has failed in at least two respects to give it the meaning it must bear if it is to be accepted as truly representing the essential character of religious experience.

In the first place, Schleiermacher fails to bring out the *qualitative* difference between the religious feeling of dependence and the feeling of dependence in ordinary life—i.e. the dependence that consists in being subject to the control of circumstances and environment. There is more here than a difference of *degree*, which is all that Schleiermacher's account seems to allow. The moment of religious feeling that is being sought after is well exemplified in Abraham's 'I have taken upon me to speak unto the Lord, which am but dust and ashes'. The expression 'dust and ashes' points to something far deeper than the mere feeling of subjection (however 'total') to extraneous forces. The note that is struck is rather that of what one may best call 'creature-feeling' —the creature's consciousness of illimitable inferiority when confronted by its Creator. The authentically religious 'feeling of dependence is at bottom' (in Otto's words) 'the emotion of a creature, abased and overwhelmed by its own nothingness in contrast to that which is supreme above all creatures'. [2] The religious and the natural feelings of dependence are thus not identical in quality, though they have sufficient similarity for the term 'dependence', drawn from ordinary experience, to serve as a useful pointer to the quality of the actual religious feeling.

---

[1] P. 8 of English translation by J. W. Harvey under the title *The Idea of the Holy.*   [2] *Op. cit.* p. 10.

The second respect in which, according to Otto, Schleier-macher's interpretation is defective is that he speaks as though this religious feeling of dependence were *primarily* a phase of *self*-consciousness; a consciousness of self as absolutely dependent, from which we pass by inference to the idea of God as a cause beyond our self which will account for this feeling of dependence. But the psychological facts, Otto insists, tell a different story. The religious experience has 'immediate and primary reference to an object outside the self' [1]—a *numen praesens*. The feeling of utter dependence, the self depreciatory 'creature-feeling', is not that from which we reason to a *numen praesens*, but rather the sub-jective reflection cast by the religious experience in its primary aspect, which is direct awareness of the *numen*. In other words, for religious experience God is not an inference from certain feelings of ours, but an immediate object.

Otto proceeds now to attempt a more detailed determination of the numinous experience, broadly characterised so far, as we have seen, as 'the emotion of a creature, abased and overwhelmed by its own nothingness in contrast to that which is supreme above all creatures'. His method is, as always, introspection supple-mented and safeguarded by reference to historical records of the religious experience of others, and by reference in particular to the utterances of those outstanding representatives of the great religions in whom, by common acknowledgment, the flame of religion has burned with a peculiar radiance and intensity. The fundamental determinations which he discovers he has com-pendiously summed up for us in the now classic phrase *mysterium tremendum et fascinans*.

Each of the three constituent terms here has its 'natural' meaning, derived from the experience of ordinary life. Otherwise, of course, they could be no guide to us at all. But it is of the essence of Otto's argument to bring out that this 'natural' meaning is never more than an analogue to the meaning which the term has for us within religious experience. Its function is to suggest, but not to portray, a corresponding moment in the numinous, and thus to facilitate the direct experience in which the numinous is alone discerned.

Otto's detailed elucidation of the several moments of the

[1] P. 10.

numinous is probably the most remarkable part of a remarkable book. One feels that the only way of doing real justice to it would be to quote in their entirety a dozen or more pages of *Das Heilige*. There is hardly a sentence in these pages that is not laden with significance; and they must be read as their author wrote them if their persuasiveness is to be in any adequate measure appreciated. The bald outline which is all that I am able to offer here cannot do much more than serve as a reminder to those who have read Otto of the riches of the original. To others I can but earnestly commend first-hand acquaintance with Otto as among the most rewarding experiences that anyone with a concern for religious understanding is likely to enjoy in a life-time.

To take first the noun term, *mysterium*. We are aware of the Holy, in its numinous aspect, as a profound mystery. But it is 'mysterious' not just in the sense that certain events in the natural world which are puzzling and incomprehensible to us are dubbed 'mysterious'. The mystery of the numinous is felt to baffle conception altogether, to elude the very possibility of rational enquiry. We feel ourselves in contact with something 'wholly other', something 'whose kind and character are incommensurable with our own, and before which we therefore recoil in a wonder that strikes us chill and numb'. [1] It is a mystery before which the emotional reaction of the creature is, in one aspect, sheer stupor, 'amazement absolute'.

The two adjectival terms, *tremendum* and *fascinans*, give us the *quale* or content of the *mysterium*. Within the *tremendum* itself, however, Otto finds three distinguishable strands revealing themselves to introspective analysis. The numen is experienced (in this aspect of it) as uniquely daunting and awe-inspiring; as of overwhelming might and majesty; and as superabounding in living energy and 'urgency'. The numinous emotions which are the correlates of these objective characteristics have their counterparts in ordinary life, and we can recognise the analogy between them, but in their numinous context the emotions are raised, as it were, to a new dimension. Consider, e.g. the kind of 'fear' that is the emotional correlate of the 'daunting' aspect of the *tremendum*. This 'numinous' fear is experienced by us as specifically different from, though also resembling, the 'natural' fear that is evoked

[1] P. 28.

by real or supposed dangers from objects in the natural world. The difference is not just one of degree. Numinous fear is closest akin to the 'shudder' we feel in the presence of the 'uncanny'; in the presence of what (as it seems to us) 'has no place in our scheme of reality, but belongs to an absolutely different one'.[1] Something of this 'inward shudder of the soul' is characteristic of all numinous fear. At the same time the numinous fear of religious experience cannot be simply assimilated to fear of the 'uncanny', if only because in religion it is but a single strand in a complex emotional whole which includes the emotional correlates of the other features of the *tremendum*—its might and majesty and living urgency—and includes also the emotional correlate of the *fascinans* aspect.

The qualitative difference between the numinous and the corresponding natural emotions, just illustrated in the case of 'fear', it is crucial to bear in mind when we try to describe in words drawn from ordinary experience the objective characteristics that belong to the numen. These objective characteristics are the correlates of the *numinous* emotions, and we must resist the temptation to interpret them as though they were identical in quality with the objective characteristics that are the correlates of the corresponding *natural* emotions. We must never lose sight of the fact that whatever nameable characteristic is ascribed to the numen, it is always a specific *quale* of the '*mysterium*'—of that which has 'a kind and character incommensurable with our own'.

The complex emotive state aroused by the numinous has, however, not only *different* elements within its unity, as we have just seen in the analysis of the *tremendum*, but also, in a sense, *opposing* elements. For the *fascinans* element of the numen, equally integral to religious experience, stands in vivid contrast with the *tremendum* element. While the soul shrinks in bottomless humility from the mysteriously awful might and majesty of the numen in its *tremendum* aspect, it is at the same time entranced and filled with blissful rapture by the mysterious enchantment and allure of the numen in its *fascinans* aspect. This 'dual character of the numinous consciousness', Otto writes, 'is at once the strangest and most noteworthy phenomenon in the whole history of religion'.[2] Fear of the Lord has as its essential complement

[1] P. 29.   [2] P. 31.

Praise of the Lord. For the object of religious worship is felt to possess transcendent *worth* or *value* no less than transcendent power and majesty, to be the ideal goal of all our desiring, communion with which brings to the soul 'the peace that passeth understanding'. And here too, Otto reiterates, it is crucial to bear in mind that the *fascinans* is a specific *quale* of the *mysterium*, and to recognise how feeble at best are the analogies we draw from our ordinary experience to describe it. The glory of God is something that eye cannot behold, or tongue tell. The universal testimony of the saints is to beatitude inexpressible before a Perfection that is indescribable; and this testimony finds its echo, so Otto would maintain, in the soul of every man to whom religion is a reality.

This very brief resumé, pale shadow though it be of the original, is all that our time will allow for Otto's psychological analysis of the religious consciousness in respect of its *non*-rational or numinous aspect; an aspect which Otto believes, surely with justice, theology as a 'scientific' discipline has been prone to subordinate unduly to the rational aspect. Shortly we shall be attempting to describe how Otto deals with this second, rational aspect of the Holy, and how he conceives its relation to the non-rational aspect. But meantime let us follow Otto a little further in his account of the non-rational aspect by noticing what may be called his epistemology, as distinct from his psychology, of the numinous consciousness.

3. The outstanding feature of Otto's epistemology of the numinous is his claim that the numinous consciousness is *a priori*. '*A priori*' is a term of somewhat ambiguous import in philosophy, but at least it always means 'independent of experience' in *some* sense of that phrase. The following excerpt makes reasonably clear, I think, in what sense Otto takes the numinous consciousness to be 'independent of experience', and at the same time how he understands its relation to experience.

'The numinous', he tells us, 'issues from the deepest foundation of cognitive apprehension that the soul possesses, and, though it of course comes into being in and amid the sensory data and empirical material of the natural world and cannot anticipate or dispense with those, yet it does not arise *out of* them, but only *by their means*. They are the incitement, the stimulus, and the "occasion" for the numinous consciousness to become astir, and, in so doing, to begin—at first with a naïve immediacy of reaction —to be interfused and interwoven with the present world of sensuous experience, until, becoming gradually purer, it disengages itself from this and takes its stand in absolute contrast to it.' [1]

The 'incitements' or 'stimuli' from the natural world here referred to, one gathers, are primarily the situations which evoke in unusual measure those 'natural' emotions which are most markedly analogous to the numinous emotions. Just as, by reason of the close analogy between the feeling of constraint by custom and the feeling of constraint by moral obligation or duty, 'the former can *arouse* the latter in the mind if it—the latter—was already potentially planted there',[2] *despite* the latter's qualitative uniqueness, so too 'natural' experiences of the exceptionally strange or the exceptionally daunting or the exceptionally enchanting can excite the corresponding numinous emotions, awaking the potentiality of our numinous consciousness into activity.

As Otto is careful to point out, it is not strictly the numinous consciousness, but rather the *potentiality* or *capacity* for numinous consciousness, that is (on his view) an *a priori* endowment of the human soul. Manifestly this potentiality is actualised in very different degrees in different persons; partly because incitements to it may be more or less frequent and more or less powerful in different types of experience, partly also because the original endowment, the predisposition to numinous experience, may be stronger in one man than another. Again, the numinous consciousness need not, and historically it does not, emerge 'all at once'. 'The numinous only unfolds its full content by slow degrees, as one by one the series of requisite stimuli or incitements becomes operative.' [3] There are many manifestations of the numinous, prior to religion proper, in which one particular moment of the numinous is exclusively evoked—most commonly the *mysterium* element. And even when the numinous is awakened in sufficient completeness for it to be legitimately identified with religion, the several moments may still be present in very unequal proportions.

[1] P. 117.   [2] P. 45.   [3] P. 136.

The *tremendum* element may preponderate over all others, as in the 'daemonic dread' that is so prominent a feature of many primitive religions: or the *fascinans* element may preponderate, as in certain 'sentimental' forms of religion more characteristic, perhaps, of modern than of ancient times; or the *mysterium* element may preponderate, as it manifestly does in all forms of mystical religion.

So much for how Otto understands the *a priori* status which he attributes to the numinous consciousness. But it will naturally be asked what *reasons* he offers for the contention that the numinous consciousness is *a priori* in this sense. To this question Otto has a direct enough answer to give—though whether or not it is a satisfactory one is another matter. 'The proof that in the numinous we have to deal with purely *a priori* cognitive elements' he tells us, 'is to be reached by introspection and a critical examination of reason such as Kant instituted. We find, that is, involved in the numinous experience, beliefs and feelings qualitatively different from anything that "natural" sense perception is capable of giving us.' [1] The core of the matter is that, in Otto's view, no *empirical* origin is conceivable for the numinous consciousness. If that be granted, then we are entitled to infer that, while events in the natural world may be necessary to excite it into activity, the numinous consciousness originates autonomously from an *a priori* endowment of the human mind. 'The facts of the numinous consciousness', he says, 'point . . . to a hidden substantive source, from which the religious ideas and feelings are formed, which lies in the mind independently of sense-experience.' [2]

We shall in a later lecture have to enquire how far this 'proof' of *a priority* can be accounted successful.

4.   We may turn now to the rational as opposed to the numinous or non-rational strand in the idea of the holy. From the beginning Otto has fully recognised that the 'holy' is a *complex* category, combining both strands within its unity. The very first sentence of *Das Heilige* talls us that 'it is essential to every theistic conception of God . . . that it designates and precisely characterises

Deity by the attributes Spirit, Purpose, Reason, Good Will, Supreme Power, Unity, Self-hood'.[1] And 'all these attributes' he adds, 'constitute clear and definite *concepts*: they can be grasped by the intellect; they can be analysed by thought; they even admit of definition'. Moreover (he goes on), 'we count this the very mark and criterion of a religion's high rank and superior value that it should have no lack of *conceptions* about God'.[2] The attitude thus manifested in his first paragraph Otto preserves to the end. Inevitably, since the governing motive of his whole work is to repair what he deems to be the fatal neglect of the numinous element by the customary theology, most of his chapters are devoted to elucidation of the numinous, and to warnings of the impoverishment that religion suffers from its disregard. But that there is another side to the picture is taken for granted throughout, and not infrequently is expressly emphasised. Thus after a rather long stretch almost exclusively concerned with the nature and implications of the non-rational element in holiness, Otto goes out of his way to insist that 'it is no less true that "holiness", "sanctity", as Christianity intends the words, cannot dispense with the rational, and especially the clear ethical, elements of meaning which Protestantism more particularly emphasises in the idea of God'.[3]

There can be little doubt, then, about Otto's intention to preserve a highly important status for the rational element in the religious life. The question he has to face (and of course does face) is how a consciousness for which the object of worship is *mysterium tremendum et fascinans* can also ascribe to that object definite rational qualities. How can God be deemed to be at once supra-rational and also the bearer of rational attributes?

The short answer lies in the word 'schematism'. 'The relation of the rational to the non-rational element in the idea of the holy or sacred', Otto declares, 'is . . . one of "schematization".'[4] The term is of course borrowed from Kant; but what Otto means by it in its religious context seems tolerably clear without reference to its highly technical application in the *Critique of Pure Reason*. The numinous content of the religious consciousness is the *mysterium tremendum et fascinans* that pertains to an order

[1] P. 1.   [2] *Ibid.*   [3] P. 113.
[4] P. 46.

'incommensurable with our own'. But as we have already seen, the emotions which the numinous object evokes in us, though qualitatively unique, have a *felt analogy* with certain emotions evoked in us by attributes and objects in ordinary experience of which we *can* form clear conceptions. It is on the basis of these felt analogies that a 'conceptual translation' or schematism of the pure numinous content becomes possible. The object which we experience as evoking in us the numinous emotions we spontaneously and naturally think of as characterised, in supreme measure, by those qualities which an object must have to evoke in us the emotions analogous to the numinous in our ordinary experience. By what Otto calls 'an inward necessity of the mind', we think of the Holy Being which at once so overwhelmingly daunts and entrances us as endued with Power and Value, and with whatever more specific qualities seem to us most fully to manifest these general attributes. At the same time the numinous marrow of our experience ensures our recognition that in the Holy Being the Power and the Value are *absolute*—totally free from all limitation which may be found in even their highest creaturely expressions.

Since Otto's use of the Kantian term 'schematism' has been somewhat blown upon by the critics, it is worth while pointing out that there does seem to be a sufficient resemblance between the process Otto has in mind and Kant's schematism of the categories—or, more accurately, Kant's schematism of the pure concepts of the understanding—for the term 'schematism' to have real indicative value. By an inward necessity of the mind, according to Kant, the pure concepts of the understanding are given a translation in terms of temporal consciousness and, as thus schematised, are applied *a priori* to perceived objects. By a corresponding inward necessity of the mind, according to Otto, the *mysterium tremendum et fascinans* of the numinous consciousness is given a translation in terms of 'rational' consciousness and, as thus schematised, is applied *a priori* to numinous objects. It may not be a particularly happy piece of nomenclature, but, on the whole, it is not easy to see what more fitting term Otto could have culled from the literature of philosophy to direct attention to the distinctive features of the 'rationalising' of the numinous as he understands it.

5.   Nevertheless I should by no means wish to dispute that Otto's doctrine of Schematism stands in need of clarification at certain points. There is most obscurity, perhaps, concerning the nature and basis of the alleged 'inward necessity' of the mind whereby the conceptual schemata of the numinous—the 'ideograms'—are framed. Let us look at this matter for a few moments.

Otto's position will perhaps best be elucidated by distinguishing between, and then considering how Otto would answer, three closely related questions. The questions are these. Given numinous experience, is there (1) an inward necessity of the mind to 'think' the numinous at all? If there is an inward necessity to think it, is there (2) an inward necessity to think it in some particular way, as the bearer of some specific set of characters? And if there is an inward necessity of this second sort, is it (3) an inward necessity to think the specific set of characters as *in their literal significance* predicable of the numinous object?

Now the answer to the first question seems obviously to be in the affirmative. For numinous experience is never *merely* emotional. Perhaps, outside the field of psycho-pathology, there is no such thing as a 'mere emotion', if by that is meant an emotion not directed towards an object that is in some manner, however dim, 'conceived'. At any rate the emotion characteristic of numinous experience as Otto has depicted it is assuredly not 'directionless'. There is always, he insists, awareness of an objective reality as evoking the emotion—the *numen praesens*. Numinous experience thus essentially involves *some* thinking of its object.

But is there, further, an inward necessity to think the numen in a particular way, a way which will permit the qualities it possesses to be individually and significantly named? The answer to this second question is equally certainly in the affirmative: and the basis of the affirmative answer here is, as we have seen, the felt analogy between the numinous emotions we experience and certain emotions experienced in every-day life. Were there no such felt analogy, we could say nothing specific at all by way of describing the numinous emotions, nor, in consequence, could we give significant determination to the numinous object. But because we are aware of analogy between our numinous emotions and our 'ordinary' emotions of wonder, of dread, and of entrancement, we naturally, and I think one may say inevitably, think the numinous object as the bearer of qualities analogous to the nameable qualities that evoke the ordinary emotions of wonder, dread, and entrancement. And this is the justification for describing the numinous object in the specific terms *mysterium tremendum et fascinans*.

Analogy, however, implies *difference* as well as identity; and in thinking the content of the numinous the differences must be taken account of no less than the identity. This consideration is crucial for a correct answer to our third question. Otto's analysis of numinous experience, it will be remembered, gave very special attention to the differences that mark off the numinous emotions from their counterparts in ordinary experience. There is no need to traverse again the old, familiar ground: but we may remind ourselves how in the preliminary and general characterisation of the numinous, the numinous feeling of 'absolute dependence' was distinguished from the natural feeling of absolute dependence by the former's sense of the infinitude of the gulf between the 'dependent' and that upon which it depends. It was 'the emotion of a creature, abased and overwhelmed by its own nothingness in contrast to that which is supreme above all creatures'. We may recall, again, how in the more detailed analysis that followed, the distinction between numinous wonder and its natural counterpart was found to lie in the former's sense that the evoking object belongs to an order 'of a kind and character incommensurable with our own', that its nature is 'mysterious' to the point of eluding the very possibility of rational enquiry. The fundamental difference, in fact, which makes the felt analogy of our numinous with our natural emotions only an *analogy*, and not a pure identity, is precisely that aura of the *supra*-natural, the *supra*-human, the *supra*-rational in which numinous experience is enveloped throughout. Now when this is appreciated, the question whether there is any inward necessity to think the numinous object in terms of rational concepts in their literal meaning answers itself. So far from there being any such inward necessity, the position is rather that, wherever the numinous consciousness is genuinely active, there is an inward necessity of the mind to *refrain from* interpreting the numinous object in these rational terms.

And yet the temptation to 'rationalise', let it be admitted, is almost irresistible. It is only for relatively brief spells that even the most devout of men are sustained at the white-hot temperature of numinous experience. When the cool light of common day supervenes, nothing is easier than to think of that which was felt to be daunting and entrancing beyond anything we can conceive, as though it were endued with a power and a value greater *merely in degree* than anything we can conceive. But 'greater in degree' implies qualitative *identity*, and the door is then wide open to thinking of God in terms of definite rational concepts. We interpret God, in a sense legitimately enough, in terms of 'the highest we know', ascribing to Him Justice, and Might, and Love, and Wisdom, and Compassion, and whatever other qualities are ranked highest in our ethical and cultural hierarchy; but we too readily forget that it is only *as analogues*, and not in their literal meaning, that these or any other 'rational' qualities can fitly be predicated of that which is *mysterium tremendum et fascinans*.

To sum up, then, the answers to our three questions. It seems to me reasonably clear both that and why Otto holds that, given the fact of numinous experience, there is an inward necessity of the mind to 'think' the numinous object, and to think it in terms of a specific set of characters, but at the same time to assign to this set of characters a no more than symbolic validity.

Now the upshot of all this, as regards the relation of the rational to the supra-rational in religion, is, I think, as manifest as it is to many religious thinkers unpalatable—I am not sure that even to Otto himself, as a Christian theologian, it was altogether palatable. It is that while the 'rational strand' is, as Otto declares, 'as indispensable' to the idea of the holy as the supra-rational strand, the latter is fundamental and ultimate in a sense in which the former is not. It is correct to say that the rational strand is 'as indispensable' as the supra-rational strand, for the reason that we cannot think the numinous at all—cannot therefore frame any idea of the holy—without thinking it in terms of rational concepts. But because these same rational concepts have to be understood as only analogues for the delineation of the numinous object, the 'indispensability' of the rational strand must not be interpreted as though rational theism, which applies its predicates to God in their literal meaning, were as valid an expression of religious experience as supra-rational theism, which applies its predicates only symbolically. The implication of Otto's central thesis seems to me to be, incontestably, that the only kind of theology possible is a *symbolic* theology.

6.   It was to be expected that a doctrine like Otto's, which seemed by implication to assign to theology the function of formulating not conceptual truths, but mere conceptual ideograms or symbols, about God and His relation to the world and to man, should meet with a rather chilly reception in the ranks of orthodox theology. Nor have such expectations been belied. Warm tributes have, indeed, been paid, almost unanimously, to Otto's spiritual depth and sincerity, to the sensitiveness and subtlety of his religious psychology, and to the astonishing amplitude of his resources of scholarship; and yet so far as the implications of his central thesis are concerned, his impact upon modern constructive theology, in this country at any rate, would appear to have been almost negligible. I do not find this surprising, but it does seem to me hard to justify. Of course, as I have already indicated, and shall later illustrate, I by no means take the view that Otto's religious theories are free from serious blemish. There is much in his metaphysic and epistemology of religion that seems to me ill-founded; and as for the curious doctrine that there is a development of the numinous 'which works itself out purely in the sphere of the non-rational', but with the stages of which development the 'process of rationalization and moralization' somehow or other 'nearly, if not quite, synchronizes and keeps pace',[1] I can only say that I share to the full the mystification of so many other of Otto's readers. But all that, I suggest, is not really to the point. For it is not Otto's highly questionable teachings on these matters, but rather his almost universally admired religious psychology, which carries with it such profound implications for constructive theology. It is the *mysterium tremendum et fascinans* of Otto's psychological analysis (untouched, so far as I can see, by the apparent errors to which I have just alluded) that forces the vital question whether theology can ever claim more than a symbolic validity for its concepts and doctrines. If religious experience is admitted to answer to Otto's description of it, then surely theology cannot be absolved from the duty of facing up to the question how a literally

[1] P. 114.

conceived theology is to be reconciled with the dominatingly supra-rational character of actual religious experience?

There have, of course, been a few critics who have appreciated that at bottom it is Otto's psychology that is the real menace to the orthodox theology of theism, and who have directed their attacks accordingly. I am bound to say, however, that adequate answers to all the criticisms on this score with which I am acquainted seem to me to lie, and usually not too deeply hidden, within the pages of *Das Heilige* itself. Nevertheless, it may be instructive to conclude this lecture with a brief comment upon one such criticism; one which, by reason of its author's great and deserved reputation as a religious thinker and the special bent of his theological interest, and also—one must add—by reason of the uncompromising and even somewhat contemptuous language in which the criticism is couched, has probably had the unfortunate effect of deterring not a few youthful students of theology from troubling themselves to become acquainted with Otto's works at first hand. I refer to Professor John Oman's attack (for as such I can only regard it) in *The Natural and the Supernatural*.[1]

7. The burden of Oman's complaint is that Otto separates the basic religious experience entirely from the ethical, so that he is able to explain the conspicuous fact of their actual union in all developed religions only by an external and implausible device; to wit, 'schematization'. And if Otto's actual account of the numinous (the 'innermost core of religion', as he calls it) were in fact as Oman reports it to be, the charge of completely dividing the religious from the ethical would have much substance. For here is the way in which Oman thinks it fair to describe that account:

'Professor Otto relates the holy to what he calls the *numinous*. The name will serve as well as any other, for it is the mere impression of *an awe-inspiring something*, the mightier for stirring intense feeling the vaguer it is.' [2]

Or again: 'Professor Otto holds this *awesome* holy to be the one essential religious feeling.' [3]

[1] P. 60 *et seq.*
[2] *Op. cit.* p. 61. Italics mine.
[3] *Op. cit.* p. 60. Italics mine.

Now of course the 'awfulness', or 'awe-inspiring' character, of the numinous is given great prominence by Otto. It relates in his analysis of numinous consciousness to a major aspect of the numen, viz. the *tremendum*. But surely it is the merest caricature of Otto's position to put forward this one major aspect as sufficiently defining what Otto means by the numinous? Otto speaks of 'that *element or factor* of the numinous which was the first our analysis noted and which we proposed to name symbolically the 'aweful' (*tremendum*)'.[1] What of the *other* major element or factor, the other of what Otto expressly calls the 'two poles' of the numinous consciousness, viz. the *fascinans*? It seems incredible, but it is sober truth, that Oman consistently writes as if the whole of Chapter VI of *Das Heilige* on the *fascinans* aspect of the numinous, not to speak of a multitude of later passages depending upon it, simply did not exist.

Yet as soon as we call to mind what Otto has called 'the *dual* character of the numinous consciousness',[2] the hollowness of the charge that he 'entirely divides' the ethical from the religious becomes apparent. The *fascinans* aspect is that in virtue of which the numinous consciousness is enraptured and entranced by the transcendent *worth* or *value* of the numen. If we choose to abstract from this aspect, and to forget that essential to the numinous consciousness as Otto portrays it is this element of valuation, then, naturally, nothing is easier than to present Otto's view as 'entirely dividing' the religious from the ethical. For it is precisely the *fascinans* aspect that provides the link between the two, ensuring that we cannot but think the object of religious experience as endued with supreme excellence. That the ethical concepts can, for Otto, be applied to God only as ideograms is of course true. But I must protest that no criticism of Otto on the ground of separating the religious from the ethical deserves to be taken seriously if (like Oman's) it does not even attempt to examine the nature and status of these ethical ideograms, and their basis in Otto's thought. Otto may conceivably be mistaken in believing that there is an 'inward necessity' of the mind to frame ethical ideograms of the numinous, and in believing, accordingly, that his 'schematization' is not external but internal. Mistaken or not, however, this is an integral and fully articulated part of his

[1] P. 65. Italics mine.   [2] P. 31. Italics mine.

system, and in my opinion no responsible critic has any right to ignore it.

I urged earlier that Otto's religious psychology imperatively points in the direction of a supra-rational or 'symbolic' theism. Much remains to be done, however, before the notion of such a theism can be made really plausible. In particular, the nature, significance, and validity of a merely analogical knowledge of God demands the closest possible examination. That perplexing problem—or cluster of problems—will be the central topic of our next lecture.

SUPRA-RATIONAL THEISM AND 'SYMBOLIC' KNOWLEDGE

1. My exposition of and incidental comments upon Rudolf Otto's religious thought in the last lecture will have made it clear, I think, that, however dubious about certain elements in his metaphysics and epistemology of religion, I have nothing but admiration for his religious psychology. I accept his delineation of the *mysterium tremendum et fascinans* as the object of religious experience; and I accept what I take to be the implication of this, viz. that the authentic theoretical expression of the religious consciousness is not Rational but Supra-rational Theism; i.e. a Theism which proclaims that the Nature of God is in principle incapable of being conceived in terms of rational concepts in their literal significance, but that certain of these concepts are validly applicable to God when understood not as literal portrayals, but as appropriate symbols, of the Divine Nature.

Now there are manifest difficulties in the notion of a supra-rational theism. The whole conception of 'symbolic' knowledge especially clamours for elucidation, and we shall have to deal with it as systematically as time permits later in this lecture. Until that has been done, the claim that supra-rational theism is the authentic theoretical expression of the religious consciousness will rightly remain to some extent suspect. But even now there is one consideration, apart from the merits of Otto's psychological analysis, which might reasonably dispose one to look at that claim with a good deal of favour. If the argument of Lecture V was sound, then Rational Theism is internally inconsistent, and hence cannot be objectively true. It would be extremely unfortunate, therefore, if Rational Theism did happen to be the authentic theoretical expression of the religious consciousness, for we should then have no alternative but to conclude that religion is not objectively true. If, on the other hand, it is Supra-rational Theism that is the proper theoretical expression of the religious consciousness, then whether religion is objectively true or not is at least still an open question.

The root of all the troubles that beset Rational Theism lies, I believe, in its failure to do justice to the *mysterium* aspect of religious experience. It would, of course, be quite unfair to suggest that Rational Theism simply ignores this aspect. Apart from sporadic pronouncements, already referred to, which have too much the character of *obiter dicta*, there is some reflection of the *mysterium* even in its formal doctrine. Thus it is, I think, largely under the compulsion of the *mysterium* aspect that Rational Theism is led to proclaim that God is Perfection *Absolute*, utterly free from all limitations and defects of finitude; and so, one would presume, beyond finite comprehension. But unhappily, in the interests of clear conceptual formulations, Rational Theism throws away what it had seemed to gain by insisting upon interpreting God's Absolute Perfection as though it could find literal illustration in modes of experience like thought and will which in fact imply finitude and defect. Thus to interpret Absolute Perfection makes Rational Theism at once inconsistent with itself and untrue to the religious experience it is concerned to formulate.

Rational Theism could, of course, achieve internal consistency, in large measure at any rate, if it were frankly to drop the *mysterium* aspect altogether, thus releasing itself from the pressure to maintain the *absoluteness* of God's perfection. But to do this would be too plainly at variance with the testimony of religious experience, and very few theists have had recourse to so drastic a remedy. They have rightly preferred to retain an unsolved problem rather than to take an easy way out which entails clear conflict with religious experience. A fact we have already noticed is significant in this connection; namely, that even among the less well-disposed of Otto's theological brethren tribute is constantly paid to his outstanding perspicacity as a religious psychologist. This applause would be hardly intelligible if it were combined with decisive disapproval of the very thing which Otto's analysis of religious experience is chiefly concerned to establish, viz. that for religious experience the object of worship is of a might and majesty and worth that transcend all human power of conception—of 'a kind and character incommensurable with our own'. The note struck in Tersteegen's dictum that 'a God comprehended is no God' has seldom been absent for long from the course of theistic theology, and it is certainly not lacking today. What *is* lacking, in my opinion, is sufficient ruthlessness and candour in following out its implications in the systems of doctrine that Rational Theists elaborate and present to the religious public as entitled to acceptance.

If I have somewhat harped upon what seems to me a fatal defect in Rational Theism, it is because I suspect that there will be little disposition to view sympathetically the claims of theism in its supra-rational form until the grounds for dissatisfaction with its orthodox, rational form are thoroughly appreciated. But I must confess I find it hard to see how intellectual dissatisfaction can really be avoided by anyone who reflects impartially upon a doctrine that is at its best so equivocal—on the one hand prepared to acknowledge, when the question is directly faced, that the Divine nature cannot be comprehended by finite minds, and on the other hand assuming throughout its systematic theology that we can know a great deal about God's attributes and qualities. I am far from denying that religion, on any discerning view of it, has its 'paradoxes'—inescapable paradoxes. Even so, I cannot help feeling that it savours a little of obscurantism to use that term when what we appear to be confronted with is something that in plain English is called a self-contradiction.

2. And yet—may we perhaps be going too fast in taking for granted that a theism which is internally inconsistent cannot be the authentic expression of the religious consciousness? Is it a possible alternative that the religious consciousness itself involves self-contradiction, that it is intrinsic to religious experience *both* to recognise the supra-rational character of its object *and* to think it in terms of rational concepts in their literal sense? Desperate as this expedient seems, there are some religious minds to which it appears as at least less repugnant to believe that religion involves

theoretical inconsistency than to believe (with supra-rational theism) that religion cannot legitimately mean just what it says when it calls God wise, and just, and merciful, and loving. To them this is to empty religion of all genuine significance; and it is not to be denied that it does indeed entail the jettisoning of much that is taken by many good and devout minds to be central to religion. Nevertheless, the acceptance of internal inconsistency in religion *is* surely a quite desperate alternative. There is no way of avoiding the conclusion that religion, if it involves this defect, is objectively false. If religious experience intrinsically requires subscription to logically incompatible propositions, such as that God is beyond all human powers of conception and that God can legitimately be described by rational concepts in their literal sense, then the question of 'the truth of religion' will for most people be already settled, in the negative.

For my own part, however, I do not at all accept that religious experience involves subscription to logically incompatible propositions. It is, I believe, a mistake (though an easily understandable one) to suppose that religion is emptied of all meaning if we are denied any knowledge of God in terms of rational concepts literally interpreted. The demands of religion on its 'rational' side are very real; but they are adequately met, in my submission, if certain rational concepts can be shown to be valid *symbols* of the Divine Nature, as is maintained by supra-rational theism. So I shall be arguing in what now follows. It will be a chief part of my endeavour to lay the spectre of *nescience* which seems for so many to haunt the notion of a 'knowledge' of God that is 'merely symbolic'. To establish that these concepts, though not literal portrayals of, can yet reasonably be taken to be truly significant of, the nature of God, seems to me to be the chief thing required in order to break down the resistance to the acceptance of supra-rational theism as the true theoretic expression of religious experience. The further and all-important question whether supra-rational theism can be substantiated as *objectively valid* will be taken up thereafter, and will occupy us almost exclusively throughout the last three lectures.

Now manifestly everything turns here upon the notion of 'symbolic validity'. Let us then look for a little at the nature of symbols, and try to specify the character as religious 'symbols' of the rational concepts which are our concern, with a view to bringing out the precise sense in which these concepts may be said to possess 'symbolic validity' for the knowledge of God.

3. A 'symbol' may be roughly defined as anything that is mentally accepted as standing for something other than itself. There are a great many different kinds of symbols; but we shall try to keep our discussion within manageable bounds by noting only those distinctions most germane to our purpose.

We should distinguish first between 'conventional' symbols and 'natural' symbols. We may call a symbol 'conventional' if it is instituted as a symbol by a more or less formal act of agreement. This is perhaps the commonest type of symbol. Very often, however, some object or event is accepted by one or more persons as standing for something other than itself, and as thus symbolising it, without there being any formal agreement so to regard it. Thus a Rolls-Royce car is regarded by many persons as a symbol of worldly prosperity, simply because, as a striking and familiar manifestation of wealth, it has a natural tendency to suggest worldly prosperity to their minds. We may call such symbols 'natural' as opposed to 'conventional'. Conventional symbols in the nature of the case have a certain publicity of character. Natural symbols may be highly personal, and indeed need not have force for more than a single person.

The line between conventional and natural symbols is not, however, a sharp one. In some cases it is hard to say with any confidence whether a particular object has or has not received a sufficiently formal sanction as a symbol to be properly styled 'conventional'. Perhaps this is true, indeed, of the example we have just taken of a natural symbol—a Rolls-Royce car. Moreover, what has once been only a natural symbol may in the course of time acquire formal sanction as a symbol and qualify as a conventional symbol.

A second and (for our purpose) more important distinction is that between 'arbitrary' symbols and 'analogical' symbols. We may call a symbol 'arbitrary' if there is nothing in the intrinsic meaning of the symbol to suggest that which it is chosen to symbolise—its *symbolizandum*. Mathematical symbols are of this kind. There is nothing in the English letter x which suggests an unknown quantity, nothing in the Greek letter π to suggest the ratio of the circumference of a circle to its diameter. And most, though not all, words of most languages are 'arbitrary' symbols in this sense. We may call a symbol 'analogical', on the other hand, if there *is* some recognised identity of character between symbol and *symbolizandum*, in virtue of which the symbol has an intrinsic tendency to suggest to the mind what is to be symbolised. It is clear that only conventional symbols can be 'arbitrary', since those we classified as 'natural' depend for their acceptance as symbols upon some supposed identity of character between symbol and symbolised, and are thus essentially analogical. But a great many conventional symbols also are analogical, or at least have an analogical element. Flags are a familiar example of a conventional symbol, but they are often also analogical symbols, as in the 'Skull and Cross-bones' of the Pirate's flag, or the 'Hammer and Sickle' of the Communist flag. The Parliamentary Mace is another obvious example of a conventional symbol with a strong analogical element. So is the circle as a symbol of infinitude. The presence of an analogical element in so many conventional symbols is not, of course, in any way surprising. There are manifest advantages in choosing as a symbol something that will tend by its intrinsic character to suggest that which we wish it to stand for.

It is clear also that if the analogical element in the symbol is to achieve its maximum effect, the affinity of character between symbol and *symbolizandum* should be of a conspicuous sort, and that the symbol itself should be something easily grasped by the mind. For this reason the symbol is most commonly something capable of *sensory* representation; not necessarily, of course, a sensory 'object'; it may be an act or a gesture (e.g. raising one's arms in token of surrender), or perhaps a set of acts and gestures, a 'performance' (as in many of the symbols of ritual). But *conceptual* elements are often present along with the sensory, and they may be important. Allegories and parables are essentially symbolic, but they require a measure of conceptual thinking for their apprehension. However, the conceptual element in symbols tends to be kept as simple, and as close to the sensuous, as the nature of the case will allow. Clearly the symbol would lose its value as a symbol if it were itself no easier to grasp than what it symbolises.

One further distinction must be made to complete our necessary preliminaries. The thing to be symbolised is usually complex in character, and is often something highly abstract, but it is in most cases susceptible of clear conceptual grasp (though to attain this grasp may well involve a laborious and difficult intellectual operation). Sometimes, however, the nature of the *symbolizandum* is such that it *cannot* be grasped conceptually. In a work of art (in so far as a work of art can be taken as not merely containing symbols but as itself symbolising something—an obscure and perplexing question which I am happy not to have to discuss), what is symbolised does not admit of conceptual apprehension. It is told of the celebrated danseuse Tamara Karsavina that once, when asked the 'meaning' of some more than usually complicated item in her repertoire, she replied 'If I could tell you in words, I should not go to the so great trouble of dancing it'! An important consequence of this impossibility of conceptually apprehending the *symbolizandum* is that the symbol in such cases cannot be accepted by the mind *as* a symbol on the ground of a conceptually apprehended identity between it and the *symbolizandum*. And yet it is certainly not an arbitrary symbol; an identity is certainly recognised; but it must be a *felt* identity, not a *conceived* identity.

4. Let us turn now to the symbols that are our especial business; those rational concepts like Power, Value, Love, Justice, Wisdom, Mercy, and Personality which theistic religions almost all predicate of God in some sense, and which supra-rational theism insists ought to be regarded, and can significantly be regarded, as *symbols only* of a God whose ultimate nature transcends human powers of conception. It is easy enough to see under which of the distinctions we have marked they will fall. Evidently (if symbols at all) they will be natural rather than conventional symbols. They have not been deliberately instituted by any common agreement to serve as symbols for aspects or facets of the Divine, but are (by some) accepted as such in virtue of their own intrinsic meaning. Again, like all natural symbols, they are not arbitrary but analogical symbols. Again, they are by definition conceptual, not sensory, symbols (there are any number of sensory symbols also in religion, but with these we are not here concerned). Finally, it is plain that

they belong to the class of symbols whose *symbolizanda* are not amenable to conceptual apprehension, and whose identity with their *symbolizanda* must be felt rather than conceived.

But though these rational concepts, regarded as religious symbols, share the last-mentioned important characteristic with works of art regarded as aesthetic symbols, we must be careful not to press too far the parallel between 'religious' and 'aesthetic' symbols. There are several important differences, and one that is fundamental for our present theme. The relation of symbol to *symbolizandum* in the work of art raises peculiarly baffling problems, and I must confess to a good deal of doubt as to whether the language of symbolism is appropriate in this connection at all. But in so far as the work of art can be regarded as a symbol of anything, it at least seems certain that it is not a symbol which is felt by the artist to be a weaker version of, a 'falling away from', that which it is intended to symbolise. If the work of art is successful, it is felt by the artist to express *perfectly* what he wants to express. Now it is obviously quite otherwise with the rational concepts that are accepted as symbols of the supra-rational God. It is of the very essence of the situation that they are taken to be *im*perfect representations of the *symbolizandum*, merely 'the best we can do' if we are to 'think' God at all. The *symbolizandum* is the *mysterium tremendum et fascinans* in its numinous meaning, and our inadequate conceptual pictures or 'ideograms' fall inevitably far short of that which they 'symbolise'.

5. And now we are in a position to attack the crucial problem of symbolic *validity*. In what sense satisfactory to religion (if in any such sense) can these rational concepts be presumed to be *valid* symbols of their *symbolizanda?*

In an obvious sense, of course, *all* symbols are valid symbols, in that (whether conventional or natural) they are genuinely indicative of their *symbolizanda* for those who accept them as symbols. But symbolic validity of this sort is only a subjective or personal validity, holding good for some minds. This is quite inadequate to the needs of the present case. For religion clearly could not be content to accept a rational concept as a valid symbol of a supra-rational God simply on the ground that for some minds which happen to be circumstanced in a certain way it is taken to have sufficient identity of character with such a Being to serve as a symbol of Him. In order to be able to accept it as a valid symbol of God, religion would rightly insist that its identity with God be shown to be not a 'subjective' identity conditioned by the particular circumstances of particular individuals, but an identity that is in some intelligible sense *objective* or *necessary*. It must be a symbol that is valid not just for some minds, but for *mind*. In short, what has to be shown, if these rational concepts are to be established as having symbolic validity in any sense that will be satisfactory to religion, is that they have objective and not merely subjective validity as symbols of their *symbolizanda*.

But a word of caution should perhaps be interposed here. It must be borne in mind that it is the objective validity of these concepts *only as symbols of their religious symbolizanda*, i.e. as symbols of the *mysterium tremendum et fascinans* of religious experience, that is our present concern. This is not to be confused with the question of the objective validity of these concepts as symbols of a reality that exists independently of religious experience. That is quite a different question—the question (in one form) of the objective validity of religious experience itself, which we shall come to in due course. Our present question is a necessary prelude to this. It is the question whether *from the standpoint of religion* these concepts can be regarded as having objective validity as symbols of the Divine nature.

Very well then. Can it be shown that, from the standpoint of a supra-rational theism (like Otto's), there is some kind of necessary identity between certain rational concepts and a supra-rational God, and that these concepts have accordingly an objective validity as symbols? It seems to me that this can be shown. It was, indeed, the whole point of Otto's contention, which we discussed in the last lecture, that certain rational concepts are applied to God through what he calls an *a priori* schematism of numinous experience; that it is by 'an inward necessity of the mind', not by the accidental circumstances of particular minds, that the identity (despite the difference) of these concepts with the nature of the supra-rational object of religious worship is affirmed. The basis of this inward necessity, it will be recalled, was the felt analogy between the emotions evoked by the numinous object and the emotions evoked by the 'rational' qualities in question. Whereas, for example, the emotion evoked by the 'value' aspect of the numinous object, the *mysterium fascinans*, is different not merely in intensity but in quality from the emotion evoked by value or goodness as we apprehend it in finite embodiments—a difference partially marked by the difference between such terms as adoration and reverence on the one hand, and admiration, love and respect on the other—there is a felt identity as well as difference between the two emotive responses. Anyone reflecting on a moment of deeply felt religious experience will, I think, confirm that his emotion of adoration felt *like* the natural emotions of admiration and love—that it pointed, as it were, in the same direction—while feeling not merely *un*like but *clean contrary to* such natural emotions as contempt and hate—pointing, as it were, in the opposite direction.

Moreover, that the recognition of such analogies is not just something fortuitous, depending upon the personal circumstances of the individual, but is an inner necessity of the mind, would seem to find illustration in the whole history of religious experience. Everywhere and always, on the basis, presumably, of this felt identity, the religious consciousness interprets the object which evokes the religious emotion in terms of 'the highest it knows'; i.e. in terms of the qualities that evoke such 'natural' emotions as admiration, respect, and love. This uniformity in the response of the religious consciousness throughout history, may, indeed, be disguised by the almost infinite variety of the specific qualities that are ascribed to God by different religions. But the disguise is superficial. It would be absurd not to expect such variety, since inevitably the qualities that are taken as manifesting the highest values will vary enormously according to the level of knowledge and culture and ethical enlightenment of different religious communities. Even if we took no account (as of course we can, and in the end must) of the complication introduced by the *tremendum* element in religious experience, which will undergo equally with the *fascinans* element a conceptual translation appropriate to the particular culture, there would still be nothing strange in the fact that the gods of primitive communities have many features that to modern eyes are gross and repellent. Shocking as the cruder conceptions of deity may seem to us, there is no theoretical difficulty in understanding them to be the worshipper's conceptual translation of the numinous. There is a long road to travel in the development of *homo sapiens* before he can be expected to interpret the *mysterium tremendum et fascinans* as an Infinite and Eternal Spirit with the attributes of the God of Christianity; and startling differences in overt content should not be permitted to blind us to the underlying, but very real, identity of substance.

Now if this be indeed the situation, if the religious consciousness is subject to an inward necessity of the mind to symbolise its object in terms of certain 'rational' concepts, at the same time as it humbly acknowledges that the real nature of God transcends all possible human conception, then it seems to me that there is good justification for the claim that these concepts have objective validity as symbols of their *symbolizandum*. For their propriety as symbols is determined, not subjectively by anyone's personal choice and private history, but objectively, by the very constitution of the human mind. The human mind, *qua* religious, *cannot but* think its object in these terms even while it fully recognises their utter inadequacy as literal representations.

And after all, is there from the religious point of view anything at all surprising, or at all objectionable, in the notion that the Creator has so made us that our knowledge of Him is not, so to speak, face to face apprehension, but only through the medium of symbols which are indicative of the Divine Nature but not literal portrayals of it? For myself I can see nothing strange, and nothing derogatory to the dignity of God or man, in such a situation. I should have thought that this kind of knowledge was eminently appropriate to the creature in respect of its Creator. Would not the strange thing rather be (I am tempted to say the *incredible* thing) if finite, temporal man *were* capable of comprehending, as He truly is, the Infinite and Eternal Spirit that is God?

6. It may help to elucidate further the position of supra-rational theism with respect to knowledge of God if we now compare it briefly with the familiar doctrine of *via negativa*, so much favoured in mystical writings. The essence of this doctrine is that since the positive ascription to God of determinate predicates implies a

limitation in that which is *ex hypothesi* completely perfect, the least misleading way of talking about God is by the denial to Him of all determinate predicates whatsoever, no matter how exalted. 'God is neither this nor that' says Eckhart. 'He, the Self, the Atman, is to be described by "No! No!" only,' say the Upanishads.[1]

But while there is important truth in this doctrine of universal negation, it must, I think, if it is not to mislead, be supplemented by the equally important truth that not all of the negations have for the religious consciousness the same status. *Positive* value terms—Justice, Love, Mercy and the like—are negated because of their felt inadequacy to God, whose value is transcendent and ineffable; whereas *dis*value terms—Injustice, Hatred, Cruelty and the like—are negated not just because of their felt *inadequacy*, but also, and primarily, because of their felt *contrariety*, to the Divine nature. Clearly there is a vital difference between negations which proceed upon such different principles; and it is precisely because there *is* this difference, to which the religious consciousness bears consistent witness, that it makes sense to say that the value terms, e.g. Justice, Love, and Mercy, though not literally applicable to God, are applicable to Him in a 'symbolic' significance. Were it not for this felt difference of principle within negation, there would be no case for holding that there is even symbolic knowledge about God. It would be no more justifiable to think of Him in terms of what human beings deem good, than in terms of what human beings deem bad. We should then indeed be left with sheer nescience.

Just as it is misleading to say that God's nature can only be indicated by negation of all determinate predicates, and leave it at that, so too it is misleading to say, without careful qualification, that God, because supra-rational and supra-moral, is 'beyond good and evil'. For such language can easily be taken to mean that the Divine nature has no more affinity with the one than with the other. And this, as I hope I have shown, is by no means an implication of supra-rational theism. On the contrary, the recognition of the special affinity of the Divine nature with goodness is implied in the recognition of the analogy between the emotion which the conception of *good* evokes in us and the emotion which

[1] Quoted by William James in *The Varieties of Religious Experience*, p. 416 (26th impression of edition by Longmans, Green & Co.).

the *mysterium fascinans* evokes in us; a felt analogy that is in the sharpest contrast with the felt *antithesis* between the emotions which the concept of *evil* and the *mysterium fascinans* respectively evoke in us. To be *supra*-moral is by no means to be *non*-moral. A God that is neutral between good and evil is emphatically *not* the God of supra-rational theism.

7. I shall be forgiven, I hope, if I dwell a little longer on this perplexing but utterly central problem of symbolic or analogical knowledge in religion. In my judgment at any rate, it is almost impossible to exaggerate its importance for any serious theistic philosophy or theistic religion. I doubt whether even the naïvest forms of fundamentalism can in the end avoid pronouncing or implying at some point that the human mind has to be content with symbols, or analogies, or ideograms, or metaphors—the particular term preferred is immaterial—for its knowledge of God. We ought therefore to spare no pains to assure ourselves that symbolic or analogical knowledge does really mean something in religion, and mean something important.

I want therefore to look rather carefully now at an argument which might, it seems to me, be directed against our position with considerable plausibility; an argument which, if sound, carries with it the conclusion that analogical knowledge in the particular case that is our concern is virtually worthless. It might perhaps be stated as follows:

Analogy implies difference as well as likeness between the analogates. Now it would seem, on reflection, that if analogical knowledge of a quality is to be of any real worth, it is vital that we should be in possession of information (as we generally are) about the respects in which the particular quality is like its analogate and the respects in which it is unlike it. For suppose we know only that there *is* a likeness. In that event, it may well be the case, for all we can tell, that the likeness to the analogate is quite trivial as compared with its unlikeness. For example, stinginess is in some respects like thrift, and in some respects unlike it; but the unlikeness so far outweighs the likeness in importance that we take up totally different attitudes towards the two qualities, condemning the one as a vice while approving the other as a virtue. Now the peculiarity of the case that is our special concern, our analogical knowledge of the 'value' pertaining to the supra-rational God, is that we do *not* know in what respects the Divine 'value' is like its analogate, 'value' as we ordinarily conceive it; for *ex hypothesi* we have no conceptual knowledge of the Divine nature which would enable us to institute the necessary comparison. It follows that the unknown difference between Divine value and its analogate may be of such a sort that, *if* it were known to us, our attitude towards them would be transformed—just as in the case of stinginess and thrift, where we do know in what respects the analogates are like and unlike one another, our attitude towards the one is utterly different from our attitude towards the other. But if that is so, does it not follow that our analogical knowledge of Divine value is virtually worthless?

I think the answer to this objection lies, in principle, in seeing that value is not the kind of quality that can be 'like' another quality at all; that, in fact, *nothing can be like value save value itself.* In order for any quality A to be like another quality B, there must be at least one more general quality X of which both A and B can be regarded as species; as, e.g. stinginess is like thrift in that each can be regarded as a species of the quality 'saving'. And that, obviously, is the condition of the great bulk of qualities— that there is at least one genus of which they are species. But is *value* a quality of this kind? I think not. A particular *form* of value such as economic value, aesthetic value, or moral value, of course *is*. Each is a species of the genus value, and is accordingly like (and unlike) each of the other species of the genus. But the genus of which they are species, value as such, cannot, it seems to me, be so regarded. For there is no more general quality (so far as I can see) of which value can be said to be a species, and which would make it possible for us to say that value is 'like' (and 'unlike') some other species of that quality. (This is not necessarily to imply, it should be noted, that those philosophers are in the right who say that value is a 'simple' quality, where 'simplicity' is understood to exclude relations. Value may very well be a *relational* quality, intrinsically involving, perhaps, a relation to human desire. What is important for the argument is not that value be simple, but that it be ultimate, in the sense that there is no genus of which it is a species.)

Now if this be granted, and nothing is like value save value itself, it follows that the Divine quality which we take to be analogous to value as we ordinarily conceive it *is* in fact value as we ordinarily conceive it. But in one respect this result looks rather disconcerting. It would appear as if we had escaped from one difficulty only to land ourselves in another just as formidable. For have we not all along been insisting on the significant difference, as well as identity, between 'human' value and Divine value? Indeed was it not on that very account that we found it necessary to say that we have only 'analogical' knowledge of the Divine quality? How can we maintain that nothing is like value except value itself and at the same time assert that value as ascribed to God is genuinely different from value as we conceive it in ordinary human experience?

But a solution of this difficulty is perhaps not so very hard to seek. For does not value as we ordinarily conceive it *point beyond itself* for its own perfect realisation? Our human aspirations after value cannot find absolute fulfilment so long as any imperfection remains in our state. Now this entails that absolute fulfilment is achievable not in any finite mode of being, but only in an infinitude or self-completeness of being that transcends our human condition. In other words, the ideal consummation of 'human' value *itself* lies in a state qualitatively different from any conceivable human value. But if that be the situation, the recognition that nothing is like value save value itself is not incompatible with the recognition that Divine value is 'like' human value and is yet in a very important sense different from it. For the 'difference' in the case is a difference *within* a general identity. It is the difference between the value man aspires after in its imperfect expressions in finite life and that *same* value in its completely perfect realisation.

This way of interpreting the likeness and the difference between value as we ordinarily conceive it and Divine value seems to me to solve our problem, and also to coincide perfectly with the testimony of religious experience. What for religious experience distinguishes the value of the religious object from value in any finite embodiment is precisely that the former is value *absolute*— the perfect satisfaction or consummation of our value aspirations. As such, as absolute, it is felt to be a value that transcends human conception, since all conceived value has the limitations that attach to the finite mode of being, and is accordingly incapable in principle of completely satisfying our value aspirations. Appropriately this value absolute which transcends human conception has for religious experience the note of mystery that belongs to the numinous.

There is no need to defend in detail against the same criticism the significance of analogical knowledge of God in respect of the other of the two ultimate qualities ascribed by religion to the Divine *mysterium*, viz. Power. For it seems clear that a precisely parallel line of argument is in order. Power, like value, though it *has* species, is not itself a species of any more general quality, and thus cannot be 'like' any other quality. And Power too points beyond any finite embodiment of itself for its own complete fulfilment; so that power 'absolute' is qualitatively distinct from power as finitely embodied, and yet is rightly deemed to be 'like' power as finitely embodied since the difference between the two falls *within* the power concept itself. And, as in the case of value, this interpretation of the likeness and difference between human and Divine power seems to correspond perfectly with the testimony of religious experience.

8.   Let me now bring this lecture to a close with a few words of reminder about what we have been trying to do in it. We have *not* been trying to prove that supra-rational theism is objectively true. The discussion of that problem will be begun in the next lecture. We have been trying to show only that supra-rational theism is valid as the theoretical expression of religion; valid in the sense that we have in it the logical *terminus ad quem* of reflection upon the object of religious experience and its implications. The most formidable obstacle to acceptance of this view, we considered, was its entailment that theological doctrines are debarred from claiming anything better than a 'symbolic' knowledge of God. We therefore devoted most of our time to trying to remove misgivings about the significance and value of 'symbolic' knowledge in a theistic context, and to trying to show that this is as clearly distinguishable from mere nescience as it is from knowledge in the strict sense. If it be so distinguishable, our submission is

that religion has nothing whatever to lose, and has very much to gain, by a frank recognition that the qualities it ascribes to God have to be understood as only symbols or ideograms of the Divine Nature. I do not myself believe that this conclusion conflicts in any way with the general mood of religion, however sharply it may conflict with the main trends of dogmatic theology. When the plain question is put, 'Which is the more fit object of worship, a God whose power and goodness are in principle beyond human comprehension, or a God whose power and goodness differ not in kind but only in degree from the power and goodness to be found in His creation?' I confess I find it difficult to understand how a religious mind could hesitate long about giving its preference to the former.

THE OBJECTIVE VALIDITY OF RELIGION (I)

1. In my last lecture I was concerned with the question 'Is supra-rational theism valid as the theoretical expression of religion?'—and I tried to show that, despite the reluctance which people naturally feel towards having to make do in religion with a knowledge that is of a merely symbolic or analogical kind, there are good reasons for returning an affirmative answer. Today I begin discussion of the different question, 'Is supra-rational theism *objectively* valid, i.e. *true*?' At the stage the general argument of this course has now reached, this can be seen to be in fact the original question we set out to answer in these lectures; the question 'Is religion true?' For religious experience (so our argument ran) finds its developed theoretical expression in theism; and the only form of theism that can adequately meet the demands of a religious experience from which the *mysterium tremendum et fascinans* has not been illicitly expunged is supra-rational theism.

For us, so far, the God of supra-rational theism has only the status of an abstract possibility. In this respect, however, it has the advantage over the God of Rational Theism, which, if the argument of Lecture XV was sound, is not even abstractly possible. For Rational Theism, while ascribing to God Absolute Perfection, ascribes to Him also, in their literal significance, various qualities which presuppose in Him thought and will; and thought and will, we tried to show, since they imply imperfection in the thinking and willing subject, are incompatible with absolute perfection. The God of Rational Theism, therefore, involves a self-contradiction; and a self-contradictory Being is not even abstractly possible. This fatal disability does not attach to the

God whose existence we are now to debate. According to Supra-rational Theism, qualities presupposing thought and will in their highest conceivable manifestations—qualities like Wisdom, Love and Justice—are also ascribable to God, but only as 'ideograms' which symbolically represent, and do not literally portray, the Absolute Perfection of the Divine Nature. Such a God we can posit, I think, at least without self-contradiction. His existence is at least an abstract possibility. But are there substantial reasons for holding His existence to be not merely possible but actual? That is what we are to consider for the remainder of this course.

2. We may best begin, I think, with arguments from the nature of religious experience itself.

It is common ground to all parties that religious experience carries with it a very powerful subjective assurance of the real presence of its object—the 'Numen' or 'God'. No one, indeed, subscribes today to the proposition, in any *general* form, that subjective feelings of certainty are of themselves a guarantee of objective truth. Yet there are always those who appear to think that, however absurd elsewhere, the proposition does somehow have a valid application in religion, and that the man who enjoys 'religious experience' stands in no need of any other support for his belief in God.

In the light of the rather lengthy discussion, in the opening lectures of the first course, of the rights of reason in the field of religious truth, I may perhaps be excused from dealing with this view in much detail. The only defence of it that seems to me to have even superficial plausibility consists in arguing that the feelings of certainty in religion are of a quite unique sort, which the critic who does not know religion 'from the inside' is incompetent to assess. Probably everyone who has ever ventured to criticise the claims of religion, or of any particular form of it, is familiar with this rather irritating device for reducing him to silence. 'You just don't understand', he is told, 'because you have never yourself experienced this unique certainty.'

But the device is surely as specious as it is irritating. In the first place, it seems to be forgotten that, even in the ranks of those whose acquaintance with religion 'from the inside' is beyond challenge, there are many who frankly acknowledge that the certainty they feel stands in need of support from other considerations if an assertion of objective validity is to be justified. *They* at any rate do not find the alleged uniqueness in their feelings of certainty. In the second place, it is surely fair to assume that if there *is* an unique kind of certainty attainable in religious experience, there will be some indication of this uniqueness in the descriptions of religious experience given by those who have been privileged to enjoy it, and perhaps some indication also in its effects upon behaviour. In fact, however, no evidence whatever of such uniqueness seems discernible. Everyone agrees that there are multitudes of putative religious experiences which, though accompanied by strong feelings of certainty, are spurious, in the sense that they are not really, as the experients proclaim, apprehensions of the Divine. (Obviously this must be so, if only because putative religious experiences frequently contradict one another.) In *some* cases, therefore, the feelings of certainty in putative religious experience are admittedly delusive. But no one has ever succeeded in pointing to any specific *quale* among the feelings of certainty in different putative religious experiences which might serve to mark off the authentic from the spurious, the objectively valid from the objectively invalid. On the contrary, I think it is fair to say that, the more closely one studies the reports of religious experiences within different and mutually exclusive religious communions, the clearer it becomes that the attendant feelings of certainty are identical, irrespective of the differences of content. The critic, so far as I can see, does not require to have himself enjoyed religious experience in order to draw a legitimate inference that, if no such difference as alleged is discernible, no warrant exists for talking of an unique sort of religious certainty which obviates all need of justification on objective grounds.

All this seems extremely obvious. And probably there are few religious thinkers who, if it were formally put to them, would care to deny its truth. It is a matter of common observation, however, that many of those who are themselves well aware of the folly of trusting to uncriticised private feelings in religion, and who are in the habit of submitting their own convictions to rigorous scrutiny by reason, are strangely averse to preaching what they practise. They condone in others—at least in the sense that they do not condemn—a faith that asks no questions and never has asked any; no doubt on the principle that since religious conviction is something very central and very dearly cherished in a man's life, one ought not to make suggestions liable to disturb it, and cause the believer distress of mind, unless for exceedingly strong reasons. But the answer to that is obvious. There *are* exceedingly strong reasons for discouraging an uncritical mind in religion, for it is beyond all question that this has brought untold calamities upon mankind. Where people imagine that 'faith' is the guarantor of its own truth, and that to raise a doubt about its validity is idle and even impious, an intolerance more or less bitter towards all opposing faiths is well-nigh inevitable. Critically-minded seekers after truth can be expected to acknowledge, more or less as a matter of course, the possibility that their beliefs may, after all, be wrong; for to them it will have become overwhelmingly clear that, in view of the great multitude and complexity of the problems raised, an attitude of dogmatic assurance is impossible except for the very ignorant and the very arrogant. Those, on the other hand, who consider their subjective, private feelings to be a self-sufficient and final criterion, just 'know' that they are right and all who differ from them wrong. Mediation by way of argument being ruled out, the upshot, inevitably, is sheer deadlock. Now a state of deadlock is something to be deplored in any field of human experience; but in the emotive atmosphere of religion it has peculiarly pernicious consequences. 'Unbelief'—the title which the bigot blandly assigns to beliefs that differ from his own—tends to be regarded as an offence against God, which it is the pious duty of 'the faithful' to eradicate. And since the appeal to the civilised technique of persuasion by reasoned argument is rejected, there is only one way of eradicating opposing views, viz. *force*. One may well be shocked, but one has no right to be surprised, at the number and the bloodiness of the religious wars that stain so many pages of human history. It would be naïve to expect anything else where the appeal to reason in matters of religion is accounted not a virtue but a vice.

Moreover, it ought not to be forgotten that respect for reason is, in the end, indivisible. If men are allowed to believe that in religion subjective feelings of certainty need no supplementation by rational evidence, they will with difficulty be dissuaded from adopting the same attitude towards other momentous questions —moral, social, and political—about which they happen to feel passionately. And surely no one can be indifferent to that consequence who has any concern for the fate of civilisation itself? It is an essential precondition of any way of life that can be called 'civilised' that there should have grown up in the community a strong tradition of appealing to reason for the settlement of disputes. To encourage, or even to condone, habits of mind that tend to weaken that tradition—as, e.g. most if not all forms of religious revivalism most certainly tend to do—is to incur a responsibility of whose gravity some notable religious leaders seem to me to be strangely and deplorably unaware.

But we have already spent over-much time on a topic which, despite its surpassing human importance, is, to say truth, of somewhat slender philosophic interest. I would only remind you in a final word, of the two propositions confusion between which, I suggested in my first course,[1] was at the bottom of most of the distrust of reason in religion. There is the proposition (1) that reason is competent to apprehend God; and the proposition (2) that reason is competent to assess the evidence as to whether an ostensible apprehension of God is an authentic apprehension of God. The first proposition seems to me almost certainly false. But it should be clearly distinguished from the second proposition, which it does not entail, and which is in my judgment almost certainly true.

3.   Turning now to philosophically more weighty endeavours to establish the objective validity of the religious consciousness (without, as it were, passing beyond the bounds of that consciousness), there is one very attractive line of argument which it seems to me important to explore with some thoroughness. It is a line of argument analogous to that which we advanced in the concluding lecture of our last course in proof of the objective validity of the moral consciousness. Let me very briefly recall to you the general form which the argument took as applied to the moral consciousness.

The moral consciousness, we there tried to show, is a mode

---

[1] Lectures I and II.

of human experience that is ultimate and unique. Consciousness of moral oughtness is consciousness of an unconditional obligation —a 'categorical imperative'; and this consciousness is incapable of being explained in terms of any combinations and permutations of non-moral ideas and feelings. The ultimacy of moral experience can be rejected only if we are prepared to deny that the moral consciousness does involve consciousness of an unconditional obligation; and alternative analyses which seek to dispense with this element, it seemed to us, are inadequate to the actual facts of moral experience. But if the moral consciousness has thus to be accepted as an ultimate mode of human experience, its testimony cannot reasonably be rejected. One may fairly ask what one *is* entitled to believe in if not in something which by the very constitution of our nature we are obliged to affirm. And the testimony of the moral consciousness, we argued, is unmistakably to the objective reality of the moral order.

Now it is entirely natural and proper to ask whether a parallel line of argument may not be valid with respect to the religious consciousness. We can distinguish a common religious consciousness from its different and sometimes mutually contradictory manifestations in particular religious experiences, just as we can distinguish a common moral consciousness from its different and sometimes mutually contradictory manifestations in particular moral experiences. It was, indeed, the nature of this common or basic religious consciousness that we were chiefly concerned to portray in our earlier lecture on 'The Concept of Religion'. What then if, as many religious thinkers have held, this religious consciousness is an ultimate and unique mode of human experience no less than the moral consciousness, every bit as incapable of being derived from anything but itself? It will follow, surely, that we must accept *its* internal testimony too. And its internal testimony is just as unmistakably to the reality of the object of worship as the testimony of the moral consciousness is to the reality of a moral order.

It is a tempting line of argument; the more so since we so often speak of 'the moral consciousness' and 'the religious consciousness' with an implication of parallelism between them. Unfortunately doubts emerge about there being any such parallelism as soon as we seriously reflect on the matter. I shall try to show this first in a general way, and shall then examine more rigorously what would appear to be the crucial point at issue.

The religious consciousness, we may perhaps assume in the light of earlier discussions, is essentially the awareness of a supernatural being or beings of a power and value transcending all human conception. Is there any constituent in this complex state which can be said to be *peculiar* to the religious consciousness, any constituent that has an uniqueness or underivability corresponding to the uniqueness or underivability of the experience of 'unconditional obligation' characteristic of the moral consciousness?

Prima facie, at any rate, this must be accounted very doubtful. The most promising candidate for the necessary uniqueness is the *mysterium* element in the religious consciousness, and Otto has rightly emphasised how impregnation by this element distinguishes religious emotions from certain 'natural' emotions which resemble them. But, as we shall see later, it is very difficult to prove, and Otto certainly has not succeeded in proving, that the sense of the 'mysterious' even in its numinous meaning of the 'other worldly', the 'supernatural', cannot have its origin in non-religious contexts. Yet nothing less than this would entitle us to regard the *mysterium* element in the religious consciousness as underivable, and the religious consciousness, in consequence as ultimate or autonomous. If we should be compelled to concede that neither this nor any other constituent of the religious consciousness is incapable of occurring in a non-religious context, the door is open to the many theories (some of them certainly not implausible) which try to explain in 'naturalistic' terms how the various constituents come, or can come, to be combined in the specific way in which they are combined in what we know as 'the religious consciousness'.

It is important to remember, of course, that even if a 'naturalistic' explanation of the religious consciousness *is* possible, that is far from proving that the 'object' of the religious consciousness has no real existence. It does not even prove that religious experience is never what it seems to itself to be, i.e. an experience directly evoked by the real presence of its object, the 'Numen'. Nevertheless, if religious experience is even *capable* of being naturalistically derived, we cannot appeal to the mere *fact* of

religious experience (so-called) to establish the real existence of
its object; as we can, in my view, appeal to the mere fact of moral
experience to establish the real existence of *its* object.

4. We shall take up shortly this question of the ultimacy of the
religious consciousness; but meantime let us notice another
circumstance that raises doubts about a relevant parallelism
between the moral and the religious consciousness.

The moral consciousness would appear to be a *universal*
characteristic of mankind. It is true that a man will sometimes
tell us that he does not know what it means to be conscious of an
'unconditional obligation'. But there are good reasons for thinking
that his disavowal of the experience arises from one or other of
certain removable misunderstandings—a matter to which we
made some reference in an earlier lecture, and upon which Henry
Sidgwick has some very pertinent observations in his *The Methods
of Ethics*.[1] That the moral consciousness should be universal as
well as ultimate is a matter of some importance for the proof of the
objective validity of a moral order. Obviously the proof offered
can carry no weight for a man who is devoid of a moral consciousness. But in so far as a man has, and acknowledges that he has, a
moral consciousness, it seems clear that he can deny the objective
reality of a moral order only on pain of self-contradiction, since,
qua moral consciousness, he himself implicitly affirms what (no
doubt from the standpoint of some theory) he also feels called
upon to deny.

It is a very great deal more open to doubt, however, whether
the *religious* consciousness is a universal mode of human experience. That it is so is a proposition which looks at first sight as
though it had widespread support among authoritative writers on
religion. But on closer inspection it usually turns out that what
these writers really mean when they tell us that religion is 'a
universal characteristic of mankind' is merely that there is no
sizeable community of men known to us, of any time or any clime,
that does not practise a religion of some sort. And that, of course,

[1] Book I, Chapter III, § 4. It is pleasant to see signs today of a revival of
interest in a work which must have a fair claim to rank as the best ethical
treatise in the English language.

even if true, is perfectly compatible with there being any number of *individuals* who are without religion. And here we are bound to notice a phenomenon that looks a trifle ominous for religion. It can reasonably be held that in *primitive* communities even individuals without religion are very few, if indeed they exist at all; but he would be a bold man who would say the same thing of communities which we ordinarily think of as 'civilised'. Indeed such a contention would seem to become less and less plausible the higher we ascend in the scale of civilisation. The appearances certainly suggest that the more habituated people become to the free exercise of reason in the formation of their beliefs, and the more extensive becomes the range of well-accredited knowledge available to them, the less prevalent among them is anything recognisable as 'religion', or 'the religious consciousness'. Of course, this *proves* nothing. All the same, I think the apologists of religion ought to be a good deal more disquieted than they usually seem to be by even the *appearance* of a close correlation between the increase of irreligion on the one hand, and the increase of well-informed and disciplined intelligences on the other hand.

At the same time, appearances can be extremely deceptive when we are trying to compute the extent to which the religious consciousness is present in a community—even where the community is the one we know best, because we happen to belong to it. Two of the commonest sources of deception are worth a passing notice.

I shall first touch upon one which encourages people to imagine that religion is *more* prevalent than it actually is. In most of the communities with which we are acquainted, religion, whether widely believed or not, has the support of 'public opinion'. It is not very 'respectable' to be an atheist or an agnostic. In many countries, including our own, a particular form of religion even enjoys the official sanction of the State—perhaps that is why we in Britain are wont to speak of ourselves, albeit a little wryly, as 'a Christian country'—and lip-service at least is accorded to it by the main organs of public opinion. In consequence, not only are expressions of anti-religious opinion subject to the fairly effective deterrent of social disapprobation, but also the media for such expressions of opinion are narrowly limited. Militant critics of religion who may be ready to brave the vilification of their fellow-men still have to overcome the formidable difficulty of securing a reasonable public hearing. It is obvious that neither our 'free' Press nor the B.B.C., for example, can be said to be really 'open' to opinions hostile to religion; though, as we are all aware, there have of late been signs (by many people viewed as deeply sinister) of a more venturesome policy by the B.B.C. The only substantial exception, however, is the highly significant one of 'The Third Programme', which, it is well appreciated, will reach only a very small section of the community, and that a section which is in any event determined to apply its intelligence to religious no less than to other matters of moment. The situation has an interesting parallel in the 'taboo' upon expressions of anti-monarchist opinion, which is also thus made to appear far rarer than it probably is. The chances that the editor of an important newspaper, or of any journal with a wide circulation, will extend the hospitality of his columns to an assault upon either religion or the institution of monarchy, no matter how brilliant its reasoning or how choice its literary form, may fairly be said to be almost negligible. This virtual, if covert, censorship may or may not be a good thing. I am not here concerned to pass judgment, but only to point to facts which have a bearing upon the capacity to assess accurately how far the religious consciousness really permeates a community. The ordinary reader of the newspapers, and the ordinary listener to the radio, could hardly be blamed if they formed the impression that the Christian Church in this country is an institution warmly approved by everyone except, perhaps, members of the criminal classes and a few crack-brained intellectuals.

The second common source of deception, however, is one that tells in exactly the opposite direction. When people say, or even think, that they 'do not believe in religion', do they always really mean what they say (or think)? It seems pretty certain that they do not. Very often what they really mean is that they do not accept the doctrines of the particular religion that finds favour in their community. I referred in an earlier lecture [1] to the common if, somewhat slovenly, tendency in ordinary speech to identify 'religion' with the particular form of it practised in one's own community; and it is easy to understand how, in our own country for example, a man should disclaim religious belief on

[1] Lecture XI, p. 236.

the inadequate ground that he disbelieves the central doctrines of Christianity. I do not of course suggest that those who in a Christian country disclaim religion are in fact devotees of Islamism or Hinduism or some other specific religion. Mostly they do not subscribe to any specific religion. But I am much disposed to think that at least some of them, and possibly many, would, if suitably interrogated, turn out to believe vaguely in some sort of mysterious, yet just and benignant, Power at the heart of things. Their belief is not formalised, and there is no appointed ritual of worship in which it can find overt expression. But it would, I think, be a mistake to regard anyone who has even this much as wholly devoid of a religious consciousness.

The lesson to be learnt from such considerations (and it would be easy to add others of like import) is that, so far as the empirical evidence is concerned, dogmatic pronouncements are out of place with regard to the extent to which the religious consciousness is characteristic of mankind generally. It is not *impossible* that, in germ at least, it is a universal characteristic; though one would have to concede that, if so, there are very many persons in whom it does not attain to a degree of development and definition which enables it to be clearly recognised as such even by themselves. One thing, however, I think we *can* say. *If* the religious consciousness should turn out to be an *ultimate* mode of experience, implying a specific power or 'faculty', it is very likely that it is also a *universal* mode of experience. For if the religious consciousness should turn out to be ultimate, it is reasonable to accept its testimony as veridical: but if its testimony is veridical, we must acknowledge the God of religion to be a reality; and if we acknowledge the God of religion to be a reality, it seems hardly possible to reconcile the pre-eminent goodness that is ascribed to God in religion with His provision for only *some* persons, and His denial to others, of the specific native endowment which makes communion with Himself possible. A proof of ultimacy may therefore with some reason be said to be, in the case of the religious consciousness, a proof of universality also.

The primary question, then, is manifestly that of the *ultimacy* of the religious consciousness. Can or can not its characteristic features be satisfactorily explained as arising out of non-religious elements in human experience?

5. It might be well, however, to preface the formal discussion of this question with a brief reminder on a point which, though obvious enough, is a little apt to be forgotten. Even if the religious consciousness is not ultimate, but has a non-religious basis, it does not follow that this non-religious basis is of that 'subjectivist' sort which provokes natural doubts about the objective validity of what is built upon it. Doubtless in many psychological studies of religion it is so presented. Most commonly, perhaps, the religious consciousness is 'explained' as the product of certain subconscious desires which demand, and (because they cannot in the ordinary way procure) project in phantasy their own fulfilment. But 'explanation' *need* not be of this subjectivist sort. Those who deny the ultimacy of the religious consciousness may wish to argue that belief in God arises out of straightforward reflection upon certain phenomena in the world about us, and/or in the history of mankind, and/or in our own souls. Once belief in God has been thus implanted, they would suggest, it is easy to understand how certain crucial experiences in a man's life come to be interpreted as experiences in which God is directly present to and operative upon him (which they may well be). Now such explanation of the religious consciousness in terms of intelligent reflection will clearly not throw doubt upon the reality of its object in the same way as does explanation in terms of imaginative projections excited by the pressure of unfulfilled desire. *Prima facie* there is every reason why we should trust the inferences arrived at by reflection, provided they are drawn with due regard for logic and from an adequate range of relevant facts. It follows that even if we find ourselves forced to reject the ultimacy of the religious consciousness, no necessary presumption is thereby created against its validity, against the reality of its object. On the other hand, if it should turn out that its ultimacy *can* be established, we shall have available an agreeably simple, and yet (I think) cogent, proof of its objective validity.

6. Among the foremost of the champions of religion's ultimacy is, of course, Rudolf Otto. I have already expressed my unqualified admiration for the brilliance and penetration of Otto's psychological description of the religious consciousness. Has he also

produced good reasons for assigning to that consciousness the status of an ultimate mode of human experience? I do not myself think that he has; but as it seems to me not easy to find anyone with anything better to offer in defence of that thesis, it will be worth while to examine his view with some care.

Otto's reasons for holding the religious consciousness to be ultimate or autonomous are one with his reasons for declaring the numinous consciousness—or to speak more strictly, the capacity for numinous consciousness—to be *a priori*. 'The proof that in the numinous we have to deal with purely *a priori* cognitive elements', he tells us, 'is to be reached by introspection and a critical examination of reason such as Kant instituted. We find, that is, involved in the numinous experience, beliefs and feelings qualitatively different from anything that "natural" sense-perception is capable of giving us.' [1] 'The facts of the numinous consciousness point therefore', he goes on, 'to a hidden substantive source, from which the religious ideas and feelings are formed, which lies in the mind independently of sense-experience.' That is to say, the religious consciousness cannot be understood as a product of 'natural' or non-religious experience, but must be accounted underived, ultimate, autonomous.

It is clear, I think, that everything depends in this argument upon the premise that numinous or religious experience involves elements that are qualitatively different from anything appearing in a non-religious context. The argument will stand or fall according to the measure of Otto's success in justifying this premise. Does he in fact show convincingly that no empirical origin is conceivable for the *mysterium tremendum et fascinans* of religious experience? The issue turns, I think, upon the character of the *mysterium* element. It is of course true that both the *tremendum* and the *fascinans* elements, according to Otto's analysis, have also qualitative uniqueness. There is something in them not merely greater than, but other than, the power and the entrancement to be found in 'natural' experiences. Nevertheless, since it is through their integration with the *mysterium* that these elements acquire this uniqueness, it is upon the *mysterium* that we must especially concentrate our attention. It will be convenient to have before us

[1] *The Idea of the Holy*, p. 117.

at this point what is, I think, a key passage for the understanding
of Otto's attitude; a passage in which he expressly distinguishes
the *mysterium* of religion from the *mysterium* of ordinary, non-
religious experience.

'Taken, indeed' (Otto writes), 'in its purely natural sense,
"mysterium" would first mean merely a secret or a mystery in
the sense of that which is alien to us, uncomprehended and unex-
plained; and so far "mysterium" is itself merely an ideogram, an
analogical notion taken from the natural sphere, illustrating, but
incapable of exhaustively rendering, our real meaning. Taken in
the religious sense, that which is "mysterious" is—to give it
perhaps the most striking expression—the "wholly other"
(θάτερον, anyad, alienum), that which is quite beyond the sphere
of the usual, the intelligible, and the familiar, which therefore
falls quite outside the limits of the "canny", and is contrasted with
it, filling the mind with blank wonder and astonishment.' [1]

The crux of the matter, then, is this. Granted that the religious
consciousness is impregnated through and through with the
'mysterious' in the sense of the 'wholly other', is the 'mysterious'
in *this* sense something peculiar to the religious consciousness, so
that the religious consciousness cannot conceivably be explained
in terms of anything other than itself?

Unfortunately Otto's treatment of this question, which is
clearly vital for philosophy, is most disappointingly perfunctory.
One gets the strong impression that on this particular matter he
does not expect to be called in question by those whom he is
addressing, who are, after all, primarily theologians rather than
philosophers. A thorough examination of the ways in which the
'mysterious' can present itself *out of* a religious milieu seems
urgently called for, but Otto nowhere supplies it. In point of fact,
so far from its being impossible to locate apprehension of a 'wholly
other' in non-religious experience, most of Otto's critics have
thought this a comparatively simple matter. Otto (as we have just
seen) baldly asserts that the 'mysterious', if 'taken in its purely
natural sense'—by which he can only mean, if his argument is
to have point, 'taken in a purely non-religious sense'—refers
merely to that which presents itself as 'uncomprehend*ed* and
unexplain*ed*'. But surely it is not difficult to point to instances in

[1] *Op. cit.* p. 26.

which it extends also to that which presents itself as *incomprehensible* and *inexplicable*, to that which seems to the experiencing subject to cut clean across the foundations of the rational or natural order of things.

The most common, though by no means the only, instance of this is to be found, I think, in the human reaction to certain kinds of dream, where the dream is as yet not known to be a dream. Often the weird creatures that inhabit our dreams come and go and change their dim shapes in ways that are grotesquely at variance with the familiar patterns of behaviour in the 'natural' world. To us sophisticated moderns this is not (once we have awakened) particularly mysterious or disturbing. For what we have before us in the dream, we have learned, are not independently existing things, but a mere phantasmagoria projected out of the depths of our own 'subconscious'. To the primitive intelligence, on the other hand, unversed in psychological explanations, these objects will be as independently real as anything in waking experience. And in so far as they are taken as real, they can hardly fail to impress the mind as profoundly disturbing and mysterious. For here are 'realities' (the awakened dreamer must feel) which yet do not conform at all; to 'reality' as he ordinarily knows it 'realities' whose manner of being is in many striking respects so dissimilar from that of the familiar objects of every-day life that his intelligence cannot even begin to cope with them; 'realities' endowed with powers, apparently, not merely greater than, but of a totally different order from, anything with which he is acquainted in his normal experience. He is confronted, in fact, with the 'mysterious' not merely in the sense of the uncomprehended but in the sense of the incomprehensible; with the 'super-natural', the 'wholly other', that 'which has no place in our scheme of reality but belongs to an altogether different order'.

Moreover, dream experiences seem quite sufficient to account for the notion of the mysterious in its 'wholly other' sense even in the mind of modern man, with all his psychological sophistication. For after all, every modern man was once a child, as innocent of psychology as any savage. There must be few among us who cannot recall the state of indescribable terror in which we awakened from some childish dream, so altogether different in kind from any terror evoked by dangers in the 'natural' world; and who cannot recall also how well-nigh impossible we found it to believe the assurances of our elders that the grisly forms that so vividly confronted us had no 'real' existence. Indeed even the adult experience of most of us is visited from time to time by the numinous-like terror of the dream. Witness the few evanescent moments that follow in the wake of an especially horrible nightmare before we have had time (as we say) to 'collect our wits' and to realise that it was 'only a dream'.

It seems to me, therefore, that one need not look beyond dream phenomena to find ample justification for those who think that man's sense of the mysterious, even in its non-natural or supernatural meaning of the 'wholly other', is easily enough accounted for independently of religious experience. The situation, of course, would be radically altered if it were possible to take the view that, wherever we have the kind of experience commonly designated by words like 'uncanny' or 'weird' or 'eerie', there we are in fact enjoying an inchoate form of religious experience itself. If that were the case, then no doubt the sense of the 'wholly other' mysterious *could* be regarded as something uniquely religious. But although there are passages in Otto which it is difficult not to interpret as suggesting this view, I must confess that it seems to me the kind of view to which no one would incline except to save a theory. If the experience of the 'uncanny' is to be regarded as not just (as on the customary view) an *element within* religious experience, and within certain forms of non-religious experience likewise, but as actually itself an inchoate form of religious experience, there must presumably be such identity of nature between the experience of the uncanny and full-fledged religious experience as will make intelligible the development of the latter out of the former. But can such identity plausibly be maintained? What is there in the uncanny as such that corresponds even in germ to that aspect of *surpassing value* which religious experience discovers in its object? I am aware, of course, that Otto has made much of a certain inherent 'attraction' which the uncanny exercises upon the human mind. He tells us that the 'ghost' has an attraction for us which 'consists in this, that of itself, and in an uncommon degree, it entices the imagination, awaking strong interest and curiosity'; [1] and again, that the ghost 'arouses an

[1] *Op. cit.* p. 29.

irrepressible interest in the mind'. Possibly this kind of attraction
is always present in the uncanny; though I fancy it will continue
to excape our notice when we awaken from a nightmare in a cold
sweat of terror. But in any event this kind of attraction seems
poles apart from the *fascinans* aspect of the religious *mysterium*.
The 'value' which the religious object has for religious experience
lies not in its being something we hunger to *understand*—an object
that excites 'interest and curiosity'—but in its being something
that we hunger to *commune with*, to be *at one with*. In the light of
so fundamental a difference of principle, it really seems a rather
desperate expedient to try to interpret experience of the uncanny
as in itself an inchoate form of religious experience.

So far as I can see, then, it is not possible to establish the
ultimacy or autonomy of the religious consciousness on the
ground that the sense of the mysterious which is integral to the
religious consciousness is something unique, and hence incapable
of being derived from non-religious experiences. Is there any
more hopeful way of trying to establish it? For myself I know of
none; and I am forced in consequence to conclude that no line
of argument parallel to that by which the objective validity of the
moral consciousness is proved is possible in the case of the
religious consciousness. The religious consciousness may very
well *be* objectively valid; but its objective validity is not provable
on the ground of its ultimacy or autonomy.

7.   But of course this is not the only, nor, historically speaking,
anything like the most common, ground upon which religious
thinkers have tried to prove the objective validity of religion. What
are we to say of the 'classic' arguments for God's existence—the
Ontological, the Cosmological, the Teleological, and the Moral
Argument?

On two of these at any rate I propose to say very little. The
Ontological and the Teleological arguments ought, I think, now
to be allowed to rest in peace. They were slain by Immanuel Kant
over 150 years ago, and I see nothing to be gained by dissecting
their stone-cold corpses. Metaphor aside, the Ontological Argument, I venture to assert, has never yet persuaded anyone who
has really understood the point of Kant's criticism that 'existence

is not a predicate'. As for the Teleological Argument, all the critics since Kant have pointed out that it would at best establish a God Who is a designing craftsman working upon a partly recalcitrant material. But a 'finite' God of this sort is not the God even of *Rational* Theism. Still less can it be the *mysterium tremendum et fascinans* of Supra-rational Theism.

The Cosmological and the Moral Arguments, on the other hand, do both seem to me to contain much that is still of real significance for philosophical theology. Neither of them, I think, succeeds in *proving* God's existence, but I believe that each contributes something of value towards its probabilification. My sympathy with the general purport of the Cosmological Argument will come out pretty plainly in the metaphysical argument I shall be developing in my next lecture. The Moral Argument I propose to discuss briefly in what remains of this lecture.

8.   The basis of the Moral Argument is the proposition that Duty or The Moral Law is an objective reality. The most historically famous form of it is no doubt that given to it by Kant in the *Critique of Practical Reason*, where arguments are led from the basic proposition to prove the existence not only of God but of Freedom and Immortality also. But since probably the majority of philosophers today would judge this to be among the least effective forms of the argument, and as I take that view of it myself, I propose here to pass it by. The Moral Argument in the form in which it seems to me to have chiefly influenced religious thought (and incidentally, it is worth recalling, the form in which it commended itself best to Kant himself in his last years) is much less ambitious and elaborate. Perhaps the following might be accepted as a fair summary of it.

Consciousness of duty is consciousness of a law that unconditionally claims our obedience—a ' categorical imperative '. Now a 'law' implies a 'law-giver', and 'imperative', an' imperator'. Where are we to look for the giver of this moral law that confronts us with the categorical imperative of duty? Obviously we do not make the law ourselves. What *we* make, *we* can unmake: but the moral law presents itself to us as something objective, existing quite independently of our subjective interests and wishes. Still more obviously, the moral law is not imposed upon us by any other human person, or by any human power or institution. Of laws from these sources we can always intelligibly ask 'Why should we obey them?'. But we cannot ask this intelligibly of the *moral* law, of an imperative we recognise as *unconditional*. Now if there must be *some* imponent of the moral law, and if this imponent is yet neither our self nor any other human person, nor any human power or institution, who or what can this moral law-giver be? Must we not posit some supra-human 'Moral Governor' of the world; a Spirit manifestly endowed with thought and will, since only for such a being can the issue of moral decrees have meaning; a Spirit who can speak to us through our moral consciousness, because he is himself the author of our nature; a Spirit, moreover—it is reasonable to infer—himself supremely good, since (as an eminent theist of an earlier generation has expressed it) he would not 'have made us to hate and despise what is characteristic of his own nature'.[1] In short, does not reflection upon the implications of the objectivity of Moral Law lead the mind irresistibly to the notion of *God* as its imponent?

Even in so bald a summary the Moral Argument seems to me to show itself worthy of respect. Nevertheless it has, I think, a fatal weakness. It depends vitally upon an assumption which, while it looks reasonable enough, becomes on reflection something more than doubtful; the assumption, viz. that the reality of the moral law intrinsically implies an 'imponent' of it, a 'moral law-giver'.

At first glance it may appear almost self-evident that 'law' implies a 'law-giver'. But it appears so only, I suggest, because of our natural proneness to think of 'law' in its highly familiar— in these days all but ubiquitous—form as a social institution. There can be little doubt that law in this its most typical form does imply a law-giver. In the definitions of law offered us by jurisprudents there are very important differences with respect to the ultimate identity of the law-giver, but reference to *some* person or body of persons as imponent of the law is, so far as I am aware, common to all definitions. Now 'moral' law is like 'human' law in certain salient features—that is the justification of our calling it moral *law*. In both cases there is a demand that our conduct

[1] *Theism*, by Robert Flint, pp. 220-1.

should conform to certain principles or rules. But there is a vitally important difference in the *sort* of 'demand' in the two cases; and what the moral argument for God's existence has, it seems to me, failed to appreciate is that an essential difference of the 'moral' demand from the ordinary 'legal' demand is that the former does *not*, like the latter, carry with it an intrinsic reference to an imponent. It is of the very essence of moral obligation or moral oughtness, as we experience it, to be self-sufficient, to carry its authority wholly within itself. There is no need whatsoever for us to think of the demand as made upon us by anything or anybody in order that it be recognised by us *as* morally obligatory, *as* moral law. In contradistinction to all human law, the question 'Who (if anyone) made it?' is totally irrelevant to the recognition of its authority over us. In short, moral law, as known in moral experience, does *not* imply an imponent of it. An imponent there well may be. And we may perhaps, on other grounds, justify a confident belief that there is. But we cannot logically infer an imponent simply from the nature of moral law as such.

That the moral law carries with it no intrinsic reference to an imponent seems to me to be the undeniable testimony of our moral experience. At the same time one can easily understand why the contrary has so often been taken for granted. It is not merely that we tend to be misled by the analogy between 'moral' law and 'human' law. It is due also to the fact that we tend to approach the analysis of moral experience with presuppositions derived from elsewhere. Thus a great many persons who would not claim to be in any formal sense 'religious' believe that there is *some* sort of Creator of the world who is the author of their being. If we undertake our analysis of moral experience against such a background of belief, it is well-nigh inevitable that we shall interpret the *de*mand of moral law as though it were a *com*mand, laid upon us by our Creator. This, as I have already admitted, may very well turn out to be the true view of the matter. But we cannot strengthen the argument for it by appealing to a non-existent intrinsic implication of 'moral law' with 'moral law-giver'.

Wherein, then, lies the value of the Moral Argument for philosophical theology? Its value has been hinted at in what has just been said. It lies, as I see it, in its capacity to combine with arguments of a different, metaphysical character to constitute a

o

more complex argument for God's existence that does have a very real force. *Per se* the analysis of moral experience yields no more (not that this is of less than superlative importance) than that there is a moral order rooted in the very nature of reality. If, however, there should also be justification, on metaphysical grounds, for positing an Infinite Being who is the ultimate source of all that is, it will follow that this Being (to whom we perhaps could not otherwise, on theoretical grounds, ascribe any 'moral' significance) is the source of a moral order, the 'author' or 'imponent' in some sense of the moral law that unconditionally demands our allegiance. Clearly the extension of our concept of the Ultimate Being to include this ethical relationship to man is an enrichment which brings far nearer the legitimate identification of this Being with the God Who is worshipped in religion. But the fuller development of the thought here vaguely foreshadowed must await the outcome of certain somewhat intricate metaphysical discussions in our next lecture.

THE OBJECTIVE VALIDITY
OF RELIGION (II)

1. In the concluding moments of my last lecture I suggested that the knowledge we possess (if, as I believe, we really do possess it) that the moral order is rooted in objective reality might make a significant contribution towards a philosophical corroboration of the truth of religion, *provided that* we were in a position to interpret this 'moral' knowledge in terms of certain metaphysical propositions about the nature of ultimate reality. In the remaining two lectures I want to explain and develop this suggestion. I want to show, if I can, that metaphysical enquiry leads us to a view of the general nature of ultimate reality which is at least consistent with, though it is not (and indeed could not be) identical with, what religion means by God; and that when we supplement the knowledge got through metaphysical argument by what we know of reality from the moral argument, we come very substantially nearer to the actual identification of the ultimate reality of philosophy with the God of religion.

The argument I am about to deploy is based on an analysis of the nature and implications of 'the contradictory'; for it is with myself a conviction of long standing that save through such analysis there is no gateway to sound metaphysical construction. The full grounds for this conviction cannot, of course, be made apparent in advance of the analysis itself, but this much may be said at once. Whatever more specific criteria the intellect may from time to time accept in its endeavours to know the real, there is one general and over-riding criterion from which its allegiance can at no point be withheld, viz. 'non-contradiction'. An 'object' that is self-contradictory, in the sense that the characters we ascribe to it in our conception of it contradict one another, cannot as so conceived be accepted by thought as the reality it is seeking to know. It goes without saying that, pending analysis of the nature of contradiction, the mere knowledge that what is real has the formal character of non-contradiction is of very little account. But I shall try to persuade you that when the nature of the contradictory is correctly elucidated, certain conclusions of the utmost importance follow about the nature of a reality which, whatever else it may be, must be assumed to be at least such that it does not contradict itself.

2. I want to begin, however, with some discussion (though I shall keep it within the briefest possible limits) of the status of what is traditionally known as 'the Law of Contradiction' (or the 'Law of *Non*-contradiction'—which expression is used is merely a matter of point of view). Is it really a 'law', and if so, what kind of a law? Wherein resides its authority as law? And, if a law, is it a law of thought only, or also a law of things? The present state in philosophy makes it imperative that I should define at the outset as clearly as I can, and offer some justification of, my position in these matters.

Now in actual practice (whatever a man may be driven to say in defending a theory) everyone agrees in rejecting as false a proposition which he believes to involve self-contradiction. The 'Law' of contradiction is one whose authority is accepted in all thinking, and in that sense is an ultimate for human thought. But just because it is 'ultimate' for thought, thought cannot 'prove' its validity, if by 'proof' we mean deductive demonstration from some principle more ultimate than itself. Manifestly any reasoning directed to its proof must presuppose the very principle it is purporting to prove. And there are some who would have us suppose that the validity of the principle is rendered doubtful by its not being amenable to this formal kind of proof.

It would surely be foolish, however, to limit the term 'proof' to deductive demonstration. If complete and final theoretic satisfaction that a principle is true can be gained in other ways, it is a little pedantic to refuse to call that 'proof'. And such complete and final theoretic satisfaction about the validity of the principle of contradiction as a law of thought does seem to me to be easily gained. If we make the appropriate ideal experiment, we shall find that to 'think' a contradiction is, strictly and literally, not even possible. This anyone may verify for himself if he takes the principle in one of its better formulations—say 'S cannot both be P and not be P', and tries to think, in defiance of this principle, S as both being P and not being P. Attempt this, and what do you find? You find, do you not, that you just have *no* determinate thought about S at all. The expression 'Laws of Thought', I am well aware, is one which (like some other useful expressions) is taboo in certain quarters today. But it is surely hard to see how more fittingly—indeed how otherwise—to designate a principle which all thinking accepts as authoritative upon it, and which in fact it cannot disobey without ceasing to *be* thinking.

These last words, however, introduce us to something of an *aporia*. We are saying, apparently, that there *is* no such thing as self-contradictory thinking. But in that case the Law of Contradiction must be merely a positive law descriptive of human thinking, not a normative law formulating an ideal. There could be no sense in exhorting anyone to try to avoid contradiction in his thinking if in fact he cannot contrive to think a contradiction at all. Yet it is obvious that we do constantly condemn thinking, in ourselves and in others, that is, as we say, 'self-contradictory'; and this practice is surely not without solid foundation. How is the paradox to be resolved? What justification can be offered for calling any thinking self-contradictory if there cannot in fact be a thinking of S as both being P and not being P?

I think two main types of case can be distinguished in which we can quite properly call the thinking involved self-contradictory even though it is not strictly a thinking of S as both being and not being P. The simplest type of case is where, in the course of a longish argument (which may of course be conducted entirely within one's own mind) one forgets that one has previously recognised S to be P and now asserts that S is not P. But manifestly what we have here is not an *act* of thought that contradicts *itself*, but *two* acts of thought, an earlier and a later, that contradict *one another*. It is natural, however, to call this 'self-contradiction', since we assume it to be one and the same self who thought the past thought and who thinks the present thought that contradicts it.

A less simple, but correspondingly more insidious, and certainly much commoner way of contradicting ourselves is as follows. We assert that S is P, and that it is also Q, failing to notice that at another point in our argument we have already agreed that Q, directly or indirectly, entails the exclusion of P. Our opponent will then be in a position to point out that in asserting S to be P and *also* to be Q we are really involved in asserting S both to be P and *not* to be P—a self-contradiction. Against this type of self-contradiction we are all of us aware that we have constantly to be on our guard. But here again it is evident that our thinking, though legitimately enough called self-contradictory, involves no act of thought in which we accept S as both being P and not being P. On the contrary, as soon as we are reminded that Q entails the exclusion of P, and that to assert that S is P and that S is also Q involves us in asserting that S both is and is not P, we straightway either abandon our original assertion or reconsider the entailments we had already, perhaps too hurriedly, admitted.

Enough has been said, I hope, to show that there is only a seeming, not a real, incompatibility between saying that men frequently fall into self-contradiction in their thoughts, and saying that the Law of Contradiction is a law which thinking cannot disobey without ceasing to be thinking at all. We may now observe that if the Law must be so understood, this disposes completely of what seems to me one of the least defensible among recent philosophical innovations—the doctrine that all logical laws, including the law of contradiction, are mere 'conventions'. According to our argument above, a man cannot *not* accept the principle of contradiction if he is to think at all. But where we have a principle which we have literally no choice but to accept, to talk of that principle as a 'convention' is nonsense. Acceptance of it is a matter of *necessity*, not convention. As Aristotle pointed out a long time ago, 'a principle which everyone must have who understands anything that is, is not a hypothesis'.[1]

Just as obviously untenable, it seems to me, is the view still advanced on occasion that though the Law of Contradiction may

[1] *Metaphysics* 1005*b* (Ross's translation).

be a law of *thought*, we are not entitled to assume that it is also a law of *things*, holding good of 'reality'. This view, if sound, would of course be fatal to the ultimate objective of the present lecture. But it is surely open to decisive rebuttal. If once we admit that we cannot *think* S both to be and not to be P, i.e. that Contradiction is a law of *thought*, must it not be mere verbiage to say that, nevertheless, S might in *reality* both be and not be P—i.e. that Contradiction may not be a law of *things*? For, by our own admission, the 'hypothesis' we are putting forward, that in reality S both is and is not P, is one which we cannot *think*. Its formulation can only be (at its crucial point) a matter of words. It seems to me clear, therefore, that this logical law, and other logical laws (if such there be) of like status, are unavoidably metaphysical as well as logical in their import.

I conclude that the Law of Contradiction is a genuine 'law', an ultimate law, and a law both of thought and reality. And let me add that if I have not debated these matters extensively, this is less for lack of space than because the traditional arguments for the conclusions I accept have nowhere to my knowledge been met, but would appear rather to have been simply forgotten, by those contemporary philosophers who, explicitly or by implication, accept contrary views. It is not easy to know what sort of supplementation of them would be useful until their defects as ordinarily presented are clearly exposed. Here—as I am afraid rather often elsewhere in these lectures—I find myself embarrassed by what one can only describe as the virtual obliteration from the contemporary philosophical mind of a whole philosophical tradition. I may very well be mistaken in my belief that many elements of value can still be recaptured from that tradition. I do not think I am mistaken in my belief that secure advances in philosophy are unlikely to be made if one simply averts one's gaze from a movement of philosophic thought which for several decades, in a by no means remote past, commanded the allegiance of almost all the leading philosophers in the English-speaking world.

3. It is one thing, however, to see that the Law of Contradiction is a genuine 'law', is an ultimate law, and is a law both of thought and of things. It is quite another thing to see what precisely it is

that constitutes contradiction. This latter task, to which we must now address ourselves, is in fact about as difficult as the former task was easy. As was pointed out by F. H. Bradley (whose account in Note A of the Appendix to *Appearance and Reality* I shall be following very closely in the early part of this lecture), it is surprisingly hard to avoid a *petitio principii* when one attempts to define contradiction. Everyone agrees that contradictory propositions cannot both be true. But when one asks what it is that makes propositions contradictory, what is the essential nature of contradiction itself, almost all the stock answers seem covertly to presuppose the very thing that is to be defined.

Consider, for example, the common suggestion (which has many variants of detail) that contradiction can be defined as the uniting of 'opposite' predicates in the same subject. Immediately the question forces itself upon us, what is to be meant here by 'opposites'? And on reflection it is difficult to give any answer save that opposite predicates are predicates whose union in the same subject we find that thought rejects. But then is this not just another way of saying 'predicates whose union in the same subject thought finds to be contradictory'? Are we not in effect defining the concept of opposition in terms of the contradictory, and then using the concept of opposition in order to define the contradictory —a circular procedure which gets us nowhere? If we are to define contradiction without circularity, clearly we must seek an answer to the prior question, what sort of union of predicates in the same subject does thought find itself obliged to reject?

The trouble is, however, that if we may not use 'opposition', or any equivalent term, in order to designate the kind of predicates whose union in the same subject thought rejects, it is not at all easy to see what terms we *can* use to designate it. It certainly does not look as though it would do simply to replace the term 'opposition' by the term 'difference', and to say that thought rejects the union of differences in the same subject. For thought is uniting differences constantly; indeed, where it does not do so, it appears to be reduced to sheer tautologising, which is not thinking at all.

Now it is just at this point that Bradley makes his distinctive and (as I think) decisive contribution to the problem of what constitutes contradiction. Beyond a doubt, he agrees, thought requires the uniting of differences for its very life. But it does not follow that thought is prepared to accept a union of differents irrespective of the manner of their union. 'Thought demands' Bradley reminds us, 'to go *proprio motu*, or, what is the same thing, with a ground or reason'.[1] A merely external union of differences (such as we get in sense perception, where the togetherness of certain differents seems given to us from without) is not in the end acceptable to thought. It is of the very essence of thought to seek some *ground* for their union; and so long as no adequate ground is discoverable, intellectual dissatisfaction persists. A *bare conjunction* of differents, unmediated by any ground, thought rejects as alien to its nature, as 'irrational'. Here then, Bradley argues, is the sort of union in the same subject that thought rejects, and here, by the same token, we find our answer to the question of what constitutes contradiction. Contradiction consists in uniting differences *simply*, in and as a bare conjunction. What the concrete nature of the differences happens to be is not of the essence of the matter. The crucial point is that thought cannot, *qua* thought, accept their union unless it conceives some actual or possible ground for their union.

One can hardly exaggerate the extent to which the course of Bradley's thought throughout all its well-known sceptical ramifications is determined by the analysis of contradiction here briefly sketched. It is profoundly unfortunate, therefore, that this analysis should have been almost consistently ignored by Bradley's critics. Time and again criticisms are launched against Bradleian doctrines which betray failure to grasp that underlying the positions criticised is Bradley's theory of what constitutes a contradiction. It may be instructive to consider briefly an outstanding example, both for its own sake and because it may help to throw into relief what is central in Bradley's analysis of contradiction.[2]

---

[1] *Appearance and Reality*, p. 562. Here as elsewhere my references are to the 7th impression.

[2] Another outstanding example would be the usual criticism of Bradley's condemnation of external relations. It is not appreciated that his condemnation rests upon his doctrine that contradiction consists in the uniting of differences in and as a bare conjunction. I have dealt with this in some detail in my *Scepticism and Construction*, pp. 23-30.

If Bradley has, as I think he has, been much misunderstood (not seldom by thinkers of his own 'school'), he himself must bear some responsibility. Had his analysis of the contradictory been presented in the early pages of

I refer to the common, but surely mistaken charge that the difficulties Bradley notoriously finds in the judgment-form are due to his confusing the 'is' of predication with the 'is' of identity. It is merely this confusion, the critics allege, that leads him to impute self-contradiction to the judgment-form' S is P'. *If* one chooses to commit Bradley's mistake of interpreting the 'is' of predication as though it were the 'is' of identity, then *of course*, we are told, one will find contradiction in the judgment-form; for no one denies that it is contradictory to *identify* S with P—or with any *other* not-S. But one has only to refrain from falling into this elementary logical blunder (so it is said) for the alleged contradiction to vanish utterly.

Now it would be extremely odd if a great logician had really gone blindly on repeating the same elementary logical blunder for a full forty years of active philosophising; and all the more odd where that logician's critics have been so good as to indicate to him the error of his ways not once but many times. The real oddity in the situation, however, is, I suggest, the unanimity with which Bradley's critics have missed his point. It will presumably be agreed that on *any* theory the 'is' of predication implies that the differences S and P are at least being *united* or *combined* in thought. The distinctive point that Bradley is concerned to make when he imputes contradiction to the judgment-form as ordinarily represented is that to unite differences without any conceived or implied ground for their union—to unite *bare* S with P, as the formula S is P suggests—is unacceptable to reflective thought, and is *therefore* (on his view of what constitutes contradiction) a contradiction. In other words, he does not assume that the 'is' of predication means identity. He assumes, like everyone else, that it means at least *union*; and he insists that thought can no more accept a bare union of differents than it can accept their identity. Indeed the bare union of differents turns out, when we reflect upon it, to be *tantamount* to their identification. 'It is idle', Bradley tells us, 'from the outside to say to thought, "Well, *unite* but do not *identify*". How can thought unite except so far as in itself it has a mode of union? To unite without an internal ground

Appearance and Reality, instead of in an Appendix 'Note' added in the second edition, the reader's task, though it could never be easy, would have been vastly simplified.

of connection and distinction is *to strive to bring together barely in the same point*, and that is self-contradiction.' [1]

Some further clarification of this doctrine of the contradictory —and also, I think, important justification—may be gained if we comment now upon an objection from the side of 'Common Sense' (to which, of course, most philosophers appeal eagerly when it seems to support them). 'You speak very freely', it may be said, 'of *thought* rejecting a bare conjunction, and *thought* being dissatisfied with any union of differences that rests on no "ground". But what is this *thought* of which you speak? It can hardly be thinking in general, for does not ordinary thinking constantly accept without a qualm bare conjunctions of differents?—e.g. in the realm of sense-perception to which you have yourself alluded. Your analysis of contradiction seems to rest entirely on the dogmatic assertion that "thought" rejects what common-sense observation shows us "thought" has often no compunction whatever in accepting.'

But I think there is no real difficulty of principle here. Everyone will agree, I take it, that much of our ordinary thinking is carried on with no pretence at self-criticism by strict intellectual standards; and will agree also that this uncritical thinking often fails to notice contradictions that are apparent enough to critical thinking. In other words, critical thinking often finds itself obliged to reject what uncritical thinking accepts 'without a qualm'. Now when we spoke above of thought rejecting 'bare conjunctions of differents', it was, of course (as was surely legitimate), *critical* thought we had in mind, thought that is going about its proper business of seeking *theoretical* satisfaction. Undoubtedly the demands that are intrinsic to the intellect are much obscured from us in ordinary experience, since there our thinking is guided primarily not by the motive of theoretic satisfaction but rather by the needs of practical living; and we are normally content to stop at the point where these needs seem adequately met. But thought's intrinsic demand for a 'ground' is surely plain enough in those activities of thought, such as science and philosophy, in which the theoretic interest dominates; in which truth, not practical convenience, is our goal, and in which, therefore, if anywhere, we might expect to discover the authentic nature of the intellect's demands. In

[1] P. 566. Italics mine.

science and philosophy 'brute facts', 'bare conjunctions of differents', are not just 'accepted'. On the contrary, intellectual unrest persists so long as we see no way to deliver them from so 'irrational' a status. 'Brute facts' are for science and philosophy *problems*: problems not solved to our satisfaction until we have mediated the 'bare conjunction' through what appears to us an adequate 'ground'. Just as 'Nature abhors a vacuum', so 'the intellect abhors a bare conjunction'.

Before proceeding to the next phase of the argument from the nature of the contradictory it may be well to pause for a moment to observe the implications for metaphysics of the argument at its present stage.

Metaphysics, we assume, seeks conceptual knowledge of the ultimate nature of the real; and conceptions of this real, we may further assume, cannot be knowledge (since they cannot be true) if they are self-contradictory. Now self-contradiction, we argued (following Bradley), consists in uniting differences without a ground for their union. If, then, any object before the mind is such that, as conceived, it involves the uniting of differences without a ground for their union, that object, *as* conceived, is not a reality. The form in which we conceive it may serve well enough for all the practical purposes of ordinary life. But metaphysics is concerned with ultimate truth, not with mere pragmatic validity. From the standpoint of metaphysics, accordingly, objects as so conceived stand condemned. They are ways in which the real *appears* to us; but as it so appears it appears falsely; the appearances are, in that sense, 'mere' appearances.

4.   But can thought *ever* get its objects into a satisfactory form, a form in which the differences are *intelligibly* united? This brings us to the second main phase of the argument. There is no great difficulty in seeing how in general thought proceeds in its endeavour to secure grounds which will make the union of differents intelligible. If we take our clue from the way in which those disciplines in which the theoretical interest predominates, viz. philosophy and the sciences, pursue their objective, the key-word, it seems clear, is 'system'. Reflective thought aims at exhibiting

the differences A and B, whose apparent connection sets the problem, as no longer separate 'units', but as distinguishable members of the same system X, the structural principles of which are such that given A, we necessarily have B, and given B, we necessarily have A. The ground of the connection or union lies in the system to which the differences belong; and the ground is adequate, one which really does 'explain' or render intelligible the connection, if the system can be seen to be one in which A and B really are mutually implicatory members. But the question arises, is a ground that is adequate capable of attainment, even in principle, by the human intellect? Bradley is convinced that it is not: and I believe him to be right.

The argument which (in this context) Bradley advances for his sceptical conclusion, is simple enough in form. In the nature of the case any 'ground' to which the intellect can appeal must be something beyond, and thus at least partly external to, the complex of differences it is to explain. For if it lay *within* the complex before us, the complex would be *self*-explanatory, and would set us no problem. But if the ground is in any way external to the complex, then it 'becomes for the intellect a fresh element, and it itself calls for synthesis in a fresh point of unity. But hereon, because in the intellect no intrinsic connections were found, ensues the infinite process'.[1] There can be for the intellect no final halting-place. Every achievement of a ground is in the nature of the case the basis of a further problem.

An example, even if a rather rough and ready one, will, I think, be helpful to elucidate this ascription of radical and inherent defect to the 'grounds' by which the intellect seeks to make unions of differents intelligible. Suppose we find the sliding roof of our car jamming in hot weather. We want to understand, to explain to ourselves, the S-P connection in the proposition that is here implied. Our first 'solution' will doubtless be that since the roof and the car body are of metal, and since metals expand under the influence of heat, the adjacent sections of roof and body will necessarily, when the weather is hot, tend to approach one another, and, at a certain degree of heat, to jam. And with this answer our intellect undoubtedly achieves a partial satisfaction. But only partial. The core of the explanation, the 'ground', is the expansion

[1] P. 568.

of metals under the influence of heat. But this introduces 'a fresh element', calling for 'synthesis in a fresh point of unity'. The proposition 'all metals expand under the influence of heat' is one in which the union of differents S and P is no more self-explanatory than the union of differents in the proposition 'The sliding roof of our car jams in hot weather'. The intellect is obliged therefore to ask *why*, to look for some ground for this new connection; and obviously it has not secured a satisfactory ground for the *first* connection to be explained if it has not secured a satisfactory ground for this *second* connection, in terms of which it sought to explain the first. Our problem has now become, why do metals expand when heated? And at this stage a ground in terms of traditional physical science is still easily enough available. Heat is a form of energy, we may remind ourselves, and in proportion as a body becomes 'hotter' the motions of the constituent molecules increase in violence and tend by their jostling of one another to disturb the existing cohesion and to create a 'bulging' beyond the normal boundaries—i.e. the body expands. With this answer again the intellect attains a partial, but only a partial, satisfaction. However well-accredited, there is nothing self-evident about the propositions implied in our new ground. Why, e.g. *should* one moving body (say, a molecule) impinging upon another moving body (another molecule) affect the motion of the second body in this way—or indeed in *any* way? A vast multitude of observed facts can be pointed to in support of such generalisations, but it is a philosophical commonplace that they do not and cannot make the connections intrinsically intelligible. It remains entirely conceivable that a case should arise in which the connection in question does not hold. Hence the intellect is forced once more to ask why, to search for a 'ground' for this new union of differents. By this stage we are coming within the region of basic laws of the traditional physics, and there is perhaps little to be gained by carrying the illustration further. The result will be the same however far we take it. Neither the primary laws of motion, nor any 'paramechanical' laws to which more recent scientific achievements may allow us to appeal, have the status of self-evident truths, propositions in which subject and predicate are united in a way that satisfies the intellect. In the course of our search after grounds we acquire a deeper intellectual satisfaction by seeing the coherence of our original connection with a progressively wider range of connections in the total field of experience. But at every stage the new ground merely sets us at a higher level the same problem that confronted the intellect at the beginning.

Now if this account of the matter be substantially correct, as I believe it to be; if every ground for the union of differents achieved by the intellect merely presents us, at a higher level, with differents united *without* a ground; then Bradley would seem to be justified in his contention that the human mind is incompetent in principle to know the reality it seeks to know. Any ideal complex by which it seeks to characterise reality, no matter how high its degree of systematic coherence, will still be a union of differents that requires a ground beyond itself for its intelligibility. Asserted *as it stands*, it contradicts itself: whereas an ideal complex that *truly* characterises reality must be non-contradictory. There would seem to be one way only in which the intellect can avoid falling into self-contradiction; and it is a way that does not yield *truth*. The intellect can assert the complex before it not as absolute, but as conditioned by unknown factors in the as yet unfathomed 'background' of reality; frankly accepting the implication that in the complex as it stands we have not got the real, but only an appearance of it, 'less or more false in proportion as the unknown conditions, if filled in, less or more would swamp and transform it.' [1]

The position, then, would seem to be as follows. *Qua* thinking beings, we have no alternative but to accept thought's criterion of truth and reality, viz. non-contradiction. In the real, differences are united, and they must be united intelligibly, in a way that would satisfy thought. But this 'way' cannot be the way of systems of terms in relation, the only way the intellect has of setting about its task of uniting differences intelligibly. For any such system, we have seen, points beyond itself, requires a ground partly external to it for its own justification. It follows that we are forced to recognise a radical discrepancy between, on the *one* hand, the kind of unity at which the intellect ideally aims, and which it can alone accept as giving us reality—viz. a unity *in* difference, in which the ground of the union is in no way external to the differences—and, on the *other* hand, the kind of unity which the intellect

[1] P. 564.

can alone achieve; a radical discrepancy, therefore, between reality 'as it is', and reality in any form in which the intellect, however far it advances *proprio motu*, is able to conceive it. In other words, Reality must be held to be *supra*-rational.

5. We cannot properly proceed, however, to ask what further conclusions the argument from the nature of the contradictory warrants about the nature of ultimate reality, and how these conclusions bear upon the religious view of ultimate reality, until we have come to grips with an objection of far greater force and of far greater consequence than any we have so far encountered. The importance of this new objection lies not merely in the threat it carries to the conclusion already reached—that reality is supra-rational. It lies also in the fact that, when due account is taken of it, it suggests an envisagement of the relationship between finite minds and ultimate reality which has, I think, very great significance for religion. This objection I shall now formulate, and thereafter discuss.

The intellect's demand for a 'ground' beyond any given union of differents, with the ensuing infinite process, arises from the apparent inability of the intellect to find satisfaction in any such union merely as it stands. If in such a union 'no internal connection of diversity natural to the intellect can be found', Bradley declares, 'we are left with a diversity belonging to and conjoined in one undistinguished point. And this is contradiction, and contradiction in the end we found was this and nothing but this.' [1] The trouble, as Bradley sees it, is that the required 'internal connection' is nowhere to be discerned—or at any rate that he is himself not able to discern it. 'I cannot say that to me any principle or principles of diversity in unity are self-evident.' [2] Hence the intellect's demand for a ground 'beyond' any given union remains insatiable. Any union of differents is for the intellect, as it stands, self-contradictory, and thus inadequate to portray the real.

Now though Bradley is, unhappily, very sparing of examples, one gets the impression that it is thinking in the empirical sciences that he has had chiefly in mind. There, undoubtedly, his case is a very strong one. No one, I take it, now claims that the unions

[1] P. 572.   [2] P. 569.

of differents formulated in science's basic 'laws'—and *a fortiori* in its special laws—'satisfy the intellect' and provoke no further question. But there are other fields of knowledge in which it is much more difficult to be persuaded that there are not connections which the intellect finds satisfactory as they stand. If it should turn out that there *are* any such intellectually satisfactory connections, then here at any rate the criterion of non-contradiction is fully honoured, truth is achieved by the intellect, and the doctrine that the real is supra-rational must call for drastic revision.

As an example of the kind of connection that raises difficulties for Bradley's view let us take the judgment, made with reference to the space in which objects are perceived, that 'any given space is part of a larger space'. We have here, as in all judgments, an S and a P that are different from one another, and the assertion in thought of their union. Now is there really anything in this union of differents that the intellect finds unsatisfactory, and that impels it to seek justification in some ground beyond the complex itself? Do we not have here a union of differents that is intrinsically self-evident to the intellect? If we accept as our test of intrinsic self-evidence that the contradictory of the proposition is inconceivable, there are, I think, strong reasons for answering in the affirmative. For it seems true that we just cannot attach meaning, in terms of perception, to the suggestion that some given space might *not* be continuous with space beyond it, and thus might *not* be part of a larger space. Of this 'continuous' character of the space of perception we can only say that such is the way we apprehend space, and cannot help apprehending it, when we are perceiving physical objects. The case here is altogether different, in respect of intellectual necessity, from that of even the best-accredited physical 'law'. In the latter it is always possible in principle to suppose the union or connection of differents false. The 'law' gets its evidence from a multitude of observations, and is subject to revision or even abandonment from further observations. But in the case of the proposition that the space of perception is continuous, or that any given space is part of a larger space, 'further observation' seems irrelevant. The only 'observations' to which we seem able to attach meaning are observations conducted within the framework of a space which is continuous in character, and thus themselves presuppose the truth of the proposition that is in dispute.

Or again, take a proposition from the cognate field of 'time'. 'Different times within the time-order in which events are perceived are not simultaneous but successive' (substantially one of Kant's 'axioms of time in general'). Is it not the case that here too we see on reflection, and for similar reasons, that the search for a 'ground' for the connection affirmed is completely pointless? To the contradictory of the proposition we can attach no intelligible meaning. The connection is one that is directly implied in the nature of time as we apprehend it, and cannot help apprehending it, when we perceive events as 'in time'.

In the face of these apparent instances to the contrary, can Bradley really be justified in his contention that every union of differents is, as it stands (i.e. as a bare conjunction), intellectually unsatisfactory, and therefore, if affirmed as it stands, a self-contradiction?

Now I am certainly not going to suggest that Bradley would have no answer to give to criticism of his doctrine along such lines. On the contrary, I think it is fairly easy to see how, if challenged on the matter, he would seek to show that even these unions of differents are intellectually unsatisfactory and point beyond themselves for their explanation. I do wish to suggest, however, that if he had considered such cases explicitly in the context of his discussion of contradiction he would have been forced to recognise an important difference of principle between the 'intellectual unsatisfactoriness' of connections of the kind we have just been noticing and the 'intellectual unsatisfactoriness' of connections of the kind enunciated in the empirical sciences. With a view to bringing out the precise nature of this difference let us, then, ask how Bradley might be expected to defend his doctrine against the sort of objection we have been raising.

Bradley would point out, I think, that we ought to distinguish carefully between what is intellectually *incorrigible* and what is intellectually *satisfactory*. It may be granted that such a proposition as 'The space in which objects are perceived is continuous' is intellectually incorrigible, in that the intellect cannot even conceive the space of perception as otherwise constituted. But that is by no means to say that the proposition is intellectually satisfactory. The proposition is, after all (like, on the last analysis, all propositions),[1] about reality. It is, in a fuller formulation, the proposition 'reality is such that the space in which objects are perceived is continuous'. Now if the words 'such that' stand here, as they apparently do, merely for an unknown x, how can we reasonably claim that the union of differents in the proposition is an intellectually satisfactory union? The proposition would be intellectually satisfactory in any final sense only if we could see *how* reality is such that space has this character. And if it be said, 'Well at any rate, even if we don't know *how*, we do know *that*, space is thus', Bradley's reply would be, I think, that we do not even know *that* space is thus. There is no certainty at all that if the reality within which space is but one feature became (*per impossibile*) fully intelligible to us, so that space was apprehended as integrated within a system that is a genuine unity *in* difference, space would then be apprehended to be just as it now appears to us. The presumption is rather the other way. It is more than doubtful whether any member of a truly coherent whole could be the same when apprehended in isolation from that whole as it would be when apprehended in integral relation to it.

6. Is this way of defending the doctrine that there are *no* connections of differents intrinsically satisfactory to the intellect one that we can accept? Up to a point I think that it is. I think we must admit that a connection is never fully satisfactory to the intellect if it remains at the level of brute fact, even if the brute fact be of such a kind that we can see the impossibility of our ever transcending it. It is a perfectly intelligible question, and one to which the intellect would *like* to know the answer (one indeed to which some philosophers, as I think mistakenly, have sought to *give* an answer), how space and time stand to the reality within which they fall. We should *like* to be able to clear up the mystery of the 'such that' in propositions of the type 'Reality is such that space and time are continuous'. But the point I want now to emphasise is as follows. Even if we grant all this to Bradley, surely we must go on to recognise that there is nevertheless a profound difference in epistemological status between the 'intellectual unsatisfactoriness'

[1] See Lecture III.

of connections which it is in principle possible for the intellect to correct, and the 'intellectual unsatisfactoriness' of connections like those we have just been discussing, where this is *not* possible in virtue of the fact that all finite thinking presupposes their acceptance? The *former* are faulty even by the standard of theoretical satisfaction which is concretely attainable by finite thinking. The *latter* are faulty *only* by a standard of theoretical satisfaction which finite thinking is in principle incapable of attaining. So strong, indeed, is the element of intellectual *satisfactoriness* in propositions of the latter sort, propositions which admit of no correction without transcending the very conditions of finite thinking, that it would be seriously misleading simply to dub them 'false'. We require a name for them which will indicate their aspect of intellectual *satisfactoriness* no less than their aspect of intellectual *un*-satisfactoriness. We might perhaps best bring out their ambivalent character by calling them 'phenomenal truths'; or, to anticipate the possibility that phenomenal truth admits of degrees, '*final* phenomenal truths'.[1]

Now to speak of a 'truth' that is merely 'phenomenal' has, I am aware, a somewhat paradoxical ring. I am persuaded, nevertheless, that the human situation is such that we are obliged to recognise two distinct—though of course closely related—*kinds* of truth, noumenal truth and phenomenal truth. 'Noumenal' truth pertains to that which would fully and finally satisfy the aspirations of the intellect, a union of differences in which the unity and the differences are in no way external to one another. Only differences so united can the intellect accept as giving truth or reality *simpliciter*. But this 'noumenal' truth must remain for the intellect only an ideal, though it operates *negatively* upon the intellect in forcing the relegation of all that falls short of it to the realm of 'appearance'. 'Phenomenal' truth pertains to unions of differents that reach as far as can be reached in the direction of theoretical satisfaction without transcending the conditions of finite thinking as we know it. In some few cases this 'phenomenal' truth can be final; in those cases, namely, where propositions affirm unions of differents that are presupposed in all significant experience and

---

[1] The two instances I have given by no means exhaust the list of propositions falling into this category; and in another context than the present it would be of great importance to make the list complete.

which can thus be said to constitute the basic framework of our human situation. *Within* that framework, however, the possibilities of advance in phenomenal truth are limitless. There is, as we have seen, no end to the process, illustrated best by the physical sciences, of seeking adequate grounding for connections through more and more comprehensive and coherent systems of terms in relation.

The *affinity* between noumenal and phenomenal truth—that which justifies us in using the same term 'truth', with due qualifications, of both of them—lies in their analogous relationship to the intellect's quest for satisfaction. Noumenal truth would yield intellectual satisfaction absolute. Phenomenal truth yields intellectual satisfaction in so far forth as that is positively attainable under the conditions of finite experience.

This affinity, so far as I can see, is not something which it is open to a man to believe in or to disbelieve in as he thinks fit. It would seem rather to be an affinity which man *must* believe in if he is to function intellectually at all. For it is surely by something we can only call 'an inward necessity of the mind' that our aspiration after intellectual satisfaction, after that non-contradictory union of differents in which noumenal truth and reality consist, seeks its fulfilment in these progressively more coherent and comprehensive systems of terms in relation in which, in its degree, phenomenal truth consists? Our finite minds being constituted as they are, the ideal of noumenal truth *impels* us to take the path that leads to phenomenal truth. The affinity, in short, seems grounded in the very nature of our human condition. It is, in a not seriously misleading sense of that term, an *a priori* affinity.

7.   Now if this, in principle, be indeed the nature of the affinity between noumenal and phenomenal truth, we can see what promises to be a most interesting parallel beginning to emerge between, on the one hand, the cognitive attitude towards God which we earlier judged to be appropriate to the religious consciousness, and, on the other hand, the cognitive attitude towards ultimate reality which we now discern to be appropriate to the intellectual consciousness. For the *religious* consciousness, the

object of its worship transcends human conception; but by reason of the recognised affinity between the emotions which that object evokes and the 'natural' emotions felt towards the highest conceivable exemplifications of 'power' and 'value', the religious mind is impelled to interpret its object *symbolically* in terms of the highest conceivable power and value; and because this affinity has nothing subjective or arbitrary about it, but is based on 'an inward necessity of the mind', this symbolism, we argued, has objective validity as symbolism. We can even speak significantly, it seemed to us, of a symbolic 'knowledge' of God. For the *intellectual* consciousness, as sanctioned by metaphysics, the ultimate reality transcends human conception likewise—is 'supra-rational'; and because of the recognised affinity between noumenal and phenomenal truth, based on 'an inward necessity of the mind', there is a like objectively justified impulsion to interpret the perfect union of differences that characterises noumenal truth *symbolically* in terms of the highest unions of differences attainable along the path to phenomenal truth. Here, I suggest, we have something more than the bare elements of a *rapprochement* between metaphysics and religion, something that promises a genuine, if partial, metaphysical corroboration of the objective validity of the religious consciousness. In my next, and final, lecture I propose to follow up this suggestion; and then, gathering together the several strands of the argument of this course, I shall try to summarise as clearly as possible the general conclusions which the argument seems to me to warrant concerning 'the truth of religion'.

LECTURE XX

THE OBJECTIVE VALIDITY
OF RELIGION (III)

1. At the close of my last lecture I pointed to what seemed to
me a highly significant parallel between, on the one hand, the
religious view of the ultimate reality it calls 'God' and, on the
other hand, the philosophical view of ultimate reality which
followed from the metaphysical argument we had just, at some
length, deployed. For both, the ultimate reality transcends all
possible conception—is 'supra-rational'. But for neither does this
entail sheer, blank, ignorance of its nature. For the religious
consciousness, we saw earlier, there is an affinity between its
object, the *mysterium tremendum et fascinans*, and certain 'rational'
qualities, which justifies the symbolic representation of its object
in terms of power and value in their highest conceivable manifestations.[1] For the intellectual consciousness, we argued in the
last lecture, there is an affinity between that perfect unity in
difference which must characterise reality (if reality is to satisfy
the criterion of non-contradiction) and the most comprehensive
and coherent, but still in principle imperfect, unities actually
attainable under the conditions of finite experience.

Of the former, the 'religious' affinity, we have already in past
lectures said perhaps more than enough. But I may be permitted
to remind you in just a sentence or two of the justification for
asserting the 'intellectual' affinity. The crucial point is that it is
in the process of seeking to attain that perfect unity which its
ideal of non-contradiction implies, that the intellect takes, and

---

[1] For some discussion of the relationship between the symbolist doctrine
I advocate and the scholastic 'Doctrine of Analogy', see Appendix D.

must take, the path of advance that leads to the increasingly comprehensive and coherent, but still in principle imperfect, unities of relational systems. The mind's acceptance of this affinity is spontaneous, and it cannot, in the nature of the case, be justified in terms of any conceptually apprehended identity between the perfect and the imperfect unities. But I suggest that it is no more possible for a man in the operations of his intellectual experience to disbelieve in this affinity than it is possible for him in the operations of his religious experience to disbelieve in the affinity between the Divine *mysterium tremendum et fascinans* and the 'rational' qualities of power and value in their highest conceivable manifestations.

2. Now as we have so far developed it, the philosophical corroboration of religion relates to no more than the most general picture of the human situation; the picture of man separated by an intellectually impassable gulf from the ultimate reality, yet at the same time rightly claiming that certain concepts are valid as symbolic representations of the ultimate reality. Our task in this concluding lecture is to consider how far philosophic corroboration (and it will be appreciated that we must inevitably, with whatever appearance of immodesty, mean thereby corroboration by our own philosophical views) is capable of extending to the more specific features of the theistic creed. Theism in general, it will be recalled, we took to be sufficiently defined as belief in one God, an Eternal and Infinite Spirit, Perfect in power, wisdom and goodness, who is the ultimate source of all that is, who is the Moral Governor of the world, and who is yet a Living Presence in the hearts of men. Supra-rational theism (with which we are now alone concerned) we distinguished from Rational Theism in virtue of its insistence that the Divine nature transcends all possible human conception, and that while the qualities Rational Theism ascribes to God are truly ascribable, they are so only when understood in a symbolic significance. Our present question is, just how far does the ultimate reality of philosophy, viewed from the standpoint of the metaphysical argument of the last lecture, correspond with the ultimate reality of religion, viewed from the standpoint of supra-rational theism?

3. Let us make a beginning with the closely connected characteristics of unity, infinity, and eternity.

Granted certain premises which we sought to establish in the last lecture, viz. that thought can accept nothing as real which involves self-contradiction, and that any bare or ungrounded union of differents involves a self-contradiction, the *unity* of the real follows almost as a corollary. For suppose reality not to be one, but to consist in a plurality of independent reals, A, B, C, D, etc. If we try to think reality in this wise, we find we are uniting in our thought differences A, B, C, D, etc., which, since *ex hypothesi* each is real independently of the others, are without an even implied ground for their union. But that means that we are uniting the differences A, B, C, D, etc., *simply*—in and as a bare conjunction. And this is of the essence of contradiction. We cannot therefore without self-contradiction conceive reality as consisting of a plurality of independent reals. If the real is non-contradictory, reality must be *one*.

Given the *unity* of reality, its infinity is deducible with equal ease. Whatever is finite, we may assume, is limited by something other than itself. But if there is only *one* reality, there is nothing other than itself that can limit it. It must be self-limited, self-complete; not finite but infinite.

The *eternity* of the one infinite reality requires a deduction only slightly more complex. It follows from the conjunction of the two propositions (a) that reality cannot be *in* time, and (b) that time must somehow be *in it*. As to (a), the one infinite reality cannot be conceived as something that is *in* time, for then time would be a reality other than it; which is self-contradictory if the real is one and infinite. And as to (b), if time were not somehow *in it*, time would again be something other than the one infinite reality, and we should again have contradiction. But if reality is not itself in time, and yet time is somehow in it, it follows that reality transcends and yet includes time; and what transcends and yet includes time can, I think, fairly be called 'eternal'.

The unity, infinitude, and eternity of ultimate reality, then, seem to follow simply enough from the metaphysical argument with which we have identified ourselves. What is not so simple a matter is the truth-status of the propositions which assert these characteristics of ultimate reality. Are they *literally* or only *symbolically* true? Neither position seems quite satisfactory. If we say they are literally true, we seem to contradict our own contention that ultimate reality transcends all possible concepts. If we say that they are only symbolically true, this is hard to reconcile with our having apparently deduced them as straight implications of the principle that reality is non-contradictory—which principle we are presumably accepting as not merely symbolically but literally true.

The solution of the dilemma I take to be as follows. The propositions which affirm respectively unity, infinitude, and eternity of the ultimately real have each a negative as well as a positive aspect. In each we intend to deny something of the real, and we also intend to affirm of it some positive content. What I suggest is that these propositions are literally true in respect of what they *deny*, but only symbolically true in respect of what they *affirm*. Let me illustrate. When we say that reality is a unity, we deny that there is a plurality of reals; and there is nothing merely symbolic about this negation. But in so far as we are also, in saying that reality is a unity, assigning to it a positive character, this positive character can have only symbolic significance. For no *thinkable* unity can be appropriate to the kind of unity that reality possesses. Unity as a positive concept, exemplified in experience, gets its meaning for us in contradistinction from plurality. It is always a unity of differences where the differences (or plurality) are something apart from and in contrast with the unity. The unity possessed by *reality*, on the other hand, is a unity not 'over against' its plurality but a unity which comprises all plurality within itself. It is a unity *in* difference, where the differences have no being save as manifestations of the unity and the unity has no being save as self-manifested in the differences. Of such a unity we have no exemplars in actual or conceivable human experience. Unity as a positively meaningful concept, then, we cannot literally ascribe to reality. At the same time, if our principle be accepted of the necessary affinity between noumenal and phenomenal truth, between the unity which thought seeks and the unities which in that seeking it can alone achieve, we are entitled to regard the highest conceivable forms of unity as symbolic of the nature of the perfect unity of the real. Symbolically, therefore, though *only* symbolically, it is legitimate to ascribe unity as a positive character to the real.

The religious counterpart of this unitary reality which comprehends all differences within itself is the one God who is the ultimate source of all that is—and who therefore *some*how comprehends the whole plurality of being within Himself. As to the 'how' of this ultimate unity, there will be no demurrer from the side of religion (in so far at any rate as it is represented by supra-rational theism) to the philosophic contention that in the end it remains for the human mind an impenetrable mystery.

Mutatis mutandis, the same principle holds of the propositions that assert infinity and eternity respectively of the ultimately real. They have literal truth in respect of what they negate, viz. limitation from without and duration in time. But in so far as positive content is concerned, literal truth is out of the question. Of a being that is totally free from external limitation, and is thus infinite or self-complete, or again of a being whose mode of existence transcends and yet includes time, we can frame no positive conceptions whatsoever. Positive conceptions are applicable only as symbols; as e.g. the 'everlasting' as the symbol of eternity. And once more, for religion as represented by supra-rational theism (though surely it must be so also for any theism that directly faces the question?), there will be no demurrer to the proposition that to frame positive concepts literally applicable to the Infinite and the Eternal is a project totally beyond the reach of the human intelligence.

4. So far, then, it seems fair to say that our metaphysical standpoint confirms the position of supra-rational theism. Like the God of the latter, the ultimate reality of metaphysics is a being that transcends all conception, and yet can in a legitimate, though qualified, sense be characterised as one, infinite and eternal.

And now what of the further characterisation of God as a Spirit, perfect in goodness, wisdom and power? Is corroboration from our philosophical standpoint possible here too? I think that it is—always bearing in mind that the religion we are concerned to corroborate claims no more than a symbolic significance for the ascription of these characters to God. But from this point onwards our arguments will have to assume somewhat more complex forms than have so far been necessary.

The argument for the symbolisation of the ultimate reality of metaphysics as *spirit* must be based, I think, on our doctrine of the affinity between noumenal and phenomenal truth, between the unity which thought seeks and the unities which in that seeking it can alone achieve. In virtue of that affinity, we claimed, we are entitled to regard the highest conceivable forms of unity as symbolic of the perfect unity of the real. Now there is good ground for holding that it is in mind or spirit (there is no special need to distinguish between these in the present context) that the highest conceivable unity of differents is exemplified. Whether we look to the range and variety of the differences that can be included within its unity, or to the intimacy in the manner of their union, mind would seem to have no serious rival among the entities actually known to human experience. Perhaps this superiority, alike in comprehensiveness and internal coherence, will best be brought out if we institute a brief comparison of the unity characteristic of mind with the unity that seems closest to it in the scale of perfection, viz. the unity of the organism.

That the unity of mind holds the advantage over the unity of organism in sheer range and variety of the items that can be embraced within it needs little demonstration. There is indeed, in principle, no assignable limit to the mind's comprehensiveness. There is nothing in the whole world of space and time that cannot in principle be incorporated in the form of ideas into the living texture of the mind and constitute differences within its unity. Now it is true that the organism also can, and must if it is to survive, absorb into its unity a great deal of material from its surroundings. But inasmuch as it is a purely physical unity, even the largest and most complex organism can absorb at best but a minute fraction of the world that lies about it. If the unity of ultimate reality is a unity that comprehends all plurality, there can hardly be any question that it is mind that of all entities known to us is best fitted to serve as its symbol.

It is in respect, however, not so much of comprehensiveness as of internal coherence, of the intimacy of the relation between whole and parts, that the unity of organism approaches nearest to the unity of mind in the scale of perfection. In the perfect unity that characterises the ultimate reality, there must be no externality whatsoever of the differences to their unity. That is to say, it must be such that the differences are nothing but manifestations of the unity, and the unity nothing but its own self-manifestation in the differences. Now in the organism, as in no other physical thing, we can discern some sort of approximation to this ideal. There is a genuine sense in which the unity of the organism may be said to *constitute its own differences*. Everything that the organism receives from without and incorporates into its unity suffers 'a sea-change'. It is acted upon by the organism and reconstituted in a form subservient to the life-process of the individual whole. Thus in the organism not merely is every part in the whole, but the whole is, in a real sense, in every part.

When we turn to the *mind*, however, we find that what has just been said of the organism can now be said with still greater truth. Mind too is in a real sense constitutive of its own differences. Nothing can enter the mind simply from without, but only as subjected to a transforming and integrating activity from within. And the mind is a still 'closer corporation' than the body, still less impervious to the operation of purely external forces upon it. For while the organism adapts to its own nature whatever it accepts into its unity, that acceptance may itself be compelled from without. There is, after all, such a thing as 'forcible feeding' of the animal body. But for the mind forcible feeding is strictly an impossibility. The degree of pressure brought to bear upon a mind to accept certain content may be very great indeed, but in principle it is free to reject or to accept whatever is offered it. What confronts it in sensation, for example, it must no doubt think in a certain way, which is partly determined by the nature of the sensory stimulus and partly by its own nature, *if* it is to think it at all. But it *need* not think it at all. It can, if it so desires, passively ignore what is presented to it, refuse to incorporate it as a new difference within its own unity. Hence it can be said with still more truth of the mind than of the organism that, in Professor Reyburn's words, 'all that it is and has results from its own action'.[1]

In so far, then, as the unity of the ultimate reality of metaphysics is a unity *in* difference, a unity of which the differences are its self-manifestations, it would appear again that it is the unity of a mind that is by far our best symbol.

[1] *The Ethical Theory of Hegel*, p. 78.

But, it must never be forgotten, *only* a symbol. The mind falls short not merely in degree but in principle of that perfect unity in difference that characterises the ultimate being. Thus, in point of comprehensiveness, I suggested that, so far as mind is concerned, there is no assignable limit to the determinations of space and time that can be incorporated within its unity. But the ultimate being, if perfect unity in difference, must somehow incorporate *space and time themselves* within its unity. And this, even in principle, mind cannot do. Again, in point of internal coherence, it is not enough for the ultimate being that, like mind, it should be *a* factor—even, if you like, the dominant factor—in constituting its own differences. It must be the sole and sufficient factor. The differences must spring *wholly* from its own nature. Otherwise it would be conditioned by something beyond itself, point beyond itself for its own explanation; in other words, would *not* be the ultimate reality. But mind as we know it is in principle debarred from achieving such internal coherence if only because, as I tried to show in an earlier lecture,[1] it inevitably presupposes an 'other', something not itself, in its fundamental modes of manifestation as thought and will.

Mind or spirit, then, I think we must agree, cannot be more than a symbol of the perfect unity in difference that characterises that non-contradictory ultimate reality which we may for convenience designate 'the supreme being of metaphysics'. It is perhaps worth noticing further that the adequacy of spirit as a symbol—preferring now the term 'spirit' in order to be free from the cramping intellectualist associations of the term 'mind'—will naturally be contingent upon the *kind* of spirit we contemplate. For though spirit is potentially the most comprehensive and coherent of all knowable forms of unity, it is evident that spirits as we know them are exemplified at many different stages in the realisation of their potentialities. There are very 'low-level' as well as very 'high-level' spirits. We must think of spirit at its highest conceivable level of realised potentialities of thought and will if it is to be the most appropriate symbol for the perfect unity of the 'supreme being' of metaphysics.

Now a spirit which *fully* achieved its own ideal would enjoy

[1] Lecture XV.

a thought that is all-comprehensive and completely coherent. It would in that sense be 'perfect in wisdom'. Again, if it fully achieved its own ideal, it would have a will in absolute harmony with its 'perfect wisdom'. In that sense it would be 'perfect in goodness'. Again, if it fully achieved its own ideal, there would remain nothing in the universe not subservient to it. In that sense it would be 'perfect in power'. May we then say that the symbolisation which metaphysics finds legitimate and appropriate for its 'supreme being' accords exactly with the theistic symbolisation of God as a Spirit 'perfect in wisdom, goodness and power'?

Not quite. For we must bear in mind that it is not in fact possible to conceive spirit in terms of the *complete* realisation of its potentialities. If thought and will were fully to achieve their respective ideals, so that no element of opposition or otherness remained, thought and will would themselves cease to be; and with them would vanish 'spirit' in any meaningful sense of that term. Hence we are not able from the standpoint of metaphysics to endorse *au pied de la lettre* the theistic symbolisation of God as a Spirit *perfect* in wisdom, goodness and power. Strictly speaking, this combination of words stands for nothing that we can conceive and which could therefore serve as a symbol. The legitimate symbol for the supreme being of metaphysics cannot be more than a spirit of the *highest conceivable* wisdom, goodness, and power.

This divergence, however, is not serious, and indeed is more verbal than real. All that is required to reconcile the religious with the metaphysical viewpoint is a minor revision in the terminology in which we have so far been content to formulate the faith of supra-rational theism. We need merely substitute 'highest conceivable' for 'perfect'. And a revision of this kind, so far as I can see, sacrifices nothing that supra-rational theism can have any special concern to retain.

5.   So far, in considering the extent to which our philosophical theory coincides with, and in that sense confirms, the faith of theistic religion, we have not found it necessary to go beyond the implications of the metaphysical argument deployed in our last lecture. But though the metaphysical argument can thus, I think, fairly be induced to yield a great deal of confirmation, we come

now to an extremely important aspect of all theistic religions about which, so far as I can see, the metaphysical argument *per se* can tell us nothing. It can tell us nothing about any *specific relationship* between its supreme being and finite selves. Of a very *general* relationship it can of course inform us. Like everything else in the universe, man is in *some* sense a 'manifestation' of the supreme being, a 'difference' *some*how comprised within its absolute unity. But the 'somehow' remains completely unspecified; as indeed it must where the notion of absolute unity has confessedly no positive import, save in a symbolic sense. On the other hand, the relationship between God and man for *religion* certainly does *not* remain completely unspecified; not even where, as in supra-rational theism, it is fully conceded that the ultimate nature of the Divine unity is an impenetrable mystery.

Now it is just here, it seems to me, that philosophy can call upon the Moral Argument (as formulated in the closing section of Lecture XVIII) to supplement the metaphysical argument with very great profit and illumination. According to the moral argument, we are entitled to regard the moral law or the moral order as an objective reality. We saw, however, that *per se* the moral argument does not entitle us to say anything about an 'imponent' of the law, a 'moral legislator'. The law's authority for the moral consciousness resides wholly within the law itself. But having now, on other grounds, arrived at the conception of a supreme being, one, infinite, and eternal, who is the ultimate source of all that is, we cannot, surely, do other than take this supreme being to be the source of, and thus the imponent of, that moral law which all rational beings recognise as unconditionally binding upon them. And from this situation, I want now to suggest, several important things follow about the relation of finite selves to the supreme being of philosophy which have the effect of bringing that supreme being into much closer accord with the God of religion.

In the first place, the supreme being, *qua* author of this moral law which we acknowledge to be unconditionally binding upon us, must be accepted as having absolute *authority* over us. So far as the supreme being's mere *power* is concerned, there is no need to wait for the moral argument to give us assurance. Absolute power is already implied in a being that is the ultimate source of all things in the universe. But that the supreme being stands to finite selves in a relation of *authority*, as a *de jure* sovereign with rightful claims to the unqualified allegiance of his subjects—that is a development which philosophy can endorse only when the metaphysical argument is supplemented by the moral. But it *can*, I think, endorse it then. And thereby it confirms that vital aspect in the theistic faith in virtue of which God is the *Lord* God, the Moral Governor of the world.

In the second place, the conjunction of the moral with the metaphysical argument strongly suggests that the relation of man to the supreme being of philosophy is one of creature to creator. When we reflect on the fact that the supreme being is the source both of man's existence and of the moral law binding upon him, and when we further appreciate that a moral law is completely meaningless for beings who are not free agents, we come to see that man's relation of 'dependence' upon the supreme being must be of a very remarkable sort. It must be somehow at once an absolute dependence, and yet carry with it a genuine *in*dependence. Now there would seem to be only one way in which we can think a relationship of this kind, and that is as a relationship of creature to creator, where the creator has endowed the creature with a 'free will'. If a being owes its whole existence to another being, and to nothing else besides—and that is of the essence of the creaturely status—it can fairly be said to be in a relation of absolute dependence upon that second being. And if we suppose this created being to have had free will conferred upon it by its creator, it can fairly be said to stand in a relation of genuine independence of its creator at the same time as it is absolutely dependent upon him. That the relationship of man to the supreme being of which it is in *some* sense a manifestation is that of creature to creator, the metaphysical argument could give us no inkling whatsoever. But when it is supplemented by the moral argument, this becomes, I think, a reasonable inference. And again, thereby, our philosophical view is brought into much closer conformity with the religious interpretation of the universe.

And there is yet a third point of interest that follows from this same general situation. For religion, the supreme goal of human life is self-surrender to God and communion with Him; and channels conducting to this end are open to man in the religious

P

way of life. Now from the philosophical standpoint, as we have so far developed it, since the moral law is taken as laid upon us by the supreme Being (symbolised as a spirit of the highest conceivable goodness, wisdom, and power), devotion to duty, to the moral law, is at the same time a mode of self-surrender to, and even of self-identification with, that supreme being; just as dereliction of duty is at the same time a mode of self-assertion against and of self-alienation from him. This may or may not be recognised by the moral agent himself. Very probably it will not be. But the point is that it will be a legitimate philosophic interpretation of the significance of the moral life. Now of course it would be idle to pretend that self-identification with the supreme being through the medium of moral endeavour is tantamount to that actual communion with God as a Living Presence which the religious man believes to be open to those who truly seek it. I shall be referring to that aspect of religious faith later. On the other hand it is not, I think, extravagant to claim that we have in this further, philosophically deducible, relation between man and the supreme being a not inconsiderable advance towards the further harmonisation of philosophic doctrine and religious faith.

6. We must pause here, however, to try to answer an important and difficult question. What is the status, from our philosophical standpoint, of these propositions that embody our conclusions about the relationship between man and the supreme being of metaphysics? Have the propositions which affirm this supreme being to stand to finite selves in the relation of creator and creature, and of moral sovereign to moral subject, like the propositions that ascribe spirit and qualities of spirit to this supreme being, no more than a *symbolic* validity?

I am disposed to claim that they have much more than this. Briefly stated, the ground for so claiming is that the two principles from whose combined force these propositions are deduced as implications, the moral principle as well as the metaphysical principle, are principles that are true in their *literal* significance— not merely 'symbolically'. The ontological status of the moral order affirmed on the testimony of the moral consciousness is not, I think, that of a phenomenal symbol of reality. The moral order is *itself* a reality; and none the less genuinely so because, as will appear later, a distinction has got to be drawn between the reality it enjoys and 'ultimate' reality.

But that this position is not free from difficulties I am well aware. *Prima facie* there is the strongest possible objection to the contention that *both* the metaphysical *and* the moral principle possess literal truth; viz. that on reflection they seem to contradict one another. Let me try to bring out the precise nature of the dilemma that here confronts us.

The moral consciousness, if our account of it in the first course be accepted, is a mode of experience no less intrinsic to our nature than the theoretic consciousness. Its fundamental deliverance, therefore, has an equal right with that of the theoretic consciousness to be respected in any constructive philosophical theory. Now the fundamental deliverance of the moral consciousness is that there is an objectively real moral law unconditionally binding upon the human will. The fundamental deliverance of the theoretic consciousness, on the other hand, is that only what is non-contradictory is real; and we found this to entail, when we worked it out, that there is but one ultimate reality, an infinite and eternal being upon whom all things in the universe in some sense depend. Clearly a major difficulty arises as to how we are to reconcile these two deliverances, the moral and the metaphysical, with one another. For if, as the moral consciousness requires, the moral law is accepted as a reality, the reality must be accepted of whatever is implied in the reality of moral law; but the moral law's reality plainly implies the reality of moral agents upon whom it is binding, and implies, accordingly, the reality of *finite* beings living in a *temporal* order—since only a temporally ordered world can provide a possible milieu for moral endeavour. The problem is, how can we consistently maintain the reality of the finite temporal order, as thus required by the moral consciousness, while we also maintain, as required by the theoretic consciousness, that the sole ultimate reality is an Infinite and Eternal Being?

Is there any way out from this impasse? I believe that there is. The one possible solution of the problem (or so I have come to think) lies in taking in full earnest the hypothesis of *creation*. If the relationship of the finite temporal order, which the moral life presupposes, to the infinite and eternal being is interpreted as that of created being to its creator, the finite temporal order will have a reality of its own, even though the only *ultimate* reality is the infinite and eternal Being. For it is implied in the very notion of a genuine 'creation' that what is created, despite its dependence on its creator, is endowed with a relatively independent existence. It is not just (so to speak) *a phase or mode of its creator's being*. On the hypothesis of creation, the world of finite temporal being is not indeed an *ultimate* reality, inasmuch as it depends for its being upon a being beyond itself; but neither is it a mere *appearance* of the ultimate reality, something which on a fuller understanding of it would lose its essential character *as* finite temporal being. In other words, given that the supreme being has created a world of finite beings in time, that world really is a world of finite beings in time.

I suggest, then, that on the hypothesis that the finite temporal order stands to the infinite and eternal as created being to its creator, there is no inconsistency in our imputing to it the genuine reality which the moral consciousness posits, at the same time as we acknowledge that it falls short of 'ultimate' reality inasmuch as it depends upon the infinite and eternal for its own being. And if this be granted, the only weighty objection vanishes, so far as I can see, to the claim that it is no mere 'symbolic' validity that attaches to the propositions which assert that the supreme being of metaphysics stands to finite selves in the relation of creator to creature and moral sovereign to moral subject.

7. And now there remains uncorroborated from our philosophical standpoint but one important item in the faith of theism, the conviction that God is a Living Presence in the hearts of men— an 'indwelling Spirit'. Can we say anything about this? Is there any ground for supposing, in the light of our constructive philosophical theory, that the supreme being deduced therein directly operates on and within the human soul as the religious man believes that God does? One cannot doubt that for most religious faiths this is nothing less than vital. If the average religious man were to be told that he is entitled to all his major beliefs about God *except* that God is ever directly present to him, sustaining, guiding, admonishing, comforting, he would surely feel that the very kernel of his religion was being denied him.

Nevertheless, I am afraid I am able to make no claim that the correspondence of supra-rationalist philosophy with theism extends to this last article also.

We cannot, in the first place, get the required philosophical corroboration by way of direct inference from the nature of the supreme being that is the ultimate reality for supra-rationalist metaphysic. For *ex hypothesi* we do not have, on that metaphysic, the kind of knowledge of the nature of the supreme being that would enable us to deduce any of its specific manifestations—such as that being's periodic ingressions into finite centres of experience. One may point out in passing, however, that rationalist systems of metaphysics are in no better case here, though for different reasons. For it seems clear enough that a supreme being whose specific manifestations *were* capable of being deduced as logical implications of its nature must wholly lack that qualitative transcendence of man's finite capacities which is surely inseparable from the God worshipped in religion. Kierkegaard's strictures on 'the God of the philosophers' are to my mind unanswerable where his target is the supreme being of any rationalist metaphysic.

In the second place, we cannot on this matter, I think, hope to derive any aid from the *ethical* supplement to the metaphysical argument. Certain implications of the objective reality of moral law that are of great importance for religion we thought that philosophy could legitimately deduce. But it is no implication of the objective reality of the moral law that the supreme being of metaphysics not only is the ultimate imponent of moral law but also, on occasion, helps us to obey it. Any suggestion to that effect must come, if it comes at all, from the religious consciousness itself.

The only kind of corroboration, so far as I can see, that the supra-rationalist philosophy could offer would be by way of a very general and highly speculative argument. It might conceivably be argued that, if the nature of the supreme being is such that it can legitimately be symbolised by the highest spiritual concepts we can frame, it is reasonable to expect that this being will have solicitude for the creatures He has brought into existence, and that this solicitude will be manifested in some such forms as are indicated by the various terms used by the religious man in testifying to his experience of God's presence. An argument of this sort is not, I think, wholly negligible; but it does seem to me that a due appreciation of the limitations inherent in our symbolic 'pictures' of the nature of the supreme being ought to make us cautious about attaching very much weight to it.

I must frankly say, therefore, that so far as our constructive philosophic theory is concerned, there is precarious support at best for the religious claim to actual communion with God as a Living Presence; though it should be added that nothing in our philosophical theory seems directly to contradict it. The only positive evidence of much significance there can be on the matter must come, I think, from religious experience itself. There seems no clear reason, apart from the testimony of that experience, why anyone should suppose that the supreme being makes specific ingressions of this sort into human souls. And this again, I take it, is one of the things that are meant when it is said that the God of the philosophers is not the God of Abraham, Isaac and Jacob.

But acknowledging to that extent an 'impotence' inherent in philosophy, I by no means admit that this entails, as some religious thinkers have eagerly but over-hastily concluded, that on the aspect of religious faith with which we are now concerned philosophy has no just claim to say anything at all. For philosophy has a critical no less than a constructive function; and in the exercise of that critical function it has not only a right but a duty to ask 'Is the evidence from ostensible religious experience for the actual presence of God to man *good* evidence? Does the experience upon which the religious man bases his belief really warrant that belief?' If such questions can be intelligibly raised at all, to what court can they possibly be taken for adjudication except the court of philosophy?

And it is surely obvious that such questions *can* be intelligibly raised. There is *no* question, of course, that the man who claims that God is directly present to him does (unless he is an impostor) have a certain peculiar sort of experience. But the experience is one thing, the interpretation he places on the experience quite another thing. The validity of his interpretation is manifestly open to question. No doubt it was on the basis of a perfectly genuine experience of an 'inner voice' that the prophet Samuel adjured Saul 'Thus saith the Lord . . . "Now go and smite Amalek, and utterly destroy all that they have, and spare them not; but slay both man and woman, infant and suckling, ox and sheep, camel and ass" '.[1] But that Samuel actually heard these words, in some sense of the term 'hearing', does not entail that they were addressed to him by God. That is Samuel's *interpretation* of his experience; and as most people would say (I hope), a false interpretation. One does not need to have much acquaintance with the literature pertaining to 'inner voices' to be quite sure that at least very many of them are not what they seem to be to the person who experiences them. The content of the message conveyed is usually sufficient evidence in itself that, wherever they come from, their origin is certainly not divine.

Is it, then, really possible to doubt that there is a task of the utmost importance to be done here in the critical appraisal of evidence? But the critical appraisal of evidence is everywhere the business of reason: and where the question to which the evidence relates bears, as here, upon the most ultimate problems of human experience, it is the business of philosophy, of reason in its philosophical manifestation. I must frankly say that, with the best will in the world, I can find little excuse for the attitude of those religious thinkers who denounce the entrance of philosophy into this field as an unwarrantable intrusion. The alternative to admitting the 'intruder' reason into the field is surely none other than sheer religious anarchy, with one man's 'hunch' as good as another's. And it is not merely that a man has no right to expect others to be persuaded by an ostensible religious experience which he has had, but for whose validity he is prepared to offer no objective reasons. In all earnestness I submit that he has no right to be persuaded of its validity *himself*. It is only by turning a completely blind eye to the fact—which we all know very well to be a fact—that there are countless cases of ostensible religious experiences that are spurious, that any man can be convinced, without the most careful and critical reflection, of the veridical character of his own ostensible religious experience.

Claims to direct experience of the Divine presence have got to be subjected to appraisal each on its own individual merits. Moreover, no criteria are available, it seems to me clear, that will enable us to attain certainty with respect to any particular case.

---

[1] I Samuel xv. 3.

We have to be content, whether we like it or not, with probabilities, more or less strong, one way or the other. At this late date, however, with the twelfth hour of this course almost about to strike, it would be absurd to try to deal systematically with the general question of the criteria of appraisal that are appropriate. I shall confine myself to two brief observations, which I feel under some compulsion to make, since the respective points to which they draw attention, obvious as they are, appear to me to be very insufficiently appreciated by many of those (even in high places) who write and talk confidently about the 'experience' of God's presence.

The first is that it is no kind of guarantee of the validity of an ostensible experience of God's presence that the experiencing subject is 'changed' by it and becomes a dramatically new and better man. It is obvious that illusory beliefs can have enormous potency in transforming behaviour (witness the psychotic), and that the transformation they effect can be most valuable (witness some converts to some 'false' religions). That a man's whole way of life can be revitalised, even revolutionised, by a belief that God has been actually present to him may be an argument for the *practical* value of such belief. It provides not a scintilla of evidence for its *truth*-value.

The second observation is that an indispensable tool in the appraisal of evidence here is an informed understanding of the vagaries of the human mind as so far revealed, and in process of being further revealed, by the science of psychology; and in particular by that branch of it known as 'abnormal psychology'. The defenders of religious experience are apt to adopt a rather disparaging attitude towards modern psychology and modern psychologists. This seems to me unwise. I should be the last to deny that too many practitioners of modern psychology have invited disrespect for their science by an undiscriminatingly clinical approach to human behaviour; often producing astonishing psycho-analytic explanations for actions that are perfectly intelligible in the light of principles that have been familiar and well-authenticated since the very dawn of psychology. But there is nothing unusual in the spectacle of scientific pioneers intoxicated by the excitement of their discoveries and seeking to apply them beyond all reasonable limits. We should not allow the irritation it provokes to blind us to the fact that any competent enquirer will find in modern psychology not only much that is doubtful, and a certain amount that seems downright silly, but also a body of well-authenticated, novel and important information about the human mind that has the most obvious relevance to some of the central phenomena in ostensible religious experience.

8. We have now reached the end of our journey. What, then, is our final and formal answer to our fundamental question 'Is religion true'?

It is that, granted that religion finds its proper theoretic expression in theism, and that this theism must be interpreted in supra-rational, not rational, terms, there is good philosophic corroboration for all the major articles of the theistic creed save one. I have contended that objective philosophical thinking, in which straight metaphysical argument is supplemented by reflections upon the implications of man's moral consciousness, leads independently to belief in an infinite and eternal being who is the sole ultimate reality, the creator of the finite temporal world, and the source of the moral law which has absolute authority over man's conduct in that world; a being who, moreover, though he transcends in his nature all human powers of conception, is yet legitimately symbolised as a spirit endowed with the highest conceivable goodness, wisdom and power.

As regards the one remaining article of the theistic creed, however, constructive philosophy can in my opinion neither sustain nor refute the general principle of specific Divine manifestations in human lives, and critical philosophy can do no more than assess, rather roughly, the probabilities one way or the other in the case of individual claims. This will seem to many a somewhat disappointing note on which to close; for I am under no illusions concerning the great importance that most religious minds attach to the conviction of God's 'Living Presence'. Like, I am afraid, a number of other things that I have been obliged to say in the course of these addresses, this part of my conclusion can scarcely fail to be unpalatable to many with whom I should be glad, if it were possible, to find myself in agreement. But the duty of a Gifford Lecturer, as I understand it, is not to be a committed defender of any faith, but to be a critical enquirer after the truth—following the wind of the argument whithersoever it may lead. The wind of the argument has driven the present lecturer into waters at times no less turbulent than deep; waters all but unnavigable, perhaps, even for a pilot of far superior skill. It may well be, and many will not doubt, that the voyage has ended in shipwreck. Even so, I should still take a little comfort from my unshakable belief that, where the quest is for truth, it is infinitely better to set sail and sink than never to set sail at all.

APPENDIX C

ON 'SPIRITUAL PRIDE'

I wish to add a few observations here about a concept which has in my opinion done a great deal to darken counsel in religious ethics, not least within recent times. I refer to what is called 'spiritual pride'.

The essence of spiritual pride in general is, I take it, an excessive self-satisfaction with one's own moral and spiritual attainments. In the religious context (with which we are alone here concerned) spiritual pride is a deadly sin, for it denotes, in greater or less degree, a failure in the person who exhibits it to make due acknowledgment of his creaturely relationship to God. Such failure may disclose itself in at least two distinguishable forms. In the first place, a man may claim much more than is its due for the efficacy of his personal effort in, e.g. a successful resistance to temptation, recognising only inadequately or not at all the rôle of divine grace. In the second place, even if there be no reason to presume a specific operation of divine grace in the situation, even if the man is to that extent justified in attributing his success to the free exercise of his own personal effort, his very sense of personal achievement may beget in him a tendency to glorify himself and to forget that, in the last resort, all that he is and has—including his 'free will'—comes from God the Creator.

Now concerning the second of these manifestations of spiritual pride I have no particular observations to make. Given religious premises, the sin is grave, and the temptation to commit it very real. No one would wish to hold that, from the standpoint of religion, it is of less than paramount importance that men should be admonished to 'remember their Creator', and above all in those moments of high personal achievement when the inducements to forget are especially powerful.

But concerning what we distinguished as the first form of these manifestations there are, I think, some things that very much require to be said.

It ought for example to be said plainly, and at whatever risk of giving offence, that a certain view with much current appeal is, despite its popularity, totally inadmissible. I mean the view that man is guilty of spiritual pride if he takes any credit to himself at all for a 'good' act, since in so doing he is arrogating to himself a power that is not his but God's. This view has plausibility only on the assumption that man is utterly incapable of resisting moral temptation by his own unaided effort. But as I have already argued, not only is that assumption completely at variance with the most fundamental intuitions of moral experience, it is hardly less at variance with the premises of religion itself. For in making nonsense of human goodness, the assumption must equally make nonsense of human badness, and hence of the religious concept of sin. If a man can do nothing on his own part to resist temptation, it is just as absurd to hold him blameworthy if he succumbs to it as to deem him praiseworthy if he resists it. And it would be a Pickwickian sense indeed of the term 'sin' which did not imply the blameworthiness of the sinner!

Let us take as agreed, then, what is really implied in the very possibility of sinning, that man does have *some* power of his own to resist temptation. If that is so, it follows that when he takes credit to himself for resisting temptation he need by no means be arrogating to himself a power that is not his. On the other hand, of course, he *may* be. Even if he has made a personal effort, and that personal effort has had some efficacy, its efficacy may have been supplemented by an operation of divine grace which his claim to credit does not acknowledge.

Whether or not, however, in any given case of successful resistance to temptation, a man claims for his personal effort more than is in fact its due, there would seem to be no external way of telling. Where a man's personal effort receives divine reinforcement, this influx of aid from without will presumably be felt as such by the man himself. If there is in fact no experience of it, it is hard to see on what grounds its occurrence can be alleged; hard to see, therefore, on what grounds one can condemn the man's belief—which is then wholly natural if not indeed inevitable—that it is the personal effort which he *does* experience that is the direct source of his success. To accuse the man of spiritual pride in these circumstances seems quite gratuitous. If, on the other hand, aid from without *is* experienced as such by the man, it might no doubt happen that overweening self-conceit induced in him disregard of it, and perhaps oblivion of it, and thus led him to claim for himself a credit to which he was not entitled. In that case he would, admittedly, be guilty of spiritual pride. But whether in a given case of claim to personal credit this hypothetical state of affairs is actualised seems to me a matter upon which the external observer simply has not the data upon which to pronounce a judgment.

It comes to this, then. If we agree that God has endowed man with a power to resist temptation by a moral effort which he is absolutely free to exert or refrain from exerting, then man is, in general, justified in a claim to personal achievement when he resists temptation, and he is guilty of spiritual pride in making the claim only where that claim ignores or fails to take due account of empirical evidence of an *ad hoc* intervention of divine grace. He is not guilty of spiritual pride merely in virtue of claiming credit, for he *need* not thereby be arrogating to himself a power that is not his. It is natural, indeed, that he should feel 'pride'— for how can he fail to enjoy a certain enhancement of self-respect in having (as he believes) won a battle against his 'lower nature'? But this pride of achievement is not 'pride' in any dyslogistic sense of that term. Why should he *not* feel such pride so long as (like pride of achievement in other fields) it is kept within reasonable bounds? There is surely nothing irreligious about taking pride in ourselves for using the freedom given us by God in the way that we know God wants us to use it, any more than there is in despising ourselves when we use that freedom in a way we know that God would disapprove? And this pride of achievement, be it noted, is completely compatible with humbly and reverently acknowledging that the power which makes our resistance possible itself comes from God. It in no way entails that man arrogantly disowns his creaturely status and asserts in himself a power comparable to the power of the Creator from whom he derives all that he has and is.

It goes without saying that pride of moral achievement, like pride of achievement in other fields, *may* find exaggerated expression. It *may* beget the 'worthier than thou' attitude which is what perhaps most people have in mind when they speak of 'spiritual pride'. But there seems no particular reason why it should. Indeed there would seem to be rather greater likelihood of a 'worthier than thou' attitude afflicting the man who believes that whatever good thing he achieves is directly due to God working in him. For suppose that such a man is (or fancies he is) more than ordinarily successful in 'doing good'. He may then well be tempted to fancy himself one of 'God's elect'—a specially chosen vessel for the execution of Divine purposes—and 'to thank God that he is not as other men'. Whether we regard this as a third distinguishable form of spiritual pride, or prefer to give it some other name, is little to the point. It is a sufficiently ugly and pernicious thing whatever we choose to call it: and I suggest that there is at least as much risk of *its* occurrence where men reject the efficacy of personal effort, as there is of *spiritual pride* occurring (in the senses earlier distinguished) where the efficacy of personal effort is accepted.

APPENDIX D

THE DOCTRINE OF ANALOGY

Some surprise may not unreasonably be felt that, in grappling with the problem of how man can talk meaningfully about God, I have found no occasion to mention the celebrated 'Doctrine of Analogy', in terms of which scholastic theologians have formulated the officially approved solution of what is fundamentally the same problem. The omission is certainly not due to any lack of respect. On the contrary, holding the views that I do, I cannot but deem it an outstanding merit of the scholastic theology that it has shown itself so consistently and conspicuously aware of the paramount importance of this problem, and I admire profoundly the concentration of intellectual power that has been directed, not least in modern times, to evolving and elaborating a solution that might satisfy the demands of faith and reason alike. An extensive examination, however, was not practicable in these lectures; and it seemed to me plain that nothing short of a very extensive examination indeed could hope to do even approximate justice to a doctrine which is not only supported by extremely subtle and complicated reasoning, but which has the further difficulty for most students of philosophy and theology outside the Catholic communion of being formulated within a somewhat unfamiliar framework of ideas. Add to this the fact that even among Catholic scholars themselves there is very far from unanimity as to the exact interpretation of the doctrine, and the futility of attempting to say anything worth while about it in brief compass becomes too glaring to ignore.

Nevertheless I am loth to leave altogether unnoticed a solution of our problem which has such high authority. I am the more loth to do so since it is common knowledge that the official sponsors of the 'Analogy' type of solution condemn with some vehemence the 'Symbolist' type of solution which is the type I have myself preferred. A symbolic theology is condemned, I understand, primarily on account of its dangerously agnostic tenor; and plainly *some* element of agnosticism is inseparable from it in whatever form it may be propounded. But the element of agnosticism in the symbolic theology for which I have argued in the foregoing pages seems to me to be certainly no greater, and quite possibly less, than the element of agnosticism implicit in the Analogical theory. It is the main purpose of this short note to try to show that such is the case.

As already indicated, there is considerable diversity of opinion among the authorities themselves concerning the precise significance of the doctrine of analogy for our problem. Since a choice of interpretation must here be made, I cannot do better, I think, than follow in its main lines the critical exposition offered by Dr. Mascall in his recent *Existence and Analogy*, a distinguished work which has elicited respectful tributes from Catholic and non-Catholic thinkers alike.

The problem may be posed as follows. How is it possible to predicate significantly of God, who *ex hypothesi* transcends the finite and temporal, qualities which are derived from experience of the finite and temporal, and which in their literal meaning seem inseparably bound up with the finite and temporal? How, to take a single important example, can we significantly describe God as 'good'?

The solution in general terms is that significant predication about God is possible only in virtue of certain analogical relations which obtain between God and man.

Two kinds of analogy—each a sub-type of the general type *unius ad alterum*—have a special relevance for the solution. The first is the Analogy of Attribution (or Proportion); the second is the Analogy of Proportionality.

In the case of the Analogy of Attribution 'the predicate belongs formally and properly to one of the analogates . . . and only relatively and derivatively to the other'.[1] Thus we can say intelli-

---

[1] *Existence and Analogy*, pp. 101-2.

gibly both that St. Andrews is healthy and that its inhabitants are healthy, though it is clear that 'healthy' has not the same, but only an analogous, meaning in the two propositions. Health is present 'formally and properly' in the inhabitants only. When we call St. Andrews 'healthy' we mean no more than that in virtue of its climate St. Andrews is the source of health in its inhabitants.

But this type of analogy, it seems clear, is inadequate to justify the ascription to God of predicates like goodness in the way that we want to ascribe them. If we assume that we are entitled to assert a relation of creative causality between God and man, we can no doubt say that, inasmuch as there is goodness in the creature, goodness must in *some* sense be present in God the Creator. But we want to be able to ascribe goodness to God as a quality that belongs 'formally and properly' to Him—in the same manner as we ascribe goodness to man. In terms of the Analogy of Attribution the sense in which we are justified in ascribing goodness to God apparently amounts to no more than saying that goodness (and of course other 'finite perfections' likewise) 'exist *virtually* in God, that is to say, that He is able to produce them in the creatures'.[1]

The second type of analogy, however, the Analogy of Proportionality, may help us over this hurdle; if, at any rate, it should prove capable of application to the God-man relationship. For 'in the strict sense an analogy of proportionality implies that the analogue under discussion is found formally in each of the analogates but in a mode that is determined by the nature of the analogate itself'.[2] Suppose, for example, that 'life' be the analogue. We can assert life to be formally present both in a cabbage and in a man; but not univocally; it is present in each of the analogates *in the mode appropriate to that analogate's specific nature*. The 'proportionality' is brought out if we express this in the form 'life of man is to essence of man as life of cabbage is to essence of cabbage'.

Now may we not apply this analogy of proportionality to God and man in respect of the analogue 'goodness', and say that Divine goodness is to the essence of God as human goodness is to the essence of man? If so, we would seem to be getting much nearer to what we are after, since goodness is now being predicated

---

[1] *Op. cit.* p. 102.   [2] P. 104.

of God's nature formally, not just virtually—precisely as it is of human nature. God, we are saying, is characterised by the goodness that is appropriate to Divine nature as man is characterised by the goodness that is appropriate to human nature.

On reflection, however, it does not look as though we were succeeding after all in saying thereby anything intelligible about the Divine goodness. Divine goodness may bear the same relation of appropriateness to the Divine essence as human goodness does to the essence of man, but that seems to tell us nothing about the Divine goodness *unless* we are in a position to frame some concept of the Divine essence. How can we have any inkling of what kind of goodness is appropriate to the essence of a being if that essence is wholly unknown to us? But we cannot frame a concept of the Divine essence. It looks, therefore, as though the analogy of proportionality leaves us in a state of sheer agnosticism.

Dr. Mascall is of course well aware of the difficulty; but he thinks it can be overcome. The first step (if I understand him aright) is to recall that though we cannot frame a concept of the Divine essence, we do know something very important about it. For we know that God is a being whose essence is identical with His existence; and we know further that, as the necessary being upon Whom all contingent being entirely depends, He stands in the Creator-creature relationship to finite man. Now in virtue of our knowledge that the Creator-creature relationship holds, we can apply the analogy of attribution and say (as we have already seen) that the quality of goodness which characterises the creature is somehow present in God also; and because in God, in contradistinction from finite beings, there can be 'no accidents, no qualities that are not included in His essence',[1] we can say that goodness characterises the Divine essence; and because in God essence and existence are identical, we can say that in God 'goodness exists self-existingly'.[2]

If these steps be granted, it follows that in saying that God's goodness is appropriate to His essence as man's goodness is to the essence of man, we *are* saying something significant about the Divine goodness. 'The goodness of God is thus declared to be self-existent goodness, and, as such, identical not merely with God's essence but with the act by which God exists. Analogy does

[1] *Op. cit.* p. 119.   [2] P. 120.

not enable us to *conceive* God's goodness as identical with his essence but to affirm it as identical with his existence.' [1]

This brief paraphrase, I need scarcely say, does scant justice to the subtlety and refinement of Dr. Mascall's presentation of the case. I may even (though I trust not) have unwittingly mis-represented links in his chain of argument. Fortunately that is not of any great present consequence. For my purpose here is not to pick a quarrel either with Dr. Mascall's premises or with the steps in his argument. My purpose is simply to point to the outcome of his argument in the form in which he himself acknow-ledges it. 'God's goodness'—the same applies to His possession of other finite perfections—'exists self-existingly'. And we are expressly told that of self-existing goodness we can frame no concept. We can only affirm that this inconceivable kind of goodness is the kind of goodness that God has. 'All our assertions about God are grossly inadequate in so far as they apply concepts to him.' [2] Indeed they are, on this showing. But how it is supposed that we can maintain this position—denying by implication that, when the ordinary believer speaks of God's Will, and Purpose, and Wisdom, and Compassion, what he has in mind (the literal signification of his words) has any conceivable resemblance to these qualities as they exist in God—and at the same time maintain a theology that can escape being what the ordinary believer would describe as dangerously agnostic, I confess I cannot see. And what is more to my present point, I cannot see one single respect in which the knowledge of God justified by this doctrine of analogy is *less* agnostic than the 'symbolic' knowledge of God which I have sought to justify in the present work.

Of course one can well enough imagine, and indeed there have not been wanting instances of, Symbolist theories to which the Catholic Church's strictures upon Symbolism are clearly applic-able; and it is no doubt such theories that the Church has especially in mind. Let me here quote Dr. Edwyn Bevan's summary of the Symbolist theory as depicted by the distinguished Dominican philosopher, Father Sertillanges:

'The theory of Symbolism is said to be erroneous because it is really only Agnosticism in disguise. The terms by which God is

[1] *Op. cit.* p. 120.   [2] *Ibid.*

represented—wise, loving, just—are adopted, according to the symbolic view, we are told, simply to satisfy certain human cravings, as useful fictions, helping to produce desirable modes of conduct or sentiment. But there is nothing in the Reality, on this view, apart from human fancy, to correspond with them. Some people regard it as quite legitimate to satisfy human cravings in this way, and since there is nothing in the great Unknown Reality to which these symbols correspond, any symbol which satisfies human craving, or produces desirable conduct, serves the purpose, and the Symbolist theory can thus extend a general blessing to all contradictory varieties which human religion shows according to differences of time and race.' [1]

I hope it will have been evident to the reader that to this kind of Symbolist theory the symbolic theology I have been advocating bears no resemblance. Everything turns on the nature of the connection held to exist between symbol and *symbolizandum*. According to the Symbolist theory just described, this connection is purely subjective. The symbols are factitious and arbitrary, adopted not on account of any inherent compulsion upon the human spirit so to construe the ultimate reality, but from frankly utilitarian motives. This is hardly even 'Agnosticism in *disguise*', and I should heartily agree in condemning it as offering the merest pretence of religious knowledge. But from it the view I have been endeavouring to establish in this work differs *toto coelo*. It has been with me from first to last a major preoccupation, whether dealing with the problem within the framework of the religious consciousness (the relation of ideograms to the *mysterium tremendum et fascinans*), or from the standpoint of metaphysical theory (the relation of the imperfect unities attainable by thought to the perfect unity taken to characterise the ultimate reality), to show that the connection of symbol with *symbolizandum* rests on an inner necessity of the mind. Between symbol and *symbolizandum*, I have argued, there exists a natural 'affinity' which the human mind finds itself obliged to accept even while it cannot 'understand' it. It is this that confers on symbols like wisdom, love and justice objectivity and necessity as symbols of the Divine nature, in the sharpest possible contrast with the capricious subjectivity of symbols invented to 'satisfy human cravings' or 'produce desirable modes of conduct'.

---

[1] *Symbolism and Belief*, p. 311.

I conclude, then, that the 'knowledge of God' founded on the Symbolist principles enunciated in the present work is no more agnostic than the 'knowledge of God' permitted by the Doctrine of Analogy. On the question whether it is perhaps *less* agnostic I should not care to express an opinion without a much more detailed understanding than I can at present claim both of the doctrine itself and of the actual use to which scholastic theologians put it in the exegesis of credal formulae.

INDEX OF PROPER NAMES

GEORGE ALLEN & UNWIN LTD
London: 40 Museum Street, W.C.1

Auckland: 24 Wyndham Street
Sydney, N.S.W.: Bradbury House, 55 York Street
Cape Town: 109 Long Street
Bombay: 15 Graham Road, Ballard Estate, Bombay 1
Calcutta: 17 Chittaranjan Avenue, Calcutta 13
New Delhi: 13–14 Ajmeri Gate Extension, New Delhi 1
Karachi: 254 Ingle Road,
Toronto: 91 Wellington Street West
São Paulo: Avenida 9 de Julho 1138–Ap. 51

MAN AND MATERIALISM
By FRED HOYLE

'A materialist', writes Fred Hoyle, 'is not a person who gobbles babies for breakfast.' Nor is it some kind of Communist. Rather it is one who does not necessarily separate material and spiritual values, who regards everything in the universe, whether a distant galaxy or a great-uncle, as an expression of the same natural laws.

To understand the behaviour of men, we have to know something of the natural laws that govern men. In this book Mr. Hoyle makes an attempt to discover what these laws might be by looking at large human communities over long periods of time, and noting the patterns which become evident.

Mr. Hoyle explores these patterns with characteristic wit, an informal and readable style, and with a wide range of knowledge. His analysis covers some of the phenomena of communism, the crisis in food and population, the significance of industrialism, man and his religious impulses, the crucial present stage of evolution. To every topic he brings a fresh viewpoint and a provocative intelligence. He does not claim to offer final answers. He does offer a challenging intellectual experience to any reader who wishes to understand the broad historical trends that determine the future of humanity on this planet.

Man and Materialism is an outstanding example of Hoyle's ability to present important and complex problems in a way that the non-scientific public can grasp. He has written of the great issues of our time with humour and understanding, as well as with deep originality and authority.

Crown 8vo. World Perspectives Series. 12s. 6d. net

A HISTORY OF PHILOSOPHY
By FRANK THILLY

The first edition of the late Professor Thilly's book appeared over thirty-five years ago. Few books in the fields of philosophy or history have maintained undiminished popularity as texts and usefulness as reference works over so long a period.

'This very comprehensive one-volume history of philosophy can be warmly recommended to students who need to orientate themselves historically in preparation for the study of the great philosophical masterpieces . . . for so large a volume it is very reasonably priced.' *Congregational Quarterly*.

Medium 8vo. 45s. net.

FAITH AND LOGIC

Edited by BASIL MITCHELL

There have been lively debates on the air and in the Press, about the bearing of modern philosophy upon Christianity, but there has been relatively little sustained discussion of the subject. This book of essays is the product of a small group of Oxford philosophers and theologians, who had met and talked informally for some years before they decided to write it. It is not a piece of systematic philosophical theology in the old style, but an attempt to discuss with care and candour some of the problems raised for Christian belief by contemporary analytical philosophy.

The questions raised are not altogether new; what is new is the rigour and precision with which they have been formulated. They cannot, therefore, be lightly dismissed as the product of a philosophical fashion. Nor are they of merely academic interest. In asking them philosophers are making articulate the perplexities of many intelligent people, both believers and unbelievers.

Philosophical criticism and defence of theology often takes the form of asserting or denying some very general theory of meaning. The contributors to this book think it more useful to concentrate on the way such concepts as God, Revelation, the Soul, Grace are actually used. In this way they hope to make some positive contribution to the understanding of them.

The contributors are Austin Farrer, I. M. Crombie, M. B. Foster, J. R. Lucas, Basil Mitchell, G. C. Stead and R. M. Hare.

'. . . the Oxford philosophers of the book address themselves first in the form of philosophical examinations of the language of theological statements, and then from the points of view of revelation, morals and divine grace. It sounds as though it would make formidable reading, but in fact the book is made fascinating if not exactly easy, by the sheer grace and wit of the writing. Almost all the contributors seem to have determined to make the reader's path as easy and as pleasant as they could, and certainly they have succeeded in this aim.' *Time and Tide*.

'. . . Nevertheless, along different lines, they persuasively argue that, while belief in the grace of God cannot be established by empirical evidence, it can, once accepted, be seen to have empirical justification and application.' *Birmingham Post*.

Demy 8vo.   21*s. net.*

DESCARTES RULES FOR THE DIRECTION OF THE MIND

By *HAROLD H. JOACHIM*

These are the long-awaited lectures on the *Regulae* of Descartes, the original manuscripts of which were lost after the death of Professor Joachim. Here again, as in his earlier works, we find Joachim's minute scholarship and his penetrating thought at work on a critical examination of the main rules for the direction of the mind and the expositions by which Descartes explains them. After a brief introduction on the history of the manuscript, the commentary concerns itself with five main topics: the power of knowing, the nature of the intellect, Descartes' account of deduction and induction, Descartes' method of analysis and synthesis, and the notion of *vera mathesis*. Joachim then goes on to criticise Descartes' method and to expound his own doctrine of philosophical analysis.

His critique of the idea of analysis, besides supplementing what he has written in *Logical Studies*, is particularly interesting at the present time, for it provides valuable material for criticism of much current theory of philosophical method. Of the views here expressed it may well be said, as Joachim himself said in his preface to the second edition of *The Nature of Truth*, that they are still 'not only alive, but kicking', and unless they are taken seriously by contemporary thinkers, a good deal of recent writing may well be written off as 'worthless, however ingenious, and rooted in sheer confusion'.

The last chapter is a valuable addition to the theory of the concrete put forward by Joachim in other works. The lucidity with which he explains and illustrates his thesis, as well as the clarity and thoroughness of his commentary on Descartes, will appeal to every student of philosophy.

Crown 8vo. *10s 6d. net.*

SOME MAIN PROBLEMS OF PHILOSOPHY

By *G. E. MOORE*

In these lectures Professor Moore presents two typical philosophical problems—that of the external world and that of what it is for a thing to be of a certain kind. With the directness and love of clarity for which he is famous he tries to make his exploration no harder than it must be. But anyone who accompanies him will soon realise that philosophy is no picnic, and will have before him a lively example of those qualities which are called for in those who seek philosophic truth.

Demy 8vo. *Muirhead Library of Philosophy.* *30s. net.*

BRITISH PHILOSOPHY IN MID-CENTURY

Edited by C. A. MACE

British Philosophy in Mid-Century is not only an authoritative review of some of the outstanding recent developments in British Philosophy; it is also a significant contribution to these developments. The papers here published had their origin in a course of lectures at Cambridge arranged by the British Council, but many of the contributions have been revised and extended so as to present the latest views of the authors.

Of outstanding interest is a contribution written especially for this volume by G. E. Moore who has exercised so profound an influence not only on the theory of the subject with which this paper is concerned but also on the whole course of philosophical thought in Britain and elsewhere.

CONTENTS

The Local Historical Background of Contemporary Cambridge Philosophy by C. D. BROAD; Recent Developments in British Ethical Thought by A. C. EWING; Some trends in the Philosophy of Mind by C. A. MACE; Some Types of Philosophical Thinking by S. KÖRNER; Probability and Induction by R. B. BRAITHWAITE; Philosophy of Science: A Personal Report by KARL R. POPPER; Some Philosophical Problems of Cosmology by H. BONDI; Perception by A. J. AYER; Visual Sense-Data by G. E. MOORE; The Theory of Meaning by GILBERT RYLE; The Interpretation of Language by STUART HAMPSHIRE; Metaphysical and Ideographic Language by MARGARET MASTERMAN; and Some Problems of Modern Aesthetics by THEODORE REDPATH.

'It was high time that some such book became available to lift the subject out of the hot-house atmosphere of academic debate and lay it before the ordinary intelligent reader—free from the forbidding technicalities of symbolic logic. Here we have a bird's eye view of British thought from the Hegelian idealism of Ellis McTaggart, at the turn of the century, down to the logical positivism and linguistic analyses of today.' *Press and Journal, Aberdeen.*

Demy 8vo. 30s. *net.*

THE WAYS OF KNOWING

By WILLIAM PEPPERELL MONTAGUE

'Packed with thought; it covers an incredible amount of ground; it is a book that will make a difference in philosophy.' *Church Times.*

Demy 8vo. *Muirhead Library of Philosophy.* 21s. *net.*

IBN KHALDUN'S
PHILOSOPHY OF HISTORY

By *MUHSIN MAHDI*

Have our historical and cultural science made philosophy superfluous, or are they themselves, on the contrary, in dire need of a philosophic foundation? This book attempts to clarify this problem through the study of perhaps the only great thinker who considered the problems of history and culture, and founded a special science to deal with them, based on the philosophy of Plato and Aristotle and their Muslim followers.

It is the first study of Ibn Khaldun which is not an apology either for the modern social sciences or for the 'modern' character of Ibn Khaldun's thought, but a thoroughgoing analysis and interpretation of his text. To achieve this end, it draws upon the methods of many disciplines: Islamic studies, cultural history, the social sciences and political philosophy. It concentrates on examining the principles of Ibn Khaldun's new science of culture and explaining the precise nature of these principles against the background of Classical and Islamic philosophy. How these principles, applied to the field of history, led to the foundation of the new science, and defined its place among the sciences in general and its relation to traditional political philosophy in particular is brilliantly done.

Demy 8vo.   30s. *net.*

PHILOSOPHICAL ASPECTS
OF MODERN SCIENCE

By *C. E. M. JOAD*

'A book which will delight all lovers of mental gymnastic. But apart from the exercise the hunt is really a good one, leading through a varied and exciting line of country, under a guidance which is clear and determined.' *Manchester Guardian.*

'A valuable criticism of these contemporary movements. . . . Deserves the attention of all those who are following the thought of our times.' *New Statesman.*

Demy 8vo.   12s. 6d. *net.*

BERTRAND RUSSELL

OUR KNOWLEDGE OF THE EXTERNAL WORLD

The lectures in this volume are designed to show, by means of examples, the nature, capacity, and limitations of the logical analytic method in philosophy.

'This brilliant, lucid and amusing book which . . . everyone can understand.' *New Statesman.*

'It is in every sense an epoch making book; one that has been needed and expected for years.' *Cambridge Magazine.*

'The author maintains the fresh and brilliant yet easy style which always makes his writings a pleasure to read.' *Nature.*

Demy 8vo. 18s. *net.*

AN OUTLINE OF PHILOSOPHY

Contents include: Philosophic Doubts; Man from Without: Man and His Environment; The Process of Learning in Animals and Infants; Language; Perception Objectively Regarded; Memory Objectively Regarded; Knowledge Behaviouristically Considered; The Physical World; The Structure of the Atom; Physics and Perception; Physical and Perpetual Space; Man from Within: Self Observation; Images; Imagination and Memory; Consciousness? Emotion, Desire, and Will; Some Great Philosophers of the Past; Truth and Falsehood; Events, Matter and Mind; Man's Place in the Universe.

Demy 8vo. 21s. *net.*

ANALYSIS OF MIND

From the tendency of many psychologists to adopt an essentially materialistic position, while the physicists, especially Einstein, have been making 'matter' less and less material, the author has developed a view reconciling the two conflicting tendencies, according to which the ' stuff ' of the world is neither mental nor material, but a 'neutral stuff' out of which both are constructed.

'A most brilliant essay in psychology.' *New Statesman and Nation.*

Demy 8vo. *Muirhead Library of Philosophy.* 18s. *net.*

BERTRAND RUSSELL

HUMAN KNOWLEDGE:
ITS SCOPE AND LIMITS

This book is intended for the general reader, not for professional
philosophers. It begins with a brief survey of what science professes to
know about the universe. In this survey the attempt is to be as far as
possible impartial and impersonal; the aim is to come as near as our
capacities permit to describing the world as it might appear to an observer of miraculous perceptive powers viewing it from without. In
science, we are concerned with what we *know* rather than what *we* know
We attempt to use an order in our description which ignores, for the
moment, the fact that we are part of the universe, and that any account
which we can give of it depends upon its effects upon ourselves, and is
to this extent inevitably anthropocentric.

Bertrand Russell accordingly begins with the system of galaxies, and
passes on, by stages, to our own galaxy, our own little solar system, our
own tiny planet, the infinitesimal specks of life upon its surface, and
finally, as the climax of insignificance, the bodies and minds of those
odd beings that imagine themselves the lords of creation and the end
of the whole vast cosmos.

But this survey, which seems to end in the pettiness of Man and all
his concerns, is only one side of the truth. There is another side, which
must be brought out by a survey of a different kind. In this second
kind of survey, the question is no longer what the universe is, but how
we come to know whatever we do know about it. In this survey Man
again occupies the centre, as in the Ptolemaic astronomy. What we
know of the world we know by means of events in our own lives, events
which, but for the power of thought, would remain merely private.

The book inquires what are our data, and what are the principles by
means of which we make our inferences. The data from which these
inferences proceed are private to ourselves; what we call 'seeing the sun'
is an event in the life of the seer, from which the astronomer's sun has
to be inferred by a long and elaborate process. It is evident that, if the
world were a higgledy-piggledy chaos, inferences of this kind would be
impossible; but for causal inter-connectedness, what happens in one
place would afford no indication of what has happened in another. It is
the process from private sensation and thought to impersonal science
that forms the chief topic of the book. The road is at times difficult,
but until we have traversed it neither the scope nor the limitations of
human knowledge can be adequately understood.

Demy 8vo.   *Muirhead Library of Philosophy.*   3os. *net.*

GEORGE ALLEN & UNWIN LTD